Yankee Ingenuity, Yankee Know-how

Yankee Ingenuity, Yankee Know-how

Walter Edwin Lewis

VANTAGE PRESS
New York

All tables and figures from *Iron Age* and Moody's Investor Service are reprinted by permission.

Published by Vantage Press, Inc.
516 West 34th Street, New York, New York 10001

Manufactured in the United States of America
ISBN: 0-533-12408-5

Library of Congress Catalog Card No.: 97-90449

0 9 8 7 6 5 4 3 2 1

To Vera, Patricia, and Adrienne

Contents

Tables

Figures

Preface

In 1892, the United States began an expansion in industrialization unmatched at that time by any other country in the world. Ten years later, by 1902, the United States had become an industrial power equal to any in the world. In 1946, at the end of World War II, the United States was the greatest superpower that the civilized world had ever known. It was producing more steel than the combined production of all other nations in the world. In 1962, seventy years after the expansion began, the industrial leadership began to wane.

What started the unparalleled industrialization of the United States in 1892 that placed it on an industrialized plane above all other nations in the world? What happened after World War II that caused the United States to lose its superpower status? Why did the industrial leadership last for seventy years and then wane? As briefly as possible, this book relates what triggered the industrialization, why it lasted for seventy years, and the sequence of events following the Truman administration that caused America to lose its world industrial leadership. Selected events in history are discussed that had a major impact upon the minerals industry.

For over ninety years citizens of the United States have enjoyed the highest standard of living of any nation in the world. A large percentage of the public came to regard this high standard of living as the result of "Yankee ingenuity and Yankee know-how," and therefore they believed they were absolutely entitled to reap the fruits of their industriousness. The mood of the nation during the pursuit of the "abundant life" after World War II was what caused the populace to drift away from recognition of the minerals industry as the roots of our modern industrial civilization. It led directly to placing in political offices individuals who had no knowledge whatsoever of the basic industry that fueled America's industrial leadership. This lack of knowledge in the political leadership persists to this day, and there is no indication that the situation is likely to change in the near future.

The opinions expressed by the author on events were formed from one-half a century of experience in the minerals industry and from a detailed diary on national and international affairs started during the Coolidge administration. The author is highly critical of the manner in which presidents following President Truman administered the minerals industries but is also just as critical of the public during that period in their constant quest for the "abundant life" as promised by Pres. Franklin D. Roosevelt. The majority of the public placed each administration in office, and they must share the blame of the United States' lost dominance in industrial superiority.

Acknowledgments

The writer wishes to acknowledge his indebtedness to the following, who typed, reviewed, and edited the manuscript, prepared the table and index sections, assisted in the library research, and offered suggestions for re-writing various paragraphs in the chapters and appendixes to make them understandable to nontechnical readers: Vera E. Lewis, Patricia C. Lewis, and Adrienne L. Lewis, the writer's wife, daughter, and grand-daughter, respectively. The writer also wishes to record his indebtedness to the Oregon State Law Library in Salem and employees of the library who supplied him with the publications that contained the production, import, and export data on mineral commodities reported in the tables included in this book. The writer must also give special thanks to his coworkers in the Federal Bureau of Mines, Department of the Interior, whom he worked with from 1949 to 1975. Many of their written reports and ideas and opinions expressed in discussion of various facets of the minerals industries have been invaluable information in preparation for writing this book.

Yankee Ingenuity,
Yankee Know-how

1

Introduction

1.1. Agriculture, fisheries, and minerals are the three basic industries in our society. Agriculture furnishes the commodities obtained from the land that produce foods, natural drugs, cultivated and animal textile materials, rubber, and forest products. Fisheries furnish the fish, crustaceans, and mollusks obtained from oceans and freshwater bodies. The minerals industry furnishes the metallic and nonmetallic mineral commodities that are used to manufacture all products we use in our everyday life, including energy, synthetic rubber, manufactured drugs, plastics, and feedstocks for synthetic textile materials. Equipment and products used in obtaining agricultural and fisheries commodities are developed from mineral industry commodities. The higher the technology in the minerals industries, the higher the yield in agriculture and fisheries.

1.2. *In the form of rocks, minerals make up the solid matter of the Earth's crust; thus rock is a mineral or an aggregate of minerals.* Rocks are of three general types as follows: (1) igneous rocks, formed by solidification from a molten state; (2) sedimentary rocks, formed by the deposition of other solid materials; and (3) metamorphic rocks, formed by pronounced changes of temperature, pressure, and chemical environment on igneous and sedimentary rocks causing them to flow in a plastic state. Excellent examples of each are as follows: (1) Granite (plutonic, intruded deep in the Earth) and basalt, ash, and pumice (volcanic, extruded at the Earth's surface) are igneous; (2) limestone, sandstone, sand, and gravel are sedimentary; and (3) gneiss and marble (originally granite and limestone, respectively) are metamorphic. Minerals, which form rocks, are naturally occurring substances containing two or more elements having definite chemical and physical properties. *A mineral, a rock, or an element, if it is bought and sold, is a mineral commodity.* Items manufactured from mineral commodities are termed *products.* Mineral commodities are most commonly depicted in their refined state, grouped

1

as elements according to increasing atomic numbers in the Periodic Table. Some of these elements are the exact same elements that make up the human body—for example, oxygen, carbon, hydrogen, calcium, potassium, sodium, iron, and zinc. Only a few of the elements, such as gold, silver, copper, platinum, and mercury, occur in economical amounts in natural form. The elements, almost universally, occur in the Earth's crust as minerals. The minerals are in the well-known sulphide, oxide, chloride, and hydrocarbon forms containing only two elements or in complex forms containing three, four, or more elements.

1.3. Mineral commodities can be either metal, nonmetal, gas, liquid, or any of the hydrocarbon fuels in liquid, gaseous, or solid form; in brief, they are everything that is mined from the Earth, including the sea and atmosphere. The metal minerals are termed *metallics* and nonmetal minerals *nonmetallics*. Certain mineral commodities (other than fuels) are often termed *rocks* and *industrial minerals*. They are commodities used in their mineral form. Metallics are further classified as ferrous and nonferrous. Table 1 in appendix 1 lists the metallic and nonmetallic mineral commodities, and table 2 lists in more detail the mineral commodities that are classified as industrial minerals and rocks. It should be noted in table 1 that the hydrocarbon fuels are classified as nonmetallic mineral commodities. *A large percentage of the mineral commodities listed in table 1 and many in table 2 are priced on an international basis, and in peacetime if a domestic mine cannot produce a commodity profitably at the international price, the only option it has is to cease operating until the international price rises to a level wherein it is again profitable to mine.* During war and emergency periods domestic strategic mineral commodities may be mined under a government subsidy even though their cost may be double or triple the international price; also, some governments may subsidize mining of a nonstrategic mineral commodity to avoid making outright cash payments to import the commodity.

1.4. Mercury is a nonferrous metal, and it is the only metal that is liquid at room temperature. Mercury occurs in nature as a liquid, but it occurs most frequently as cinnabar, a mineral in sulphide form. The hydrocarbon fuels, coal, petroleum, and natural gas, are nonmetallic minerals in solid, liquid, and gaseous form, respectively. Uranium is a metallic, but its primary end use is energy. It is often listed with the hydrocarbon fuels as an energy source. The United States uses about 150 mineral commodities in metallic, nonmetallic, and industrial form

2

to produce the various products needed in our industrial society. Some familiar names will be noted in appendix 1, such as iron, steel, aluminum, gold, silver, copper, petroleum, coal, lime, cement, corundum, emery, gemstones, fluorine, iodine, salt, and talc.

1.5. *Breaking rock is the basic step necessary to our industrial society.* Some sedimentary rocks contain coal deposited as layers in the sedimentary series. The overlying rock layers must be broken or removed to recover the coal deposit by surface mining methods or shafts sunk through the overlying rocks to mine the deposit by underground methods. Sedimentary rocks under certain conditions contain petroleum, natural gas, and sulfur deposited at various depths in the Earth's crust; mining these commodities requires gaining access to the deposits by drilling through the overlying rocks and thence pumping the minerals to the surface. Some igneous, sedimentary, and metamorphic rocks contain concentrated amounts of metallic and nonmetallic minerals (other than fuels) deposited in a relatively small area within a large rock mass. These concentrated mineral deposits are termed *ores* by mining engineers and geologists to differentiate the deposit from the surrounding rock mass. The term is misleading because it indicates to the layman that only "ores" are being broken and not rocks. In actuality, "ores" are rocks that are being broken to obtain a mineral that may be and often is less than a fraction of 1 percent of the whole. *Breaking rocks is the only way in which we can mine mineral deposits to obtain mineral commodities to produce products necessary to sustain our industries and the way of life to which we have become accustomed.*

1.6. Anthropologists have divided the progress of mankind into the "stone, bronze, and iron ages," each age being defined by the product that was developed and most in use at that specific time. However, the phrases are misleading; they connote that at a certain period of time bronze and iron became the dominant basic material. Nothing could be further from the truth, because in reality the so-called stone age has never ended. It has been continuous ever since early man started using rock as a tool. The only change that has been made is in the selection and recovery of certain minerals from the rock. Today it is safe to say that the U.S. minerals industry breaks more rock in one minute than was ever used in the stone age.

1.7. Mineral commodities are the roots of our modern civilization; they touch every facet of our everyday life. The extent of their use is a direct measure of the state of mechanization and industrial power of a nation and the standard of living of its citizens. Our medicines, clothes, plastics, the surgeon's smallest scalpel, X rays and magnetic resonance spectroscopic imaging machines, hand tools, machine tools, engines, industrial machinery, automobiles, motor trucks, railways, aircraft, boats and ships, and agricultural fertilizers and pesticides are produced from mineral commodities. Newspapers, magazines, and papers of all kinds are produced by using mineral commodities to convert the raw wood and produce the colors and inks used in printing. Everything in which the use of electricity is involved, including power generation and distribution, lighting, heating, radio, television, and computers, is produced from mineral commodities. All forms of construction, including paved and unpaved roads, dams, bridges, and buildings, are constructed with mineral commodities. Mineral commodities are the foundation of our armed forces. The minute heat-seeking sensor, machine pistol, rifle, artillery, gun, tank, guided missile, aircraft, naval surface and undersea warships, and atomic bomb are all produced from mineral commodities.

1.8. A nation operating under a program of fear and paranoia can by deliberate mineral industry program option reach a high degree of sophistication in the development of armed forces, atomic bombs, rockets, and outer space exploration and yet still be woefully deficient in the development of its own infrastructure. This deficiency shows up in the statistical data on the minerals industries by recognition of the tonnage of mineral commodities required for the building and maintenance of the armed forces and the relative small tonnage remaining for other purposes; also, this small tonnage is normally reflected in comparatively small production and use of the industrial minerals such as sand and gravel, cement, limestone, and fertilizers. The nation that chooses to go this route courts disaster. On the surface its armies and navies appear huge and powerful, but because of the internal weakness of the nation the armed forces' strength rests on a bed of quicksand. Nations that choose this mineral industry program option are dangerous to world peace, because as they approach bankruptcy their tendency is to use the available war matériel and huge armies for land expansion and personal aggrandizement of their leaders.

1.9. The communist nations, recognizing that their industrial might can be accurately measured from the use of mineral commodities, often will not publish, even in peacetime, production, use, import, and export statistics on their minerals industries. In contrast, the United States in peacetime publishes detailed statistics on domestic production, use, imports, and exports of mineral commodities; however, during wartime, for obvious reasons, all statistical data on the minerals industries becomes classified information under one of the secrecy codes.

1.10. In our industrial civilization certain mineral commodities are required in much greater volume than others. These commodities are the metallic mineral commodities: iron and iron alloys, copper, and aluminum, and the nonmetallic mineral commodities: coal, petroleum, natural gas, coke, cement, sand and gravel, asphalt, and fertilizers. They are the primary commodities in use for construction, transportation, power generation and distribution, machine tools, warfare, and the basic industries. *Iron is the most abundant, most useful, most important, and least expensive of all metals. It is the only metal that can be tempered, that is, hardened by heating and sudden cooling.* The most important use of iron in our industrial civilization is for making steel. Steel is an alloy of iron, and for practical purposes the use of steel in the United States may be classified under three types of alloys as follows: (1) carbon steel, (2) stainless steel, and (3) all other alloy steel. Carbon steel constitutes about 90 percent of the total steel produced; stainless and all other alloy steels make up the remaining 10 percent. *Every product that is in use today is made from one of the three types of steel and/or by machinery made of one of the three types of steel.* The ferrous ores, bituminous coal, coke, limestone, and other fluxing mineral commodities needed to produce the three types of steel are bulk freight materials, and they constitute a major percentage of the tonnage freighted annually in the United States. *The annual production of steel in the United States is a direct measure of our industrialization. To gain an understanding of the minerals industry it is not necessary to plow through the statistics of 150 mineral commodities. The annual production of steel and the basic mineral commodity from which steel is produced, iron ore, is a mirror image of the industrial activity of the nation.* The annual production statistics will show panics, depressions, recessions, the ups and downs of Wall Street, and serious labor strikes and brutally portray the mistakes made by administrations and congressional bodies in governing the nation.

1.11. Political actions by the U.S. government have often had as profound and lasting effect upon the minerals industry as research and technology developments. Such actions include government organization, government interference in the marketplace, setting of border lines, acquisition of new territory, mining laws, environmental laws, public land withdrawals, active wars, threatening wars, social programs, and, in general, political inaction by the government when action is needed. Some political actions have had highly beneficial effects and others severely detrimental; political inaction when action is needed has been the most devastating, and it has set a course for the future that is almost politically irreversible. Political inaction is usually the result of the president, the president's cabinet, and Congress failing to recognize that the minerals industry is undergoing a massive change either in available ore reserves, insufficient investment capital, or intense competition from foreign sources. The effects of political action and inactions are discussed in later chapters.

    1.12. The six primary and accompanying secondary process systems for obtaining mineral commodities are shown in table 1.1. *All of the primary systems, with the exception of three, require breaking rock, either mechanically or chemically.* In the sequence of all these processes, transportation is a necessary part of the process, and in total it may be and often is an expensive component in the recovery and marketing of a commodity. Table 1.1 is shown in more detail in table 1 in appendix 1. The subsystems under the secondary systems are presented in considerable detail, in table 1 in appendix 2, in order to convey the complexity of a mining operation and the wide range of scientific knowledge required to produce a mineral commodity. Table 2 in appendix 2 shows the various components of managing a mining plant, the complexity of the operation, the range of scientific knowledge required for operation, and the constant and never-ending effort to hold costs to a minimum by continuously keeping abreast of new technology and research in progress.

    1.13. In the prospecting system, the mining engineer, petroleum engineer, or geologist of the prospecting team is faced with the problem of finding a mineral deposit often buried deep in the Earth, somewhere within a landmass that may be hundreds of square miles in area. When a deposit has been found, then the design of the plant and the commercial value of the deposit must be predicated on the information gleaned under the prospecting system. Not an easy task by any measure, because a mistake here can cost a company millions of dollars. The planning processes are discussed in more detail in table 1–2.1 in appendix 2. The management of a petroleum or gas field or mine plant is an extremely difficult task. The line between profit and loss can be easily breached. A suddenly caved bore hole, destruction of a drill platform, underground cave, open pit slope failure, fire, dust explosion, rock burst, or minute

6

Table 1.1
Primary and Secondary Process Systems to Obtain Mineral Commodities

1.	PROSPECTING	
	1.1.	Search processes
	1.2.	Discovery processes
2.	PLANNING	
	2.1.	Plant design processes
3.	VALUATION	
	3.1	Environmental analyses processes
	3.2	Economic analyses processes
4.	DEVELOPMENT	
	4.1.	Preparation for mining processes
5.	MINING	
	5.1.	Extraction processes
6.	REFINING	
	6.1.	Extraction and purification processes for petroleum, natural gas, and natural gas liquids
	6.2.	Extraction and purification processes for solid fuels, metals, and nonmetals
	6.3.	Material development processes

change in grade of ore downward often can be the difference between profit and loss and, at times, even bankruptcy.

1.14. In the search and discovery of minerals other than liquid and gaseous fuels, many mining companies will, depending upon the location, size, and type of the mineral occurrence, spend between $1 and $20 million in process systems 1, 2, and 3. An additional amount of $5-500 million or more is required in process systems 4, 5, and 6. In the search and discovery of liquid and gaseous fuels, the initial costs are even greater. In the United States the oil companies have to bid for tracts of land on the coastal continental shelf. These bids are made primarily on the structure of the tract as determined under the prospecting system. What may be considered a low bid on some of the tracts may be $25 million. High bids are often in the $75–100 million range. However, no matter what the bid is and the total costs of process systems 1 through 6, the eventual user of the final product is the one who pays for it all, including an additional amount for profit to the operator.

1.15. Environmental laws in general and land use, withdrawal, and exclusion laws have a definite effect in the planning and valuation systems. All such laws must be reviewed and analyzed prior to proceeding with any of the search processes in the prospecting system (see tables 1:1.113 in appendix 2). If there effect is found to be too adverse, it may require abandonment of that particular target area.

1.16. A mineral deposit discovered in the crust of the Earth under the prospecting system has a basic value that is measured in dollars, which is the prospective wealth of the deposit to the mining company

7

or corporation. This value is established in the valuation system. The value must be sufficient to bear the cost of systems 1 through 6, plus taxes and profit, together with redeeming of all capital expended at a fair rate of compound interest.

1.17. However, not only do the mineral deposits have a value to a mining company or corporation, but they also are, if occurring within the boundaries of a nation, a basic source of wealth to that nation. The wealth is measured not only by the personnel employed, equipment required, and taxes paid to produce the mineral commodity but also by elimination of the need for an expenditure of funds to import the commodity, which in effect transfers wealth from the importing to the exporting nation.

1.18. Technological developments in the minerals industry have the effect of producing more wealth through the production of improved and new products, which results in higher yields in agriculture and fisheries and improved manufactured products for all other uses. Because the production of a mineral commodity produces wealth, the full value or wealth of a mineral deposit contributed to a nation is realized by obtaining a marketable mineral commodity utilizing all of the process systems shown in table 1.1. The amount of wealth that a mineral deposit contributes to a nation is determined by the required number of primary process systems utilized to obtain the mineral commodity; if all required primary systems are used to obtain the mineral commodity, the maximum wealth of the mineral deposit to the nation has been realized. In brief, for a nation's obtaining the maximum value or wealth from a mineral deposit requires that the mineral deposit be situated within its borders and all of the required system processes of table 1.1 be utilized to obtain the mineral commodity.

1.19. Mineral commodities are imported into the United States as mined material in their crude state (primarily petroleum) or as commodities that have been processed through one or more of the subsystems under the refining secondary systems (see tables 1:6.1, 6.2, 6.3 in appendix 2). Table 1.2 shows the ten ferrous mineral commodities that were imported in 1993 and the net import reliance of each (U.S. Bureau of Mines 1993). The net import percentage reliance on iron and steel is combined.

1.20. All of the imported ferrous mineral commodities in table 1.2 require a transfer of wealth from the United States to the importing nation. Some of the European countries and Japan have to import almost

Table 1.2
Net Import Reliance on Ferrous Mineral Commodities in 1993 (U.S. Bureau of Mines 1993)

Mineral Commodity	Percentage Reliance
1. Columbium (niobium)	100
2. Manganese	100
3. Tantalum	86
4. Tungsten	84
5. Chromium	82
6. Cobalt	75
7. Nickel	64
9. Iron ore	12
10. Iron and steel	15

100 percent of the first nine mineral commodities to maintain their industrial base.

1.21. The value of the total nonfuel mineral production in the United States is shown in table 1.3 for years 1989 to 1991. The value of the mineral commodity production, excluding fuels, averages over $30 billion per year and for the three-year period is over $96 billion. This is a tremendous input of wealth by the nonenergy mineral commodities into the nation, and table 1.3 demonstrates that the attention of the president, his cabinet, Congress, and the public should not be riveted only upon petroleum, which then refined provides motion to the automobile. After all, the automobile has to be built before it can run.

1.22. Manufactured products produced from metallic mineral commodities are discarded at the end of their industrial life. At this point the metallic material comprising the product is termed *scrap*, and it becomes a valuable mineral commodity. Scrap may be classified roughly as ferrous, nonferrous, and precious metals scrap. The scrap enters the process system at one of the secondary systems under refining, depending upon its classification (see tables 1:6.221 in appendix 2). There are problems in assembling and collecting scrap, so that 100 percent return of

Table 1.3
Value of the Total Nonfuel Mineral Commodity Production, 1989–91 (U.S. Geological Survey and U.S. Bureau of Mines 1992)
(value in thousands of dollars)

Mineral Commodities	1989	1990	1991
Metals	$11,863,000	$12,442,000	$10,950,000
Nonmetals and Industrial	20,357,000	20,895,000	19,539,000
Total	32,220,000	33,337,000	30,489,000

scrap is never obtained. The highest percentage return of scrap metal is probably gold. However, lead, because of the strict environmental laws governing its use, now has a recycling rate of over 90 percent (Spitzer 1996).

2

The First 100 Years (1775–1875) (Staff of the Bureau of Mines 1956, 1965, 1975, 1985; Perke's and Urdang 1974; Morse 1956; Smith 1984)

2.1. General Cornwallis's surrender to American forces on October 19, 1781, brought an end to the military operations of the American Revolution. However, peace negotiations, which began in 1782, dragged on for almost two years after the end of the war. In 1781 Benjamin Franklin, John Adams, and John Jay were appointed to conclude a treaty of peace with Great Britain. The treaty, known as the Treaty of Paris, was signed September 3, 1783, in Versailles, France.

2.2. The length of the negotiations was testimony to the difficulty experienced in obtaining any kind of reasonable agreement out of Great Britain. Actually, Britain regarded the peace negotiations as little more than a delaying tactic until they again asserted their rule over the colonies. As subsequent events proved, no matter what the terms of the agreement, Great Britain had no intention of complying with them.

2.3. It is doubtful if the new country could have found three better negotiators than Messrs. Franklin, Adams, and Jay. Messrs. Franklin and Adams were both signers of the Declaration of Independence. Mr. Jay was a lawyer and strongly allied to merchant business interests in the colonies, much more so than either Messrs. Franklin or Adams. Each had a different viewpoint of what they wanted out of the peace treaty, but at the same time all were fully aware of the stakes involved. They were prepared to give to achieve an overall end that could be deemed satisfactory.

2.4. The treaty achieved British recognition of the independence of the states and defined the boundaries of the United States; however, the Treaty of Paris did not stop the controversy between Great Britain and the United States. In 1794, war was becoming almost a certainty because of unsettled differences. Pres. George Washington appointed John Jay, then Chief Justice of the Supreme Court, to negotiate a final settlement with Great Britain.

2.5. The result of Mr. Jay's negotiations with Britain in 1794 was what was called Jay's Treaty. Many Americans were highly critical of the terms, including James Monroe, who later became the nation's fifth president, but President Washington felt it was the best agreement that could be reached under the circumstances. However, no matter what one thought of both the Treaty of Paris and Jay's Treaty, in the end Great Britain was "royally snookered."

2.6. At the times that the Treaty of Paris and Jay's Treaty were signed neither side could have known that the largest deposit of iron minerals in the world lying on and just below the surface had been placed within the boundary lines of the United States. That Messrs. Franklin, Adams, and Jay managed to negotiate the boundary line north of the Mesabi Iron Range in what was later to become the state of Minnesota was probably due in part to Great Britain's unyielding attitude of "no matter what we sign, we will not comply with it," dogged determination and patience by the American negotiators, and then both mixed with a large dash of good luck. It was a fortuitous historical political action that a century later was to be the primary force that triggered and sustained an industrial dominance that would last for seventy years.

2.7. In 1803, the United States purchased the Louisiana Territory from France for $15 million. This political action doubled the nation's area, and it also removed a barrier to westward expansion. However, it presented another problem with Great Britain. Just a few short years ago the thirteen colonies were part of Britain's domain. Now they were doubled in area, with apparently unlimited resources at their disposal. It was abundantly clear that Britain was not satisfied with the outcome of the Revolutionary War and that they still considered the United States as their thirteen colonies. Their continuous violations of the United States' neutrality came to a head in 1812, when war was declared against them by the United States. In 1814 the Treaty of Ghent ended the war, but the last battle was fought at New Orleans in 1815, before news of the peace signing arrived. It is indeed fortunate that Gen. Andrew Jackson's troops defeated the British army soundly in this battle, because if they had not, Great Britain would have in all certainty revoked the Treaty of Ghent and continued the war. Great Britain's treatment of the colonies

Table 2.1
Annual Population Estimates for the United States in Ten-Year Intervals, 1790–1875
(Bureau of the Census)
(in thousands)

Year	Total Resident Population	Year	Total Resident Population	Year	Total Resident Population
1790	3,929	1820	9,379	1850	23,261
1800	5,297	1830	12,901	1860	31,513
1810	7,224	1840	17,120	1870	39,905
				1875	45,073

before and after the Revolutionary War was the most ill-advised sequence of actions ever undertaken by that country.

2.8. The successful ending of the War of 1812 with Great Britain had a beneficial effect on the United States, Great Britain faced the fact that the colonies were lost forever and turned its attention towards Africa for colonization. The other European nations recognized that the United States was indeed a potent power in the New World. The United States continued to solidify its borders and remove European colonies on the continent by the Adams-Onis Treaty in 1819, in which Spain ceded their holding in Florida. There were good reasons for Europe to recognize that the new nation in the Western Hemisphere was going to be a real power in the New World. The land area had increased from 864,746 square miles in 1790 to 1,749,462 in 1820, and the population had more than doubled in the same time period; if the population growth continued at the same rate for fifty years, the United States would have as large a population as the larger countries in Europe. The population growth is shown in table 2.1: "Annual Population Estimates for the United States in Ten-Year Intervals, 1790 to 1875" (*World Almanac* 1993).

2.9. In 1816 James Monroe, who was fifty-nine years old, was elected the fifth president of the United States. President Monroe had wide public experience prior to becoming president. He had been an officer in the Revolutionary War, a member of Congress, a member of the Virginia legislature, governor of Virginia, and a minister to France, England, and Spain. While in France he had assisted in the negotiations for purchase of the Louisiana Territory from France. President Monroe was elected to two terms. He was a strong proponent of the United States expanding westward.

2.10. Near the end of his second term, in 1823, President Monroe made a bold move by promulgating the Monroe Doctrine. It was one

13

of the most important political actions made by the United States up to that time. This doctrine spelled it out clearly to the European powers: any further European effort to colonize the Americas (both North and South) or to interfere in their affairs would be considered a hostile act by the United States. The European community had never seen or heard of anything like this. For years they had plundered the world outside Europe at will. If force was necessary, then force was used, but here was a new nation, barely thirty years old, flexing its muscles as if it owned the Western Hemisphere.

2.11. With the Monroe Doctrine in force and Great Britain and France concerned with colonizing Africa, the United States made additional moves in adding to their area. In 1836, Texas declared its independence from Mexico. Texas agreed to join the United States, and it was annexed in 1845. In 1846 the Mexican War broke out, and by 1847 the United States had captured Mexico City. The Treaty of Guadaloupe Hidalgo was signed in 1848, establishing the Rio Grande as boundary, Mexico ceding New Mexico and California in return for $15 million, and also Mexico recognizing the United States' claim to Texas. In 1853, land now included in New Mexico and Arizona was purchased from Mexico in the Gadsden Purchase. The acquisition of additional territory was interrupted by the Civil War, from 1861 to 1865. In 1867, Secretary of State William H. Seward negotiated the purchase of Alaska for $7.2 million.

2.12. In little more than four decades since the promulgation of the Monroe Doctrine, the United States had moved its western boundary to the Pacific Ocean and in the process eliminated France, Spain, and Russia from the contiguous continental landmass of North America. The land area had increased from 1,749,462 square miles in 1820 to 2,969,640 square miles in 1860 (Bureau of the Census 1944). Acquisition of these new territories had gained the new nation tremendous agricultural, fisheries, and mineral resources. They had only to be exploited.

2.13. While the United States was engaged in the political actions described above, there were also technological advances that were critical to its economic strength. In 1793 Eli Whitney invented the cotton gin, which immediately proved to be one of the most important inventions connected with cotton manufacture. In 1807 Robert Fulton was the first to achieve practical success in applying steam to power boats and ships, and he was granted a U.S. patent for the construction of a steamboat.

The government recognized the significance of his invention and later employed him to construct the first steam-propelled warship.

2.14. In 1831 Cyrus H. McCormick invented the reaping and steam-powered threshing machine. It was the first successful machine that could be used for harvesting field crops, and it marked the beginning of mechanization in agriculture. It contributed greatly to technological development of labor-saving machinery in agriculture. Through the rest of the nineteenth century and in the first quarter of the twentieth century the mechanization of agriculture would create a strong demand for ferrous mineral commodities, which were the basic materials for construction of the machinery. Cyrus McCormick's reaper was so successful that it kept in motion continuous agriculture machinery development over a period of fifty-five years. From the end of the Civil War to 1925 the United States' rate of mechanization in agriculture far exceeded that of any other country in the world. John Deere also made a strong contribution to agriculture. In 1838 he designed a plow shaped by bending with a cutting point or share, as it was called, made of steel. The moldboard, which was used for lifting and turning the soil, was made of polished wrought iron. In 1846 in Pittsburgh, Pennsylvania, he produced the first American-cast steel plow.

2.15. In the same year that Mr. McCormack invented the reaper, Michael Faraday, an English experimental scientist, invented the electric generator. Faraday's invention was based on the research by Hans Oersted in 1820, which established the existence of a magnetic field around a conductor carrying an electric current. The electric generator was a stunning discovery, and it was solid proof that Faraday was a genius far ahead of his time with a remarkable ability to transfer basic research into a viable operating technology.

2.16. In 1836 Samuel F. B. Morse invented the magnetic telegraph (Jesperson and Fitz-Randolph 1981). In 1843 Congress appropriated $30,000 for the construction of an experimental telegraph line between Baltimore and Washington, D.C. The telegraph was the first long-distance communication device invented, and messages were transmitted over iron wire by a code devised by Mr. Morse. The telegraph communication method developed by Mr. Morse was accepted readily by both government and industry. The railroads started using the system immediately for communications between cities and towns along their right-of-way.

2.17. Cyrus W. Field, the owner of a paper-merchandising firm, became interested in the possibility of transatlantic telegraphy. In 1856, in collaboration with some New York financiers, Mr. Field established separate companies in the United States and England for the purpose of laying a transatlantic submarine cable. Through the two companies he received grants from both governments, which gave him the necessary funds to complete the project in 1866. It was a remarkable achievement in view of the technology that existed at that time. It was the first attempt at laying a submarine cable, and the technology for the project had to be developed as the work proceeded. Lord Kelvin, a noted British scientist, was associated with Mr. Field in the English company that had been set up to undertake the project. He was the key figure in solving the problems of laying and protecting the submarine cable (Jesperson and Fitz-Randolph 1981). The participation by both government and industry in what was really an experimental project at a high cost was indicative of the deep desire for better and faster communication between nations.

2.18. History of the period from 1775 to 1875 shows that many of the elected presidents and legislators were individuals of acute vision. There is little doubt that there was corruption and some did not measure up to what are termed *statesmen* today. However, year after year there seemed to be always enough intelligence within the government body to move it to back inventions and projects that, if successful, would be highly beneficial to the newly emerging nation.

2.19. By 1875 European scientists had added tungsten, tellurium, molybdenum, uranium, zirconium, titanium, yttrium, beryllium, chromium, columbium, tantalum, vanadium, selenium, cadmium, ruthenium, cesium, rubidium, thallium, indium, and gallium to the Periodic Table of elements. The importance of these mineral commodities was not known at the time, but years later several of them would prove to add greatly to technological development in the United States. Chromium alloyed with steel produced rust-resisting stainless steel, and molybdenum, tungsten, columbium, tantalum, and vanadium became valuable alloying elements to produce special types of steel. At the time that uranium was added to the Periodic Table of elements, nobody, including the most noted scientists, had even an inkling that it would be a mineral commodity that would unleash the greatest destructive power ever developed by mankind. The little-known element zirconium became the necessary mineral commodity in the fabrication of fuel elements in nuclear power plants.

2.20. During the first 100 years most of the nation's mineral commodities were being produced in the area east of the Mississippi River. The northeastern United States produced iron, zinc, lead, and copper. In the southern Appalachians the most important metallic ore deposits were the Clinton iron ores, which occurred in many localities from New York to Alabama. Anthracite coal was produced in Pennsylvania and bituminous coking coal in the Appalachian region. In the midcontinent region iron, lead, and zinc were produced in Missouri, lead and zinc in Wisconsin, zinc, and copper in Tennessee, and iron and native copper in the Upper Peninsula of Michigan.

2.21. Pennsylvania, Alabama, Missouri, and Michigan were important iron-producing states. Iron ore was discovered in the Upper Peninsula of Michigan in 1845, about ten miles southwest of Marquette. The area was named the Marquette Iron Range, Lake Superior Iron Region, and active mining started in 1852. It was called a range because the orebody was located in a series of heights above the surrounding land surface. This was the first known production of iron ore from the Lake Superior Iron District, which was to become one of the great iron–producing regions in the world. The ore was shipped out of Marquette, a port on Lake Huron, to Erie, Pennsylvania, and then by railroad to the blast furnaces in Pittsburgh. The second discovery of iron ore in the Lake Superior District was the Menominee Range, also in the Upper Peninsula of Michigan, near the northeastern border of Wisconsin, in 1867. The earliest record available in the reference *Mineral Resources of the United States* on production from the Lake Superior District and importation of iron ore is shown in table 2.2 (U.S. Geological Survey and U.S. Bureau of Mines 1992). By 1875 production was close to a million long tons per year. However, this was only about 25 percent of the annual production of the nation, and starting in 1872 iron ore had to be imported to meet the needs of the growing nation.

2.22. The discovery of gold in California in 1848 set off the California gold rush in the latter part of 1848 and 1849. By the end of 1849, the population of California was estimated to be greater than one hundred thousand. The state was admitted to the Union in 1850. With a large part of the population searching for gold, it was not long before mercury was discovered at New Idria in 1853; also, the massive movement of people to California in 1849 had a beneficial effect on the neighboring territories.

Table 2.2
Iron Ore Production in the United States in 1875, from the Lake Superior District, 1857–75, and Iron Ore Imported for Consumption 1872–75 (U.S. Geological Survey and U.S. Bureau of Mines 1992)
(in thousands of long tons)

Year	Total Long Tons Produced	Long Tons Produced Lake Superior District	Long Tons Imported for Consumption
1857		26	
1858		23	
1859		69	
1860		114	
1861		114	
1862		124	
1863		203	
1864		247	
1865		194	
1866		297	
1867		466	
1868		511	
1869		639	
1870		859	
1871		814	
1872		949	24
1873		1,195	46
1874		900	58
1875	4,018	881	57

2.23. Closely following the gold rush, gold seekers fanned out from California in a wide semicircle into the new territories as far north as Montana and east to Colorado and Utah seeking the yellow metal and finding not only gold but also discovering copper, lead, zinc, and silver in the following locales: Central Mining District, Grant County, New Mexico, in 1858; Virginia City, Nevada in 1859; Pioche District, Nevada, in 1864; Park City and Main Tintic Districts, Utah, in 1869; Western San Juan Mountains, Colorado, in 1870; Leadville District, Colorado, in 1974; Gilson, District, Colorado, in 1878; Magma and Banner Districts, Arizona, in 1875; and Butte, Montana, in 1864. By 1967 gold mining in Butte was finished, in 1874 silver was discovered, and within a year Butte became the leading mining district in the western United States.

2.24. In 1860 Henry Bessemer invented the Bessemer steel-making process in Great Britain, and in 1864 the open-hearth steel-making process was developed in France (see appendix 4: "Iron and Steel-Making Processes"). Three years later Alfred Nobel in Sweden developed dynamite. In 1868 Andrew Carnegie introduced into the United States the Bessemer steel-making process. Mr. Carnegie had a remarkable insight into what was making America run. He recognized early in life that the way to become rich and powerful in America was to control the iron ore mines and the iron- and steel-producing plants, because every industry would need the most important of all metals, iron and iron alloys, for construction, transportation, and communication. He positioned his companies so that they would become the primary providers of these metals. He became the principal owner of the Homestead Steel Works in Pennsylvania and had a controlling interest in seven other large steel plants. By 1875 his companies were producing more Bessemer steel than any other company in the world. The recorded production of pig iron and steel prior to 1875 in the reference *Mineral Resources of the United States* is shown in table 2.3 (U.S. Geological Survey and U.S. Bureau of Mines 1992).

2.25. Table 2.3 depicts the growth of the iron and steel industry in the United States after 1810. The growth in the production of pig iron was slow and somewhat erratic in the years between 1810 and 1863. After the inventions of the Bessemmer and open-hearth steel-making processes in 1860 and 1864, respectively, growth became more stable, and some of the pig iron was being used to produce steel. The first steel production is shown in 1860, but it is known that steel was produced before that time. John Deere used steel in the share of his plow in 1838, and he cast the first steel plow in 1846. The 1860 production of 13,000 tons is the first reliable number available. By 1875 over 2 million tons of pig iron and over four hundred thousand tons of steel were being produced—a phenomenal growth in a fifteen-year period. The market for the iron and steel being produced was growing at such a rate that pig iron had to be imported starting in 1871 and steel in 1872 to satisfy the increasing demand. Andrew Carnegie was well aware of the tremendous demand for these mineral commodities, and with this knowledge he made a decision that set him on the course of becoming a multimillionaire in a period when a mere millionaire was an exceptionally rich man.

2.26. Petroleum was discovered at Titusville, Pennsylvania, and the first oil well was drilled in 1859. The completion of this oil well was the beginning of the petroleum industry in the United States (Staff of the Bureau of Mines 1956, 1960, 1965, 1970, 1975, 1980, 1985). A year later the first petroleum refinery was built near Titusville. After the well at Titusville was completed, drilling for oil spread rapidly throughout the United States and the world. The most important early use of petroleum

Table 2.3
U.S. Production and Imports of Pig Iron, 1810–75, and Production and Imports of Steel
1860–75
(in thousand short tons)

| Year | Pig Iron | | Steel | |
	Production	Imports	Production	Imports
1810	60			
1820	22			
1828	146			
1829	159			
1830	185			
1831	214			
1832	224			
1840	321			
1842	241			
1846	857			
1847	896			
1848	896			
1849	728			
1850	631			
1852	560			
1854	730			
1855	784			
1856	813			
1857	798			
1858	705			
1859	841			
1860	920		13	
1861	732			
1862	788			
1863	948		9	
1864	1,136		10	
1865	932		15	
1866	1,350		19	
1867	1,462		22	
1868	1,603		30	
1869	1,917		35	
1870	1,865		75	
1871	1,912	245	82	
1872	2,855	296	160	150
1873	2,868	155	233	160
1874	2,689	61	242	101
1875	2,267	84	437	18

was for illumination, and the primary product up to about 1910 was kerosene. At that time gasoline and lubricants would become the primary products; they would be used to power and lubricate the automobile, which began to roll off of a manufacturing assembly line in 1908.

2.27. In the period from 1860 to 1875 an average of about 5 million forty-two-gallon barrels of petroleum were produced per year, to total

20

about 75 million barrels over the fifteen-year period. The average price over this period was $2.91 per barrel at the well-head, for a total value of about $15 million. Coal was the primary energy commodity in use for home and industry needs in the period from 1775 to 1875. In 1870, 17.4 million short tons of bituminous coal and lignite were produced, valued at $2.34 per ton at the mine. By 1875 production had increased to 29.9 million tons, valued at 1.84 per ton.

2.28. The first Homestead Law was enacted by Congress in 1862, during the administration of Abraham Lincoln. The purpose behind the Homestead Law was to enable citizens without capital to acquire land. The initial law provided that any clients twenty-one years of age or older or the head of a family could acquire 160 acres of land on the public domain. The conditions were simple. To acquire title to the land the homesteader had to settle on and cultivate the land for a period of fourteen months. Also, the homesteader was protected by a clause in the law that forbade creditors from levying against the land for debts contracted prior to the issuance of the land grant (Morse 1956).

2.29. The first mining claims to land that later became part of the public domain were staked in Nevada and California by miners to protect the property upon which they were mining. The rules were based essentially on three principles as follows: discovery, development, and mining (see appendix 2:1.2, 4.1, and 5.1). Discovery of the mineral in itself was insufficient right to hold the claim. The claim had to be developed and the mineral mined to retain the rights (Peele 1941).

2.30. During the presidency of Andrew Johnson, Congress enacted the First General Mining Act, on July 26, 1866. After Ulysses S. Grant became president in 1869, this act was largely superseded and repealed by subsequent legislation on May 10, 1872, by the Mining Act of 1872 (Peele 1941). This law was titled as follows: "An Act to Promote the Development of the Mining Resources of the United States." The law was specific and carried through on the three principles of discovery, development, and mining.

2.31. The Mining Act of 1872 and the Homestead Act of 1862 were overwhelming successes. They said to one and all, including the European and Asian immigrant who desired to become a citizen of the United States: seek the farmland and mineral resources of western America that are in the public domain and they are yours. The recent immigrants had never seen anything like this. Where they came from, the king, kaiser, czar, or mandarin held the land and mineral deposits for their own disposal. The new immigrants following in the footsteps of the 1849 gold seekers flooded westward, traversing virtually every square foot of western America. If there was a mineral showing on the surface, they found it. Those that found economic mineral deposits started to mine them, utilizing the technology that they had learned in their home country and the technology that had been developed over a century in the eastern and central United States. Those that were not so lucky worked for those that were or took advantage of the Homestead Law and settled on 160 acres of farmland. The Mining Law of 1872 and the Homestead Law of 1862 had set the stage for America's giant leap forward in industrial superiority.

2.32. The massive search for mineral resources by the early adventurers in western America started by the discovery of gold in California and later the Mining Act of 1866, revised in 1872, had a deleterious effect upon Native Americans. Miners searching for minerals encroached upon their tribal lands in many of the western states, regardless of the treaties that had been reached with the Indians by the U.S. government. The search for metallic minerals was primarily in the mountainous areas of the West. Mountains in the American Indian culture were a dynamic and living land. They were an eternal source of water, food, and clothing. Their rushing streams gave life to the migrating salmon and other fish, and animals migrated into the lowlands from the mountains during the winter when food was scarce. The Indians viewed the mountains with religious awe, because violent storms always appeared to originate at their peak and there were movements on them, such as rolling stones and rock- and snowslides, with no apparent reason behind their occurrence. Thus mountains became the Indians' hunting, burial, and religious grounds. As miners swarmed in on the tribal mountain lands they invaded these areas, digging up the earth and fouling the streams. Even the most peaceful of tribes would rise up in anger at such desecration. The resulting territorial wars usually ended with the U.S. Army attempting to place the Indians on a reservation at a considerable distance from their original tribal land. Miners and Indians absolutely could not coexist in an area. It was a most unfortunate aspect of the settling of the West. However, if it had not been the American settlers, it would have been other invaders from some Asian or European countries seeking mineral resources and land with the same intensity. The era of holding vast areas of land to sustain a small group by hunting was past; it could

22

not possibly exist as population burgeoned on the Asian and European continents.

2.33. The adventurous Americans who traveled westward in the early years were faced with tremendous problems of making the places where they settled civilized communities suitable to live in. They lived in minute segments or enclaves of America within themselves, as if the rest of America did not exist. They had to make their shelter and furniture, be their own bankers, blacksmiths, and carpenters, build their roads and bridges, grow and hunt their food, find sources of drinking water, and provide means for disposal of their wastes, and in many isolated areas they often had to make their own tools. When their work was done for the day they had no place to go but in the shelter that they had built. Barter was a common way for individuals to obtain goods that they wanted. Lawlessness was always a problem. There were those who coveted what others had, and the new settlers or miners had to be ready to protect what they owned by law, because they could not be protected by the nation that had enacted the law.

2.34. The standard of living of these isolated settlers changed dramatically whenever their settlement became a station or was within a radial area of twenty-five to fifty miles of a transcontinental railroad. The first transcontinental railroad, the Union Pacific, was completed in 1869 (Smith 1984). The construction of the transcontinental railroads in the United States was rife with graft and corruption, and the Union Pacific was no exception. However, managing to get one railroad through to the Pacific Ocean by 1869 was for the United States a herculean task. The granting of ten alternate sections of land along the right-of-way to help defray the costs has often been criticized, but at that time there was no other way to induce investment to construct the railroad.

2.35. The achievement of getting the railroad built in 1869 was almost miraculous. Oklahoma, North and South Dakota, Montana, Wyoming, Colorado, New Mexico, Arizona, Utah, Idaho, and Washington were still territories (Smith 1984). The drain on the iron mineral resources of the nation was tremendous. A total of 1,780 miles of track had been laid, and the amount of locomotives and railroad cars, both freight and passenger, to service the line required every iron- and steel-producing area in the East and Midwest to produce at full capacity during construction.

2.36. In the period from 1775 to 1875, the populace in general were highly aware of the value of mineral resources to the nation. Individuals might not be able to read or write and if they signed their names it was with an x, but they were acutely aware of the part that mineral resources, especially iron, played in their daily life. During this period the populace dealt regularly with shortages in food, hardware, tools, horseshoes, and various types of machinery. Nails were a scarce product, and handmade wooden pegs were substituted for them. Often a desired tool or nail had to be hand-forged from a piece of scrap iron. A blacksmith was the most important tradesman in a community. Dealing with product shortages constantly made the masses highly aware of how these products were produced and the basic mineral resources that were needed to produce them. No matter what an individual's education level, he or she could not help but realize the value of a plentiful supply of mineral resources; they recognized that mineral resources were the roots that nourished their well-being and exercised a definite control over their standard of living. Tools and supplies, such as hammers, saws, axes, shovels, mauls, wedges, picks, and nails were treasured like gold and silver.

2.37. An individual who lived in the western part of America was also acutely aware of the tremendous difference in his or her standard of living when he or she lived near a railroad. Not only was transportation available but also fast telegraphic communication with the East. They had a market for the fruits of their labor, and sales and purchases could be made with money rather than by the never satisfactory and often time-consuming system of bartering.

2.38. The populace was also well aware that mineral resources were behind the continuous and tenacious efforts to colonize the Americas by European nations. Europe wanted the mineral resources so that they could be manufactured into products and exported back for sale. This high awareness of the value of mineral resources by the populace was reflected in many of their elected politicians having the same level of awareness. The Monroe Doctrine and the Mining Act of 1872 were political actions that were the result of the populace's knowledge of the value of mineral resources. The Monroe Doctrine kept the would-be colonizer out of the continent, and the Mining Act assured a plentiful supply of mineral resources for the nation to produce their own marketable products.

3

The Next Forty-five Years (1875–1920) (Peele 1941, Ridge 1968, Perkes and Urdang 1974, Morse 1956)

3.1. The Mining Law of 1872 and the Homestead Act of 1862 proved to be the most important laws enacted by the United States since the promulgation of the Monroe Doctrine. The Mining Law established a rule of order in the mining districts of the West, and it was the catalyst that was needed to continue after the 1849 gold rush the exploitation of America's mineral resources other than gold. In Europe and Asia there was no incentive for an individual to search for mineral resources; if an individual did find minerals, he was reluctant to report it, because in all probability he would be charged with poaching or trespassing on the supreme ruler's domain. The result was that only a few individuals were authorized to search for minerals on these continents or in Africa, whereas in the United States, with the Mining Law of 1872 in force, there were thousands searching for minerals in the public domain.

3.2. The mining law's effect was to make the far western part of the nation an integral part of the United States. Within a few years after its enactment, Butte, Montana, had become a major producer of copper, gold, silver, zinc, and lead and had known reserves of cadmium, bismuth, selenium, tellurium, and manganese. The Coeur d'Alene District in Idaho was producing lead, zinc, and silver, and the Homestake Mine, in South Dakota, was producing gold. Other mining districts were being discovered in Washington, Nevada, Utah, Arizona, Colorado, and New Mexico. The East needed the mineral commodities that the West was producing, and the West was dependent upon the East for new machinery, parts, and supplies.

3.3. In March of 1876, Alexander Graham Bell sent his first message by telephone (Jespersen and Fitz-Randolph 1981). Thomas Edison, who already had several inventions to his credit, improved upon Mr.

Bell's invention. The telephone system of communication, unlike the telegraph, was not adopted as readily by the public, primarily because of the need of a central system to relay calls; however, as soon as relaying calls through a central system proved to be feasible, the use of the telephone spread rapidly (Jespersen and Fitz-Randolph 1981). Also in 1876, the gasoline engine was developed in Germany. This invention, along with the diesel engine, which was patented in 1892, was to have a profound effect on the United States. In less than half a century these two inventions would create a massive demand for ferrous and hydrocarbon mineral commodities. In 1880–82 Thomas Edison built a central electric power station in New York City to power the incandescent light bulb, which he had invented. Thomas Edison had taken Michael Faraday's invention and put it to practical use. This proved to be the dawn of the electrical age, and it created a huge market for steel, copper, and nonmetallic materials. The growing demand for copper was filled by the rapid expansion of production from the Butte, Montana, copper mineral deposits.

3.4. The gold rush of 1849 and the continuous news of new mineral discoveries in the West raised public concern for more transcontinental rail service. This concern was also heightened by the fear that England would take over the Washington Territory in the Northwest. The result of this concern was government sponsorship of additional transcontinental railroads under somewhat the same terms as those under which the Union Pacific was constructed.

3.5. There was a downside to this expanding industrialization with a correlative expansion in the minerals industry, and that was the formation of trusts. The Standard Oil Company was formed in 1870. In 1882 the first trust was formed when John D. Rockefeller and his associates merged their petroleum companies to form the Standard Oil Trust to control production and prices and drive out competitors. To stop the forming of trusts Congress enacted the Sherman Antitrust Act of 1890.

3.6. With the advent of electrical power the electrical-powered vertical hoist began to slowly replace the steam-powered hoist for transporting workers, supplies, equipment, and ore in mines. Also, electrical power hastened the development of the modern elevator, which radically changed the architecture and the manner in which the larger cities of that time developed by making practical the multistoried building. The skyscrapers, as they were later called, were constructed with a steel metal frame and usually an exterior masonry of dimension stone or cement. A tremendous amount of steel and stone or cement could be placed on a small acreage of land to create either living or business space.

3.7. By 1883, everything was in place for a massive industrial surge forward. A transcontinental railroad and telegraphic communications system had spanned the nation, an instant communications system (telephone) was developing at a fast rate, Edison's electrical power plant was proving to be the beginning of the electrical age, more rail transportation was under construction, and with the additional railroad mileage came better and faster mail service. Also, with the electrical-powered elevator the cities could grow in three dimensions instead of just two, thus eliminating sprawl over acres and acres of land. The production of aluminum for industrial use started in 1893. Prior to 1893, production of aluminum was reported in troy ounces, the same units as gold, and even up to 1910 production was reported in pounds avoirdupois. The growth in the production of aluminum is shown in table 1 in appendix 6.

3.8. Coal and petroleum were in plentiful supply, and the West was producing copper, lead, zinc, silver, and gold at a high rate. However, there was one key ingredient missing, and that was a plentiful supply of iron and steel. In all parts of the nation, products and machinery made of iron and steel were in huge demand. The underground iron mines that were supplying the nation with iron ore were having difficulty meeting the rising demand. Companies operating in the western mining districts were experiencing critical shortages of iron and steel products. The companies could develop their mineral discovery, but their output was controlled by the machinery they could purchase. There was a continuous and never-ending scramble for new machinery, parts, and supplies.

3.9. The heavy demand for products made of iron and steel spurred the search for iron ore deposits in all parts of the United States and especially in the Lake Superior District. Two major iron ore deposits, the Marquette and Menominee Ranges, had already been discovered in the Upper Peninsula of Michigan, and with the intense prospecting in progress in the area, a third, the Gogebic Iron Range, was discovered in 1884. The Gogebic Range was located in the southwest corner of the Upper Peninsula and extended into Wisconsin. Apparently the discovery of the Gogebic westward from the Marquette and Menominee Range encouraged prospectors to trek westward into Minnesota. The Vermilion Iron Range was discovered in northeastern Minnesota near the Canadian border in 1885. The principal mines on this range were eventually owned by Andrew Carnegie.

3.10. Five years after the discovery of the Vermilion Range, iron ore containing an average of 52 to 57 percent iron was discovered in northeastern Minnesota on the Mesabi Iron Range in the Lake Superior Region, in 1890 (Ridge 1968). The setting of the northern boundary of the United States in 1783 by Messrs. Franklin, Adams, and Jay, the affirmation of this boundary by Jay's Treaty in 1794, enactment of the Mining Law of 1872, and the discovery of the Mesabi Iron Range had melded together in 1890 to create an industrial giant. The discovery of the Mesabi Iron Range, which would prove to be one of the great iron ore deposits in the world, was to make the greatest change in the United States of any other event in history prior to that time or in the future. The change that America was to undergo from this discovery would be far greater than that caused by World Wars I and II or atomic energy development. The effect of the Mesabi would be subtle over a number of years, and few, if any, politicians would recognize that it was occurring. The mechanization and industrialization that resulted from the discovery would be accepted as a natural course in the chain of historical events.

3.11. The northern part of the Mesabi Range was located twenty miles south of the Vermilion Range and fifty miles northwest of Duluth, Minnesota, a port on Lake Superior. The significance of the discovery of the Mesabi Range was that the deposit was enormous in size, with almost unlimited reserves, the ore was direct shipping—that is, it required no beneficiation—and it could be mined by surface mining methods as opposed to underground methods. Table 3.1 shows the explosive annual production growth after the Mesabi Range came on line in 1892 (U.S. Geological Survey and U.S. Bureau of Mines 1992). In 1890 the nation was producing 16 million long tons of iron ore; by 1902, just twelve years later, total production had more than doubled to 35.5 million long tons. In the third-decade period from 1890 to 1920 annual production of iron ore increased over 4 times to 67.5 million long tons, with the Mesabi producing 54 percent of the total. However, even with the explosive growth in production, there were still some companies continuing to import iron ore from their regular foreign suppliers. The annual long tons imported for consumption are shown in table 3.2. The import tonnage varied depending upon the demand. In 1910 and 1913 it was over 2.5 million tons. At the end of the third-decade period, in 1920, it was slightly below 1.3 million tons.

Table 3.1
Total Annual Production of Iron Ore in the United States, 1880–1920, Compared to That Produced by the Lake Superior District, 1876–1920, and the Mesabi Iron Range, 1892–1920 (U.S. Geological Survey and U.S. Bureau of Mines 1992) (in thousand long tons)

Year	Total Tons	Lake Superior District		Mesabi Iron Range		
		Tons	Percentage of Total	Tons	Percentage of Total	Tons Accumulated
1876		993				
1877		1,025				
1878		1,111				
1879		1,376				
1880	7,120	1,909	27			
1881	7,120	2,307	27			
1882	9,000	2,965	33			
1883	8,400	2,353	28			
1884	8,200	2,519	31			
1885	7,600	2,468	32			
1886	10,000	3,572	36			
1887	11,300	4,731	42			
1888	12,063	5,055	42			
1889	14,518	7,520	52			
1890	16,036	8,944	56			
1891	14,591	7,621	52			
1892	16,297	9,564	59	29		29
1893	11,588	6,594	59	684	6	713
1894	11,880	7,683	65	1,913	16	2,626
1895	15,958	10,269	64	2,839	18	5,365
1896	16,005	10,566	66	3,083	19	8,448
1897	17,518	12,206	70	4,220	24	12,668
1898	19,434	13,779	71	4,838	25	17,506
1899	24,683	17,803	72	6,517	26	24,023
1900	27,553	20,564	75	8,158	30	32,181
1901	28,887	21,446	74	9,304	32	41,485
1902	35,554	26,977	76	13,080	37	54,565
1903	35,019	26,573	76	13,453	38	68,018
1904	27,644	20,198	73	11,672	42	79,690
1905	42,526	33,325	78	20,159	47	99,849
1906	47,750	37,876	79	23,565	49	123,414
1907	51,721	41,527	80	27,245	53	150,659
1908	35,925	28,108	78	17,725	49	168,384
1909	51,155	41,863	82	27,878	55	196,262
1910	56,890	46,329	81	30,576	54	226,838
1911	43,877	35,550	81	23,127	53	249,965
1912	55,150	46,369	84	32,605	59	282,570
1913	61,980	52,377	85	36,379	59	318,949
1914	41,440	33,540	81	19,808	48	338,757
1915	55,527	46,944	85	30,802	55	369,559
1916	75,168	63,735	85	41,325	55	410,884
1917	75,289	63,481	84	41,127	55	452,011
1918	69,658	59,780	86	39,056	56	491,067
1919	60,965	52,392	86	33,263	54	524,330
1920	67,604	57,861	86	36,642	54	560,972

Table 3.2
Iron Ore Imported for Consumption in the United States, 1876–1920
(in thousand long tons)
(in thousand dollars)

Year	Long Tons	Value	Year	Long Tons	Value
1876	17		1901	967	$1,659
1877	31		1902	1,165	2,583
1878	28		1903	980	2,260
1879	284	$ 681	1904	488	
1880	493	1,437	1905	846	
1881	783	2,223	1906	1,060	
1882	590	1,641	1907	1,229	
1883	491	1,208	1908	777	
1884	488	1,334	1909	1,696	4,579
1885	391		1910	2,591	7,832
1886	1,309	1,912	1911	1,812	5,413
1887	1,194	2,207	1912	2,105	6,500
1888	587		1913	2,595	8,337
1889	854	1,852	1914	1,351	4,484
1890	1,247	2,854	1915	1,341	4,182
1891	913	2,457	1916	1,326	4,567
1892	807	1,796	1917	972	3,655
1893	527	907	1918	787	3,464
1894	167		1919	476	2,386
1895	524		1920	1,273	
1896	683	1,037			
1897	490	679			
1898	187	256			
1899	674	1,083			
1900	898	1,303			

3.12. The blast furnace and steel mill capacity to refine the increasing annual domestic production and imports of iron ore had to also expand correspondingly in the third-decade period. This expansion is seen in table 3.3 (U.S. Geological Survey and U.S. Bureau of Mines 1992). It was a remarkable period of industrial expansion in the United States. The surge in industrialization in America in the period from 1890 to 1920 was not matched anywhere else in the world at that time for the simple reason that no other nation had discovered an iron ore deposit comparable to the Mesabi Range or had available unlimited quantities of coking coal and other fluxing materials available for the blast furnaces and steel mills.

3.13. The "Tons Accumulated" column in table 3.1 provides the most significant number in the third-decade period; it shows that by 1920 the Mesabi Range had produced in total over .5 billion tons of iron ore. In fact, the number is solid proof that the Mesabi Iron Range,

Table 3.3
U.S. Production, Imports, and Exports of Pig Iron and Steel, 1876–1920
(in thousand short tons)

Year	Pig Iron Production	Imports	Exports	Steel Production	Imports	Exports
1876	2,093	83		597		
1877	2,315	67		638	35	
1878	2,577	75		820	10	
1879	3,071	341		1,048	25	
1880	4,295	785		1,397	158	
1881	4,642	521		1,779	249	
1882	5,178	605		1,945	182	
1883	5,147			1,874		
1884	4,590	206		1,737		
1885	4,530	164		1,917		
1886	6,365	405		2,870		
1887	7,187	524		3,740		
1888	7,269			3,247		
1889	8,516			3,792		
1890	10,307			4,790		
1891	9,273			4,373		
1892	10,256			5,519		
1893	7,979			4,502		
1894	7,456			4,941		
1895	10,580			6,849		
1896	9,658			5,915		
1897	10,811			8,016		
1898	13,187			10,005		
1899	15,255			11,917		
1900	15,444			11,411		
1901	17,784			15,090		
1902	19,355			16,237		
1903	20,170	672	23	16,279		
1904	18,477	89	55	15,523		
1905	25,751			22,427		
1906	28,344			26,206		
1907	28,875			26,166		
1908	17,848			15,706		
1909	28,891			26,830		
1910	30,580			29,226		
1911	26,487			26,517		
1912	33,294			35,001		
1913	34,682			35,057		
1914	23,332			26,335		
1915	33,506			36,009		
1916	44,167	152	680	47,907		
1917	43,256	86	735	50,468		
1918	43,471	39	302	49,798		
1919	34,737	115	360	38,832		
1920	41,357	208	243	47,189		

31

and only the Mesabi Iron Range, was the reason for America's industrial surge starting in 1892. If there had been no Mesabi Range, America's industrial surge would have been delayed at least thirty years, until many of the iron ore deposits of South America had been discovered and were beginning to supply the world. At that time, America would have been in head-to-head competition with Europe and Japan for the available iron ores, and it would have been impossible for America to achieve the dominance that it attained with the Mesabi for seventy years. History as we know it today would have been completely rewritten.

3.14. Table 3.3 shows that in 1875 pig iron was the dominant mineral commodity produced from ore. Most of the products produced were made from iron, such as iron rails, cut nails, wire nails, iron shapes, plates, bars, and iron wire. The growth in production of pig iron and steel was gradual up to 1892, and then the growth in both resembled the explosive growth of the production of iron ore. By 1902, ten years after the Mesabi came on line, the nation was producing 19 million tons of pig iron and 16 million tons of steel. A decade later, in 1912, when the automobile was coming off the assembly line, the production of steel exceeded that of pig iron, and from that date forward the production of steel continued to increase as more and more marketable products were being made with the mineral commodity steel in place of iron. As the demand for steel products continued, a substantial amount of the pig iron production was being utilized to produce steel. By 1912 no nation in the world could match the United States in the production of the most important of all metals, iron, and the alloy of iron: carbon steel. America without question had become the most dominant industrialized nation in the world.

3.15. Prior to discovery of the Mesabi, underground methods of mining ore in the Lake Superior Region had been well established primarily because of the physical characteristics of the deposits being mined; their depth below the surface and relatively narrow width economically prohibited utilizing surface mining methods. Based on previous experience, it was natural for the companies to start mining on the Mesabi by underground methods; however, as development proceeded and the size and shallow depths of the ore deposits became apparent, surface mining methods (open pit) were adopted (see appendix 2:5.14). The massive occurrences of iron ore where the initial discoveries were made generated considerable activity along the southwest trending range, and by 1900 the extent of the range (110 miles) was known. Open pit mining became the dominant method of ore extraction by 1902 (Ridge 1968).

3.16. For forty years prior to the discovery of the Mesabi Range, iron ore was being shipped from underground mines on the Marquette Range in Michigan to lower Great Lakes furnaces in Pittsburgh, Pennsylvania; thus transportation on the Great Lakes had been well established prior to discovery of the Mesabi Range. The location of the Mesabi close to Lake Superior guaranteed iron ore delivery at lower Great Lake ports without excessive transportation charges. New and additional blast furnaces and steel mills were constructed in Illinois and Indiana, ports on Lake Michigan, and Detroit, a port on Lake Huron. In addition, in the Appalachian Region were the vast bituminous coking coal fields of the eastern United States. Limestone was found in Michigan in huge quantities. All of the raw materials needed for the furnaces were for all practical purposes lying next to one another. No other place in the world had at that time or has now such a fortuitous placing of iron deposits and the necessary other raw materials for making steel.

3.17. Andrew Carnegie had succeeded in obtaining some of the largest deposits to be found on the Mesabi in the vicinity of Hibbing, Minnesota. The open pits owned by Mr. Carnegie were of sufficient size so that the railroad cars could be loaded in the pit directly at the point where the ore was broken; the ore was quite soft and needed only to be shaken up by relatively small charges of dynamite.

3.18. With the change from an underground method of mining to open pit Mr. Carnegie must have recognized that he now was the owner of something that could be imagined only in one's wildest dreams: mines that could produce iron ore on demand. That is, he could turn production on and off almost like a water faucet. Production of iron ore from the pits could be raised or lowered in a matter of a few days. If the demand was heavy, add another steam shovel and more railroad cars; if the demand fell off, pull the steam shovel out of production and store the extra railroad cars on a siding. There was no other iron ore deposit in the world where this on-call demand could be met so easily.

3.19. By 1894, as production was steadily increasing from the Mesabi, Mr. Carnegie must have recognized that he had the wherewithal to drive his competitors in iron and steel out of business in short order. He had mines that could produce a huge volume of iron ore at a cost that no other mining company would meet, and thus his iron and steel mills could undersell all competitors. The exact point in time when Mr. Carnegie became aware of this is unknown, but it is certain that he did recognize it. Moreover, the exact time of the subsequent action that he took in light of this knowledge is unknown, but it must have taken place sometime between 1894 and 1896. The action by Mr. Carnegie was to set a policy for his own company whereby everybody in the iron and steel–producing business would survive. Instead of going the route of driving everybody else out of business, which was attempted by John D. Rockefeller and associates in petroleum, Carnegie went in the exact opposite direction. He made it possible for those companies that were in the iron ore and steel–producing business to stay in business, and also for them to develop new iron ore discoveries when they were found. The policy that was set in motion even allowed new companies to enter the steel and iron ore–producing business, if they had discovered an iron ore deposit that could be economically mined.

3.20. Mr. Carnegie set the policy for his mining company on the Mesabi to market the direct shipping iron ore sold to his blast furnaces and on the open market at a price per long ton (2,240 pounds) that would allow all the companies obtaining iron ore by underground mining methods or from foreign suppliers to continue in operation. By this policy, the underground iron mines that were then in operation could continue to supply the demand for iron ore to their own integrated system or on the open market to their regular clients. In addition, companies that had been using foreign ores in their furnaces could continue to import just as they always had done. Mr. Carnegie's company would supply his own furnaces and mills, supply the shortage that was then in existence, and supply the additional demand that would develop by growth in the nation's economy. By 1900, this live and let live policy had made him the wealthiest man in the United States. In 1899, he consolidated his interests in the Carnegie Steel Company, which was merged into the United States Steel Corporation in 1901. He retired at age seventy-one in 1901. Although there were millionaires at that time, Mr. Carnegie was not just a millionaire when he retired; he was a multimillionaire. In today's dollars he would easily be considered a multibillionaire or possibly a trillionaire. The manner in which he collected this vast wealth in such a short period of time is discussed below in paragraph 3.21.

3.21. As stated in chapter 2, the Marquette Range was discovered in 1845 and mining started in 1852 (see paragraph 2.21). The range contained two types of iron ores, which were classified as hard ore and soft ore. A different method of underground mining was used for each ore. The open stope method was used for the hard ore and sublevel caving for the soft ore (see appendix 2:5.). The average mining costs plus royalty per long ton of these two types of ores from the Marquette Range on railroad cars or other vehicles at the mine varied from year to year. Table 3.4 shows the data available on pricing before and after discovery of the Mesabi Range. By 1893, after the Mesabi started producing, the price per long ton of ore quoted in Minnesota was $1.55, reaching $1.75 in 1903, which corresponds reasonably to the average charged by all mines in the United States and that charged in Michigan. This price range spread over ten years quite likely included a profit on each long ton of iron ore produced of about $1.25 to $1.50—a stunning amount when it is realized that in just twelve years, from 1890 to 1901, the Mesabi mines, most of them owned by Andrew Carnegie at that time, shipped 41,485,000 long tons, as shown in table 3.1. This amount of tonnage would net him a profit of $50 to 65 million on the iron ore shipments alone. At the same time he would also gain an additional profit from his iron and steel mills. It is understandable why he decided to retire in 1901: he had more money than he could ever spend or endow to worthy programs in the remaining years of his life; however, he did manage to give away most of his wealth before he died.

3.22. This massive inflow of dollars to the United States Steel Company made it the strongest company in the world financially. Financial panics or slowdowns in the economy had very little effect on it. When the Mesabi Range first started to come into production it served to eliminate the shortages that were occurring in iron ore and at the same time fill the rising demand as the economy continued to grow.

3.23. Between 1890 and 1920, as the iron ore started to flow from the Mesabi, the iron and steel mills started producing an endless river of moderately priced iron and steel products, such as shapes, forms, bars, beams, rails, angles, rods, pipes, wire, cable, sheets, and plates. The ready availability of these products had a profound effect upon the minerals industry. Mining and refinery machinery manufacturers seized the opportunity to double and triple their output. The use of the machinery was automatic by mining operations in all parts of the United States. Many, even in the Far West, had been in operation for years, and such machinery had been in short supply, forcing them to keep operations at a level commensurate with the machinery they could obtain. Now with the opportunity to purchase what they needed, they expanded operations

Table 3.4

Average Value per Long Ton of Ore of Iron Ore Produced in Various Years from 1898 to 1916 (U.S. Geological Survey and U.S. Bureau of Mines)

Year	Average Value Per Long Ton of Ore at Mine		
	Michigan	Minnesota	All Mines in United States
1889			$2.30
1892	$2.20	$2.46	2.04
1893	1.84	1.55	1.66
1894			1.14
1895			1.14
1896			1.42
1897			1.08
1898			1.14
1899			1.42
1900			2.42
1901			1.71
1902	2.40	1.58	1.84
1903	2.40	1.75	1.84
1904	1.97	1.43	1.56
1905			1.77
1906			2.11
1907			2.55
1908			2.27
1909			2.15
1910			2.47
1911	2.66	2.07	2.11
1912	2.27	1.80	1.88
1913			2.19
1914			1.81
1915	2.07	1.77	1.83
1916	2.58	2.32	2.34

and moved aggressively toward expanded exploration and development programs.

3.24. Slowly but surely many small mines became large ones, and by 1900 America's industrial dominance was off and running. The basic technology was all in place when the unlimited supply of iron and steel products was made available, and it was just a matter of applying the known technology. The Spanish-American War, which lasted from April 25 to August 12, 1898, caused hardly a ripple in the upward-trending production curve of iron ore because of the strong steadily increasing demand prior to the beginning of the war. From 1900 to 1910 production from the Mesabi increased yearly, and by 1912, when the Mesabi was almost 100 percent surface-mined, the machinery manufacturers could supply almost any amount and type of machinery and equipment needed

36

by any industry in the United States. The flood of machinery available in the United States was unmatched anywhere else in the world at that time.

3.25. Even with the Mesabi producing iron ore at a high rate, the industrial expansion of the United States was expanding at such a rate that production from new iron ore mines could enter the market. An important one, the Birmingham District, Alabama, started producing iron ore in 1899, mostly from underground mines. Since the initial discovery the district produced on an average about 6.0 million long tons per year until imports of iron ore from South America forced closure.

3.26. At Bingham Canyon, Utah, underground mining for copper started in 1904, but within two years surface waste stripping was begun while the underground mining was in progress. Surface mining began in 1907, and by 1914 all the porphyry coppers of the Bingham District were being mined by open pit (Ridge 1968). The Bingham District, Utah, supplemented the copper being produced in Butte, Montana, and after consolidation of the many small properties more than one hundred thousand tons of ore were being mined per day (Pfleider 1968). The Bingham Canyon open pit mine became one of the largest in the world. In the later years of the life of the mine, one ton of the ore contained roughly 1,986 pounds of waste rock and 14 pounds of copper.

3.27. Although many new mineral deposits other than gold were coming on line, the western prospector still had a fascination with gold. This was amply proven when in 1896 gold was discovered in the Klondike, a region in the Yukon, Territory, in Northwest Canada. An estimated thirty thousand gold seekers invaded the Klondike in 1897–1900, in what has been called the Klondike Gold Rush. The event received considerable publicity at the time and even now is romanticized in the movies and on television, but in actuality it was nothing more than a minor event, a momentary blip on the screen, in the mineral industry history of North America. Much more important were the discoveries of petroleum in Pennsylvania, iron ore on the iron ranges in Michigan, copper in Montana, Utah, and Arizona, and, most important of all, iron ore on the Mesabi Range in Minnesota.

3.28. During the period from 1890 to 1910, as the metallic minerals were being discovered, developed, and produced at an increasing rate, new discoveries and increased production was occurring in the nonmetallic minerals. Prospecting for petroleum was helped by the tremendous surge of people westward searching for all types of minerals. In 1894 the first oil field near Santa Barbara, California, was discovered. In 1908 the first discovery of oil in the Middle East was reported.

3.29. These discoveries all made news as they occurred, but none made news comparable to that by Guglielmo Marconi when, in 1901, he was successful in communicating between Cornwall, England, and Saint Johns, Newfoundland, by a wireless electrical method. Mr. Marconi had taken the scientific studies of Oersted, Ampere, and Hertz and developed a practical method of wireless electrical communications called radio (see appendix 3). His wireless system became standard equipment on ships using the Morse code for communication; about twenty-five years later, after wireless transmission of voice had been developed, radio would become a major part of the entertainment industry.

3.30. Development of engineering technology for mining and refining the metallic and nonmetallic deposits as the industrial dominance grew was steady. The most rapid technological developments were taking place in petroleum. In 1901 motor oil was marketed by Mobil Oil Company. Prospecting methods for search and discovery of petroleum were being improved as each new oil field was discovered. Borehole drilling methods were being improved constantly, and in 1910 the first on-shore drilling for oil in water was started in Louisiana. The United States was the undisputed leader in the world in technology for prospecting and drilling for petroleum.

3.31. Advancement in technology in the metallic deposits centered mainly around the development of more efficient rock-breaking methods, new underground mining methods, faster underground transportation of the broken rock, and obtaining higher recovery of the minerals from the rock by improved technology of minerals separation. The hydrometallurgy process development that proved to be the most successful was froth flotation (see appendix 2: 6.212). The first commercial froth flotation refining plant was built in 1911. At this mill only one mineral was separated from the rock. By 1925 almost all of the copper, lead, and zinc mining camps were using the selective flotation process to separate two, three, or more minerals from the rock. This hydrometallurgical process made possible the treatment of low-grade and complex ores, which were not economical to treat under the methods listed under 6.211 in appendix 2. Development of the process had the effect of doubling, tripling, or even quadrupling the ore reserves in many mining districts. E. H. Crabtree and J. D. Vincent in the AIME volume on froth

38

flotation describe the process as the major technological breakthrough in the history of the mining industry (Fuerstenar 1962).

3.32. From 1875 to 1920 the United States was a leader in the development of improved technology of hydrometallurgy processes; however, it was not the leader in development of improved technology of pyrometallurgical processes. Also, there was little, if any, basic research under way in the United States during this period. Almost all of the basic research was being done in Europe. There were a series of basic research discoveries in Europe in the decade from 1895 to 1905 that at that time were not viewed as sensational but later proved to be fundamental to the development of the atom bomb during World War II. Henry Semat, Ph.D., in his book *Introduction to Atomic and Nuclear Physics* considers the decade from 1895 to 1905 as the beginning of modern physics (Semat 1958). During this period, J. J. Thomson discovered the electron as one of the constituents of the atom, Bequerel and Roentgen discovered natural radioactivity and X rays, and Planck developed his theory on radiant energy, which led to the development of the quantum theory of radiation and later to quantum mechanics. It was also during this period that Einstein developed his theory of relativity.

3.33. In addition to the scientific and technological developments, significant political actions that had great effect on the minerals industry were also taking place. The period from 1900 to 1914 could be termed the period of "trust busting." The greatest offenders in forming trusts were corporations in the minerals industry. To shore up the Sherman Antitrust Act of 1890, Congress passed the Clayton Act in 1914. In the same year Congress also established the Federal Trade Commission. This agency was given broad regulatory powers over corporate structure.

3.34. In 1903 Wilbur and Orville Wright made the first flight in a motor-driven airplane. In 1907 Pres. Theodore Roosevelt authorized construction to begin on the Panama Canal across the Isthmus of Panama. At the time the canal was started, surface mining had been in progress on the Mesabi Range for fifteen years; thus the technology for moving huge amounts of earth and broken rock by steam shovel and railway haulage had been well established. The construction of the Panama Canal was one of the great engineering feats of that time. A total of seven years was required to complete construction, at a cost of close to $367 million.

3.35. In 1903 Henry Ford founded the Ford Motor Company, and ten years later, in 1913, he introduced into the plant standard parts and assembly line techniques. Although Mr. Ford was not the first to employ such practices, he was the first to apply them practically. With this technological development in the automobile industry, gasoline and lubricants instead of kerosene became the primary products of the petroleum industry and the United States went into an orbit of industrialization far above that of any other nation in the world. As the automobiles began to roll off the assembly lines, a subtle change in the infrastructure of the United States began to take place. To accommodate the automobile, roads were being graded and paved, bridges built on wide rivers to replace the river-current-driven ferries, and homes constructed with an attached building to shelter the family's most precious possession.

3.36. By 1913, just twenty-three years after the discovery of the Mesabi Iron Range, the United States indisputably had become a world power. The continuous development of the automobile industry from 1913 was totally dependent upon the never-ending stream of iron and steel products that were being produced from iron ore obtained from the Mesabi Range and the continuous flow of crude oil from an expanding petroleum industry. Between 1910 and 1920, in addition to the demand for steel by the automobile industry, there was also a strong demand for steel by the railroads and for expansion of the navy. There were many other iron-mining operations in the nation mining by underground mining methods, but their production was static. The underground mines operating at that time did not have the ability to meet an on-call increase in production. The ability to meet an on-call demand was solely the characteristic of the Mesabi Range. To expand production from an underground mine requires redesign of haulage ways and often a change in underground mining methods, which entails a high cost and a time period often measured in years. The underground mines in the Lake Superior Region and in other mining districts were producing at their maximum rate, and any increase in demand for iron ore had to be met by the Mesabi Range.

3.37. The development of the assembly line technique to produce automobiles at a high rate in addition to increasing the use of steel products also increased the amount of petroleum products needed to run them. Fortunately, the thermal cracking process to treat petroleum was developed in 1913. This process increased the yield and quality of products from petroleum.

3.38. World War I started in 1914, and before peace was declared in 1918 it involved thirty-two nations. The United States entered the war in 1917. During the period from 1914 to 1917, the United States increased its army and naval strength and also exported war matériel to Great Britain and France. Mechanization in agriculture was proceeding at a high rate. Tractors were replacing draft animals, and the most casual observer could note that the flatbed truck was replacing the horse-drawn wagon. Even the last bastion of the horse-drawn conveyance, the milk wagon that delivered milk from door to door, was being replaced, although the gasoline-powered milk truck was never as efficient as the wagon drawn by a horse that knew the milk route.

3.39. The phrases *Yankee ingenuity* and *Yankee know-how* were coined to describe America's industrial position in the world. The discovery of the Mesabi Iron Range had the effect of diminishing the awareness of the general populace of the value of mineral resources in their daily lives. The lower Great Lakes blast and open hearth furnaces were producing iron and steel products at such a rate that shortages were not a problem. With no shortages to deal with, a large proportion of the populace no longer recognized the fact that a plentiful supply of mineral commodities was the key to their standard of living and America's industrial might.

3.40. The populace lived with the shortages caused by World War I, but they did not really have the grasp of the importance of mineral commodities in their minds that the populace had prior to the discovery of the Mesabi Range. The individual appeared to be unaware of the roots that nourished his standard of living. The products that he needed were always there; why worry about where they came from? It was easy, too easy.

3.41. This attitude was compounded by the continuous growth in population from 1875 to 1920. In this forty-five-year period, the population expanded from 45 million to over 106 million. This population gain is shown in table 3.5 (Bureau of the Census 1944). The table shows that on an average the population of the United States was increasing by over 1 million a year or, more accurately, about 6 million in each five-year period. There is little doubt but what this rate of increasing population was one of the factors contributing to the industrial surge that was experienced between 1875 and 1920.

3.42. As the nation entered the decade of the twenties, there were few, if any, politicians who recognized what was taking place in the United States. They knew that America was the dominant industrial nation in the world and were intensely proud of the dominance, but

Table 3.5
Annual Population Estimates for the United States in Five-Year Intervals, 1875–1920
(Bureau of the Census)
(in thousands)

1875	45,073	1890	63,056	1905	83,822
1880	50,262	1895	69,580	1910	92,407
1885	56,658	1900	76,094	1915	100,546
				1920	106,461

they had no idea of the responsibilities that this dominance invoked. Most failed to recognize that a nation that was the dominant industrial power in the world could not sit on the sidelines and watch other nations attempt to establish a world order that would be peaceful.

3.43. With the most dominant industrial power as a nonparticipant in the peace-keeping processes after World War I, a massive depression hit the world in less than a decade, and a war even bigger than the one that had just ended broke out again in less than two decades. Would our presidents, our cabinets, and our Congress be any wiser at the end of the depression or at the end of World War II? Would a Washington, Jefferson, Monroe, or Lincoln come on the scene who would be able to understand how the nation had attained the world-dominant position it held and the responsibilities to the world that accompanied the dominance? If there was to be such a person, by now it had become obvious that it would have to be somebody who understood the basic industries, especially the minerals industry. This industry built the dominance, provided the engines for war, provided the engines for peace, and was the roots of our standard of living and the base for every product produced in the United States. How could it be ignored? But sadly, ignored it was.

Summary of the Era from 1875 to 1920

3.44. The period from 1875 to 1920 was a remarkable era in the history of the United States. It included the first seventeen years, from 1875 to 1892, when the nation was experiencing its first need for more iron ore, and the subsequent twenty-eight years of explosive industrial growth, when a massive iron ore deposit was found to fill the need. The period from 1892 to 1920 can be aptly identified as explosive years in industrial growth.

3.45. This explosive industrial growth is best illustrated in graphic form. Figures 3.1 and 3.2 show how the growth was attained. In figure

42

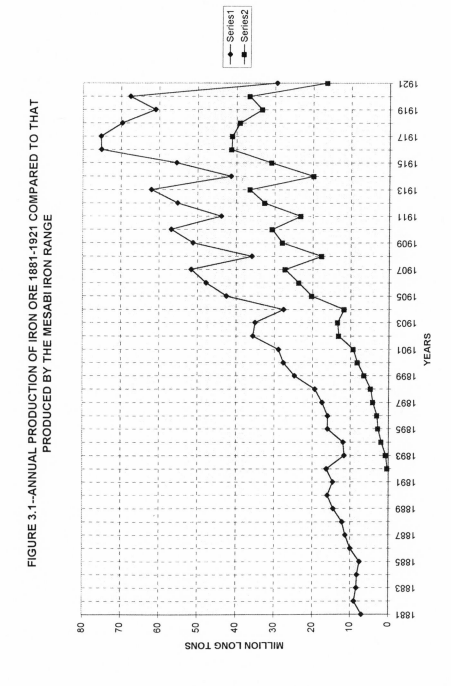

FIGURE 3.1--ANNUAL PRODUCTION OF IRON ORE 1881-1921 COMPARED TO THAT PRODUCED BY THE MESABI IRON RANGE

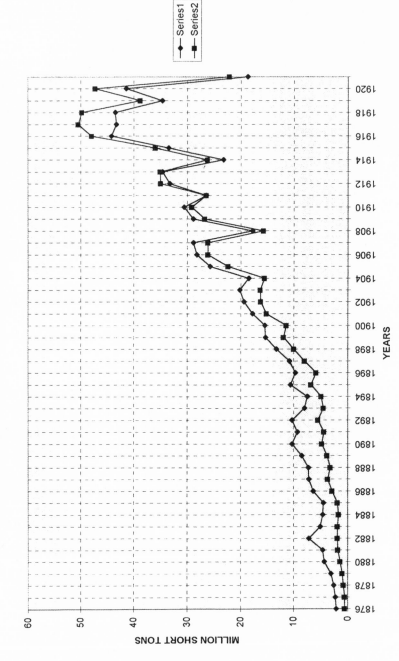

FIGURE 3.2--ANNUAL PRODUCTION OF PIG IRON AND STEEL 1876-1921

3.1, series 1 is the total tons of domestic iron ore produced annually and series 2 is the contribution to the total made by the Mesabi Iron Range. What should be noted in figure 3.1 is the amount of iron ore contributed to the total by the Mesabi Range. If there had been no Mesabi, the total production line (series 1) would have remained between 10 and 20 million long tons through the range of years on the x-axis in the graph. Without the Mesabi the explosive years of tremendous growth would not have occurred and the United States never would have attained the industrial capability that it did by 1902.

3.46. In figure 3.2 series 1 is the domestic annual production of pig iron and series 2 is the domestic annual production of steel. With the Mesabi Range feeding the blast furnaces with iron ore at a high rate, the graph shows a sharp upturn in pig iron and steel production in 1897, and by 1902 the United States was well on its way towards becoming the industrial leader of the world. Ten years later, in 1912, the production of steel exceeded that of pig iron, which cemented America's industrial leadership over the rest of the world. The upward trend in production that started between 1896 and 1897 continued until 1920.

4

The Next Twelve Years (1920–32): Harding, Coolidge, and Hoover (Morse 1956, Perkes and Urdang 1974, Davis 1968)

4.1. In accordance with naval disarmament treaties after the war, the United States demilitarized or scrapped almost two-thirds of its total tonnage. It would be more than a decade before naval construction started up again under the Roosevelt administration. There was a succession of three Republican presidents elected in the next twelve years.

4.2. The first, Warren G. Harding, was elected president in 1920. He advocated a quick return to peace time conditions, which was expressed in his campaign theme: "back to normalcy." However, his administration was anything but normal; it was marked by a series of political scandals in domestic affairs. If there was anybody in Mr. Harding's cabinet who was aware of the value of mineral commodities, it was his secretary of the interior, Albert B. Fall. Mr. Fall was indicted with others in connection with leasing two naval oil reserve fields; he resigned from the cabinet in 1923.

4.3. Tremendous technological developments in aviation were made during the war, and by 1920 commercial air transport lines were in operation in both Europe and the United States. The primary cargo was government-subsidized air-mail service.

4.4. President Harding favored protective tariffs and opposed the entry of the United States into the League of Nations; he wanted to isolate the United States completely from European politics. He, his cabinet, and a major percentage of legislators did not appear to understand that the most dominant industrial nation in the world had to be a leader, not an observer. He made the League of Nations an ineffective body by refusing to join. When Mr. Harding took office in 1921, the nation was experiencing an economic depression that had started in 1920. President Harding attempted to combat this downturn by enacting the Emergency Tariff Act of 1921, followed by the Fordney-McCumber Act of 1922; the latter act empowered the president to increase or decrease customs duties as he deemed necessary. The trust-busting zeal that characterized the period from 1900 to 1914 diminished sharply during his administration. He died August 1923. Calvin Coolidge, his vice president, served the remainder of Harding's term and was nominated and reelected in 1924. President Coolidge, like President Harding, started very few antitrust actions.

4.5. When Mr. Coolidge took over the presidency after Harding's death, the nation was emerging out of the depression that had started in 1920 and surging forward to an even greater world industrial dominance. The leaders of the European nations did not really understand just how great an industrial power the United States had become, and for that matter, it is doubtful if President Coolidge and the elected representatives to Congress actually recognized the direction that the nation was headed. The very nature of the democratic form of government was behind the surge. There was an unlimited supply of iron and steel, and laws had been enacted that encouraged entrepreneurship. The immigrant, who had been stifled so long in his own country, was reveling in the constitutional right to own property and hold a legal right to his own inventions.

4.6. If the Mesabi Range had not been in existence, it is difficult to predict what the United States would have looked like under President Coolidge's administration. Certainly the automobile industry would not have been as advanced as it was, and the infrastructure of the nation would have resembled that of the European nations during that period. It is quite likely that the demand for steel would have generated an intense search for iron ore in Canada and South America, but with available technology in prospecting at that time the rate of discovery of mineral deposits would have been low. None of the processes cited in table 1:1.114, 1.115, and 1.117 in appendix 2 had been perfected, and the only method available was geological survey, which meant teams traversing difficult and rough terrain on foot searching for surface areas of mineralization. Certainly the time scale of the mechanization and industrialization would have been delayed at least twenty, or more likely, thirty years. Without the Mesabi Iron Range the state of industrialization in 1920 would have been delayed until about 1950.

4.7. By 1921 General Motors was beginning to mount a serious challenge to the Ford Motor Company in the production of automobiles.

By the midtwenties General Motors had become the dominant automobile manufacturer in the nation. The meteoric rise of General Motors was helped to a great extent by Henry Ford's reluctance to accept new technology that would have changed radically the original design of the Model T. Henry Ford's failure to modernize his automobile in the late 1920s would give General Motors a dominant lead in the automotive industry for many years. Also at this time, Chrysler was beginning to cut into Ford's sales.

4.8. By the midtwenties, commercial aviation was expanding rapidly, carrying not only mail and cargo but also passengers. The strong demand for steel by the airplane and especially the automobile plants was being filled by the blast furnaces and steel plants in Detroit, Michigan, Chicago, Illinois, and Gary, Indiana. Detroit is a port on Lake Huron, and Chicago and Gary are ports on Lake Michigan. Rolled products, such as plates, shapes, and bars, from the steel mills were being produced virtually on the doorsteps of the automobile factories. The increasing demand for light metallic materials for the framework of the airplane intensified physical metallurgy research in light metals, such as aluminum, magnesium, and titanium.

4.9. The second administration of President Coolidge, from 1925 through 1928, was marked by high prosperity. Mechanization of farms was continuing at a rapid rate, with a corresponding increase in arable land for growing crops other than animal food. The U.S. Supreme Court in 1920 sustained the validity of the Eighteenth Amendment and the Volstead Act, which established regulation of the distribution of hard liquor. The act eliminated the growing of grains and other crops for the liquor industry and thus made more land available for growing crops for human consumption. Mechanization of the farms and the Volstead Act released 40 to 45 percent of the total arable land then under cultivation for growing crops for human consumption. The United States did not have the population at that time to absorb the huge increase that was coming on the market, and the overproduction of agricultural products was causing disruption in the agricultural industry.

4.10. The minerals industry was experiencing great prosperity, with all mining districts in the East and West working at maximum capacity. The Mesabi Range was shipping iron ore out of the upper Lake Superior ports at a high rate. Although President Coolidge did not exhibit it outwardly to the public, he was a shrewd politician. Somebody at sometime called him Silent Cal. Mr. Coolidge appeared to enjoy the nickname, and the press picked it up and used it ad nauseam. However in defense of the media, the constant use of the nickname could have been a mechanism by which they were informing the public that there was no news, absolutely none, forthcoming from the White House. Coolidge appeared to be able to meet any criticism of his presidency and, before it became of any major dimension, quash it without undue effort or publicity. On the outside looking in, his running of the government appeared to be an effortless task, although the strains on the farmer because of overproduction were beginning to show in the latter part of his administration.

4.11. The rapid expansion of mechanization in the agricultural industry was beginning to slow, causing a correlative slowdown in the minerals industry. The fact that two of America's basic industries were beginning to experience difficulties was recognized by the individual farmer and the agriculture machinery manufacturer who were affected, but the elected politicians, even the most brilliant, appeared to have no recognition whatsoever that the great mechanization and industrialization surge that had lasted for almost forty years was slowing down to a crawl.

4.12. The prosperity of the Coolidge administration gave impetus to the use of the two phrases: *Yankee ingenuity* and *Yankee know-how*, which were in common usage prior to America's entry into World War I. They were the outgrowth of the nation's dominant industrial position in the world; however, few people appeared to realize exactly what the forces behind this dominant industrial position were. With the never-ending stream of available products to satisfy every wish and whim, why would anybody need to worry about where they came from? The "roaring twenties" were nothing more than a manifestation of the massive industrial surge that was taking place. Why worry about our industrial position in the world? "Yankee ingenuity" and "Yankee know-how" will keep us there. By the end of President Coolidge's term in 1928, a large percentage of the populace had apparently totally divorced themselves from the roots that nourished their standard of living. They appeared to have only a vague idea of the role of mineral commodities in their everyday life.

4.13. The factors behind the industrial dominance were a combination of political shrewdness, enactment of wise laws to encourage the development of mineral resources, the richest and largest deposit of iron ore in the world at that time, unlimited supplies of all petroleum products, massive deposits of copper, lead, zinc, gold, silver, and other metallic minerals, and huge reserves of nonmetallic minerals, including bituminous coal and, to cap it off, all of the mineral commodities and products produced from them selling at a reasonable market price. One would be hard pressed to say that all of these factors were the result of "Yankee ingenuity" or "Yankee know-how."

4.14. The universities and colleges of that time did not appear to be overly concerned with America's industrial dominance. They accepted the dominance as something that was due America for being a good, true, democratic, and Christian nation. If anything was taught at all on the role of the minerals industries in America's industrialization, it had to be from the professor's own notes, because no textbooks treating the subject in detail were ever published. It is indeed impossible to find any detailed historical treatment of the minerals industry, and the effect that enactment of the Mining Law of 1872 and the discovery of the Mesabi Iron Range had on the nation.

4.15. Mining companies that were active in the western part of the United States became active in the 1920s in opening up mining districts in South America, especially in Chile and Peru. The production from these mines was primarily copper, gold, silver, and zinc. The size of the mines required a large native labor force, and the high standard of living attained by the labor force made them a powerful political bloc in their country.

4.16. In 1926 Congress enacted a law that permitted petroleum producers to deduct an allowance for depletion of the resources. Under this law, depletion could be calculated in the oil industry upon one of two different bases. The base most familiar to the general public was the one that provided for a deduction for each property of 27.5 percent of its gross income. The purpose of the depletion tax provisions was to provide incentive for prospecting, exploration, and discovery of new petroleum reserves. The law achieved its purpose, as prospecting proceeded at a high rate. Its effect on petroleum production was comparable to the effect that the Mining Law of 1872 had on the western United States.

4.17. Under President Coolidge's administration the automobile was becoming a means of transport throughout the United States and tourism was starting to flourish. Motels and restaurants were being built to accommodate the traveler. The value of tourists was not lost on the mayors of cities and towns. It was "manna" from the automobile instead of heaven, and there was nothing ethereal about it, because it meant an infusion of new money into the towns, which otherwise never would have happened.

4.18. In 1928 President Coolidge surprised the nation and the Republican Party by announcing that "I do not choose to run for president in 1928" (DeGregorio 1993). Many politicians at that time were of the opinion that Coolidge's phrasing of the statement meant that he wanted the party to draft him to serve another term. If such was true, he certainly got a big surprise, because the Republican Party took him at his word, trumpeted to the world that we needed an engineer to run the nation, and nominated Herbert Hoover to run for president. If President Coolidge had stated bluntly that he wanted to run again for the four-year term, the Republican Party would have had to nominate him. It is possible that President Coolidge politically outmaneuvered himself this one critical time, but then again perhaps not. It is possible that he felt that with the prosperity of his administration at a high point there was nowhere else to go but down or was shrewd enough to see on the horizon trouble in the stock market and the massive economic depression that blanketed the nation after 1929. Whatever it was that caused him to make his "I do not choose to run" statement, it succeeded in dumping on Herbert Hoover the total blame for the stock market crash in 1929 and the ensuing Great Depression.

4.19. Mr. Hoover was secretary of commerce under Presidents Harding and Coolidge. Like Presidents Harding and Coolidge before him, Hoover instituted very few antitrust actions during his four years in office. Tourism, which was beginning to flourish under the Coolidge administration, continued during Hoover's administration, but at a reduced rate.

4.20. President Hoover's administration was noteworthy for the stock market crash of 1929. The crash and the ensuing economic depression had a devastating effect on the minerals industry. Mining districts all over the West closed down, and the Mesabi Range production dwindled to a trickle compared to what it had been. In one of the years of the depression the ad valorem tax (State of Minnesota tax on the unmined iron ore) was higher per ton of ore than the price received per ton of ore mined. President Hoover was a very able administrator, as four presidents, Harding, Coolidge, Truman, and Eisenhower, would willingly testify, but had great difficulty in dealing with the then Democratic-controlled Congress. He had no control over the events that were responsible for the 1929 stock market collapse any more than any other politician. He just happened to be the sitting U.S. president when it occurred.

4.21. Although the depression was starting to take a stranglehold, the United States was at the highest state of mechanization and industrialization of any country in the world. The automobile manufacturers were producing new models with higher-horsepower engines each year. With the more powerful engines, freight motor trucks plying the state and interstate highways were providing another method of transporting products; and the passenger-carrying motor buses were beginning to cut deeply into the passenger revenue of the railroads. By 1930 commercial aviation had expanded to 500 planes. A manufacturing firm could purchase by direct order any size or shape of rolled steel, from which a product could be developed for sale on the market.

4.22. Ideal examples of the rolled steel shapes available and products made from steel were contained in the tenth edition of the *Carnegie Shape Book*, published in 1929 by the Carnegie Steel Company (Carnegie Steel Company 1929), and the *Roebling Catalog* of wire rope (cable) and wire published in 1930 by the John A. Roebling Son's Company (1930). The *Carnegie Shape Book* listed more than twelve hundred shapes, all of different dimensions, of rolled steel products for sale. Shapes, plates, bars, and rails were listed for construction of ships, cars, buildings, and railroads. A detailed breakdown of the listings is shown in table 1 in appendix 5. No country in the world had this amount of ready to order variable-sized steel products on inventory. John A. Roebling Son's Company catalog listed over one thousand variable sizes of wire rope and wire made out of five different grades of steel and one grade of iron. Any purpose for which wire rope or wire was needed could be filled from the listed inventory.

4.23. During President Hoover's term the largest oil field in the United States was discovered in West Texas, in 1931. Also, basic research was being expanded in the state universities. In particular, the University of California at Berkeley was starting a basic research program in experimental and theoretical physics. E. O. Lawrence and Robert Oppenheimer were instrumental in starting the research at Berkeley to dissect the atom (Davis 1968). Dr. Oppenheimer, born in the United States, was probably one of the most brilliant theoretical physicists in the world at that time and, for that matter, the most brilliant the United States has ever produced. He was brought to Berkeley by Dr. Lawrence because of his knowledge of quantum mechanics, which was an extremely difficult field of theoretical physics to comprehend. Dr. Oppenheimer was to play an important role later in development of the atom bomb, during the Roosevelt and Truman administrations. Dr. Oppenheimer started teaching a graduate course in quantum mechanics at Berkeley in the fall of 1929. Although he was given a medal for his wartime service, he has never received the recognition he deserves from the public as one of the greatest scientists of the United States. The state of technology in 1930 on radiation and electromagnetic waves is discussed briefly in appendix 3.

4.24. To combat the depression President Hoover and Congress followed the lead of former president Harding and enacted the Hawley-Smoot Tariff Act in 1930. This act raised customs duties on an average of about 20 percent; the act also retained the power of the president to increase or decrease custom duties, as in the Fordney-McCumber Tariff Act, which was passed under the Harding administration. However, all efforts that President Hoover made to combat the depression were unsuccessful. The Republican Party nominated him to run again in 1932, but Franklin Delano Roosevelt during the campaign reiterated constantly that Mr. Hoover was doing nothing that would take the nation out of the economic depression. Hoover was defeated in 1932 by Mr. Roosevelt.

4.25. There were probably a combination of factors that caused the economic depression. heading them would be the almost unlimited purchases on margin in the stock markets. When the bubble burst and it was time to pay for the stock purchases, many could not meet the margin call. The change that the United States was undergoing because of mechanization did not appear to be recognized by any politician at that time. A massive change was occurring in agriculture; the automobile and aviation industries were making huge changes in methods of transportation and causing correlative changes in the infrastructure of the United States; and employment in the bituminous coal mines was being reduced annually. The changes caused by these industries were massive in character, but so subtle that they were not immediately detectable in the general economy, because there was never a shortage of iron, steel, petroleum, and other essential mineral commodities. The continuous flow of the needed mineral commodities to the automobile, aviation, and agricultural industries was silently forcing the United States into a state of mechanization whereby the combined production of these industries would be a primary factor in the state of prosperity of the nation. If these industries were in a downturn demand period, then it was almost a certainty other industries in the nation would experience the same downturn.

4.26. The bituminous coal division of the minerals industry was an ideal example of how mechanization was affecting the United States. The percentage of underground coal mechanically mined rose from 4.5 percent in 1928 to 7.5 percent in 1929; by 1939 the percentage had raised to 31.0 percent (see appendix 7: "Bituminous Coal and Lignite," table 1). The continuously increasing mechanization in the industry over a period of ten years caused a continuous reduction in the work force over the same period of time, and this is the reason by Appalachia was so hard hit during the depression: recovery just could not occur with the year-after-year reductions in employment. Instead of the work force going back to work as the depression eased, more of the work force was being laid off.

4.27. The Fordney-McCumber Tariff Act was not the best piece of legislation to have on the books during a depression, and certainly President Hoover and Congress tended to exacerbate the situation with passage of the Hawley-Smoot Tariff Act in 1930. The failure of all three presidents, Harding, Coolidge, and Hoover, to maintain rigid control over the formation of trusts may have been a factor in causing the depression, but it is difficult to put too much blame on trusts in a depression that was so deep and severe; housing was priced reasonably low, and products needed for almost any use were modestly priced and available on the market. If trusts were a factor in the depression, how they affected it is obscure. Certainly a large part of the public themselves must share some of the blame; during the "roaring twenties" they immersed themselves in breaking the Volstead Act. It was the thing to do. Millions of dollars were lost in taxes, and millions of dollars were wasted annually in trying to enforce the act. Vice and corruption were rampant. Also, almost all employees in the liquor industry were unceremoniously thrown out of work by passage of the Volstead Act; and to add to the above factors mechanization of the farms and the passage of the Volstead Act resulted in overproduction of agricultural products.

4.28. Once all the factors are enumerated they add up to quite an impressive list, and there were probably other unknown factors that were not as obvious as those in the list above. However, whatever the causes were, everything seemed to come to a boil at once. The bottom fell out of the stock market, two of the three basic industries, agricultural and minerals, were almost immediately in deep trouble, businesses were closing, and later many banks were found to be unsound. The nation lay prostrate, and the populace was frightened. They had a reason to be,

Table 4.1

Total Annual Production of Iron Ore in the United States, 1921–32, Compared to That
Produced by the Lake Superior District and the Mesabi Range (U.S. Geological Survey
and U.S.Bureau of Mines 1992)
(in thousand long tons)

Year	Total Tons	Lake Superior District		Mesabi Range		
		Tons	Percentage of Total	Tons	Percentage of Total	Tons Accumulated
1921	29,491	25,298	86	16,380	55	577,352
1922	47,129	39,716	84	26,805	57	604,157
1923	69,351	59,285	85	41,809	60	646,966
1924	54,267	44,842	83	29,819	55	675,785
1925	61,908	52,057	84	34,851	56	710,636
1926	67,623	57,143	84	37,998	56	748,634
1927	61,741	51,540	83	32,866	53	781,500
1928	62,197	52,517	84	34,856	56	816,356
1929	73,029	62,825	86	42,376	58	858,732
1930	58,408	49,383	84	31,300	54	890,032
1931	31,132	25,877	83	15,599	50	905,631
1932	9,846	8,139	83	4,255	43	909,886

because bread and soup lines were getting longer each day and the United States was at a crossroads. The final solution to the problem was not provided by the politicians; it was provided by war. In all respects the Great Depression was a baffling economic problem, but almost certainly the depression in 1920–23 was a warning that something was going wrong.

4.29. The production statistics of iron ore and iron and steel accurately reflect the depression periods in 1920–23 and 1929–32. Table 4.1 shows the annual production of iron ore compared to that produced by the Lake Superior District and the Mesabi Iron Range. Table 4.2 shows the iron ore imported for consumption in the twelve-year period, Table 4.3 shows the production, imports, and exports of pig iron and steel, and Table 4.4 shows the annual population estimates.

4.30. It took until 1944 for the nation to get completely out of the depression that started in 1920. However, the 1920–24 depression appeared to be just a prelude to the massive depression that hit in 1929 and in all probability was a warning that although the nation was prosperous, there was something that needed tending to.

4.31. Table 4.2 shows that after 1924 many of the overseas producers to maintain their shipments of iron ore to the United States dropped the price of their ore sharply. After 1929 importations dropped by about

Table 4.2
Iron Ore Imported for Consumption into the United States, 1921–32 (U.S. Geological
Survey and U.S. Bureau of Mines 1992)
(in thousand long tons)
(in thousand dollars)

Year	Long Tons	$ Value	Year	Long Tons	$ Value
1921	316	1,076	1927	2,621	6,068
1922	1,135	4,916	1928	2,453	5,428
1923	2,767	11,304	1929	3,139	8,145
1924	2,047	10,581	1930	2,775	8,113
1925	2,191	6,895	1931	1,466	3,902
1926	2,555	5,876	1932	582	1,539

1 million long tons a year until 1932, when the total imported was only
582,000 long tons, which was the smallest total since 1921.

4.32. As would be expected, the production statistics of pig iron
and steel in table 4.3 show the same downturn in demand as the production statistics of iron ore. Unfortunately, during this period and into the
late forties, the data on steel imports and exports in the published minerals yearbooks (U.S. Geological Survey and U.S. Bureau of Mines 1992)
are combined with imports and exports of steel products. The manner
in which the statistics are presented makes it impossible to separate out
the imports and exports of crude steel.

4.33. The annual population growth rate in the United States remained strong between 1921 and 1930. However, in 1931 and 1932 the
rate dropped to less than a million (Bureau of the Census 1944).

Table 4.3
Production, Imports, and Exports of Pig Iron and Production of Steel in the United
States, 1921–32 (U.S. Geological Survey and U.S. Bureau of Mines 1992)
(in thousand short tons)

	Pig Iron			Steel
Year	Production	Imports	Exports	Production
1921	18,691	49	32	22,158
1922	30,486	429	35	39,875
1923	45,204	412	36	50,337
1924	35,174	234	46	42,484
1925	41,105	494	37	50,841
1926	44,097	499	28	54,089
1927	40,954	146	57	50,327
1928	42,734	158	95	57,729
1929	47,728	165	52	63,205
1930	34,761	153	15	45,583
1931	20,107	95	8	20,059
1932	9,576	146	3	15,323

Table 4.4

Annual Population Estimates for the United States, 1921–32 (Bureau of the Census 1944)

(in thousands)

Year	Total Resident Population	Year	Total Resident Population	Year	Total Resident Population
1921	108,538	1925	115,829	1929	121,767
1922	110,049	1926	117,397	1930	123,077
1923	111,947	1927	119,035	1931	124,040
1924	114,109	1928	120,509	1932	124,840

4.34. In one respect, President Hoover's administration was difficult to understand. When he became secretary of commerce in the Coolidge administration, he had the Bureau of Mines moved into Commerce from the Department of the Interior. Mines was primarily a minerals research and statistics agency. Its mission was to promote mine safety and ensure that the nation had adequate mineral supplies for security and other needs. However, at the time it was the only bureau with direct responsibilities for the minerals industry that provided a political voice in the government for the minerals industry. This was the reason he wanted Mines in his department. Mr. Hoover was a mining engineer and was fully aware of the value of the minerals industry to the nation. Why, after he became president, he did not create a a cabinet-level Department for the minerals industry is really not understandable. He, like all others preceding him, appeared to think that the minerals industry needed no representative in the government. Minerals were so plentiful that the industry could take care of itself without a voice as a cabinet-level department.

5

The Next Thirteen Years (1932-1945): Roosevelt (Perkes and Urdang 1974, Morse 1956)

5.1. Mr. Roosevelt, like James Monroe, had wide experience in public life prior to being elected president, which occurred in 1932. He served two terms as a New York State senator. President Wilson appointed him assistant secretary of the navy, and he held that position for the duration of World War I. In 1920 he was the Democratic vice-presidential candidate and running mate of James Cox. In 1928 Roosevelt was elected governor of New York, and he was re-elected in 1930. His long tenure under Mr. Wilson as assistant secretary of the navy served to impress upon him the value of and need for a strong, well-trained navy. During his campaign for the presidency he promised the people a "New Deal," and this became the term to describe his entire tenure as president. He became president at a very critical time in U.S. history. The nation had been in the throes of a massive economic depression for three years prior to his election. Two of the basic industries, agriculture and minerals, were ailing. Roosevelt was critical of President Hoover primarily for what appeared to him to be inaction in trying to combat the economic depression and upon becoming president immediately advocated bold experimentation of economic theories to bring the nation back to prosperity.

5.2. President Roosevelt asked and received from the overwhelmingly Democratic Congress broad powers to combat the depression. He enacted the National Industrial Recovery Act to formulate a program to combat the depression, and the National Recovery Administration (NRA) was established to direct the program. Some of the economic theories that he proposed were indeed bold, especially in agriculture, in trying to deal with the surplus of farm commodities. Legalization of 3.2 beer in 1933 was a cause for celebration throughout the nation, and when full repeal of the Volstead Act was established, Mr. Roosevelt could do no wrong in the eyes of those who were certain that prohibition had been the most stupid experiment in history. President Roosevelt further endeared himself to the public by the use of radio for what he termed *fireside chats*. Radio by the early 1930s had become a major part of individuals' lives, and President Roosevelt used the medium as it had never had been used before. His "fireside chats" were written so that each listener felt that the president was addressing him personally. Roosevelt's voice and his personality would come over the air in a strong, steady baritone, often using the broad *a*, as in "the fahmah"; "the fahmah needs our help"; "we must help the fahmah."

5.3. To start the minerals industry working again, President Roosevelt began building up the U.S. Navy into a strong striking force; construction projects started under the Public Works Administration (PWA) and Works Projects Administration (WPA); construction of hydropower and flood control dams in several places throughout the United States, including the Tennessee River Valley (TVA) and on the Columbia River at Grand Coulee, Washington. These dams were expected to prevent floods, provide cheap electricity for domestic consumption, and attract industrial development because of the cheap available energy. The tourist industry received its fair share of attention by improved roads and bridges. To put young people back to work President Roosevelt started the Civilian Conservation Corps (CCC). Many cities and towns took advantage of NRA programs to improve their airfields.

5.4. President Roosevelt appointed Harold Ickes secretary of the interior. Mr. Ickes had a firm grasp of the importance of mineral commodities to the nation, more so than any of the other cabinet appointees, and became one of the most influential advisers to the president. In addition to administering the Interior Department, Ickes was also appointed administrator of the public works program, with a budget of over $3 billion.

5.5. However, no matter what programs Mr. Ickes pursued with this enormous amount of dollars, the economic depression held onto the nation with a suffocating death grip. The recovery programs appeared to lift the nation out of the doldrums for a few months, but the recovery was never constant (see paragraph 4.26, on the bituminous coal industry, and table 1 in appendix 7). Although President Roosevelt's attempts to combat the depression were only partially successful, the fact that he was at least trying endeared him to the public. The apparent inaction of Herbert Hoover from 1929 through 1932 was still fresh in the minds of the people, and President Roosevelt was easily re-elected to a second term in 1936.

5.6. President Roosevelt reversed the lenient attitude of Presidents Harding, Coolidge, and Hoover toward trusts. The Roosevelt administration became known for the antitrust actions he instituted against many corporations. These court actions against trusts had very little effect on the economic depression, because of the length of time required by the courts to come to a decision. By his programs and his own nationwide popularity he plunged the federal government into regulating the economic life of the nation to a far greater extent than ever before.

5.7. Roosevelt forced industries to collect and pay their share of Social Security and unemployment insurance benefits, gave labor the right to organize and bargain collectively, and demanded that business undertake increased social responsibilities. Those who opposed him, and there were many in the minerals industry who did, considered him a menace to society and felt that his policies would mean the end of free enterprise in the United States. However, whatever the conservative coalitions thought of him, they would admit that he had made changes in America that were irreversible. Social Security, unions, and unemployment insurance were here to stay; fight them to the last gasp, but adapt or die. John L. Lewis and Walter Reuther were two individuals who took advantage of the labor laws passed by the Roosevelt administration. Mr. Reuther was the head of the United Automobile Workers (UAW) union, the largest in the nation. Before the start of World War II he organized sit-down strikes that succeeded in gaining labor contracts with the Big Three automobile makers: General Motors, Chrysler, and Ford. John L. Lewis was the head of the United Mine Workers (UMW), and his union succeeded in gaining labor contracts with coal mine operators that substantially raised the wages of coal miners and set higher safety standards in the mines. John L. Lewis was an impressive individual as he appeared in motion picture news or speaking over the radio, relating his determination to improve the lot of the men who worked "in the bowels of the Earth."

5.8. President Roosevelt's second administration was plagued by the menacing foreign policy of three nations: Japan, Italy, and Germany. Japan had invaded China and was actively at war with them. In 1935 Italy, under the leadership of Benito Mussolini, invaded Ethiopia in defiance of the League of Nations. His successful campaign there gave him absolute power in Italy. Adolf Hitler had also gained absolute power in Germany after the death of Pres. Paul von Hindenburg. At the start of President Roosevelt's second term, Hitler was rearming Germany in defiance of the World War I treaty and at the same time waging a violent anti-Semitic campaign.

5.9. The Japanese war in China was deadly, and the American people were appalled at the news that was being carried in the press and being heard nightly over the radio. It was somewhat of a different matter with Germany and Italy. Motion picture news, which often preceded the main feature at the theaters, carried up-to-date news clips of the actions of Hitler and Mussolini. They would be seen emoting, strutting pompously, and throwing out their chests while speaking before huge crowds. Their ritual for greeting and saluting each other was a comic opera. Mussolini would click his heels, throw his right arm up and out at an angle, and hold the pose for about ten seconds. Hitler would respond by clicking his heels and raising his right arm. Then Hitler would salute first and Mussolini would respond. This would go on for two or three minutes. In American theaters a gentle titter would flow through the audience. As one sat watching it, you expected that at any moment Mack Senett's Keystone Kops would suddenly appear, brandishing their billies, and then all would take off running down the street. The American public in general appeared to have real difficulty in understanding how either the German or Italian people could allow Hitler or Mussolini to stay in power very long.

5.10. President Roosevelt was aware of the violent anti-Semitic program in Germany probably in much greater detail than was being written in the press and described on radio, but he was powerless to do anything more than protest. President Roosevelt had no power base by which he could influence Hitler. The U.S. Navy had been decimated by the naval disarmament treaties of World War I, and the regular army was a small and impotent force. The only war matériel available was that left over from World War I, and President Roosevelt's yearly efforts to increase the budgets of both the army and navy were a matter of lengthy debate in Congress. About the only thing that President Roosevelt could do was send written protests through State Department channels, and if he did send any, it is doubtful that Hitler even bothered to read them. Hitler was not one to listen to reason of any kind, and he later proved that diplomatic agreements, insofar as he was concerned, were nothing but pieces of paper. His comic opera gyrations in motion picture news proved to be no comedy. The war he started in 1939 ended up costing the world millions of lives.

5.11. In his second term President Roosevelt continued to enlarge the role of the federal government in the economic life of the nation. He established the Rural Electrification Administration (REA) and regulated working hours and wages under the Fair Labor Standards Act. The mission of the REA was to place electric power on the farms of the United States. The programs implemented by this agency placed heavy demands on the production of various mineral commodities. Roosevelt's concern for what he called the ill-housed, ill-clad, and ill-nourished led him to state that all citizens of the United States should be able to lead what he called the "abundant life." "Abundant life" to the faithful who adored him meant that in their future was not only an "abundant life" in the place where they lived but also a chance to tour the United States in their own vehicles and even possibly take a foreign jaunt just like the jet set of that era.

5.12. Consciously or unconsciously, President Roosevelt had proposed a plan of unlimited use of mineral commodities. In effect he had set a government policy on the minerals industry, which for all practical purposes was a government policy on all mineral commodities used in industry. From the very top of the government came the statement that all should have the "abundant life." Each individual could make his own interpretation of the phrase *abundant life*, but to most people, the ill-housed, ill-clad, and ill-nourished, it meant something a whole lot different than the way they were living then.

5.13. There was only one way that everybody in the United States could lead the "abundant life," and that was by the unlimited use of mineral commodities produced by the minerals industry. The policy that Roosevelt expounded meant that the minerals industry would have to produce mineral commodities in sufficient quantity for all to lead the "abundant life"; if needed mineral commodities could not be produced within the borders of the United States, they would have to be imported. The message was clear to the minerals industry: if they did not produce the needed mineral commodities, the government would. President Roosevelt's penchant for expanding the role of the government in the economic life of the nation was well known, and if they did not want interference in their affairs, they had better get on with it. However, the "abundant life" policy was not implemented by President Roosevelt. It was implemented by the people after World War II and became the policy of the United States for over fifty years.

5.14. By early 1939, President Roosevelt had to put aside the "abundant life" policy, because most of his time was being taken up by foreign affairs and, in particular, the actions of Germany and Japan. World War II began with the invasion of Poland on September 1, 1939. After Poland was occupied by both Germany and the USSR, fighting was intense on the high seas, but on land it became static nonshooting, with both sides on the western front holding the same positions they held at the start of the war. On April 8, 1940, Germany invaded and conquered Norway, not only for the U-boat seaports on the North Atlantic, but also to ensure that all iron and steel produced in Norway and Sweden would be funneled into Germany. On May 10 the inaction on the western front was broken abruptly when the German army invaded the Netherlands and Belgium and thence France.

5.15. In 1940 President Roosevelt ran for an unprecedented third term. He received virtually no support for another term from the American press; however, he once again took to the radio waves. His personality and voice were never in finer form, and he effectively counteracted the anti–third term editorials that were appearing regularly in many newspapers across the nation. The acknowledged master of the radio won again; he was re-elected in 1940. President Roosevelt had established radio as a powerful force for reaching and influencing a large number of people.

5.16. By early 1941 Germany held all of Western Europe and the Japanese army was rapidly moving to conquer all of China. Germany's position appeared to be invincible, and Hitler was threatening to invade England. An alarmed President Roosevelt managed to get the Lend-Lease Act of 1941 passed. He likened the Lend-Lease Program to a person lending a garden hose to a neighbor whose house was on fire. At that time, if any nation in the world needed a garden hose it was England. President Roosevelt described America's role in the Lend-Lease Program as serving as "the arsenal of democracy." In June 1941 Germany attacked the USSR on the western front, and four months later, in October, President Roosevelt extended the Lend-Lease Program to include the USSR. Like it or not, the United States also had become "the arsenal of communism."

5.17. The Lend-Lease Program was a tremendous success. It bolstered England at a time when they sorely needed it, and without doubt it also saved Stalin's brand of communism. The Russian Revolution, which established communism in Russia in 1917, would have died before it was thirty years old, but President Roosevelt recognized that the Lend-Lease Program would place a heavy demand on petroleum and coal, so he appointed his most able administrator, Harold Ickes, to the key posts of petroleum administrator and solid-fuels administrator. As administrator of these two new government agencies and still holding the position of secretary of the interior, which had responsibility for all mineral commodities, Mr. Ickes held the most powerful position of any appointee in the history of the nation. How he managed these responsibilities would mean life or death to England and the Soviet Union and, as events later developed at Pearl Harbor, Hawaii, the United States.

5.18. The United States received a huge shock on December 7, 1941, when a large part of the Pacific naval fleet anchored at Pearl Harbor, Hawaii, was suddenly and deliberately attacked by naval and air forces of the empire of Japan. Obviously there was a massive breakdown in the United States' intelligence gathering and communications. Somehow or other the seriousness of the situation never did get through to the army and navy commanders in Hawaii. This seems odd in view of the fact that the Fortieth Division (the Los Angeles National Guard Unit that had been activated into the regular army) under the same communications as received at Pearl Harbor was manning machine guns on the beaches in Southern California.

5.19. It is difficult to imagine two career military men who were ranked as an admiral and a general viewing the situation in Asia as abstract as the army and navy commanders in Hawaii apparently did. They appeared to have little or no knowledge of current events that were being discussed daily in the newspapers or in vivid detail nightly on the radio. Japan's actions were patently clear. They intended to make China a ready and available source of mineral commodities and a place where their manufactured products could be sold without competition. Their invasion of China was even more ruthless than when Genghis Khan plundered Asia and Europe. After their actions in Korea and the rape of Nanking, China, there should have been no doubt by anyone as to what the Japanese army would be doing after it defeated and occupied China. A large segment of the American public was viewing the developments much more seriously than the commanders at Pearl Harbor, and their only sources of information were the press and radio. If the commanders at Pearl Harbor had been listening to the same radio broadcasts and reading the same newspapers as the general public, it is possible that their state of preparedness on the morning of December 7, 1941, might have been somewhat different than it was. It certainly would not have been any less.

5.20. Regardless of who was to blame for the disaster at Pearl Harbor, it represented a massive blunder by the United States. It never should have happened. However, as massive as the American blunder was, it did not even approach in size the gigantic blunder by the Japanese. Their intelligence gathering and espionage must have been more incompetent than America's, if that was possible. The Japanese, German, and Italian leaders and their advisers did not understand the United States. They viewed its people and manufacturing production in direct relationship to their own people's problems and on the basis of their own industrial capabilities. These leaders could not tolerate dissension or publicly expressed disagreement within their countries. They believed such actions reflected a weakness in the government that could only result in overthrow; thus their reasoning was that with all the internal dissension and opposition in the United States, uniting the public to wage war would be a difficult and time-consuming task.

5.21. However, their greatest error was in underestimating America's industrial production capacity. Germany and especially Japan had no concept whatsoever of America's state of mechanization or industrial capability and the annual production of the critical commodities petroleum, steel, iron, copper, lead, and zinc. They measured America's capacity to produce energy, ships, aircraft, and tanks against their own capacity. Their intelligence agents failed completely to convey to them the actual potential of America's industrial might. The inability of the Axis powers to recognize America's industrial capability must represent the greatest failure in espionage in the history of ancient and modern warfare.

5.22. For forty-five years the industrial capacity of the United States had been increasing, with the exception of the hiatus during the Great Depression. The U.S. Bureau of Mines published annually the mineral industry production, use, import, and export data in the minerals yearbook volumes. Location and production of actively producing mining districts, oil fields, furnaces, rolling mills, smelters, and refining plants were published in detail. Industry publications, such as the *Engineering and Mining Journal, Coal, Rock Products, Concrete Products, Iron Age,* and the *Oil and Gas Journal,* covered all aspects of the industry, including political. These journals could be obtained by subscribing to them.

The U.S. Bureau of Mines and U.S. Geological Survey also published detailed investigative reports on many of the western oil fields, mines, and the Lake Superior Iron Range deposits from Ishpeming, Michigan, to Grand Rapids, Minnesota. The government publications were for sale to anybody who wanted them from the Government Printing Office.

5.23. If there was any doubt that the published material was deliberately falsified data to show high production of steel, all one had to do was visit the upper lake harbors in Minnesota and Wisconsin and count the iron ore boats departing for the lower lake ports; additional information could be obtained easily by counting the eighty-ton railroad cars loaded with iron ore leaving the Mesabi Range daily. These two numbers would give a good check on the steel production data being published in the mineral yearbooks. To get an idea of the massive reserves of iron ore available, a quick tour of the Mesabi Range and a glance at the Hull Rust Sellers open pit on the outskirts of Hibbing, Minnesota, from a tourist vantage point would provide the answer. Japanese espionage agents appeared to have been instructed that the only intelligence worth gathering was that which was obtained by stealth. Anything openly published and distributed widely was probably false and not worth looking into. The United States was able to overcome its massive intelligence blunder at Pearl Harbor, but the gigantic intelligence blunder by Japan eventually proved to be fatal.

5.24. It is almost a certainty that the Japanese military war lords were of the opinion that with one strike at Pearl Harbor, accompanied by lightning attacks on Malaya, Hong Kong, Guam, the Philippine Islands, Wake Island, and Midway Island, the war in the Pacific would be over in a few months. If they could deal a death blow to the Pacific fleet at Pearl Harbor, they would be able to establish naval and air bases in the South Pacific with little opposition, and with ready access to petroleum and all other mineral commodities they needed their position would be invincible. The United States would lie prostrate, unable to offer little more than token opposition to Japan's takeover of the South Pacific.

5.25. Japan had picked an excellent time for the attack. The United States was by that time deeply engaged in the Lend-Lease Program to both England and the USSR. However, the Lend-Lease Program continued at an accelerated rate even after Pearl Harbor. The need for petroleum and iron and steel products was enormous, but the petroleum, steel, and iron ore companies responded quickly. Petroleum companies

66

increased oil production from already-developed fields, and the steel companies stepped up production from the Mesabi and started building new blast furnaces at the lower lake ports to handle the additional iron ore. Construction of additional steel capacity was started, and the automobile industry converted to war production. The commercial air transport industry was the nucleus upon which President Roosevelt relied to meet his goal of producing 55,000 airplanes per year. This industry responded immediately and began to move fighters, heavy and medium bombers, and reconnaisance and cargo planes onto the runways.

5.26. In later years in observing Pearl Harbor Day it is common when the media discusses the attack to give credit to the workers for the quick salvaging of the decimated fleet. It is true that the United States work force did a remarkable job, but no matter how many workers were put on it, they could have done nothing except look at it without an almost inexhaustible source of petroleum, the continuous stream of iron ore that flowed from the Mesabi, and the products developed from the steel rolling mills in the lower Great Lakes ports. The Axis powers appeared to have no knowledge at all that the United States had petroleum sources and an iron deposit that could fill such a void. The American people took the disaster at Pearl Harbor in stride. In general, they appeared to feel that FDR, "Yankee ingenuity," and "Yankee know-how" would solve the problem. There was little or no recognition of what was making the "ingenuity" or "know-how" work.

5.27. The Lend-Lease Program ended the Great Depression, which had lasted for ten long years. Almost everybody on the home front was working. Agriculture, the oil fields, mines, and manufacturing plants were at full capacity. Herbert Hoover maintained to the day of his death that President Roosevelt never did bring the nation out of the Great Depression with his alphabet make-work programs. Hoover was right. The depression still held the nation in its grip up to the time the Lend-Lease Program started; it was ended by the massive demand for war matériel.

5.28. The Japanese met stiff resistance on the Bataan Peninsula, Philippines. Immediately after overtaking Bataan, Japan ran true to the form it had established in China: they reran the slaughter in Nanking. The original War Department press release revealed that 100,000 soldiers died on the Bataan death march and in Japanese prisoner-of-war camps (American Legion 1992). It did not take a military expert to see that the

United States was in a deadly fight that must end in victory no matter what the cost in lives or how long it took.

5.29. At the urging of concerned physicists, President Roosevelt authorized the Manhattan Engineer District Program in 1941 to conduct research to construct an atom bomb. The final responsibility for the project was assigned to the U.S. Army engineers under Gen. Leslie Groves in 1942. He assigned Dr. J. Robert Oppenheimer as director to the Los Alamos Laboratory. In 1943 Klaus Fuchs, a theoretical physicist from England was assigned to the laboratory to partially satisfy England's wish to have a scientist working on the project. Fuchs was later proven to be a Soviet espionage agent (Williams 1987).

5.30. President Roosevelt involved himself in the military and political strategy of waging war on two fronts with General of the Army George C. Marshall. Roosevelt had little time for domestic issues, yet he still managed to run for a fourth term and get reelected in 1944. However, the tremendous responsibilities that he had faced for the past twelve years had left him drained. He died on April 12, 1945, and he was succeeded by Vice Pres. Harry S Truman. Roosevelt never lived to see the end result of the Manhattan Project that he authorized in 1941.

5.31. The administrations of President Roosevelt had a profound effect on the American people. The nation had been developing into a massive industrialized power from 1890 up to the start of the Great Depression in 1929. The easy unlimited access of American manufacturers to products produced from the mineral commodities iron, steel, steel alloys, copper, and petroleum had never been experienced in any period of history by any nation prior to that time. The massive industrial surge culminated during the Coolidge administration. At that point the United States was a totally different nation than at any other period in its history, and the governing rules used by previous presidents could not be used as guidelines and no longer applied. In the New Deal, President Roosevelt experimented and developed his own rules and guidelines to start new and innovative programs. Whether or not they were successful is obscured by the Lend-Lease Program and America's entry into the War in 1941.

5.32. President Roosevelt's death passed on to Mr. Truman the task of ending successfully the most devastating war in the history of the civilized world, and also some unfinished domestic issues that had been put aside when the Lend-Lease Program started in 1939. President Roosevelt left a legacy that was to concern President Truman deeply but not concern any other president who followed him for the next forty years. That legacy was the "abundant life" policy that President Roosevelt had promised the people during the depression years of the 1930s.

5.33. The "abundant life" policy was destined to have a major effect on the minerals industry. Because of the ready availability of metallic mineral commodities, which were flowing into the marketplace without any difficulty, attention would be fastened on one nonmetal: petroleum. From this mineral commodity was produced the energy that moved ships, planes, tanks, trucks, and automobiles and powered many industries. It was easy for the public to grasp what a shortage of petroleum would do, because it would affect them personally. They could drive up to a service station, say, "Fill 'er up," and get a negative shake of the head, and the pride and joy of their whole life would stand lifeless in the driveway.

5.34. This high visibility of the need for petroleum products by the public was reflected in the actions of state and federal governments. Politicians were fully aware that in peacetime a lifeless car would be a millstone around their necks, which they could never get rid of. This was an unthinkable event; it must never happen while he or she was in an elected position. The final result of it all was an obsession in all channels of government with the end product of petroleum: energy. Agencies would be activated within the federal government to deal explicitly with energy problems. This attempt to develop a program on one mineral commodity without considering all other mineral commodities was doomed to failure because of the interdependency of mineral commodities. This failure was to translate in the early fifties into the Middle East becoming an area of political jockeying and intrigue and even war where the major nations of the world sought to protect what they considered their oil interests.

5.35. The Great Depression and World War II years are accurately portrayed in the production statistics for iron ore, pig iron, and steel. Table 5.1 shows the total annual production of iron ore in the United States from 1933 to 1945, compared to that produced by the Lake Superior District and the Mesabi Range, and table 5.2 shows the iron ore imported for consumption during the same period. Table 5.3 shows the pig iron production, imports, and exports and the production of steel during the Roosevelt administration.

5.36. The "Total Tons" column, immediately following the "Year" column, depicts the difficulty the nation had in escaping the death grip

Table 5.1

Total Annual Production of Iron Ore in the United States, 1933–45, Compared to That Produced by the Lake Superior District and the Mesabi Range (U.S. Geological Survey and U.S. Bureau of Mines 1992)
(in thousand long tons)

Year	Total Tons	Lake Superior District		Mesabi Iron Range		Tons Accumulated
		Tons	Percentage of Total	Tons	Percentage of Total	
1933	17,553	14,611	83	11,367	64	921,253
1934	24,858	21,031	85	14,415	58	935,668
1935	30,540	25,369	83	18,324	60	953,992
1936	48,789	41,781	86	30,205	62	984,197
1937	72,094	61,657	86	46,271	64	1,030,468
1938	28,447	21,308	75	13,257	47	1,043,725
1939	51,732	41,680	81	29,522	57	1,073,247
1940	73,696	61,471	83	45,485	62	1,118,732
1941	92,410	78,858	85	59,688	65	1,178,420
1942	126,527	91,005	72	70,288	56	1,248,708
1943	119,675	85,789	72	65,335	55	1,314,043
1944	111,020	79,111	71	61,994	56	1,376,037
1945	106,312	74,821	70	58,355	55	1,434,392

of the Great Depression. As President Roosevelt started his public works and dam building programs production picked up from 1934 to 1937, but production dropped from 72 million long tons to 28 million as the nation retreated into a recession in 1938. In the following years the effect of the war in Europe became evident. After the Lend-Lease Program started in 1941 production in that year reached 92 million tons, and after the United States entered the war production rose to 127 million tons in 1942, the highest during the war period.

5.37. In 1937 the accumulated production from the Mesabi Iron Range passed 1 billion tons. In just forty-five years the Mesabi had provided more iron ore to the blast furnaces than all other domestic iron mines combined. In 1937 it was providing 64 percent of the total produced in the nation. With these impressive statistics is it easy to understand how the United States became the greatest industrial power in the world. The industrial surge came from one great iron ore deposit: the Mesabi Iron Range.

5.38. The import statistics on iron ore reveal that imports after 1933 were reasonably stable up to the point when the United States entered the war. The drop from almost 3 million tons in 1941 to 731,000 in 1942 and less than .5 million in 1943 and 1944 reflects the difficulty in importing ore from overseas sources during the war years.

Table 5.2
Iron Ore Imported for Consumption into the United States, 1933–45 (U.S. Geological
Survey and U.S. Bureau of Mines 1992)
(in thousand long tons)
(in thousand dollars)

Year	Long Tons	Value $	Year	Long Tons	Value $	Year	Long Tons	Value $
1933	861	2,054	1937	2,442	5,842	1941	2,940	5,347
1934	1,428	3,308	1938	2,122	5,288	1942	731	2,143
1935	1,492	3,482	1939	2,413	5,866	1943	399	1,827
1936	2,232	5,280	1940	2,479	6,205	1944	464	2,008
						1945	1,197	4,116

5.39. The production statistics for pig iron and steel show the gains in production from 1933 to 1938 and then the sudden drop during the recession in 1938. From 1939 to 1945 the statistics represent the demand for the Lend-Lease Program and the nation's own war effort. In 1944 steel production reached almost 90 million tons. No nation in the world had ever produced that amount of steel under any circumstances. In 1940, production was 67 million tons; in 1941, 83 million; in 1942, 86 million; in 1943, 89 million; and in 1944, 90 million. No nation in the world had the capacity to expand steel production so rapidly. Obtaining the iron ore for the expansion is a far bigger problem than building the extra capacity in blast furnace and steel mills, and the United States was able to solve that problem with the Mesabi Iron Range. The steel expansion was tied directly to the ability of the Mesabi Range to raise iron ore production on demand.

Table 5.3
Production, Imports, and Exports of Pig Iron and Production of Steel in the United
States, 1933–45 (U.S. Geological Survey and U.S. Bureau of Mines 1992)
(in thousand short tons)

Year	Pig Iron Production	Pig Iron Imports	Pig Iron Exports	Steel Production	Steel Imports	Steel Exports
1933	14,591	178	3	26,020		
1934	17,569	128	5	29,182		
1935	23,326	147	5	38,184		
1936	33,885	186	6	53,500		
1937	40,482	125	876	56,637		
1938	20,812	34	485	31,752		
1939	34,805	43	198	52,799		
1940	46,204	11	620	66,983		
1941	55,085	4	579	82,839		
1942	59,078		111	86,032		7,672
1943	60,765	2	144	88,837		5,617
1944	61,094	6	162	89,641		4,925
1945	53,224	21	91	79,702		3,793

Table 5.4

Annual Population Estimates for the United States, 1933–45 (U.S. Geological Survey and U.S Bureau of Mines 1992)
(in thousands)

Year	Total Resident Population	Year	Total Resident Population	Year	Total Resident Population
1933	125,579	1937	128,825	1941	133,121
1934	126,374	1938	129,825	1942	133,920
1935	127,250	1939	130,880	1943	134,245
1936	128,053	1940	131,954	1944	132,885
				1945	132,481

5.40 The annual population growth from 1933 to 1941 varied roughly between 800,000 and 1 million. The figures in table 5.4 are for total resident population only; thus 1944 and 1945 show losses in population because of the large number of troops in the Pacific and European Theater of Operations during World War II.

Summary of the Era from 1921 to 1946

5.41. The end of World War II marks the end of the era that started in 1921. The era from 1875 to 1920 was one of explosive years of industrial growth, but in contrast the period from 1921 to 1946 was the roller-coaster years in industrialized America. Figures 5.1 and 5.2 are a continuation of figures 3.1 and 3.2. In figure 5.1, series 1 is the total tons on domestic iron ore produced annually and series 2 is the amount of iron ore contributed to the total by the Mesabi Range. In figure 5.2, series 1 is the domestic annual production of pig iron and series 2 is the domestic annual production of steel. The graphs depict the recession in 1921; the Great Depression, starting in 1929 and ending in 1938; the start of the Lend-Lease Program in 1939; and America's active participation in World War II, 1941–45. Noting the amount of iron ore contributed to the total production by the Mesabi Range, it is easy to see where the steel during World War II came from for supplying England and the USSR with war matériel through the Lend-Lease Program and at the same time supplying war matériel to America's own armed forces fighting on two major fronts. The Mesabi Iron Range was supplying iron ore on immediate demand, a characteristic that no other iron ore deposit in the world was capable of meeting at that time.

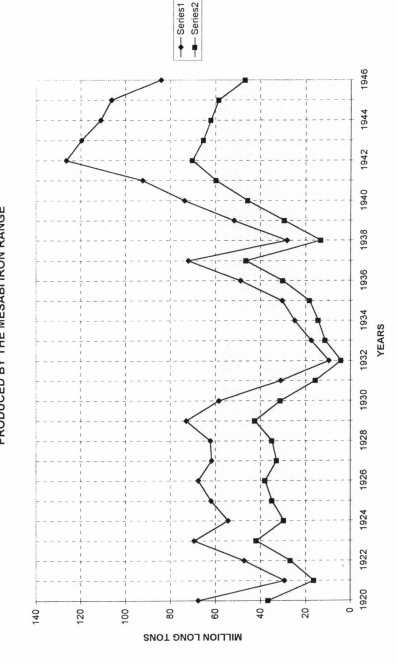

FIGURE 5.1.--ANNUAL PRODUCTION OF IRON ORE 1920-1946 COMPARED TO THAT PRODUCED BY THE MESABI IRON RANGE

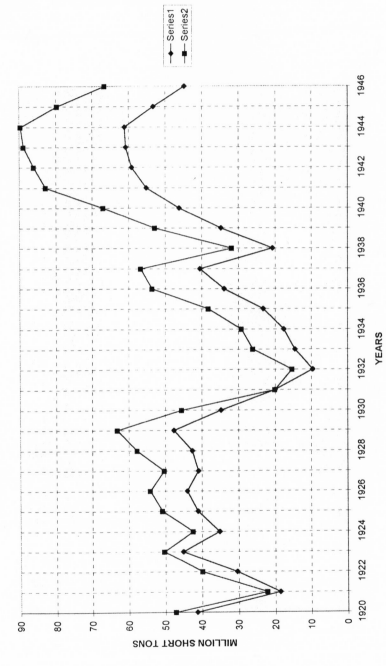

FIGURE 5.2--ANNUAL PRODUCTION OF PIG IRON AND STEEL 1920-1946

6

The Next Seven Years (1945–52): Truman (Davis 1968, Gladstone 1950, Morse 1956, Williams 1987, Pogue 1987)

6.1. On April 12, 1945, a few minutes after Mr. Truman became president, he learned the full secret of the Manhattan Project (Pogue 1987). The Japanese sneak attack on Pearl Harbor was proof that something was wrong with America's espionage and security systems, and President Truman's briefing had to be confirmation of it, because it was later discovered that the Soviet Union had been informed on atomic-energy development by Klaus Fuchs, the English scientist working at the Los Alamos Laboratory. There certainly must have been something wrong with a system that managed to keep the development of the A-bomb secret from the vice president of the United States and yet at the same time the details of development had been transferred to the Soviet Union by a mole working at Los Alamos. America tends to blame England for this lapse because Klaus Fuchs was a British citizen and thus England was responsible for him. However, there is no way that the debacle at Pearl Harbor can be laid on the British doorstep.

6.2. Those in the top echelons of government were just refusing to face up to the fact that the Federal Bureau of Investigation, Office of Strategic Services, and army and navy intelligence were allowing serious security breaches. Secretary of War Henry Stimson, Secretary of the Navy Frank Knox, Director of the Office of Strategic Services William Donovan, and Director of the Federal Bureau of Investigation J. Edgar Hoover were failing to coordinate their intelligence efforts and manage properly a very vital and important segment of the war effort. Those who were being informed on the Manhattan Program appeared to be reveling in the fact that they with the president were an exclusive club that knew a secret nobody else knew. Their elation in this knowledge apparently made them forget that there were others beside the vice president and

Congress that had to be guarded against. The failure to adequately keep secret the development of atomic energy from outsiders was to lead to a stunning Soviet Union atomic bomb test in August 1949, and also to a pathetic period of excesses during the last two years of President Truman's administration and the administration of Dwight D. Eisenhower.

6.3. If President Roosevelt had stayed alive one more month, he would have lived to hear of the victory in the European Theater of Operations. Germany unconditionally surrendered on May 7, 1945. Hitler, the mass murderer of Europe, was dead. Meanwhile Dr. Oppenheimer, director of the Los Alamos Laboratory, was preparing to test the first atomic bomb that had been developed. It was successfully tested at Alamogordo Air Force Base, New Mexico, on July 16, 1945. The United States now had a superweapon with which they could end the war with Japan.

6.4. The decision to use the atomic bomb on Japan was not reached lightly (Pogue 1987). Basically, the political and military leaders could meet and discuss the matter all they wanted to, but in the end they had no option. War is war, and Japan proved that conclusively in Korea and China, at Pearl Harbor, and in Bataan. The basic strategy of war is to inflict casualties on the enemy's armed forces, destroy their war industries, terrorize the home front, seize their land, and force surrender. Whether the enemy is killed by bayonet, pistol, rifle, machine gun, mortar, artillery, or A-bomb or run over with a jeep makes no difference. With a device on hand that would end the war virtually without another American casualty, the casualties that would have been inflicted on the United States from a land invasion of Japan could have never been defended. The first atomic bomb used in warfare was dropped on Hiroshima, Japan, on August 6, 1945. The second was dropped on Nagasaki, Japan, on August 9, 1945. The second bomb forced the emperor of Japan to regain leadership of the country from the war lords, and on August 14, 1945, he surrendered Japan. The war lords never would have surrendered. They were prepared to contest the American invasion by using the civilian population to join with the armed forces to fight on the beaches and in the towns and cities. The Japanese populace were willing participants in this endeavor, but they yielded to the emperor's rule when he resumed leadership of Japan.

6.5. Atomic energy development was not something that would have never happened if the Manhattan Project had not been started. When Max Planck expressed the hypothesis that radiant energy, in its interaction with matter, behaves as though it consists of corpuscles of quanta of energy, the development of atomic energy was inevitable (Semat 1958). Enrico Fermi produced fission in 1934, without realizing it, and two German scientists, Otto Hahn and Fritz Strassmann, discovered fission in 1939 (Glasstone 1950, Davis 1968). The Manhattan Project did nothing more than speed up the technology development by two or three years. It is common for television commentators to intone dramatically that the atomic bomb changed the United States and the world forever and they would never be the same again. The world, especially the United States, prior to the development of atomic energy was changing constantly through technological developments and scientific discoveries, and atomic energy was just one of the developments that was coming in sequence as new discoveries were made. It was merely a development in the chain that reached maturity slightly ahead of schedule because of the concentrated effort and funds spent on it. Far greater changes were made in the United States when the Mesabi Range went on line supplying iron ore to the lower Great Lake furnaces.

6.6. At the end of the war the United States emerged as the world's greatest superpower. It was producing over 50 percent of the world's steel, it had the largest industrial capacity to produce war matériel and the largest navy and air force, and at that time it was the only country in the world that could produce atomic bombs. Along with this huge capability for waging war, the populace had the highest standard of living of any country in the world. The USSR was not at all happy with the situation. Premier Joseph Stalin took a long hard look at the United States and decided that the key to "Yankee ingenuity" and "Yankee know-how" was steel and more steel. He began a crash program to produce as quickly as possible the following: (1) more steel than any other nation in the world, (2) a stockpile of atomic bombs, and (3) long-range rocketry with atomic warheads. At the same time he had on his agenda developing an army, air force, and navy equal in size or bigger in all respects than the armed forces of the United States. Stalin's intent was clear. He was going to place the armed forces of the USSR on equal footing with those of the United States on land, sea, and air, including outer space, no matter what the cost. He did not allow his industries to move toward a peacetime economy; they were kept on a war footing, producing warplanes, tanks, submarines, warships, rockets, and the neccessary war matériel to equip a giant army and navy. It was a massive effort, and all accomplished at the expense of the infrastructure of the USSR and the standard of living of the populace.

6.7. In contrast to the USSR, the United States started moving into a peacetime economy immediately after the war. Gasoline rationing, which had been in force since 1941, was canceled as soon as Japan surrendered. Factories converted quickly to peacetime production. Those on the home front had money to spend, and the United States was swept into prosperous times even greater than those experienced during the Coolidge administration. There was a never-ending demand for automobiles, freezers, refrigerators, houses, radios, home improvement products, and electrical appliances of all kinds. A large percentage of the public were on a long car-dealer list waiting to purchase a new-model car from their favorite manufacturer as soon as it became available. Cities were beginning to experience difficulty in maintaining an intercity road network that would allow everybody to ride to and from work in their own automobile. In particular, the Los Angeles area, with a large population widely spread out and inadequate mass transportation, was experiencing particulates of smoke and fog (smog) befouling the air day after day. The tourist industry was starting to boom. Those who had automobiles started to travel throughout the United States. As the airplane factories converted to passenger planes, commercial airlines expanded international and national flight schedules and major cities started expansion of their airports.

6.8. President Truman was beset with a myriad of problems on both the domestic and foreign fronts. The larger cities were encountering social problems that they had not faced prior to the war. The United States was becoming an urban society because of the movement of people from the country to the city. In addition, the migration of Negroes from the South into the larger northern cities was proceeding at an even faster rate than during the war, and their reception in many cities was one that could best be termed *rough*. Communism was spreading in the Near East, and the economies of several European countries were faltering. In 1947 Mr. Truman implemented the Truman Doctrine, which was intended to counter the Soviet arms buildup and stop the spread of communism in Europe and the Near East; also in conjunction with this program, the Marshall Plan was implemented, which was designed to accomplish the economic rehabilitation of Western Europe. On the domestic front, President Truman split with the Eightieth Congress on the continuation of presidential war powers, price controls, and labor legislation. Harold Ickes continued as secretary of the interior in Mr. Truman's cabinet after President Roosevelt's death but was unhappy with the loss of the power that he had held in the Roosevelt administration. He resigned in 1946, charging Mr. Truman with "government by cronyism." Julius Krug was appointed in 1946 to replace Ickes and served through Mr. Truman's first term. Oscar Chapman was appointed to serve as secretary for the second term. Both individuals proved to be highly capable and excellent administrators.

6.9. President Truman apparently came to a decision that the way that the government was organized at that time was inefficient and costly. In 1946 he appointed Herbert Hoover to head a commission to recommend changes in organization. Also in this same year the Atomic Energy Commission was formed to take over all the laboratories and plants of the Manhattan Project. The commission was to be run by a chairman and four commissioners. The AEC, as it was called, was to wield a considerable amount of power in the postwar period.

6.10. Comprehensive governmental reorganization changes were recommended by the Hoover Commission over a period from 1948 to 1949. However, the change that was urgently needed at that time was never recommended. Agriculture was represented in government by a cabinet-level department, but the minerals industry was not. Responsibility for this industry was under the Department of the Interior, which in 1946 was comprised of many different agencies, such as the following: Bureau of Land Management, Bureau of Reclamation, Bureau of Indian Affairs, Bureau of Mines, Geological Survey, National Park Service, Fish and Wildlife Service, and Office of Territories. The functions of these eight agencies varied widely. With this many-faceted responsibility the secretary of interior had to be a remarkably capable individual to effectively represent them all at presidential cabinet meetings.

6.11. Prior to World War II the situation in regard to mineral commodities was essentially taking care of itself. There was a steady, never-ending flow of strategic mineral commodities for any purpose needed. This had been going on for fifty years, and there was nothing to say at cabinet meetings except that there was no problem. However, the situation was now undergoing a massive change. Many of the eastern and western mining districts were beginning to show their age, and imports were going to have to be made to cover the shortages. There were going to be disruptions in the steady flow, and costs for all commodities were going to rise. The United States was in dire need of a strategic long-range plan of action on mineral resources. The time was rapidly approaching when the supply of mineral commodities would not take care of itself, and with the problems that the United States was facing, the minerals industry needed representation at cabinet level. This historical period was somewhat similiar to that of the industrialization and mechanization surge under the Coolidge administration. The nation was moving into a similiar mode, but with a major exception: Eventually a substantial amount of the needed mineral commodities would have to be imported. Wealth would no longer be created by mining and refining them in the United States; instead wealth would have to be expended to obtain them.

6.12. The Hoover Commission, charged with making changes in government organization, did not appear to grasp the changes that were taking place in the minerals industry and made no recommdation to place the responsibility for minerals at cabinet level. If ever a time was ready for the agency with the responsibility for minerals to become a cabinet-level department, it was then. AEC had been established to be responsible for the Manhattan Project installations, which were researching the radioactive mineral commodities. It would have made much more sense to place the responsibility for all mineral commodities under one agency and make it a cabinet-level department. Whether or not private mineral industry lobby groups ever attempted to influence President Hoover to recommend that the agency responsible for minerals be made a cabinet-level department is unknown, but if they did not, they were certainly remiss in not doing so.

6.13. In 1948 President Truman campaigned vigorously against what he called the "no-good Eightieth Congress." He defeated Thomas E. Dewey by 114 electoral votes. The victory gave him considerable prestige and clout, which the Eighty-first and Eighty-second Congresses could not ignore. In 1948 Bernard Baruch, who at that time was a highly respected elder statesman, remarked that the United States was engaged in a "cold war" with the Soviet Union. The print and electronic media picked up the term immediately, and they have used it consistently to this day. The term was unfortunate, and it should have never have been used. It tended to obscure what the Soviet Union was actually doing. There was nothing cold about their actions or intentions. Along with their unprecedented massive buildup in armed forces, they were behind almost every insurrection, uprising, or war that was in progress at that time or would occur in the next forty years. Their embassies all over the world were nothing more than fronts for espionage agents. They had in progress the master plan to place communism in every country in the world, including the United States. North Korea, North Vietnam, and Cuba were their surrogates in active wars. There was certainly nothing "cold" about the actions undertaken by these countries.

6.14. As the nation was continuing to move back toward a peacetime economy, it was becoming obvious that the "abundant life" policy as proposed by President Roosevelt was still fresh in everybody's mind. The public had began to implement the policy that President Roosevelt had to lay aside because of the war. Commercial aviation was growing fast, and the tourist industry had become one of the fastest-growing industries in the nation. Motor trucks on the state and interstate highways were becoming the major haulers of food products and were also giving the railroads strong competition by hauling everything from structural steel to wood chips. Passenger motor buses were leaving the large city terminals for some cross-country destination about every thirty minutes. The railroads were unwilling to meet the services offered by passenger motor bus companies and began to withdraw their passenger trains first on the short hauls and later on the longer hauls. By 1948 television was becoming the new industry in entertainment. The technology of radio and television made a huge jump forward when Bell Laboratories announced to the world on June 30, 1948, that they had developed a transistor, a three-terminal, solid-state device that was capable of providing amplification. It immediately replaced the vacuum tube in radio and television receivers.

6.15. One of the fastest-growing parts of the minerals industry was the development of synthetic resins used for textile fibers and what were termed *plastics*. The synthetic resins are *polymers*, a term applied to a molecule formed by two or more identical smaller molecules. Nylon was the first polymer, developed in 1935 by E. I. du Pont de Nemours and Company. By 1950 The United States was producing about 1 million tons of plastic materials. From 1950 to 1975 the production of various materials developed by polymerization increased by about 1 million tons every five years.

6.16. The transition from a wartime to a peacetime economy was hardly noticed in the Lake Superior District. The Mesabi continued to operate at a high rate. Several of the companies were beginning research on the lower-grade iron rock, which in Minnesota was known locally as "taconite," because the high-grade direct shipping ore was nearing depletion. U.S. Steel, through its mining affiliate, and Bethlehem Steel were active in exploring for iron ore deposits in South America. Successful discoveries of large deposits in Venezuela were reported in 1949. The open pits on the Mesabi Range had been through three wars, the Spanish-American War, World War I, and World War II. They were becoming deep, and the end to the direct shipping ore could be seen. *The era of iron ore on demand was coming to a close.*

6.17. Technological developments that occurred during and after World War II were having a strong effect upon the nation. Cemented or sintered tungsten carbide was proving to be a remarkable development for machine tools, drilling bits, cutting edges, and other applications where extreme hardness was desirable. With this development in drilling bits and the development of better alloys for drilling rods, the petroleum industry was drilling into the Earth a distance of over four miles in their search for petroleum and natural gas. Also, the development of high-strength, high-heat resistant alloys and synthetic rubber made possible the development of the jet-propelled engine for high-speed military and commercial aviation. England, France, Germany, the Soviet Union, and the United States had extensive research in progress on material development (see appendix 2:6.3).

6.18. A method of bolting the roof in underground mines made possible mechanical mining and loading of coal in many mines where mechanical mining had not been possible before, because other means of support restricted the use of machinery. Edward Thomas, a Bureau of Mines safety engineer, was the individual who was successful in transferring this rock bolt technology from the Tri-State Metal Mining District to coal mining. Striking developments were starting to occur in the tonnage capacity of off-road motor vehicles for mining and construction being manufactured by the automotive industries. Beginning in about 1947, the automotive manufacturers were, in each succeeding three-to-four-year period, bringing out new models with higher tonnage capacity. The technological developments in engines, higher-strength steel alloys, and more durable synthetic rubber tires made the increasing tonnage capacity of the off-road vehicles possible. This increase in tonnage capacity was continued up to the early 1990s, culminating in off-road vehicles with a capacity of up to 240 tons. Correlative technological development was also occurring in surface mining ore-loading machinery. Electric shovels, draglines, and front-end loaders were yearly increasing in size and mobility, and with these developments came the expanded use of surface mining methods to extract mineral commodities. The effect of roof bolting in underground coal mines and bigger and better surface loading and hauling machinery is illustrated in the data presented in table 1 in appendix 7. In the decade from 1950 to 1960 mechanical mining of underground coal increased from 67 to 86.3 percent. Developments of better surface mining machinery occurred earlier than the roof bolt, and from 1944 to 1960 the amount of coal mined by surface mining increased from 16.3 to 29.5 percent.

6.19. Paddy Martinez, a Navajo Indian, made the initial discovery of uranium in the San Juan Basin near Grants Pass, New Mexico, in 1950 (Sheppard 1993). The basin contained over 50 percent of the known reserves of uranium in the United States. The huge peacetime demand for mineral commodities was a matter of considerable concern to Mr. Truman. Conscious always of the gigantic arms buildup taking place in the Soviet Union, he established the Defense Minerals Administration (DMA) in the Department of the Interior under Secretary Oscar Chapman. The objective of this agency was to assure that the United States had a sufficient supply of mineral commodities in the event that war erupted with the Soviet Union. A branch of this agency, the Defense Minerals Exploration Administration (DMEA), undertook actual exploration and discovery assistance to strategic mineral mining claim holders and mining companies in the United States and its territories on a cost share basis.

6.20. Under the DMEA program the Bureau of Mines and Geological Survey furnished professional personnel for examination and valuation of the mining claim and, if found feasible, develop a discovery program to determine the extent of the mineral resource (see appendix 2:1.2). The mining claim owner or mining company was expected to pay half of the cost of the actual exploration and discovery program. Their half most often was paid by management of the program once it was under way. Under the Mining Act of 1872, each holder of an unpatented claim had to do a certain amount of assessment work each year. A DMEA project on a claim was always sufficient to cover the assessment work on an unpatented claim for that year. In addition, if a significant discovery was made, the claim owner had enough evidence to have the claim patented. During the period that it was active, DMEA ran all but the strongest private mining engineering and mining geology consulting firms out of business.

6.21. The situation in regard to petroleum was becoming even more critical than metallic mineral commodities. The public demand for gasoline was increasing each year after the war. By 1948 production of petroleum was over 2.02 billion forty-two-gallon barrels; the domestic industry could not meet the total demand, and imports of petroleum exceeded exports by 53.5 million barrels. As the demand for petroleum continued to grow, imports exceeded exports by 2.14 billion barrels in 1974, even with a constantly increasing domestic production. The detailed statistics of the steadily increasing domestic petroleum production and imports over a number of years are shown in appendix 8. The United States, Great Britain, France, the remainder of Europe, and Japan were zeroing in on the Middle East, with its huge reserves of petroleum. Iran, Iraq, Saudi Arabia, and Kuwait had become focal points for political maneuvering by the major powers for investment in the petroleum fields being developed. Europe was undergoing a massive resurgence in industrialization because of the ready availability of energy. The Truman administration European rehabilitation plans, aided by cheap energy from the Middle East, were moving Europe into an industrialization that it had never experienced before.

6.22. The Department of the Interior started what was called a synthetic fuels research program, which was primarily a program to produce oil from coal and shale oil. The program was successful in one respect: gasoline could be produced, but the cost per gallon was far in excess of the price of imported oil. There were huge reserves of shale oil in Colorado, Utah, and Wyoming. The process to recover oil from the shale could produce gasoline at about two to two and one-half times the price per gallon of imported oil. For a limited period of time the Department of the Interior also had a research program in progress for using finely ground coal dust to power engines. The research was successful in getting the engine to run, but its operating life was short because of the abrasive action of the coal dust.

6.23. President Truman continued to face continuous problems in converting to a peacetime economy. The first occurred in August 1949, when the Soviet Union conducted their first atomic bomb test. How the Soviets managed to develop the A-bomb so quickly became abundantly clear when, in February 1950, the United States learned from the British that Klaus Fuchs had delivered to the Soviet Union all that he had learned at Los Alamos. This information stunned the president, Congress, and the public. Even though President Truman knew nothing whatsoever about atomic energy development until 1945, he ended up taking the blame for the whole fiasco.

6.24. Congress demanded that intense security checks be made of everybody engaged in advanced scientific research and those that had access to sensitive data on the research. Ranges of secrecy codes were established, and it was necessary that each individual's background be checked thoroughly prior to receiving information listed under the codes. Under the system as it developed, every person being given security clearance was regarded as a possible communist agent until the rigid clearance testing procedure proved otherwise. Woe betide the persons that had unknowingly subscribed to a newspaper, book, magazine, or record company that the FBI had labeled a communist front organization. They would have to explain that stigma to the examining agents again and again as clearance rechecks were made.

6.25. Klaus Fuchs was undoubtedly the most successful espionage agent in world history. He had transmitted to the Soviet Union sufficient details of A-bomb construction that when they made the first test, they apparently also had attained a stockpile of A-bombs. He gave the Soviets information that was then worth at least $2 billion, and it never cost them even one ruble. Fuchs did it all in the name of political idealism. The complete documentation of his case by Robert Chadwell Williams borders on the unbelievable (1987). Fuchs accomplished his undercover work under the noses of England's Scotland Yard, America's FBI, OSS-CIA, army and navy intelligence, and the most noted and brilliant scientists in the world. The ease with which Fuchs transmitted his information and duped everybody he came in contact with is beyond understanding. He never experienced any danger to his person or encountered an obstacle to his mission until he decided to inform the British of what he had done. If he had not willingly given the information on his activities, it is very possible that his duplicity would have never been discovered.

6.26. In May 1950 the United States started a military aid program sending a small cadre of advisers to assist the French in their military action in South Vietnam. In June 1950 the Soviet-equipped North Korean army invaded South Korea. The United Nations invoked sanctions, and President Truman ordered U.S. military forces into action. Mr. Truman's immediate reaction to the North Korean invasion was understandable. China and the Soviet Union appeared to have become strong allies. The insurgent group in Vietnam had strong backing from China. The Soviet Union had never converted to a peacetime economy, and it was in the process of developing a gigantic army and navy. Pearl Harbor was still fresh in the public's mind; it had resulted in the United States having to start in New Guinea and take back island by island up to the Japanese mainland at a cost of thousands of lives. The intent behind the defense of Korea was to stop the Soviets there in their quest for dominance in Asia. There was absolutely no doubt that North Korea was a puppet of the Soviet Union. North Korea's airplanes, tanks, guns, and all war maté-riel were Soviet-made, and the North Korean army was being actively directed in the field by Soviet army personnel. The American print and electronic media disregarded the Soviets' part in the Korean War and still continued to use the term *cold war* when referring to America's relationship with the Soviet Union. The term would just not die, even with the deaths and wounding of many American servicemen.

6.27. The unmasking of Klaus Fuchs closely followed by the Korean War set off a period of excesses unmatched even by the Salem, Massachusetts, witchcraft trials. There were calls for impeachment of President Truman, and congressional committees were busy investigating communistic front organizations. Sen. Joseph McCarthy from Wisconsin utilized the situation to keep himself in the political spotlight. He was the first and only elected individual to use actual numbers. He first charged that there were 204 communists in the State Department. In citing numbers he was shrewd. He would never cite a number in even hundreds. It was always a few more, giving the impression that he had counted actual people who could be identified as communists. The print and electronic media faithfully quoted these numbers without comment or question on how he arrived at such an amount. This served to give credence to numbers that were patently untrue. Senator McCarthy would occasionally raise the number by one or two, without explanation, leaving the impression that he had made a recount. The print and electronic media would again accept the new numbers as if they had been handed down by the archangel Gabriel and dutifully publish and broadcast them. The massive publicity given Senator McCarthy gave him a halo of honesty that he did not deserve. He never did actually prove anybody he charged was a communist.

6.28. The huge demand for mineral commodities by the Korean War, military aid program to Vietnam, and the public in pursuit of the "abundant life" greatly concerned the Truman administration. This concern triggered the development of a program to determine just what the current and future status of strategic materials was under the demand that was occurring at that time. President Truman appointed a Materials Policy Commission to be headed by William S. Paley, president of CBS, Inc., to study and prepare a report on strategic materials, which included strategic mineral commodities. President Truman stated in a letter to Mr. Paley on January 22, 1951, the following:

> I believe the Commission should study, together with any other aspects deemed by it to be pertinent, such questions relating to production materials as:
>
> (1) The long-range requirements outlook.
> (2) The long-range supply outlook.
> (3) The prospect and estimated extent of shortages.
> (4) The consistency and adequacy of existing Government policies, plans, and programs.
> (5) The consistency and adequacy of private industry practices. (Paley 1952)

6.29. The president's commission was given the authority to call on all agencies in the government for data and reports that were needed to complete the study. President Truman's selection of Mr. Paley to head the commission was, in a sense, political—to assure the leaders of the Republican Party that the study would be nonpartisan. Mr. Paley responded to the president's request by producing a report on RESOURCES FOR FREEDOM in five volumes in June 1952 (Paley 1952). It was called the Paley Report, and it was the most comprehensive study ever made by the nation on strategic materials.

6.30. Development of the current status of the minerals industry by the president's Materials Policy Commission involved utilizing the mineral commodity statistics and information already compiled on the minerals industry by two agencies in the Department of Interior: the Bureau of Mines and Geological Survey. The statistical data compiled on the ferrous division of the minerals industry were the production, imports, and exports of iron ore, iron, and steel, which have been regularly presented in each chapter of this book since chapter 1. Tables 6.1, 6.2, 6.3, and 6.4, presented below starting with 1946, continue the sequence of chapter 5 that ended with 1945. These tables present the same data on the ferrous metals division that was available to the president's commission in 1952.

Table 6.1
Total Annual Production of Iron Ore in the United States, 1946–52, Compared to That Produced by the Lake Superior District and the Mesabi Range (U.S. Geological Survey and U.S. Bureau of Mines 1992)
(in thousand long tons)

Year	Total Tons	Lake Superior District		Mesabi Iron Range		
		Tons	Percentage of Total	Tons	Percentage of Total	Tons Accumulated
1946	84,194	59,042	70	46,679	55	1,481,071
1947	93,092	76,384	82	58,772	63	1,539,843
1948	101,103	82,277	81	64,072	63	1,603,915
1949	84,937	68,392	80	52,551	62	1,656,466
1950	98,045	79,292	80	60,838	62	1,717,304
1951	116,505	93,495	80	73,575	63	1,790,875
1952	97,918	76,619	78	59,371	61	1,850,250

6.31. Tables 6.1 and 6.2 must be considered together to understand what was happening in iron ore production during the Truman administration. The demand during the seven-year period was high, and by 1947 the Mesabi Range production had increased from 55 percent of the total produced in 1945 to 61 percent in 1952. Even though total production was close to or past 100 million long tons for the last three years, it did not supply the demand, and thus iron ore imports began to increase. At the end of the war, in 1945, 1.2 million long tons, mostly from Canada and South America, were imported. As soon as the seas were safe for bulk shipments, the steel-producing companies started importing from Europe and other overseas sources, in 1946.

Table 6.2
Iron Ore Imported for Consumption into the United States by Continents, 1946–52 (U.S. Geological Survey and U.S. Bureau of Mines 1992)
(in thousand long tons)
(in thousand dollars)

	North America(a)		South America(b)		Europe(c)		Remainder	
Year	Long Tons	Value	Long Tons	Value	Long Tons	Value	Long Tons	Value
1946	1,103	5,086	1,096	2,460	233	1,385	323	1,440
1947	1,553	7,587	1,670	7,747	1,287	7,756	393	2,006
1948	986	5,839	2,632	7,527	1,359	8,317	1,132	5,648
1949	1,623	10,770	2,627	6,891	2,027	12,893	1,121	6,181
1950	2,072	13,265	3,308	11,554	2,049	13,540	852	5,609
1951	2,136	14,936	4,440	21.290	2,597	17,549	967	5,745
1952	2,043	15,322	4,718	37,790	2,116	24,561	883	5,181

(a) Canada only from 1946 to 1949, others insignificant tonnage and combined under remainder.
(b) Chile only from 1946 to 1949, others insignificant tonnage and combined under remainder; Chile, Brazil, and Peru only in 1950; Venezuela started shipping in 1951.
(c) Sweden only from 1946 to 1949, others insignificant tonnage and combined under remainder.

6.32. All of the integrated steel companies, including U.S. Steel, who held a strong position on the Mesabi Range, could see the end of the direct shipping ore in the Lake Superior District and on the Mesabi Range and were actively prospecting for iron ore deposits in South America in order to have an assured and steady supply of iron ore for their blast furnaces. Chile, Brazil, and Peru had active mines that were shipping iron ore to the United States. However, Venezuela became the star of the group. It started shipping in 1951, and by 1953 it was shipping 12 million long tons, which was seven times more than Peru, four times more than Chile, and twelve times more than Brazil. As the mines in South America were developed, they increased in production, and this production forced cutbacks in the production from the domestic mines. It was a matter of simple economics. The companies wanted to have a strong and steady production from a source as the domestic supplies dwindled.

6.33. The value of the imported ore was about $10 million. At the end of President Truman's tenure, in 1952, the value of imported iron ore had increased over eight times to $83 million. This wealth used to be produced in the United States, and now it was being paid out to import the strategic mineral commodity most vital to America's industrial strength. It was not necessarily the fact that the iron ore was being imported, it was the trend that concerned the president's Policy Commission. How long would the upward trend continue? Would the lower-grade deposits of the Lake Superior District be able to compete against the cheaper foreign ore deposits? Would the integrated steel companies maintain a strong domestic production base or would they go completely foreign? The commission had to answer these questions so that a strategic long-term plan could be developed that would guide the nation into the future. Even more disturbing trends were developing in steel. These trends are illustrated in tables 6.3 and 6.4.

6.34. Tables 6.3 and 6.4, like tables 6.1 and 6.2, have to be considered together to understand the trend that was developing in steel production. The statistics presented in table 6.3 show that the United States was on a real roll. From 1950 to 1952 the nation produced 99 million, 105 million, and 93 million short tons. This is a tremendous tonnage of steel, and 1951 is the first year in which tonnage exceeded 100 million short tons. However, a different picture develops in table 6.4 when the U.S. production is compared with that of the rest of the world. The trend in steel production show that the Soviet Union had increased their

Table 6.3
Production, Imports, and Exports of Pig Iron and Steel in the United States, 1946–52
(U.S. Geological Survey and U.S. Bureau of Mines)
(in thousand short tons)

Year	Pig Iron Production	Pig Iron Imports	Exports	Steel Production	Steel Imports	Exports
1946	44,842	14	96	66,603		3,016
1947	58,329	33	40	84,894		3,207
1948	60,005	219	7	88,640		3,245
1949	53,413	100	81	77,978		3,518
1950	64,587	796	7	98,838		2,567
1951	70,274	1,067	7	105,200		2,764
1952	61,313	374	14	93,200		3,271

Table 6.4
World Production of Steel with the Production and Percentage Produced by the United States, USSR Separate from Europe, Europe, Japan, and Other Nations, 1946–52 (U.S. Geological Survey and U.S. Bureau of Mines 1992)
(in million short tons)

Year	World Tons	U.S. Tons	%	USSR Tons	%	Europe Tons	%	Japan Tons	%	Other %
1946		66.6								
1947		84.9								
1948	172.0	88.6	52	20.2	12	52.2	30	1.9	1	5
1949	176.4	78.0	44	25.4	14	60.8	35	3.4	2	5
1950	208.5	98.8	47	29.8	14	66.6	33	5.3	2	4
1951	232.5	105.2	45	34.7	15	74.3	32	7.2	3	5
1952	233.7	93.2	40	38.6	17	83.5	36	7.7	3	4

production 5 percent from 1948 to 1952 and the European nations, without the Soviet Union, had increased their production 6 percent in the same time period. While these increases were being made, the United States' percentage of world production dropped 12 percentage points, from 52 to 40.

6.35. The industrial production dominance in steel that characterized the nation before, during, and immediately after World War II was beginning to fade at a rate of about 2 percent per year, and Europe, the Soviet Union, and Japan were gaining production at about 1 percent per year each. Without doubt Europe, the Soviet Union, and Japan had embarked upon a program to produce all the steel that they possibly could. Insofar as they were concerned, they had viewed the United States perched in the dominant industrial position long enough. They all had aspirations of claiming that spot for themselves.

6.36. The trends that were developing warned that the United States was entering a critical time in its history. The industrial dominance that had been its position for sixty years was under direct challenge from both friendly and unfriendly nations. If the trends continued and the industrial dominance continued to fade, America's attitude toward all nations in the world would have to change; it would be operating on the world's diplomatic front from a position of equality or, more likely, third or fourth in rank, rather than from a position of dominance. The relationships with many countries would undergo subtle changes that had never been experienced before. Nations that had been compliant with America's wishes would tend to become more demanding. Communist nations and their satellites as their industrial production of steel rose year after year would become progressively more difficult to deal with, and their approach to diplomacy would be to regularly stage day-long parades with goose-stepping soldiers and displaying the military might of all branches of the armed services.

6.37. The Paley Report was completed in 1952, and President Truman immediately took steps to implement their recommendations. He appointed Jack Gorrie, chairman of the National Security Resources Board, to review the recommendations of the Paley Report and advise of actions deemed appropriate to be taken with respect to these recommendations (Gorrie 1952). Mr. Gorrie responded with a report on the objectives of U.S. materials resources policy and suggested initial steps in their accomplishment on December 10, 1952 (Gorrie 1952). President Truman did not run for a second term in 1952. In the election of 1952 Dwight D. Eisenhower easily defeated Adlai Stevenson, the nominee of the Democratic Party. When President Truman left office the situation in Vietnam was worsening and the Korean War was still in progress. The nation's involvement in Korea at that time gave Dwight Eisenhower a perfect campaign issue. Mr. Eisenhower was critical of the policies that involved the United States in Korea, and he pledged to try to end the war. The electorate responded to this pledge by electing him to office by a large margin in electoral and popular votes.

6.38. President Truman understood that the United States through scientific and technological developments was undergoing constant change. He recognized that America was at the time the world's greatest superpower and its role in the world had to be as a leader, not as a sideline observer. If the democracies were going to survive, America would have to accept this leadership instead of retreating into the isolation posture that was characterisitic of the administrations of Presidents Harding, Coolidge, and Hoover. More than any other president since

1920, including President Roosevelt, Truman and his cabinet understood the value of mineral commodities. They were acutely aware that minerals were the root source of the nation's stature as an industrial power and the very cornerstone of the nations's standard of living. Where the needed commodities were to come from was a matter of deep concern to him. He recognized that many strategic commodities would have to be imported and this meant not only the expenditure of wealth but also a serious military problem in obtaining them during wartime.

6.39. President Truman also understood that the nations of Europe were undergoing a tremendous industrialization surge because of ready access to Middle East petroleum production. They were constructing petroleum refineries with sufficient capacity to meet all their needs. With an unlimited quantity of cheap energy available, they were building or purchasing bulk haulage ships to import needed mineral commodities from any nation that would export them, and for the first time in sixty years they were becoming really competitive with mineral-rich and highly industrialized America. With ready access to Middle East petroleum, the European nations were moving quickly to produce steel and more steel. They, like the USSR had discovered that the secret to "Yankee ingenuity" and "Yankee know-how" was steel and in a few years would be mounting a strong challenge to America's leadership in the production of steel.

6.40. President Truman saw the changes that were coming and intended to meet these changes with a strategic materials policy that would guide America into the future. His administration was continuously plagued by the excessive anticommunist activities of Congress and the Korean War, which was sponsored by the Soviet Union. He reacted quickly and decisively to events, both foreign and domestic, that were threatening to the security of the United States, regardless of whether or not the action would cost his party votes. To head off a steel strike during the Korean War, he ordered seizure of the steel mills in April 1952. Two months later the Supreme Court negated the seizure and declared that he had exceeded his constitutional authority.

6.41. In contrast to President Truman's knowledge of the value of mineral commodities and changes that were taking place in Europe, the public's awaremess, in general, of the value of mineral commodities to their lifestyle and their relationship to the security of the job they held had diminished to almost zero. The average individual had only a vague

Table 6.5
Gross Federal Debt at the End of Year, 1946–52 (Bureau of Public Debt 1994)
(in millions of dollars)

Year	Gross Federal Debt	Year	Gross Federal Debt
1946	270,991	1949	252,610
1947	257,149	1950	256,853
1948	252,031	1951	255,288
		1952	259,097

idea as to where mineral commodities came from. What was the difference whether they were mined in the United States or imported? The end product of the minerals was all that the public was interested in. If it ended up as a car, boat, electrical appliance, woodworking tool, or airplane and there was an electrical switch to push to obtain electricity, why worry about where anything came from? "Yankee ingenuity" and "Yankee know-how" were accepted as gospel truths. America would never lose its massive industrial superiority, and it would always be able to solve and surmount any problem because it had the ingenuity and know-how.

6.42. This attitude was not too serious as long as the president and Congress were aware of the problem. However, the primary difficulty with this attitude was that the public was electing to Congress many individuals in their own image, individuals who had no idea of the necessity to maintain a strong domestic minerals industry. This lack of knowledge was to be one of the primary reasons for the nation losing its industrial dominance in the world and causing the gross federal debt to reach the astounding amount of over $4 trillion in 1993. At the end of World War II, in 1945, the gross federal debt had reached over $260 billion. Table 6.5 shows the growth in the debt during the Truman administration. President Truman managed to reduce the debt in 1947, 1948, and 1951, as shown in table 6.5.

6.43. The Great Depression, which held a death grip on the nation until the start of the Lend-Lease Program with England and the USSR did not resurface after the war was over. For some reason the market faults that had caused the depression had disappeared or been corrected during the war years. Whether it was a sufficient increase in population to assimilate the agriculture surpluses that were evident before the war or the purchasing of products by the public in pursuit of the "abundant life" that kept the depression from resurfacing is unknown. Population

Table 6.6
Annual Population Estimates for the United States, 1946–52 (Bureau of the Census 1994)

Year	Total Resident Population	Year (in thousands)	Total Resident Population
1946	140,054	1949	148,665
1947	143,446	1950	151,235
1948	146,093	1951	153,310
		1952	155,687

growth during the Truman administration averaged 2.2 million per year, as shown in table 6.6, and this could have been a strong factor in keeping the depression at bay.

7

The Next Eight Years (1952–60): Eisenhower (Staff of the Bureau of Mines 1956, 1960, 1965, 1970, 1975, 1980, 1985; Perkes 1974; Standard and Poor's Corporation 1980; Morse 1956)

7.1. By 1952, when Mr. Eisenhower was elected president, television was emerging as a means of communication unrivaled by other media. It provided public viewing of every major event occurring in the world. In a democratic society nothing could be hidden from its view, but it also could be manipulated. Candidates for election or re-election to office became adept at obtaining personnel skilled at staging and timing candidate events for the viewing public in time for the 6:00 P.M. news hour. During the Dwight Eisenhower–Adlai Stevenson race for the presidency the three major networks, ABC, CBS, and NBC, for the first time used computers to tabulate the votes and predict the winner before all the votes had been counted. However, because Mr. Eisenhower's lead was so great, there was never much doubt of who was going to win the presidency, but the computer predictions on congressional and state offices were remarkably good. From this election in 1952 to the present, computer predictions have been a fixture in all television broadcasts for tabulating the votes and predicting winners before the polls close. Although the computer cannot predict how an individual will vote, it can predict with considerable accuracy how the masses will vote on the basis of previous sampling of selected voting districts, exit polls, and other factors.

7.2. Dwight D. Eisenhower was a graduate of West Point. He filled various posts in the army during his career and attended the Army War College. From 1929 to 1933, he served as a military aide in the office of the assistant secretary of war. Eisenhower became commanding general of the U.S. forces in the European Theater of Operations in June

1942. He was named supreme commander of the Allied forces in the European Theater of Operations on December 24, 1943. This post required that he win the cooperation of not only his own commanders but also the British and Free French commanders. He demonstrated remarkable ability in this regard and molded the Allied armies into a solid fighting front, all with the objective of defeating Germany and Italy.

7.3. General Eisenhower was recalled to Washington by President Truman in December 1945 to succeed General of the Army George C. Marshall as chief of staff. Eisenhower held this post until May 1948 and then retired from the army to become president of Columbia University. In 1950 he was recalled to military duty to become the supreme commander of the Integrated European Defense Force, which was being organized to counteract the threat posed by the Soviet Union's massive armed forces buildup in Eastern Europe. If experience was a requisite for becoming president of the United States, there is little doubt but what General Eisenhower was well qualified. After he was elected president he managed to end the Korean conflict in July 1953. However, though the fighting stopped, because of the constant threat by North Korea, aided and abetted by the Soviet Union, the United States has had to maintain armed forces there for over forty years. President Eisenhower continued the arms shipments and a cadre of advisers to Vietnam, which was a succession of the program begun by President Truman.

7.4. President Eisenhower administered the presidency in essentially the same manner as he did his posts in the military when he was supreme comander of the Allied forces in Europe and the Integrated European Defense Force. Although his cabinet members were not commanders of armies, he placed on them the full responsibility for administering the departments that they headed; in addition, they were expected to monitor political problems within their departments and ensure that these problems did not get public airing in the electronic or print media. Those who allowed political problems to get out of hand were certain to have one-sided discussions with President Eisenhower's Chief White House aide, Sherman Adams.

7.5. President Eisenhower appointed Charles E. Wilson and George M. Humphrey to the key cabinet posts of secretary of defense and secretary of the treasury, respectively. Prior to becoming secretary of defense, Mr. Wilson had been president of General Motors since 1941. He was an engineer and an expert in production planning, and he had spent a large part of his life moving up the ladder in the General

Motors Corporation. Mr. Humphrey was involved in the operation and organization of the National Steel Corporation, Consolidation Coal Company, and M. A. Hanna Company (Sheppard 1993). The latter company had mines on both the Mesabi and Cayuna Iron Ranges in Minnesota.

7.6. Messrs. Wilson and Humphrey were key cabinet members in the decisions being made to counteract the continuous menacing actions of the Soviet Union. Mr. Wilson had the responsibility for developing offensive intercontinental atomic warhead missiles, maintaining the armed forces in a state of war readiness, and ensuring that the nation was defended insofar as possible with the latest technological hardware against enemy intercontinental atomic warhead missiles. With these annual massive expenditures, Mr. Humphrey was facing an almost impossible task in attempting to balance the annual budgets and make payments to reduce the gross national debt, and as if these problems were not enough, he was also confronted with the buying binge by the American public.

7.7. The American public was not only on a buying binge; it was also on a touring binge. It was "see America by automobile." People were motoring across the country, north to south and east to west, and vice versa, as never before. Accommodations for the automobile traveler were being constructed on all the major highways. The automobile had become a necessity to everybody in the United States except the Department of the Treasury's Internal Revenue Service (IRS). The touring binge also included overseas travel by airplane. Intercontinental flights were available to every major city in the world, and by the thousands Americans flocked to Europe and Japan in the spring and summer and to South America, Africa, and Australia in the fall and winter. The Eisenhower administration never did attempt to meet head-on the "abundant life" policy that was first proposed by President Roosevelt and was being implemented by the public and increasing in momentum annually. The administration appeared to have no recognition whatsoever that the public by itself was implementing a program of unlimited use of mineral commodities.

7.8. In foreign affairs President Eisenhower relied heavily on his secretary of state, John Foster Dulles. Mr. Dulles was never successful in ending the threat posed by the Soviet Union. It did not take long for President Eisenhower and Secretary Dulles to discover what President Truman had known for seven years: The Soviet Union could not be dealt with diplomatically. Their leaders seemed to have just one way of dealing with another country, and that was by a show of force with a huge well-equipped army, navy, and air force and atomic warhead rocketry. Their objective was to place their form of government in every country in the world.

7.9. Throughout the world the Soviet form of government was termed *communist,* but the manner in which the Soviets administered their government bore no similarity whatsoever to the idealistic form of government as envisioned by Karl Marx, the world's most noted socialist. Marx's often-quoted statement: "Workers of the world unite, you have nothing to lose but your chains," did not apply to the Soviet workers; they had more chains on them than they had under any czar, including Ivan the Terrible. The Soviet government was an autocracy, that is, supreme government by an individual. In addition, the Soviet government was based on a class system. There were those (a small percentage) who belonged to the Party and those who did not. Those who did not belong could go nowhere in the political system until they were accepted for party membership. Party members had a higher standard of living than the masses who did not belong. Those who did belong had to work themselves upward into succeeding class levels. At each higher level, they achieved a higher standard of living than at the level below. It was as pure a caste system as it could possibly be.

7.10. The most difficult aspect of the Soviet administration to understand was their motives and actions. The individuals in the Central Committee of the Communist Party appeared to be suffering en masse with paranoid schizophrenia or, to put it in plainer words, constant suspicion and resentment, accompanied by fear that the democratic nations of the world were hostile and plotting to destroy them. The leaders attempted to shield the Soviet people from any contact with the rest of the world and discouraged cultural exchanges with other nations. This characteristic of the Soviet government was described by Winston Churchill as an "iron curtain." If the Soviet Union had opened its borders to trade and cultural exchange after the war, it could have become one of the great superpowers of the world, but its leaders did not have the vision to grasp this opportunity. A substantial amount of the armed might that they had after the war was achieved through the Lend-Lease Program, begun in 1939 by President Roosevelt. That they pursued the course of continuous direct armed confrontation with their former allies made no sense at all, but pursue it they did without pause for almost fifty years. They used the greater part of their mineral resources to build and maintain a huge armed force at the expense of their own infrastructure.

7.11. Dealing diplomatically with the Soviet Union meant dealing with an individual who wielded enormous power. The small group in the Central Committee supported the premier at every move, realizing that if he was overthrown, all would be likely to go the same route. After Stalin's death in March 1953, Georgi M. Malenkov was premier and in 1955 was succeeded by Marshall Nikolai Bulganin.

7.12. During the Eisenhower administration, difficulties in dealing with the Soviets diplomatically were compounded, because even though Marshall Bulganin was premier, the chief architect of Soviet policy was Nikita Khrushchev. Mr. Khrushchev was an extremely emotional and volatile individual and an absolutely firm believer in the constant menacing actions that had become the trademark of the USSR. He appeared to ooze confidence that the USSR would eventually rule the world. He had solid evidence to bolster this confidence. His nation had the atomic bomb, the hydrogen bomb, advanced rocketry to deliver the bombs, a massive army, a huge navy under a successful building program, and, most important of all, a program in which steel production (Yankee ingenuity and Yankee know-how) was increasing by 4 million short tons per year. In a confrontation with Vice President Richard Nixon shown on television, Khrushchev said, "We will bury you." There was absolutely no doubt that he meant every word of it. With Mr. Khrushchev setting the policy, President Eisenhower was constantly beset by menacing actions by the Soviet Union; for eight years he was continuously acting or reacting to counteract some action by the Soviets.

7.13. Probably one of the reasons that the Soviet Union's actions were so constant and continuous against the Eisenhower administration was because they had been waiting for seven years for the United States to replace President Truman. In dealing with President Truman diplomatically they encountered a dapper, polite gentlemen, but always in the background were the vivid pictures of the ruins of Hiroshima and Nagasaki, Japan. Here was a man who had not hesitated to use the atomic bomb twice. Underneath that polite exterior was something much harder than steel. How far could he be pushed before he used it again? Thus the Soviets were never actually certain what action they could take that would move President Truman to once again push the button on the atomic bomb. He had done it twice, and the question that most concerned the Soviets was what would impel him to use it again. Although the Soviets had atomic bombs of their own, they were well aware that beginning an atomic war with the United States with Truman as president would have been a fatal move.

7.14. In 1955, President Eisenhower acted directly when a Chinese attack on Formosa appeared imminent. He deployed armed forces into the area to defend the Chinese Nationalists on Formosa. This show of force by the United States was successful, and China eased back from engaging the United States in actual warfare. In September of 1955 President Eisenhower suffered a mild heart attack, but by the end of the year he had again resumed the duties of president.

7.15. If there was anything President Eisenhower admired in Germany, it was their "autobahns," and one of his strongest domestic programs was the improvement of America's highway system. This federal program included transcontinental east–west and north–south four-lane-or-more highways. The basic Federal-State Highway Program as developed under the Eisenhower administration has continued to this day. The program placed heavy demands for mineral commodities petroleum, steel, limestone, coke, coal, cement, asphalt, crushed rock, and sand and gravel.

7.16. Douglas McKay, former governor of Oregon, was appointed secretary of the interior. He, Secretary of State Dulles, Secretary of Commerce Weeks, and the director of the Office of Defense Mobilization, Fleming, were named by President Eisenhower on October 26, 1953, to a cabinet committee on minerals policy to inquire into national problems affecting the production and utilization of minerals and metals (McKay, Dulles, Weeks, Sinclair, and Fleming 1954). The task assigned to the Cabinet Committee was essentially the same as that covered by the Paley Commission under President Truman; however, in their report submitted to the president on November 30, 1954, there is no mention whatsoever of the Paley Commission report. Many of the recommendations made by the cabinet committee were the same as those recommended by the Paley Commission, but after the report was made public there was little follow-through on the recommendations, except enlargement of the strategic stockpile and continuation of the Defense Minerals Exploration Programs (DMEA). Under the Office of Defense Mobilization (ODM) the development of a strategic minerals policy appeared to bog down in bureaucratic language and passive paper programs citing aims and goals, with stockpiling of strategic mineral commodities being the primary goal. The needed leadership in Interior and ODM to deal with the complexities of a viable minerals industry strategic program was never present.

7.17. In February 1956, President Eisenhower, the United States, and the world were baffled when Khrushchev denounced former premier Joseph Stalin at the Communist Party Congress in Moscow. This de-Stalinization, if it can be called that, of the Soviet Union made as little sense to the outside world as their continuous menacing actions. This action, which appeared to have the approval of all members of the Central Committee, probably could erase any mention of Stalin within the Soviet borders and their satellites, but it could not erase from world history Stalin's rule from 1924 to 1953, a period of twenty-nine years. If the Central Committee thought that by this action they were divorcing themselves from the barbaric actions by Stalin during his twenty-nine-year rule, they were fooling nobody but themselves. The primary effect that de-Stalinization appeared to have was for many, and certainly President Eisenhower, was wondering whether the Central Committee of the Soviet Communist Party was comprised of lunatics.

7.19. Although 1956 started out with Khrushchev's surprising denunciation of Stalin, that was not to be the most surprising event that year. Col. Gamal Abdel Nasser, who had succeeded King Farouk as ruler in Egypt, decided to gamble. He nationalized and expropriated the Suez Canal, which was the lifeline for Great Britain and France to obtain petroleum from the Middle East. This action triggered what has been termed the Suez Crisis. Great Britain and France wanted to take military action immediately, but President Eisenhower wanted a peaceful solution to the crisis, which both Britain and France regarded as unrealistic. They had solid reasons for this belief, because Nasser had tied himself directly to the Soviet Union and at the same time was harassing Israel along the Sinai Desert border. In October Israel crossed the border in the Sinai and France and Great Britain started military movement to occupy the Suez Canal Zone.

7.20. Nasser's reaction to the military action was to block the canal with sunken ships. President Eisenhower's reaction was even more drastic. He refused to support Britain and France in the action and demanded their withdrawal. With the Suez Canal blocked, the petroleum lifeline to Middle East oil cut, and no support from the United States for the action, Britain and France had only one option, and that was to withdraw.

They, along with the United States, had suffered a humiliating defeat. Nasser had won the Suez Canal Zone, and he controlled the Suez Canal lifeline for bringing petroleum from the Middle East to Europe. He had placed Europe's surging industrialization under a constant threat. Nasser now had no restraints whatsoever on continuing his menacing actions in the Middle East and promoting unrest in North Africa. He could proceed like a "loose cannon" in the Middle East without fear of retaliation, and that is exactly what he did until his death by heart attack in September 1970.

7.21. Nasser was not the only big winner. The Soviet Union ruthlessly put down a Hungarian uprising during the military effort in the Suez Canal Zone virtually without condemnation. The constant menacing actions and often erratic behavior by the Soviets had paid off handsomely. It had made President Eisenhower uncertain as to their intentions, and he must have refused to back Great Britain and France because of fear of military action by the Soviets. This is the only rational explanation for his action; apparently, above all he did not want a war with the Soviet Union virtually on their own doorstep. The successful action in Hungary and the green light to continue promoting unrest in the Middle East gave Khrushchev enormous confidence that he could mount other challenges without fear of reprisal.

7.22. The refusal to back Great Britain and France in the Suez Crisis has to be regarded as a mistake by President Eisenhower. Their military presence in the Suez would have stabilized the Middle East, that is, as much as it could be stabilized, and it would have dampered, if not eliminated, wars and unrest in that area in the following forty years. Great Britain and France had only done what the United States did almost four decades later when it invaded Iraq in the Gulf War to maintain the flow of petroleum from the Middle East.

7.23. Douglas McKay did not last out the full term as secretary of the interior. In 1956 Mr. Eisenhower appointed Frederick A Seaton as secretary. Mr. Seaton was active in Republican politics in Nebraska. He controlled newspapers, magazines, and broadcasting stations throughout the Midwest. Before becoming secretary of the interior he held two different positions in the administration, as assistant secretary of the Department of Defense and presidential assistant. Mr. Seaton's term as presidential assistant gave him an insight into the manner in which President Eisenhower's chief aide, Sherman Adams, handled the cabinet secretaries who let political problems spill over into the media. Mr.

Seaton's approach to administering Interior was, first and foremost, based on doing nothing that would "rock the boat" politically. As a result, insofar as mineral commodities were concerned, Interior coasted in neutral for the five years of his administration; in additon, Mr. Seaton appeared to have as little knowledge of the missions of the Department of Interior as his predecessor, Douglas McKay. Seaton did little in regard to mineral resources, which in effect kept Interior nicely in tune with the rest of the administration.

7.24. By the end of the first Eisenhower administration the political inaction on the minerals industry was becoming serious, especially in regard to the liquid fuels and ferrous metals divisions of the minerals industry. Petroleum and natural gas were replacing coal as an energy source in many industries; in addition, the nation was importing more petroleum than it was exporting, and the Middle East was destined to become the primary foreign supplier of petroleum, but inept handling of the Suez Crisis had destabilized the area. The situation in ferrous metals had become even more serious. To maintain a steady supply of iron ore, iron, and steel, some of the integrated steel companies, including U.S. Steel, were faced with capital expenditures of billions of dollars to develop foreign deposits of iron ore, build new furnaces and steel mills, and upgrade the technology of treating domestic low-grade iron ores and maintain the existing blast furnaces and steel plants. The huge capital investments required would increase the price of steel, which would increase the cost of all machinery and products produced in the United States.

7.25. The national security, outer space, and AEC programs were placing heavy demands on the domestic minerals industry; also, the public had implemented the "abundant life" program, which called for unlimited use of mineral commodities for any purpose, no matter how trivial, for which they might be desired. There was no action taken by the administration to determine the effect that these demands were having on the nation and develop a structured program that would meet the demands for national security and place limitations on those uses that were not essential to national security. To fill the growing demands without any restrictions whatsoever would require imports far and above what the United States had ever imported before. Importing would be an expenditure in place of creation of wealth. If large amounts of mineral commodities had to be imported, this would entail a tremendous change in the amount of wealth being produced in the United States.

7.26. Under President Eisenhower's administration, a substantial amount of military expenditures were shifted from purchase of the conventional weapons of the type used in World War II to atomic weapons. The atomic weaponry meant a nuclear-armed and powered navy and intercontinental ballistic missiles carrying atomic warheads. This shifting of emphasis to atomic weapons, coupled with the outer space program, was a massive change not only in war strategy but also in technology development. What had been satisfactory technology with conventional weapons was no longer satisfactory when applied to atomic weaponry. The need for new technology created a change in the manner in which the armed forces developed technology. They expanded their in-house research programs and entered into research and development contracts with universities and industry.

7.27. The three branches of the Department of Defense had available a tremendous amount of funds for research and development contracts. The navy was engaged in remodeling parts of the old fleet and building new atomic-powered ships and submarines to carry guided missiles; their jet-powered aircrafts were being designed specifically for use on carriers. The air force and army were both developing rocketry for outer space exploration and intercontinental ballistic missile rockets for national security. In addition, the air force was procuring under contracts the full range of jet-powered conventional cargo, fighter, and medium and long-range bomber airplanes for use from land bases. The army also had strong research and development programs on conventional weapons, such as rifles, rocket guns to replace the field artillery gun, and land vehicles of all types.

7.28. In addition to the Department of Defense contract programs, the AEC had both in-house and outside contract research and development programs in progress on the radioactive mineral commodities, atomic bomb development, conducting underground atomic explosion tests, and peaceful uses of atomic energy. During Mr. Eisenhower's administration the military-AEC-industrial-university complex was melding into a whole, which essentially dominated the scientific developments that were occurring in the minerals industry. In a large part strong emphasis was placed on material development (see table 1:6.3 in appendix 2) to develop materials with a combination of special properties, such as high strength, light weight, high resistance to heat, machinability, radiation shielding, and high resistance to fatigue. The manner in which the research and development was conducted by the different agencies resulted in duplication, but because of the massive volume of proposals and the manner in which they were prepared, duplication could not be detected easily. Each government contractor essentially carried on their agenda of research and development independent of the others.

7.29. In 1956 President Eisenhower was re-elected to a second term. Not long after his inauguration in 1957, he and the American public got a huge surprise. The USSR launched *Sputnik I*, the first man-made Earth satellite, into outer space. This was essentially the start of what could be called the Space Age, and it aroused considerable concern that the United States was falling behind in the space race. However, President Eisenhower was firm in his refusal to enter into a space race with the Soviets; he told the public that America's space program was on a specified time schedule and he would adhere strictly to that schedule.

7.30. Actually, the launching of *Sputnik I* should not have been that big a surprise to either President Eisenhower, the armed forces, or the Central Intelligence Agency (CIA). This marked another failure by America's intelligence agencies to keep the public informed that it was not only a possibility but a probability that the Soviets would be the first to launch an Earth satellite into space. Both the United States and the Soviets initially gained most, if not all, of their rocket technology from the German rocket military cadre that manned Peenemunde, the rocket base in Germany from which the German V-1 and V-2 rockets were launched. As the war was drawing to a close and the Soviet army was moving into Germany, some of the top management personnel of Peene-munde fled to the western front to be captured by the U.S. army instead of by the Soviets. However, some of the top managers and most, if not all, of the middle managers, engineers, technicians, and construction personnel were captured by the Soviets. The Soviet overrun of Peene-munde, the capture of most of the personnel, and the removal of the complete installation deep into the Soviet interior was a well-known event to U.S. intelligence and certainly an event that then-general Eisen-hower must have known about in minute detail. German scientists, chemists, engineers, technicians, and workmen were equal to or better than any others in the world, and the cadre at Peenemunde had no equal on rocket knowledge in the world. The nation that got hold of the installation at Peenemunde and most of the experienced German personnel to man it started out with the capability launching a V-2 rocket and the advanced research beyond the V-2, which meant a tremendous head start in rocket technology.

7.31. In twelve years, from 1945 to 1957, the Soviet Union, with the help of an atom spy and the capture of a German rocket base, and by their own initiative achieved a massive capability for armed conflict. In 1945 the United States was the superpower of the World. By 1957 the Soviet Union had surpassed the United States in armed conventional forces, equaled it in atomic weaponry, and surpassed it in outer space rocketry. The effort that the Soviets made in this twelve-year period concentrated solely on military superiority was all done at the expense of their infrastructure. An effort of this magnitude in such a short period of time must have required extreme sacrifices by the Soviet populace. Their standard of living for the twelve-year period in all probability regressed. Virtually all research and development was concentrated on the effort, and fully 75 percent of the mineral commodities mined would have to be funneled into the effort. The wealth produced by the production of mineral commodities was wasted on military hardware. Construction of living space, hospital facilities, communication and transportation systems, and other amenities for a decent standard of living had to go on hold while the effort was in progress. No nation in the world, even mineral-rich America, could continue at the pace set by the Soviets without eventually faltering.

7.32. The industrial surge that was occurring in the Soviet Union and Europe is best illustrated by the same set of tables that have been presented in previous chapters. Tables 7,1, 7.2, 7.3, and 7.4 accurately depict the diminishing industrial dominance of the United States and the rising dominance of Europe and the Soviet Union.

7.33. Table 7.1 shows that the Mesabi Range reached the second billion long tons of production in 1955. It took forty-seven years to produce the first billion and just eighteen years to produce the second. Without doubt this iron ore deposit was the key to America's industrial dominance. In the same year that the Mesabi had produced a total of 2 billion tons, table 7.2 shows, imports of iron ore increased sharply from North America (Canada and Mexico), South America, and Europe. The time had come when the Mesabi could no longer expand production upon demand, and essentially an era was coming to an end. Henceforth, from 1955 on, the United States would have to rely on foreign imports of iron ore to supply a substantial percentage of the total iron ore consumed. By 1960 a total of 35 million long tons was being imported per year at a value of $322 million; the tonnage imported amounted to 28 percent of the total produced and imported in that year. The United

Table 7.1

Total Annual Production of Iron Ore in the United States, 1953–60, Compared to That Produced by the Lake Superior District and the Mesabi Range (U.S. Geological Survey and U.S. Bureau of Mines 1992)
(in thousand long tons)

Year	Total Tons	Lake Superior District		Mesabi Iron Range		
		Tons	Percentage of Total	Tons	Percentage of Total	Tons Accumulated
1953	117,995	95,437	81	75,324	64	1,925,674
1954	78,129	60,836	78	45,725	59	1,971,399
1955	103,003	82,985	81	64,860	63	2,036,259
1956	97,877	77,468	74	59,346	61	2,095,605
1957	106,148	83,530	79	65,886	62	2,161,490
1958	67,709	51,577	76	40,860	60	2,202,350
1959	60,276	43,950	73	34,556	59	2,236,906
1960	88,874	71,792	81	54,442	61	2,291,348

Table 7.2

Iron Ore Imported for Consumption into the United States by Continents, 1953–60 (U.S. Geological Survey and U.S. Bureau of Mines 1992)
(in thousand long tons)
(in thousand dollars)

Year	North America		South America		Europe		Remainder	
	Long Tons	Value	Long Tons	Value	Long Tons	Value	Long Tons	Value
1953	2,363	19,904	5,616	41,716	2,109	27,360	987	7,808
1954	3,799	30,422	9,402	66,512	1,544	14,276	1,047	8,249
1955	10,398	81,134	10,765	75,836	1,223	12,393	1,086	8,094
1956	14,112	121,069	13,881	104,563	1,000	11,957	1,418	12,901
1957	12,955	144,892	18,836	149,508	677	9,614	1,183	11,037
1958	8,549	78,555	17,925	142,533	114	1,704	942	8,741
1959	13,618	128,888	20,570	167,156	171	2,100	1,258	13,303
1960	10,748	105,252	22,716	206,168	95	1,562	1,019	8,907

States now was in direct competition with Europe for shipments of iron ore from various nations throughout the world. The direct shipping ore on the Mesabi was nearing depletion, and plants had to be constructed to concentrate the lower-grade ore. Foreign ore was actually cheaper per unit of contained iron than the concentrated ore being produced on the Mesabi. The advantage that the United States had held for over sixty years was gone. The massive industrial surge from 1892 to 1929 and World Wars I and II had depleted America's Yankee ingenuity and Yankee know-how.

7.34. In the middle of July 1959, the United Steel Workers went

Table 7.3

Production, Imports, and Exports of Pig Iron and Steel in the United States, 1953–60
(U.S. Geological Survey and U.S. Bureau of Mines 1992)
(in thousand short tons)

Year	Pig Iron			Steel		
	Production	Imports	Exports	Production	Imports	Exports
1953	74,901	590	19	111,610		2,680
1954	57,948	291	10	88,312		2,534
1955	76,849	284	35	117,036		3,583
1956	75,030	327	269	115,216		3,622
1957	78,404	225	882	112,715		4,509
1958	57,155	210	103	85,255		2,429
1959	60,210	700	10	93,446	4,615	1,773
1960	66,501	331	112	99,262	3,570	4,247

on strike against the steel industry that lasted for 116 days. *Business Week* stated that "labor historians may record it as the most important strike of the midcentury" (1959). The steel industry had dug in and refused to make an additional wage offer or propose a social welfare plan. President Eisenhower wanted a quick settlement of the strike, but at the same time he wanted a noninflationary settlement. The strike lasted almost four months, and Vice President Nixon had to become part of the negotiating team to finally obtain an agreement to end the strike. However, President Eisenhower did not obtain what he wanted. The agreement that ended the strike was inflationary, and the public ended up being the big losers. At the time under the terms of the settlement most observers felt that labor had won a great victory (*Business Week* 1960), but the data presented in table 7.3 show that it was a pyrrhic victory. In 1959, the year of the strike, 4.6 million short tons of steel were imported to fill the shortage caused by the strike. These imports broke into the domestic market at an opportune time, with no competition because of the strike, and they gained a foothold that has to the present never been relinquished but increased substantially over the 1959 figure. Labor may have won the strike, but at the same time they gave away a large part of their future by losing thousands of jobs and also with an annual inflation rate that ate into their paychecks like termites into decayed timber.

7.35. The strike was called at the worst possible time. The steel industry was undergoing substantial changes in the handling of Mesabi ore, sharp increases in the importation of foreign ores, and an all-out assault on their dominant steel production position in the world by the USSR, Western Europe, and Japan. Table 7.4 shows that America's share of the world steel production was decreasing on an average about 2

Table 7.4

World Production of Steel with the Production and Percentage Produced by the United States, USSR Separate from Europe, Europe, Japan, and Other Nations, 1953–60 (U.S. Geological Survey and U.S. Bureau of Mines 1992)
(in million short tons)

	World	U.S.		USSR		Europe		Japan		Other
Year	Tons	Tons	%	Tons	%	Tons	%	Tons	%	%
1953	258.7	111.6	43	42.0	16	82.7	33	8.4	3	5
1954	246.6	88.3	36	45.6	19	89.6	36	8.5	3	6
1955	297.6	117.0	39	49.9	17	103.0	35	10.4	3	6
1956	312.6	115.2	37	53.6	17	110.6	35	12.2	4	7
1957	322.0	112.7	35	56.2	17	117.0	36	13.9	4	8
1958	298.3	85.3	29	60.5	20	113.9	38	13.4	5	8
1959	336.3	93.4	28	66.1	20	123.8	37	18.3	5	10
1960	381.2	99.3	26	72.0	20	142.8	37	24.4	6	11

percent per year, Europe's was increasing by slightly less than 1 percent per year, and the USSR's and Japan's by about .5 percent per year. In 1957 the continent of Europe, without the Soviet Union, had gained the dominant position by 1 percent. Six nations, Great Britain, France, Germany, Spain, Sweden, and Italy, were developing automotive industries, and they were making plans to market worldwide their automobiles, trucks, passenger buses, and earth-moving, railroad, mining, and agricultural machinery. The combined nations of Europe were preparing to compete in the world's market with mass-produced automotive machinery on an equal footing with the United States for the first time in over fifty years.

7.36. Although Europe was surpassing the United States in steel production, a far greater danger was the constant menacing actions by the USSR. The Soviet Union with a confident Nikita Khrushchev in control had every reason in the world now to believe that his prediction to Vice President Nixon that "we will bury you" would come true. Table 7.4 shows that the Soviets had increased their steel production from 42 million short tons in 1953 to 72 million tons in 1960. This increase in steel production was a remarkable accomplishment, but what was most troubling about the increase was that fully 75 percent or more was being applied to build an armed capability that was unsurpassed by any other country in the world.

7.37. Even though the Soviets were building their mighty military machine, the American public was in hot pursuit of the "abundant life." The executives of some of America's largest companies also seemed to be mesmerized by the success they were enjoying. The automotive industry was annually producing models that were different in body style but with few, if any, changes in anything else. The styles ranged from the sleek to the grotesque. If the executives or salesmen were asked what changes in technology had been made, they were more than likely to point out that the cigarette lighter had been moved to the middle of the dashboard, so that it would be equally convenient to both front seat occupants. The public flocked to the showrooms as the new models were annually placed on the market. They stood back admiring the new styles, got into the front seat behind the wheel, occasionally gave a perfunctory glance at the engine under the hood, kicked one of the front tires, and then started to dicker on what they could get for a trade-in on the car they were driving. The automotive companies appeared to think that this would go on forever. Who could match what they were producing? There was no foreign competition, the American public was hooked on the automobile, and there were customers galore. Gasoline was cheap, and the trend was to build longer, heavier, and more stylish models. The more metal the manufacturers could hang on the car, the higher the price.

7.38. The union leaders of the automotive industry appeared to be in the same state as the executives, believing this ideal situation would last forever. The relationship between the union and companies was always adversarial, hardly ever, if at all, concilatory. To impress the union brotherhood, it was incumbent upon the union leaders and negotiators to be adversaries, never advocates. Above all, the union leaders must never do anything that might give the brotherhood the suspicion that they were becoming "company men."

7.39. The ease with which new automobiles were accepted by the public gave rise to the era of "screw ya." If a car buyer had a complaint about his purchase, the dealer turned his back and walked away. Complaints to the manufacturer resulted in form letters to the complainant, which were polite but actually said: "Screw ya. If you don't like our product, go someplace else." The automotive companies became masters of "stonewalling" techniques, and they were ideal subjects of study on how not to conduct customer relations and, in some instances, how not to produce an automobile.

7.40. The executives of the automotive industries and also, for that matter, the union leaders appeared to be existing in a somnolent state.

They never appeared to see the foreign competition that would be entering the market in the future. They appeared to be unaware of the industrialization surge in Europe because of cheap available energy. Each company had their percentage share of automotive sales now, and insofar as they could see, nothing was on the horizon that was going to change it. Although there were signs beginning to appear that warned that strong competition was not far off, they were ignored.

7.41. One of the most obvious warning signs was the resurgence of the Japanese shipbuilding industry; this was a forerunner of the success that the Japanese were having in rebuilding their shattered economy after World War II. They had become by 1957 the primary world producers of ocean cargo ships and tankers and, at a later date, supertankers. The Japanese single-minded concentration on the shipbuilding industry in their country had paid off handsomely. Once their position in the shipbuilding industry was solidified, it had to be apparent that their next move would be with the same single-minded purpose into something that would utilize the same steel products that were used in the shipbuilding industry (see appendix 5). It was a logical transition into the production of farm and industrial machinery, machine tools, household appliances, trucks, and automobiles. For a country with a strong steel industry, the development of an automotive industry to accompany their shipbuilding industry was a relatively simple task.

7.42. However, with the economy of the United States as it was, a cloud of euphoria diffused throughout the nation masking any ominous signs of change that were occurring. The dynamic growth in the economy in America was further fueled by the development of air-conditioning machinery for factories, apartments, office buildings, residential units, ships, airplanes, trucks, and automobiles. As new buildings were built, air-conditioning units became as necessary as the heating furnaces; window air conditioners became a common item in older homes. Air conditioners in automobiles were an extra item, but more often than not, they constituted part of the original purchase.

7.43. By 1957 Secretary of the Treasury George M. Humphrey had had all he could stand of the Eisenhower administration. Humphrey had consistently sought to reduce spending, but he apparently was the lone voice in the cabinet advocating that. After seeing the administration's 1957 budget, he resigned and warned, "If we don't cut spending, over a long period, I will predict that you will have a depression that will curl your hair" (DeGregorio 1993). Mr. Humphrey had good reasons for his

Table 7.5
Gross Federal Debt at the End of Year, 1953–60 (Bureau of Public Debt 1992)
(in millions of dollars)

Year	Gross Federal Debt	Year	Gross Federal Debt
1953	265,953	1957	272,252
1954	270,812	1958	279,666
1955	274,366	1959	287,465
1956	272,693	1960	290,525

concern. Table 7.5 shows the increases in the gross national debt from 1953 to 1960. Apparently the point he was trying to make was that if a balanced budget could not be prepared for fiscal year 1957, when was the nation going to be able to balance the budget? This certainly was a logical question. By 1960 the gross national debt had risen $24.7 billion to a total of $290.5 billion. Mr. Humphrey's resignation must have had some effect on the administration, because 1956 and 1957 were the only years in which the debt was lowered.

7.44. President Eisenhower bowed to political pressure and in 1958 placed the space program under a single agency, the National Aeronautics and Space Administration (NASA). This agency as a collective unit continued the same massive contracting program to industry and universities as it had when it was in separated units in the Department of Defense. To the public, NASA became the absolute zenith of science and technology, and its successes in the outer space program lent impetus to the public's belief that Yankee ingenuity and Yankee know-how could solve everything.

7.45. On September 12, 1958, an engineer from Texas Instruments, Jack S. Kilby, invented the integrated circuit, which is known in everyday language as the microchip (McCarthy 1969). This invention most certainly must be regarded as one of the great discoveries of the twentieth century. It created tremendous changes in the computer and communications industries. It automated communication systems and made possible the development of the computer and remote control systems as we know them today, wherein it touches every facet of our everyday lives at home, at work, at play, at the library, and on a train or airplane or in an automobile. The impact on the world in advancement of technology may well prove to be greater than the development of atomic power.

7.46. In 1955 the Soviet Union started exporting petroleum to Western Europe. By 1958 the exports were in sufficient amounts to have an effect on the world market price. The Soviets cut prices to make sales.

If there was anything that could upset the delicate balance between the petroleum companies and the sultanates in the Middle East, it was a cut in the price of their petroleum. Sudden exports of mineral commodities from a type of government such as that which ruled the USSR is something to be expected. In their government structure they have no system whereby overproduction can be halted; thus when storage space is overflowing, there is no other option but export.

7.47. The dislocation of the world market price of petroleum and the Suez Crisis focused the Eisenhower administration on the liquid fuels division of the mineral industry, but the focus was on placating the sultanates and meeting the immediate domestic and European demand for petroleum while the Suez Canal was blocked, instead of on developing a structured program for the future. Petroleum by this time was providing 67 percent of America's energy needs. It was supplanting coal in many uses in industry. The imports from the Middle East were like a never-ending gusher. Huge oil field after oil field was being discovered, and the world was virtually swimming in excess petroleum at low cost. There was little doubt but what the Middle East petroleum production could have shut down at least 80 percent or more of the production in the United States, unless some means of protection was given the domestic industry. This protection came in the form of a quota system. Under the authority of the Trade Agreement Extension Act of July 1, 1954, as amended, the president by proclamation established import quotas of petroleum into the United States.

7.48. The situation in regard to petroleum is illustrated by the five tables of statistics presented in appendix 8: "Petroleum and Natural Gas." In table 5 the exports and imports are listed. The first year that imports exceeded exports was 1948, and in this year imports exceeded exports by 53.5 million forty-two-gallon barrels. Thereafter imports would continue to rise and exports to drop until, by 1960, imports exceeded exports by 590.2 million barrels, and imports continued to increase into the seventies. Table 4 shows that in 1948 the domestic production was 2 billion barrels and imports exceeded exports. In the ensuing twelve years up to 1960, domestic production rose to 2.6 billion barrels. As oil started gushing from the Middle East in the midfifties, the establishment of import quotas managed to keep domestic production in the 2.4 to 2.6 billion barrel range.

7.49. It was obvious in the decade between 1910 and 1920 that petroleum was replacing coal for many uses. The growth in the use of petroleum and natural gas as energy sources relative to bituminous coal is shown in table 1 of appendix 7. In 1930 petroleum and natural gas provided 34.1 percent amd bituminous and anthracite 34.2 percent.

7.50. The Eisenhower administration appeared to be unconcerned that petroleum was supplanting coal for many industrial uses. They set the import quotas on petroleum to protect the domestic industry and at the same time left the solid fuels division of the minerals industry to do its own fighting for a share of the market. It is little wonder that John L. Lewis of the United Mine Workers yearned for two powerful allies like petroleum had in Congress in Texas senator Lyndon Baines Johnson and Texas representative Sam Rayburn. The administration had cast the die; they apparently decided that as domestic production of petroleum declined, the United States would, by diplomatic means, be able to maintain the shipments of petroleum from the Middle East. Their actions during the Suez Crisis, when they refused to back Great Britain, France, and Israel, left them no other option.

7.51. However, the Suez Crisis was not the only mistake the Eisenhower administration made. It made a mistake when it focused on the problems of only one mineral commodity, rather than the problems of the minerals industry. A much more acute problem than that of the liquid fuels division of the minerals industry was developing in the ferrous metals division. This division, like the liquid fuels division, affects every fabric of American life. The steady technology development in materials had placed a heavy reliance by U.S. industry on the ferrous metal commodities that are listed in table 1 of appendix 1. A total of 100 percent of the columbium was being imported, at least 90 percent of the manganese, cobalt, tantalum, and chromium, over 50 percent of the nickel and tungsten, and about 30 percent of the vanadium. In addition, iron ore mining on the Mesabi was undergoing a massive change in structure and iron ore imports were starting to rise.

7.52. Although the structural change was massive in character, it was subtle. To the general public and those lacking knowledge of the minerals industry, the change was occurring unnoticed. The reason that it was going unnoticed was because there was no shortage of iron ore and no interruption of the flow of iron ore to the blast furnaces. The change was occurring in the type of iron ore that was being mined and where it was being mined. The change in structure started about 1950 and continued on into the midsixties, a period of perhaps about fifteen years. The era of iron ore on demand from the Mesabi ended in about

1955. Direct shipping ore was gone, and that which was left was a material in Minnesota called taconite. It contained about 30 to 33 percent magnetite, a magnetic oxide mineral of iron. It was necessary to mine 3 to 3.1 tons of taconite, crush and grind the rock so that 75 percent or more would pass through a screen with 325 spaces to the inch, separate the magnetic magnetite from the silica rock by electric magnets, and fuse it into pellets to obtain 1 ton of 62 percent iron ore suitable for the blast furnaces in the lower lake ports.

7.53. The capital investment to build these plants and other types of beneficiation plants in the Lake Superior Iron Region over the fifteen-year period would be billions of dollars. In addition to the increased dollar costs in mining, beneficiating, and pelletizing the ore, a tremendous increase in energy usage would be required. The administration, Congress, and the public were feeling the effects of the iron ore mining structure changes in the creeping increase in the price of steel. In turn, the increasing price of steel was increasing the price of all machinery and other manufactured products in the United States, which was causing inflation. The widespread and pervasive price increases that were occurring at that time were not being identified by the Eisenhower administration as being caused by steel price increases; in their opinion, the inflation was being caused by too much money chasing too few goods. In other words, the administration was regarding the public's pursuit of the "abundant life" as the root cause of inflation. How the administration could come to this conclusion is difficult to understand, because there were no shortages of goods; the shelves of stores and automobile and machinery showrooms were full. The public was pursuing the "abundant life" with enthusiasm, but there was absolutely no difficulty whatsoever in finding everything they wanted to fulfill their needs. To illustrate that continuous increases in the price of steel were the cause of inflation during the Eisenhower administration, table 7.6 shows the annual finished steel composite prices as reported by *Iron Age* (1929–60) in their forecast issues published after January 1 of each year.

7.54. Table 7.6 shows that the average composite steel prices fluctuated between a low of 1.851 and a high of 2.536 cents per pound between 1929 and 1940. Prices were frozen at 2.396 during the war years from 1941 to 1944, which was actually below the prices for 1937 and 1938. After the war, during the Truman administration, prices increased 1.841 cents per pound between 1944 and 1952. During the Eisenhower administration, prices increased 46 percent, a total of 1.959 cents per

Table 7.6
The *Iron Age* Annual Average of Finished Steel Composite Prices,
1929–60 (*Iron Age* 1974)
(composite prices in cents per pound)

Year	Composite Prices	Year	Composite Prices	Year	Composite Prices	Year	Composite Prices
1929	2.288	1937	2.536	1945	2.449	1953	4.518
1930	2.111	1938	2.459	1946	2.686	1954	4.716
1931	1.957	1939	2.311	1947	3.014	1955	4.977
1932	1.873	1940	2.273	1948	3.434	1956	5.358
1933	1.851	1941	2.396	1949	3.713	1957	5.800
1934	2.051	1942	2.396	1950	3.862	1958	6.060
1935	2.068	1943	2.396	1951	4.131	1959	6.196
1936	2.118	1944	2.396	1952	4.237	1960	6.196

pound, between 1952 and 1960. In brief, the price of steel increased more during the Eisenhower administration than it did under the Truman administration, when there were strong upward price pressures coming off a four-year period of frozen prices.

7.55. All of the increases during the period from 1952 to 1960 were for the steel industry to develop foreign supplies of iron ore to replace the dwindling domestic supply, develop foreign supplies of ferrous alloy ores, develop mining and concentrating methods for treating the low-grade ores on the Mesabi Range, upgrade the technology of their blast furnace and steel plants, and construct new and additional blast furnaces and steel plants to meet the growing domestic demand for carbon, stainless, and other alloy steel. Increasing the price of steel to accomplish these objectives increased the price of all machinery and every other product produced in the United States, and as a natural result inflationary pressures were constant during the Eisenhower administration. There is little doubt but what the inflationary pressures could have been lessened somewhat by reducing the national security and defense program, stockpiling of strategic commodities, outer space exploration, atomic energy program, and "abundant life" program being pursued by the American public; however, the annual steel increases would have remained the same with or without these programs. If the United States was to maintain its position as a dominant industrial power in the world, restructuring of the ferrous metals division was an absolute necessity.

7.56. By the end of the second Eisenhower administration the American public in general had only a vague knowledge of the part that mineral commodities played in their lives. They knew that somewhere, somehow, the stuff you took from mines was needed to make a car and

Table 7.7
Annual Population Estimates in the United States, 1953–60
(Bureau of the Census 1994)
(in thousands)

Year	Total Resident Population	Year	Total Resident Population	Year	Total Resident Population
1953	158,242	1956	167,306	1959	177,135
1954	161,164	1957	170,371	1960	179,979
1955	164,308	1958	173,320		

the sticky goo from an oil well was needed to make gasoline to run it. The school systems, public and parochial and from elementary schools through colleges and universities, were doing a poor job of educating the students on what was fueling their standard of living. Americans appeared to understand that their standard of living was the highest in the world, but they related it more to Yankee ingenuity and Yankee know-how than to anything as abstract as a plentiful supply of mineral commodities.

7.57. Individuals were being elected to Congress who had little or no knowledge of the minerals industry. The Eisenhower administration's political inaction on the minerals industry had set a dangerous course by inaction on the following: (1) as the economy grew, petroleum imports increasing from the unstable Middle East; (2) petroleum and natural gas continuing to replace coal in many industries, placing even more reliance on Middle East imports; (3) the ferrous metals division having to spend billions in capital expenditures to maintain a strong domestic industry; (4) these capital expenditures by the ferrous metals division forcing annual increases in the price of steel up to about 1965, which in turn would increase the price of machinery and all other manufactured products, developing inflationary pressures on the economy; (5) the advanced industrialization that was taking place in Japan and Europe because of the availability of cheap energy; and (6) the "abundant life" minerals industry policy, which had been implemented by the public and was in full swing without guidance or restrictions.

7.59. There was a tremendous number of people that were in search of the "abundant life" in the United States, and at the rate the population was growing, there were certainly going to be a lot more in the future. Table 7.7 shows that during the Eisenhower administration resident popualtion growth averaged about 2.7 million per year.

8

The Next Three Years (1960–63): Kennedy

8.1. John F. Kennedy defeated Hubert Humphrey, a senator from Minnesota, in the race to be the Democratic Party's nominee in the 1960 election. This would prove to be an unfortunate choice by the Democratic Party, because Mr. Humphrey was more mature, more intelligent, and much more aware of the changes that were taking place throughout the United States and the world; he would have been a much better president than Mr. Kennedy. In fact, if Mr. Humphrey had been the nominee and had won the presidency, history as we know it today would have been completely rewritten. Mr. Kennedy defeated Richard M. Nixon, the Republican nominee and Mr. Eisenhower's vice president, in a close race to win the presidency. Kennedy's vice president was Lyndon Baines Johnson, who had been Democratic majority leader in the Senate prior to becoming vice president. His presence on the ticket was instrumental in Mr. Kennedy winning the election.

8.2. Mr. Kennedy had served in the House of Representatives as a representative of the State of Massachusetts during most of the Truman administration. He was elected senator in 1952 and re-elected in 1958. He published two books, one of which was a best-seller, the other one a Pulitzer Prize winner. At age forty-three he was the youngest man who had ever been elected president. He was highly articulate and quick-witted in repartee. He followed the lead of President Eisenhower by setting up a group in the White House under a chief of staff.

8.3. At the time President Kennedy took office the Soviet Union was probably at the height of its military powers. At the head was Premier Khrushchev, an extremely emotional, volatile, and erratic individual, and he had complete control of the Central Committee, which set the course of the Soviet Union in foreign and domestic affairs. With Khrushchev at the head there was little doubt but what they intended to continue the menacing actions that had been characteristic of their relations with the Eisenhower administration. Actions by the Soviets would be a continuous harassing burden to President Kennedy, just as they had been to President Eisenhower.

8.4. The DOD, NASA, and AEC had research and development contracts under way with both industry and universities. As previously stated, this contracting system had developed a NASA-AEC-military-industry-university complex, which was steadily growing larger as more money was budgeted each succeeding year. Contracts for defense by the government had created a massive defense industry employing thousands of physical scientists.

8.5. The liquid fuels division of the minerals industry was facing problems that had never been encountered before. The Middle East was exporting oil to almost every country in the world, and it had become Europe's chief supplier. The Netherlands port of Rotterdam was becoming the primary port for distribution of petroleum by pipeline to Central Europe. The Middle East petroleum-producing nations had no technology for producing petroleum; thus they were totally dependent upon the petroleum companies for all of the process systems and subsystems needed to obtain the petroleum (see paragraph 1.13 and table 1.1 in appendix 2). The Middle East petroleum producers were also dependent upon the companies to market the refined products obtained from the crude petroleum. This total technology and marketing dependency by the Middle East nations gave the companies complete control of the rate of development of a specific field, the number of barrels produced, and the price they would pay per barrel.

8.6. The world was awash with petroleum from the Middle East. However, no more crude petroleum could be produced than could be refined and stored; thus the refinery and storage capacity of the world controlled how much petroleum could be produced. Annually each petroleum company had to set the volume (number of forty-two-gallon barrels) of production from all sites, based on their own refinery and storage capacity. If the company brought another field on line, the volume originally set would have to be reduced to give the new field its share of the total. The system enraged the sultans of the various Middle East nations. They considered such actions an infringement upon the sovereignty of their domain and felt that they should be able to sell their petroleum in any amount, at any price, and to whomever they chose. Their anger at the system was further heightened by the fact that they were not dealing with another foreign country but with oil company executives, whom they considered inferior to them and distrusted and disdained.

8.7. Inasmuch as the United States was one of the largest importers of Middle East petroleum, the major concessionaires with refineries in the United States had to always be aware of the barrels of petroleum that were allowed into the United States under its import quota law. This import quota restriction also angered the Middle East sultans, and they constantly badgered the petroleum companies to get the U.S. import quota increased. It was an amazing situation, representatives of petroleum companies at an annual or bi-annual meeting informing a sultan what they would pay per barrel produced and how much petroleum they would produce from each field in his country. The sultan had no recourse but to swallow his pride and anger, berate the company either publicly or privately, and accept the price and production figures. Inevitably the system created intense hatreds, which have existed to this day.

8.8 The frustration of the Middle East sultanates with the system was finally manifested in the formation of the Organization of Petroleum Exporting Countries (OPEC). Through unilateral action by this organization they hoped to gain more control over the volume produced and price of their mineral commodity. The organization accomplished little in the sixties, but in the seventies it managed to get agreement among enough members to show Japan, Western Europe, and the United States just how dependent they were on Middle East petroleum.

8.9. President Kennedy appointed the following cabinet members: Secretary of State Dean Rusk, Secretary of the Treasury C. Douglas Dillon, Secretary of Defense Robert S. McNamara, Secretary of Commerce Luther H. Hodges, Secretary of Agriculture Orville L. Freeman, Secretary of Labor Arthur J. Goldberg, succeeded later by W. Willard Wirtz, Secretary of Health, Education, and Welfare Abraham A. Ribicoff, succeeded later by Anthony J. Celebrezze, Attorney General Robert F. Kennedy (the president's brother), and Secretary of the Interior Stewart L. Udall. The cabinet differed from others in that the members were much younger than those appointed by preceding presidents.

8.10. In his inaugural address President Kennedy pointed out that a new generation was coming into power and described his administration to be the "New Frontier." He moved aggressively in accelerating the outer space program under NASA, a program to aid South America, and the development of a Peace Corps to assist Third World countries in the development of better agriculture methods and infrastructure service systems. There was considerable resistance to his social programs in Congress, primarily the House, but in 1962 he managed to gain passage of the Trade Expansion Act, which gave the president power to reduce trade tariffs to allow the United States to trade more freely with the European Common Market.

8.11. In foreign affairs President Kennedy was, like Mr. Eisenhower, always acting or reacting to a crisis brought on by the Soviet Union. In 1961 Cuban rebels with the support and approval of President Kennedy invaded Cuba at the Bay of Pigs, but they were soundly defeated by the Cuban army, led by Fidel Castro, the communist leader of Cuba. The Berlin Wall, which sealed off East Berlin from West Berlin, was erected by East Germany in 1961. President Kennedy was concerned with the concentrated effort by the Soviet Union in Southeast Asia. He expanded the number of American troops and amount of war matériel to the defense of both South Vietnam and Thailand and sent military advisors to Laos. He added about seventeen thousand troops to the nine hundred that were there at the end of the Eisenhower administration (McCarthy 1969).

8.12. The small military cadre committed by both Presidents Truman and Eisenhower essentially represented a political commitment to counteract the actions of the Soviet Union in North Vietnam; neither President Truman nor President Eisenhower ever exhibited any intent to equal the troop and war matériel commitment to South Vietnam that was being made by the Soviet Union to North Vietnam. It was a show of support to South Vietnam to encourage them to resist the spread of communism in their country. President Kennedy's expansion to about eighteen thousand troops totally changed the commitment from political to actual combat action, and, in fact, Kennedy publicly stated that U.S. troops should return fire if fired upon by the North Vietnamese.

8.13. What President Kennedy intended to do with about eighteen thousand troops in the morass of Southeast Asia is not entirely clear. Whether or not there were members in his cabinet who opposed the move is unknown, but if there were, the opposition never surfaced publicly. South Vietnam and Laos were a part of what was called French Indochina. For eight years after World War II insurgent activity against the French there was almost constant. Even with substantial aid from the United States, the French were unable to regain their prewar status in the area, and they later abandoned all of Indochina. Although a compromise plan in 1954 set boundaries among the warring factions, the insurgent activity in South Vietnam never did actually cease. The country was divided by ideological, racial, political, and religious factions that made unity almost impossible. If France, which had been a colonial power in the area for many years prior to World War II, could not regain power and restore unity to the area, the chances of a small U.S. fighting force succeeding where France had failed were virtually nil.

8.14. A majority of the public appeared to agree with President Kennedy's action in South Vietnam. Most did not want all of Southeast Asia to become communist-dominated, and that was certainly the trend after the French abandoned the area. The military commitment received strong support in Congress from both parties.

8.15. In late 1962, Premier Khrushchev of the Soviet Union made a daring move. He built missile sites in Cuba, which he intended to arm with nuclear warhead missiles aimed directly at the United States. President Kennedy imposed a blockade on Cuba, which barred the Soviet Union from arming the missile sites. It was a direct nuclear confrontation. Premier Khrushchev backed off and dismantled the missile sites and returned the missiles to the Soviet Union, although he did leave in Cuba a cadre of about two thousand advisers. President Kennedy's stature as a leader was enhanced considerably throughout the world with his handling of such a dangerous situation. The action by the Soviets in trying to arm Cuba with nuclear warhead missiles was unsettling not only to the United States but also to the rest of the world. For a short period of time nuclear war was a distinct possibility, and the government of any nation could only wonder what would be hatched next by the lunatics on the Central Committee of the Soviet Union.

8.16. In the time period of the crisis, little, if any, note appeared to be taken by the print and electronic media of the intention of Fidel Castro to permit the Soviet Union to place the nuclear warhead missiles on Cuban soil. Apparently, without any regard to the possible consequences of his action he was intent on placing such missiles in Cuba aimed at the United States under the control of an acknowledged enemy of the United States. By doing so he had made Cuba the prime target in event nuclear war broke out. If nuclear war had started, the island of Cuba would have been one of the primary nuclear targets for the U.S. Atlantic Fleet, which had virtually no opposition of any kind from Cuba. Within minutes a large part of Cuba, with the exception of Guantanamo Bay and the immediate surrounding area, could have been reduced to a sterile desert devoid of human or animal life. There is no doubt that for a few days in late 1962 the very existence of Cuba hung on the actions of a group of lunatics in the Soviet Union. Fidel Castro's apparent ignorance of the consequences of his action was appalling. He could not have had any feeling for his country or, for that matter, his own countrymen. He was intent upon his own aggrandizement and fueling his own ego rather than caring for the Cuban people.

8.17. When Khrushchev backed off from placing the missiles in Cuba, one of the terms of the agreement was a promise from President Kennedy that the United States would not invade Cuba. This indicates that Khrushchev and the Central Committee were far more aware of the consequences of Cuba's part in the action than Fidel Castro himself. That President Kennedy would promise not to invade a nation that had tried to become a launch point for nuclear warhead missiles aimed at the United States is difficult to understand, but it is possible that it was a condition that Khrushchev was insisting upon for a peaceable settlement of the matter.

8.18. Although President Kennedy received widespread acclaim for his handling of the crisis, in actuality he had no other option. The only course that he could take was a showdown. At that time the Soviet Union had a military capability fully equal in every respect to that of the United States, and at its head was an emotional and volatile individual who at times appeared to go out of sanity balance. The United States under no circumstances could have ever allowed missiles in Cuba under the control of Khrushchev and Castro.

8.19. There is no doubt that when Khrushchev took the action to place nuclear missiles in Cuba he was doing so with a considerable amount of information on President Kennedy's extracurricular activities. Khrushchev was well aware that he could not have taken such an action with Presidents Truman or Eisenhower, but with the "detailed book" that he had on Mr. Kennedy, he must have felt that he had a "patsy." It was no secret, even at that time, that Kennedy had a strong liking for "affairs" other than political ones, and all of them involved women (Miller 1977). Soviet intelligence had undoubtedly provided Khrushchev with enough information for him to reach the conclusion that here was a playboy he could face down. The only thing that Khrushchev did not seem to realize was that in attempting to install the missiles in Cuba he had placed President Kennedy in a position where he had no other option but to oppose it, even if that meant nuclear war.

8.20. Khrushchev's attempt to arm Cuba with nuclear warhead missiles effectively silenced any criticism of President Kennedy's expansion of troops in Southeast Asia. After the Cuban Missile Crisis many in Congress and a large segment of the American public was ready to admit that it would be better to stop the Soviets in South Vietnam than allow them to move into Southeat Asia without resistance.

8.21. Kennedy's supporters were lavish in their praise of his presidency. They glossed over his blunder in supporting the invasion of Cuba at the Bay of Pigs and praised his efforts in the Cuban Missile Crisis and for attempting to stop the communists from taking over South Vietnam. Those in the Democratic Party who had worked for him in his campaign openly expressed adoration and adulation for him. He had excellent publicists who released pictures of him seated alone against different backgrounds and in deep thought, supposedly pondering the problems of the presidency and the decisions that had to be made. He was greatly admired by all of South America and the predominantly Catholic countries in Europe. He had a friendly White House press corps and in general a friendly press throughout the nation; reporters were comparing his administration to Camelot, when knighthood was in flower. The publicist who dreamed up this idealistic existence of the Kennedys in Washington, D.C., should somehow be rewarded for placing upon an administration a hallowed sainthood that has persisted to this day, even in the face of historical revelations that sainthood was being stretched well beyond its elastic limit (Miller 1977).

8.22. There was little doubt but that the constant publicity about President Kennedy and his family was winning him many supporters in all sections of the country. The lavish praise for President Kennedy fell on willing ears. Homes were being constructed with attached two-car garages because the average American family was discovering that it was too inconvenient to get along with just one car. The longer the wheelbase, the more accessories it had, and the heavier the car the better. In addition, science and technology, especially outer space science and technology, were absolute proof to the public that Yankee ingenuity and Yankee know-how were flourishing as never before. It could all be seen on television in one's own home, the only cost being an advertisement about every five to eight minutes. The public related progress in science and technology directly to outer space programs. The many advances made in outer space technology gave the public confidence in the ability of their government, and they were becoming more than willing to back the president who was in charge when the the progress was being made.

8.23. The average home owner appeared to be reasonably satisfied with his or her life. Many felt that now they had attained or were reaching the "abundant life" promised them more than twenty years earlier by Pres. Franklin D. Roosevelt. Along with a couple of cars, many also had a house trailer and/or a boat to fulfill them when not working. There were power-driven mowers, saws, clippers, weed trimmers, and edgers for landscaping chores. The interiors of new houses had often two, two and one-half, or three bathrooms. Many houses were heated by gas, a heat pump, or electricity, cooled with air conditioners, and well stocked with electric-power-driven appliances, such as dishwashers and dryers, clothes washers and dryers, ranges, sewing machines, vacuum cleaners, refrigerators, freezers, hair dryers, shavers, can openers, garbage disposals and compactors, mixers, blenders, toasters, frying pans, and griddles. In many homes the basement or backyard workshop was full of power equipment for working in either metal or wood. Woodworking equipment often included a lathe, table saw, band saw, jig saw, drill, router, planer, sander, and buffer. With such equipment many individuals could make items as good or better than those produced by furniture factories. The standard of living of the average American was the envy of the rest of the civilized world. Many U.S. companies had factories overseas, and if a part on an appliance as small as an electric shaver was needed, it was quite possible that it could be obtained in the larger European cities such as London, Frankfort, Paris, Madrid, or Rome from a U.S. factory.

8.24. Stewart Udall, President Kennedy's secretary of the interior, embraced the "abundant life" program wholeheartedly. He started a new agency in the Department of Interior called the Bureau of Outdoor Recreation. This agency provided funds for renovation and construction of parks and other recreational areas. It was a well-funded and busy agency.

8.25. In 1962 the United Steel Workers Union was opening work contract negotiations with the big steel companies. President Kennedy did not want a rerun of the 1959 strike; thus he managed to get the steelworkers union to accept a contract without a wage increase. U.S. Steel Corporation after obtaining the scaled-back contract with the union raised steel prices 3.5 percent, which almost immediately resulted in an industrywide raise in steel prices. This action by the steel companies infuriated President Kennedy. When he managed to get the union to scale back their demands, he apparently assumed that the steel companies would not raise steel prices.

8.26. President Kennedy immediately went on the offensive. He denounced the steel companies publicly and demanded that they withdraw the price increase. In this effort Mr. Kennedy had the unanimous support of his cabinet, majority support from Congress and the public and, with the exception of a few business publications, almost total support from the daily newspapers and weekly news magazines. With President Kennedy's public popularity at an all-time high at that time and the congressional and media support that he received, the pressure was too great, and the steel companies rescinded completely the steel price increase. Whether or not there were efforts by the steel companies to obtain a compromise with the president to get a partial raise of steel prices is unknown, but if there was, these efforts were certainly unsuccessful.

8.27. This action by President Kennedy was a massive blunder. He had without any study of the situation interfered in the marketplace and by his action placed a strangling noose around the steel industry. He had cut off the life blood of the greatest industrial dominance that the world had ever known. President Kennedy was following through on the same mistake that was made in the second term of the Eisenhower adminstration. The steel industry that existed under the Truman administration and first term of the Eisenhower administration had changed radically. There was no longer an ability to produce iron ore on demand from the Mesabi Range. Instead, the companies on the Mesabi were making huge investments in plants to treat the taconite to produce a product suitable for the blast furnaces. In addition, they were spending more than a billion dollars annually on expansion and improvement of the steel-making processes. The annual expenditures for expansion and improvement are shown in table 9 in appendix 8.

8.28. The loss of the direct shipping iron ore from the Mesabi and the need for development of the taconite deposits to maintain a viable domestic iron ore source had erased the premier advantage that the domestic steel industry had had for seventy years over foreign competitors. With low-cost energy from the Middle East and the development of high-bulk-tonnage oceangoing ships, cheap ocean transport was an established fact, and President Kennedy by his action had given Japan and Western Europe the opening they needed. He forced the capital-starved U.S. ferrous metals division of the minerals industry to compete against the combined nations of Western Europe and Japan, whose governments were subsidizing the industrial growth of their ferrous metals industries. The governments of Western Europe were subsidizing plants constructed with Marshall Plan Funds to produce iron, steel, and ferroalloys with the latest known technology, while the U.S. steel industry was struggling with insufficient capital to modernize their plants. Japan, noted for its work ethic and ability to adapt, moved quickly to compete in both the world and domestic ferrous metals markets, often selling ferrous products at a lower price than it cost to produce them.

8.29. The steel companies had been well aware of when the Mesabi direct shipping ore would be gone. They had been preparing for that time by development of the taconite deposits over a period of twelve years prior to 1962. They were aware of the difficult position that the petroleum companies had placed themselves in by dependence on production from the Middle East and had no intention of going this route. They had positioned themselves to maintain the industrial superiority that had been in place for seventy years with a strong domestic iron ore source, and their intent was to maintain this domestic source insofar as possible, even though they had iron ore mining concessions in other countries.

8.30. The maintenance of a strong domestic iron ore source was a relatively simple matter when the Mesabi Iron Range direct shipping ores were available, but when these ores were mined out, it meant that billions of dollars were going to have to be spent for designing and building plants to treat the lower grade of ore that had to be mined. In addition, mining and milling costs of the lower grade of ore would be higher than the cost of mining the direct shipping ore. It was a massive change in operations that was affecting seriously the integrated steel companies. The very last thing they needed at this time was a strangling noose of insufficient funds to carry through on their programs.

8.31. President Kennedy and his cabinet appeared to be totally ignorant of the consequences of their action in forcing the steel companies to forgo a price rise in steel. They had no grasp at all of the fundamental changes that were occurring in the ferrous metals division of the minerals industry, both domestically and worldwide. The interference in the marketplace resulted in the sharpest drop in the stock market since 1929. Neither Mr. Kennedy nor his cabinet related the stock market drop to any action by the government. Apparently, they considered the stock market merely a sideshow action that had no relationship to the main American scene.

8.32. After the denial of the price rise, the stock of the six major steel companies, Bethlehem, Inland, Jones & Laughlin, National, Republic, and U.S. Steel, dropped sharply and started a downward price trend over the next thirty years. The detailed effect of President Kennedy's action is shown in appendix 10: "Common Stock Prices by Year of Major Steel Companies after Price Rise Denial in 1962." Along with the inflation that was occurring annually, the drop in stock prices was a devastating blow to the companies. It stripped them of the funds needed for them to maintain the nation's industrial superiority that had lasted for seventy years. With the strangling noose of insufficient funds, America's decline in industrial superiority was inevitable. President Kennedy had placed them in the position of being unable to compete on even terms with the Marshall Plan–funded and government-subsidized ferrous metals industries in Western Europe and Japan. His price denial action, made in haste, was a massive blunder.

8.33. The mistake by the Kennedy administration in depending upon price controls of the ferrous metals division products to control inflation problems was also a massive blunder and indicated that neither the president nor his advisers had any knowledge whatsoever of the basic causes of inflation. Inflation was certain to occur with the huge expenditures for defense, atom bomb research and development, expanded troop commitment and combat action in Vietnam, the Apollo Program for a manned landing on the moon, and at the same time maintaining the highest standard of living of any country in the world for its citizens. However, inflation cannot be stopped by applying measures from the top down. Reduction of the funds needed by the ferrous metals division companies to maintain a viable domestic iron ore source and for new plants and rebuilding and maintenance of old plants was not the way inflation could be reduced. Such a program may hold off inflation for a short while, but in the end inflation increases rather than decreases.

8.34. To stop inflation, a program controlling the root cause should have been started. In President Kennedy's case, he felt that he must continue the strong defense buildup and atom bomb research and development because of the menacing actions of the Soviet Union. This left him with three programs where substantial cost reductions could have been made as follows: (1) Control of the purchasing binge by the American public, (2) a substantial reduction in the Apollo Program and other

128

outer space programs, and (3) reduction in the military commitment in South Vietnam back to the original noncombatant cadre of 900 to 1,000 men. Admittedly, the first two measures would have been politically unpopular and the third would have required him to admit he had made a mistake. However, any of the three would have done far more to reduce inflation permanently than forcing the ferrous metals division of the minerals industry to forgo a price rise. In addition, it would have given truth to his inaugural statement: "And so, my fellow Americans: Ask not what your country can do for you; ask what you can do for your country" (Taranik and Trautwein 1976).

8.35. The president's cabinet and other high-level administrators appeared to have no grasp at all of the dangers of increasing the gross national debt. They were far more concerned with the facade that they presented to the public rather than actual accomplishments. In the early morning, as their chauffeurs drove them to work, gooseneck lamps inside the limousines in the back window showed the occupants diligently perusing documents. If a person happened to be following one of the backseat-illuminated limousines on Highway 50 as the traffic moved slowly into the District of Columbia, he had to be duly impressed by the occupant's intent to utilize every moment of time for study of the problems that he would expect to face during the day—although one might tend to wonder at times what document he was studying, because in several miles of slow traffic he never turned a page.

8.36. Regardless of what his supporters have tried to portray, President Kennedy did not live up to to the stirring statements in his inaugural address. He mired the nation in the morass of Southeast Asia, and by an incredible exhibition of poor judgment he applied the first strangling noose on an industrial dominance that had lasted for seventy years. Kennedy was not mature enough to be president. The New Frontier program suffered because of the lack of wise leadership. It sputtered and careened through three years of his administration rudderless. His cabinet appeared to career with it, failing to recognize the root cause of the problems that had developed in the nation, not understanding how to deal with them. Nobody in the administration appeared to recognize that nothing was being accomplished by the expanded troop commitment in Southeast Asia. Nevertheless, because of a favorable press and constant publicity, President Kennedy had become highly popular throughout the nation. The public appeared willing to overlook his immaturity and failures and concentrate solely on his personality.

Table 8.1

Total Annual Production of Iron Ore in the United States, 1961–63, Compared to That Produced by the Lake Superior District and the Mesabi Range (U.S. Geological Survey and U.S. Bureau of Mines 1992)
(in thousand long tons)

Year	Total Tons	Lake Superior District		Mesabi Range		Tons Accumulated
		Tons	Percentage of Total	Tons	Percentage of Total	
1961	71,329	53,207	75	41,199	58	2,332,547
1962	71,829	55,556	77	43,039	60	2,375,586
1963	73,599	56,132	77	43,570	59	2,419,156

8.37. President Kennedy, like President Eisenhower, was continuously acting or reacting to menacing actions by the Soviet Union. Kennedy had difficulty in dealing with the problems caused by the Soviet Union, and this tended to cause neglect of domestic issues, which had become extremely severe during the third year of his administration. He was asassinated on November 22, 1963, in Dallas, Texas. The asassination plunged the nation into a traumatic ten-day period. He was a very popular president, and over the years since his assassination a large segement of the public have been unwilling to accept criticism of his term in office. Nevertheless, like it or not, President Kennedy by government action was the first to deliberately drive a nail in the coffin of an industrial dominance that had lasted for seventy years.

8.38. The Kennedy administration lasted only three years, but even in this short period of time the production, import, and export statistics of iron ore, pig iron, and steel, when coupled with those reported under the Eisenhower administration, reveal that significant changes were taking place. With massive expenditures beginning on the Apollo Program, these changes should not have been ignored by the administration. Tables 8.1, 8.2, 8.3, and 8.4 show the production, import, and exports of iron ore, pig iron, and steel during the three-year period.

8.39. In table 8.1, the total annual production of iron ore in the United States, compared to that produced in the Lake Superior District and on the Mesabi Range, shows that domestic total production, the Lake Superior District production, and the Mesabi Range production were leveling off. That is, each year production was within about 10 percent of the preceding year. Leveling off is a sign of age in a mineral deposit, and it is significant because it indicates that expansions in production much over the 10 percent difference each year might require a period of two or three years to reach. Although the period is only for

130

Table 8.2

Iron Ore Imported for Consumption in the United States by Continents, 1961–63 (U.S. Geological Survey and U.S. Bureau of Mines 1992)
(in thousand long tons)
(in thousand dollars)

Year	North America Long Tons	North America Value $	South America Long Tons	South America Value $	Europe Long Tons	Europe Value $	Remainder Long Tons	Remainder Value $
1961	9,806	99,585	15,180	142,396	81	1,313	738	6,931
1962	16,970	170,311	15,600	146,164	33	590	806	7,508
1963	18,892	199,421	12,981	112,406	37	755	1,353	10,576

Table 8.3

Production, Imports, and Exports of Pig Iron and Steel in the United States, 1961–63
(U.S. Geological Survey and U.S. Bureau of Mines 1992)
(in thousand short tons)

Year	Pig Iron Production	Pig Iron Imports	Pig Iron Exports	Steel Production	Steel Imports	Steel Exports
1961	64,853	377	416	98,014	3,308	2,221
1962	65,638	500	154	98,328	4,297	2,266
1963	71,840	645	70	109,261	5,637	2,670

Table 8.4

World Production of Steel with the Percentage Produced by the United States, USSR Separate from Europe, Europe, Japan, and Other Nations, 1961–63 (U.S. Geological Survey and U.S Bureau of Mines 1992)
(in milion short tons)

Year	World Tons	U.S. Tons	U.S. %	USSR Tons	USSR %	Europe Tons	Europe %	Japan Tons	Japan %	Other %
1961	390.4	98.0	25	77.8	20	143.2	37	31.2	8	10
1962	397.4	98.3	25	84.1	21	143.1	36	30.4	8	10
1963	426.6	109.3	26	88.4	21	147.8	35	34.7	8	10

three years, the possibility that it may be the start of a trend should raise the red flag immediately that domestic production may not be able to meet increasing demand and an increasing expenditure of wealth for imported ore is a future possibility.

8.40. Table 8.2, showing iron ore imported for consumption, demonstrates that the leveling-off trend developing in table 8.1 was not just a possibilty but an actual fact. In the three-year period 93 million tons of ore was imported at a total value of $898 million, the imported ore filling 30 percent of the domestic demand. This meant that while massive expenditures were being made for the Vietnam War, the Apollo Program,

131

Table 8.5
Gross Federal Debt at the End of Year, 1961–63 (Bureau of Public Debt 1992)

Year	Gross Federal Debt (in millions of dollars)
1961	292,648
1962	302,928
1963	310,324

atomic energy research and development, military defense, and the "abundant life" program of the public, an additional amount of close to a billion dollars was being spent to import iron ore—an additional wealth expenditure on a resource that heretofore had been produced by the United States. It was, in fact, a double hit. The nation once it produced the wealth then had to pay the same amount in order to produce the products that were in demand. It is incredible that an administration would continue the massive expenditure of dollars without some retrenchment in view of the trend that was developing.

8.41. Table 8.3 shows that the trend that started in 1959 and 1960 was continuing. The nations that had gained a foothold for steel imports during the steel strike were continuing to import. By 1965 steel imports had reached 5.6 million tons. Exports totaled only 2.7 million tons in the same year; thus imports exceeded exports by 2.9 million tons, which represented another annual expenditure of wealth. The small amount of exports indicates that U.S. companies were not capturing much of the world market for steel outside of the United States. Table 8.4 shows that the nation making the greatest gain in the share of world production of steel during the three-year period was Japan. The increases in production by the USSR, Europe, and Japan indicate that the foreign companies in these nations were capturing the increasing world market for steel outside the United States. Companies in the United States were having real difficulty moving into the world market outside the United States because of the strangling noose of insufficient funds for expansion placed on them by the Kennedy administration.

8.42. There was no effort by the Kennedy administration to balance the federal debt. Table 8.5 shows the gross federal debt at the end of each year during President Kennedy's term in office. The federal debt increased $10.3 billion from 1961 to 1962 and $7.4 billion from 1962 to 1963. These huge annual increases were the result of expenditures for the Apollo Program, the Vietnam War, the atomic energy program, and military defense. The majority of the public were in agreement with

Table 8.6
Annual Population Estimates in the United States, 1961–63
(in thousands)

Year	Total Resident Population
1961	182,992
1962	185,771
1963	188,483

these programs, and thus the administration received favorable marks for continuing the programs regardless of the billions of dollars they were adding to the federal debt.

8.43. Population growth during the Kennedy administration was close to that of the Eisenhower administration, about 2.7 million per year. Table 8.6 shows the annual population estimates for the three-year period.

9

The Next Five Years (1963–68): Johnson

9.1. Vice Pres. Lyndon B. Johnson became president upon President Kennedy's death. Mr. Johnson was a member of the House of Representatives from 1937 to 1948 and was elected to the Senate in 1948. He was widely known for his knowledge of congressional procedures and his ability to get legislation passed. His legislative ability earned him the Democratic majority leadership in the Senate in less that five years, which was a truly remarkable accomplishment in that body. In 1960 he became Mr. Kennedy's running mate on the Democratic ticket. Johnson's presence on the ticket produced southern support, which Mr. Kennedy did not have. Mr. Kennedy would have lost the election had Mr. Johnson not been on the ticket.

9.2. Mr. Johnson brilliantly handled the tragic circumstances that thrust him into the presidency. During the mourning, funeral, and interment of the former president, Johnson appeared on television calm and poised, radiating assurance to the American people and the world that the system of succession was working and everything was going to be all right. It was a most remarkable performance. He also avoided disruption of the executive branch by retaining all of the cabinet members appointed by President Kennedy. This was the action of a master politician, because it sent the message to the nation and world that the executive branch of the United States was a stable body under any set of conditions, no matter how tragic.

9.3. In the remaining year of what was left of President Kennedy's term, President Johnson continued the social agenda that Kennedy had in progress. Johnson pushed through Congress an Economic Opportunity Act, which he declared to be the opening salvo of War on Poverty; a Civil Rights Act; and an Education Act. The enactment of these laws and the manner in which he accomplished their passage in Congress won him widespread support from independent voters and minority groups in all sections of the nation. President Johnson would sign these bills into law in full view of the television cameras. Standing behind him would be the congressional sponsors of the bill. Johnson would write one or two letters of his name and then give the pen to one of the legislators. This would go on until all had received a souvenir pen. As each legislator was handed a pen, President Johnson would lavishly praise their efforts. In the parlance of the day, "he could really lay it on."

9.4. President Johnson's success in social legislation during the last year of the Kennedy administration appeared to split the Republican Party into factions. The end result was that the conservative wing gained complete control of the party, and Barry Goldwater, an ultraconservative in terms of that time period, was nominated as their candidate to run for president in 1964. President Johnson easily won the Democratic nomination, with little or no opposition. However, his next move indicated that he was uncertain just how much support Barry Goldwater had throughout the nation. Johnson selected Hubert Humphrey, a liberal senator from Minnesota, to be his running mate as vice president. By having Mr. Humphrey on the ticket, President Johnson hoped to pick up enough liberal eastern and northern voters to counteract the losses of conservative Democrats to Mr. Goldwater. Actually, Johnson should have felt no such concern, because in a choice between him and Mr. Goldwater, the liberal Democrats had no other option but him and, in addition, independents and liberal and moderate Republicans voted for him. He won an overwhelming victory over Mr. Goldwater.

9.5. Johnson and Humphrey were alike in that each had a king-sized ego and each considered himself ordained to be president of the United States. However, at this point the similarity ended. President Johnson was pompous, moody, arrogant, paranoid, secretive, and more conservative than Humphrey, and insofar as Johnson was concerned, the Democratic Party and any person that he came in contact with were his to use for his own aggrandizement. He expected all those under him to be absolutely loyal and back any program that he proposed, whether they agreed with it or not. He had little or no use for advisers, because he expected everybody to agree with him. They were either "yes-men" or they were out.

9.6. In contrast, Mr. Humphrey was highly intelligent, idealistic, liberal, loquacious, and an optimist. His rosy optimism on just about everything and his constant gush of words could wear on many people, even though they admired him as a politician. Mr. Humphrey adored the Democratic Party. He had difficulty imagining anybody voting anything but the Democratic ticket, and in every election he was always absolutely positive that the Democratic candidate would win. He considered the election of President Eisenhower to be an aberration due to his popularity as a successful general in the European Theater of Operations. Mr. Humphrey had the ability to go well beyond his own education in understanding topics under discussion, and he retained the knowledge gained in textbooks, discussions, and congressional testimony to the point that he was almost a talking encyclopedia. His loyalty to the Democratic Party and verbosity would at times get him into situations that would cause some to doubt his ability to be president. He had three nicknames in the Senate: HHH, the Humph, and Gabby (Miller 1977). Mr. Humphrey was not at all fond of the latter, and understandably so, because in a body like the Senate, where 90 percent or more of the members could talk for an hour and say nothing that made sense, the nickname was derisive.

9.7. Why Mr. Humphrey tied himself to President Johnson in 1964 is not really understood. Having worked for Mr. Johnson for fourteen years in the Senate, Humphrey certainly knew him as well as or much better than anybody else. Humphrey knew that as vice president he would have to be loyal to Johnson's programs whether he agreed with them or not and must have been aware that Johnson would attempt to make his vice president a nonentity. Humphrey knew that in Johnson's administration there was only going to be one star on center stage. He also had to know that he would be little more than a messenger boy carrying Johnson's programs to the electorate, and in addition he had to know that anybody that served under Johnson was never going to succeed him as president. Johnson would personally see to that. Running with Johnson was one of Mr. Humphrey's decisions that had no real explanation and indicated that possibly he had either taken leave of his senses or he had overestimated his own powers of persuasion. In all probability, it was a little of both.

9.8. If there was a politician in federal or state government in 1960 who had a chance to be president and could grasp and understand the problems and importance of the minerals industry to the United States, that politician was Hubert Humphrey. If he, instead of Mr. Kennedy, had won the Democratic Party's nomination in 1960 and then won the election the following November, he would have had time to reverse the trend set by the Eisenhower administration, and as a result the ferrous metals division of the minerals industry would have been in position to fight for its share of the world's steel market. In addition, Mr. Humphrey never would have supported such an endeavor as the invasion at the Bay of Pigs and never would have increased the number of troops in South Vietnam as President Kennedy did. If Humphrey did anything in Vietnam, he would have withdrawn the cadre of advisers sent there by President Truman and retained by President Eisenhower. Humphrey's vice presidency under President Johnson was to be a millstone around his neck when he ran against Richard Nixon in 1968.

9.9. President Johnson again retained most of Mr. Kennedy's cabinet officers after his re-election in 1964 as follows: Secretary of State Dean Rusk, Secretary of the Treasury C. Douglas Dillon, later replaced by Henry Fowler, Secretary of Defense Robert McNamara, later replaced by Clark Clifford, Secretary of the Interior Stewart Udall, Secretary of Agriculture Orville Freeman, Secretary of Commerce John Conner, later replaced by Alexander Trowbridge, Secretary of Health, Education, and Welfare Anthony Celebrezze, later replaced by John Gardner, Attorney General Nicholas Katzenbach, later replaced by Ramsey Clark, and Secretary of Labor W. Willard Wirtz. In 1967 Johnson appointed Alan Boyd to a new cabinet department: the Department of Transportation.

9.10. The Democratic Party was euphoric after the election. The leaders of the party appeared to believe that the party platform and the two candidates were the primary reason for the landslide victory and envisioned Democratic victory after victory in the future. In fact, the overwhelming victory could not be attributed to the candidates, the party platform, anything that the party did, or the way they waged the election campaign. It was primarily a vote against Barry Goldwater and his far right stance. Many voters, including independents and a substantial number of Republicans, had no place to go but toward Johnson and Humphrey. Any number of Democratic Party politicians then in the Senate, House, or state governments would have garnered as many votes as Johnson and Humphrey had they been the party's nominees. Voter support for Barry Goldwater would have been confined solely to the far right wing of the Republican Party no matter who opposed him.

9.11. Immediately after his sweeping victory in 1964, President Johnson launched the United States into what he termed the Great Society program. Within two years he had pushed through a willing Congress legislation on water and air pollution, immigration reform, highway beautification, medical care for the aged, education aid, housing, and voting rights. It was a remarkable two years. Some of these acts were executive legislation—that is, they were written by the executive branch and endorsed by Congress. The Water Quality Act of 1965, the Clean Water Restoration Act of 1966, the Clean Air Act of 1965, and the Air Quality Act of 1967 marked the first determined recognition by the federal government that the environment needed protection. The effect of these laws for the first three to five years was minimal, but a series of events in 1970 placed the environmental movement on a fast track that has not slowed down in a quarter of a century. Certainly Lyndon Johnson must be regarded as not only one of the greatest social reformers of all time but also as the father of the environmental movement in America. His Great Society programs will leave an indelible mark on the United States forever.

9.12. The environmental legislation and the massive federal regulation and multibillion-dollar spending requirements by the Great Society program brought into Washington, D.C., individuals acting as agents for every conceivable type of business. The agent was expected to exert influence on members of Congress and department secretaries and assistant secretaries in the executive branch and sway them to enact favorable legislation and develop regulations that would be favorable to the firm the agent represented. These agents became permanent fixtures on the Washington, D.C., scene and became known as "Power Brokers." The more successful ones were paid fabulous sums for their services. They established firms in downtown Washington, D.C., and some would move in and out of high positions in the federal executive branch, depending on the political party in power at the time.

9.13. The primary difficulty with the environmental legislation and the Great Society programs was that they were wealth-consuming rather than wealth-producing and no provision was made to develop wealth-producing programs to cover the multibillion-dollar costs. The result was catastrophic. Inflation started on an upward spiral, which would plague succeeding administrations.

9.14. The inflationary pressures from the legislation enacted between 1964 and 1967 was also compounded by the political inaction of the Eisenhower administration and the actions of the Kennedy administration. The ferrous metals division was suffocating from the strangling noose thrown around it by President Kennedy, because of the lack of sufficient funds to modernize their plants to maintain a viable domestic industry. The price of iron ore from the Mesabi Range had increased, and imports of iron ore were at an all-time high, requiring a large expenditure of wealth, where before wealth had been created. Between 1964 and 1969 the production of aluminum was increasing by almost 1 million short tons per year (see table 1 in appendix 6). All of the bauxite ore needed to produce aluminum had to be imported. Also, between 1964 and 1969 an average of 881 million forty-two-gallon barrels of petroleum per year was being imported at a cost of about $2.6 billion; by 1969 imports had risen to over 1 billion barrels (see table 5 in appendix 8). Base metal (copper, lead, and zinc) imports were also increasing.

9.15. Another major contributor to the inflationary pressures was the "abundant life" program, which was a favorite of the American public. By this time many front driveways contained a couple more cars for brother and sister to drive to school and "cruise the gut" on Friday and Saturday nights. Vacation cruises were the rage, and tours to Europe, Africa, the Holy Land, South America, Japan, and the South Pacific were heavily utilized. Many had summer homes either in the mountains, on a lake, or on the seashore. The buying binge by the American public was in full swing, and it had not slackened, regardless of the fact that the United States was engaged in a deadly and highly expensive war in Southeast Asia.

9.16. In addition to the environmental legislation on air and water pollution, President Johnson passed the Wilderness Act in September 1964, which established a preservation system for withdrawing from federally owned areas to maintain those areas in perpetuity as wilderness. Western senators managed to keep a clause in the act that allowed mining. The flowery language in the act so impressed the public that in the quarter-century since the law was enacted no mining has ever taken place on any of the acreage withdrawn. Public pressure would have been too great for any mining company to start mining in an area withdrawn to create a wilderness.

9.17. While President Johnson was getting the Clean Air, Clean Water, and Wilderness Acts and social legislation passed, he was also escalating the Vietnam War at a huge cost of not only dollars but American lives. In 1964 President Johnson claimed that U.S. ships had been attacked in the Gulf of Tonkin. He ordered bombing of North Vietnamese PT-boat bases. Congress approved this move by the Gulf of Tonkin Resolution. There are those who think President Johnson created this incident to gain public support for his planned expansion of troops in

Vietnam. However, it makes no difference whatsoever whether the Gulf of Tonkin incident was manufactured or not. At that time, President Johnson had Congress in his "back pocket," and if he could not get an endorsement from Congress from the Gulf of Tonkin incident, he would have obtained it in some other manner.

9.18. President Johnson appeared determined to end the Vietnam War, but rather than negotiate immediately with the North Vietnamese he decided to go the force-negotiation route. Apparently his strategy was to escalate the war by bombing, which would force the North Vietnamese to negotiate for peace in order to stop the bombing. If that did not work, he would continue to escalate the bombing until they offered to negotiate for peace. It is unknown whether he decided on his strategy himself or on advice from the Pentagon; however, wherever he got it, it was flawed. Bombing by conventional means, that is, by other than nuclear bombs, has never forced any country to surrender. The infantry soldier with the bayonet has to be on enemy soil before surrender can be forced. This lesson should have been learned from the Battle of Britain and bombing of Germany. Japan would have never surrendered from conventional bombing without the United States resorting to the atomic bomb. Even then, the Japanese emperor had to wrest back control from the war lords and offer the unconditional surrender himself (see paragraph 6.4).

9.19. The manner in which it was decided to escalate the Vietnam War by bombing was bone-chilling at best. The only known source to the author was found in *Hubert, the Triumph and Tragedy of the Humphrey I Knew*, by Edgar Berman, M.D. (1979). At a luncheon meeting of the cabinet early in 1965, President Johnson took a poll on the bombing strategy. All the cabinet members voted for it. Vice Pres. Hubert Humphrey was the lone dissenting voice. In addition to voting against the bombing, Vice President Humphrey stated his reservations about the war in general, calling for a review of our involvement before expanding the effort. According to Dr. Berman, President Johnson never forgave Humphrey for this negative vote.

9.20. If this version is true, and there is no reason to believe that it is not, then the following statement can be made with certainty: THIS IS NO WAY TO RUN A NATION. Making this kind of decision casually at a luncheon meeting is the absolute zenith of absurdity, but it does illustrate that this was the way President Johnson handled his staff. His mind was already made up, and all he wanted was a chorus of "yesses" on his decision to escalate the war. At that time most of his cabinet had been with him over a year, and they knew exactly what was expected of them.

9.21. The cabinet is set up to be advisory to the president but primarily advisory on the specialty in their own department. Most department secretaries, except the secretary of defense, know little or nothing about military strategy and warfare, and certainly several members of this cabinet, which at one time served under Mr. Kennedy, had proved that at the Bay of Pigs invasion and by approval of escalation of the Vietnam War in 1962. For a cabinet secretary to vote on a war strategy would require weeks of briefing and input by acknowledged experts on the war as it was being waged in Vietnam. When asked for their vote every single individual in that cabinet should have voted "no" and, like Vice President Humphrey, called for a review of our involvement. It is quite possible that President Johnson had his mind made up and a total cabinet "no" vote would not have stopped him, but at least it was worth a try. With its unanimous sycophantic vote of "yes" the Johnson cabinet ran true to the form that they had established under President Kennedy. Thousands of young men had been sentenced to death or maiming by a casual vote at a luncheon meeting.

9.22. President Johnson's escalation of the Vietnam War was a tragic mistake. He was forced to expand the U.S. military commitment in 1966 and again in 1967. By the end of 1967 more than five hundred thousand troops had been committed to the war in Vietnam. North Vietnam leaders did not respond to his peace overtures, and public opposition to the Vietnam War was becoming intense. It crossed party lines, and although Johnson never said so publicly, he certainly had to admit to himself that his military strategy of bombing the North Vietnamese to the peace table had failed. With the failure, great harm had come to his presidency, and unless he could extricate himself from his own blunder, a second term as president was in jeopardy. His frustration with the Vietnam War was becoming obvious to a growing number of discontented people. In full view of a television audience he lost control of his temper and lashed back at a statement. Those who had seen him on television in November 1963, after the assassination of President Kennedy, calmly assuring the public that all was well, could not help but see the difference. His poise and self-assurance were gone.

9.23. On May 19, 1967, President Nasser of Egypt took advantage of President Johnson's preoccupation with the Vietnam War and demanded that the UN Emergency Force be removed from the Middle

East (World Almanac 1993). Upon their withdrawal, Egyptian forces reoccupied the Gaza Strip and closed the Gulf of Aquaba to Israeli shipping. On June 5, 1967, Israel attacked, and in six days they had won and occupied the Gaza Strip, the Sinai Peninsula to the Suez Canal, the Old City of Jerusalem, Syria's Golan Heights, and Jordan's West Bank (World Almanac 1993). This quick and humilitating victory was devastating to the Arabic nations of the Middle East. Neither the United States nor the European nations appeared to recognize the long-term consequences of Israel holding this land won by force of arms. It was to be a continuous festering sore, which would break into bloody warfare on Yom Kippur, October 6, 1973, and bring on an attempt by the Middle East nations to blackmail the United States and Europe.

9.24. President Johnson was continuously trying to hold down inflation, but he made the same mistake as President Kennedy and tried to fight it from the top down. He used the power of the presidency to intervene between management and labor in heading off strikes and walkouts. Also, he attempted to set price and wage guidelines. The result was that the guidelines had to be continuously revised upward. This need to continuously change the guidelines should have been a warning to him that the method that he was using was not working. In a address in 1968 he said that because of the Vietnam commitment the American people would have to face austerity, but he never did attempt to place an actual curb on the "abundant life" program, which would have relieved some of the inflation pressure. He, like President Kennedy, apparently considered such a move a political impossibility. Johnson's presidency was faltering, and many legislators who had previously sounded his praise were attempting to distance themselves from him.

9.25. However, President Johnson still had the support of the prominent Democrats in the party in late 1967. But in 1968 in the early March Democratic primaries in New Hampshire, Eugene McCarthy, Democratic senator from Minnesota, won over 40 percent of the vote. It was a stunning blow to President Johnson. Senator McCarthy's campaign in the New Hampshire primaries was viewed by the leaders of the party and by a large segment of the media as a joke. Reports continuously surfaced that he had no funds, no organization, and no grassroots support and that he was not really serious about running. His strong showing in New Hampshire, a strong showing in preprimary polls in Wisconsin, and a campaign speech in Madison, Wisconsin, dispelled all doubts that he was not a serious candidate or that he had no supporters.

9.26. Senator McCarthy had voiced opposition to the Vietnam War in 1966, and over the years he had become even more strongly opposed to the war. His decision to run for the Democratic nomination for president was a direct challenge to President Johnson's stand on the war. Senator McCarthy's success in New Hampshire and his strong showing in early Wisconsin polls changed completely the race for the Democratic nominee. It was now obvious that President Johnson could be beaten on just one issue, the Vietnam War. Johnson was a political realist and, realizing that he had lost the support of the people, pulled out of the race. Upon his withdrawal, Robert Kennedy and Hubert Humphrey entered the Democratic primaries.

9.27. Senator McCarthy had proven himself to be a brilliant politician. He had detected the mood of the public long before anybody else in either the Democratic or Republican parties, including President Johnson, Vice President Humphrey, Robert Kennedy, George McGovern, Barry Goldwater, and Richard Nixon. McCarthy was in the vanguard alone. Substantial numbers of the press were caught off guard by his successes in New Hampshire and Wisconsin. His addresses during his campaign were usually summarized by reporters in brief statements or were discussed in the context of the number attending, the predominant age group, and their enthusiasm for what he said. His style of oratory was not hellfire and brimstone; it was measured, calm, and deliberate. In a speech delivered on March 25, 1968, in Madison, he presented his conception of the role of the presidency. In the annals of history since George Washington nobody had ever expressed as briefly or more clearly the role of the presidency (McCarthy 1969). He cited three conditions: character, experience, and understanding that a candidate for the presidency must meet as follows (McCarthy 1969): he must be able to judge the needs and aspirations of the people, he must know and always be aware of the limitations of power and influence of the presidency, and he has to know that the office of the presidency is not a personal office. Senator McCarthy described the role of the presidency as one of uniting the nation.

9.28. Anybody hearing or reading Senator McCarthy's Wisconsin speech should have been able to grasp that he was waging a serious campaign and in the race to the very end, that is, within the limitations of the funds he could raise. No president or presidential nominee has ever publicly clearly defined the role of the president as did Senator McCarthy. At the time of his campaign speech in Madison, the print and electronic media had little to say about his conception of the role of the presidency, and, in fact, they have had little to say about it since. Even after the 1972 Watergate fiasco, wherein President Nixon and his aides wilfully abused their power and violated all the conditions of character and understanding cited by Senator McCarthy in his statement, the print and electronic media remained mute.

9.29. On March 31, 1968, President Johnson announced that he had partially halted the bombing of North Vietnam, and at the same time he appointed a team to negotiate with the North Vietnamese in Paris, France. The peace negotiations in Paris effectively tied Vice President Humphrey to President Johnson's Vietnam program. Humphrey was warned by the president to do or say nothing during the campaign that would affect the peace negotiations he had in progress in Paris. Rather than make an open break with the president, Vice President Humphrey accepted the straitjacket that tied him directly to President Johnson's Vietnam War strategy. Humphrey campaigned for the Democratic nomination and for the presidency within the parameters demanded by President Johnson. Although Humphrey stated several times during the campaign that he was his own man and would have his own ideas as president, the majority of the public failed to grasp what he was actually trying to say. He won the Democratic Party's nomination but lost a close race to Richard Nixon, who had served as vice president under Eisenhower for two terms. After President Nixon took office it soon became apparent that he was unwilling to end the Vietnam War immediately and it would be ended only on his terms and, as he termed, "with honor." In actuality, President Nixon was more pro-war than President Johnson.

9.30. Humphrey's defeat was a tragedy and a massive mistake by the electorate of the United States. It placed the nation on a course that resulted in shaming the office of the president and the resignations both the president and vice president. President Kennedy had placed a noose around the ferrous metals division of the minerals industry, and President Johnson had compounded Kennedy's mistakes with his own environmental, social, wage, and price control programs. He had effectively tightened the noose and positioned himself to place his hand on the lever for springing the trapdoor. Humphrey was the only individual in government at that time, possibly with the exception of Sen. Eugene McCarthy, who appeared to understand what was going wrong. In the end it would be President Nixon, in his first term, who would place his

Table 9.1
Total Annual Production of Iron Ore in the United States, 1964–68, Compared to That Produced by the Lake Superior District and the Mesabi Range (U.S. Geological Survey and U.S. Bureau of Mines 1992)
(in thousand short tons)

Year	Total Tons	Lake Superior District Tons	Percentage of Total	Mesabi Iron Range Tons	Percentage of Total	Tons Accumulated
1964	84,836	63,106	74	47,256	56	2,466,412
1965	87,439	66,432	76	50,280	56	2,516,692
1966	90,147	68,603	76	51,506	57	2,568,198
1967	84,179	63,229	75	48,857	58	2,617,055
1968	85,865	66,224	77	51,411	60	2,668,466

hand on the lever and spring the trap door. Within the short space of ten years three presidents would manage to destroy an industrial leadership that had lasted for seventy years. President Nixon's role in the destruction is discussed in chapter 10.

9.31. The serious situation that was developing during the Johnson administration in the ferrous metals division of the minerals industry is well illustrated in a continuation of the production, import, and export statistics on iron ore, iron, and steel in tables 9.1, 9.2, 9.3, and 9.4, from 1964 to 1968, and table 9.5, showing the effect of the price guidelines, which were used to hold down prices.

9.32. Table 9.1 shows that the leveling-off trend that was developing during the Kennedy administration continued in the Johnson administration. Total domestic iron ore production varied from 85 million to 90 million long tons. Mesabi Range production varied from 47 million to 51 million long tons. It was obvious from these statistics that the growing demand for iron ore was going to have to be met by imports. Table 9.2 shows that the increasing import trend starting under the Kennedy administration continued under the Johnson administration.

Table 9.2
Iron Ore Imported for Consumption into the United States by Continents, 1964–68 (U.S. Geological Survey and U.S. Bureau of Mines 1992)
(in thousand long tons)
(thousand dollars)

Year	North America		South America		Europe		Remainder	
1964	24,876	274,677	14,309	121,812	103	1,586	3,120	23,213
1965	23,756	264,360	18,169	154,908	57	1,108	4,135	23,412
1966	23,941	273,309	17,583	148,545	82	1,523	4,653	39,977
1967	24,214	276,597	15,825	129,909	148	1,840	4,440	35,733
1968	26,339	308,014	13,011	115,665	592	5,256	3,999	24,818

Table 9.3
Production, Imports, and Exports of Pig Iron and Steel in the United States, 1964–68
(U.S. Geological Survey and U.S. Bureau of Mines 1992)
(in thousand short tons)

Year	Pig Iron			Steel		
	Production	Imports	Exports	Production	Imports	Exports
1964	85,458	736	176	127,076	6,630	4,065
1965	88,207	882	28	131,462	10,640	2,888
1966	91,287	1,187	12	134,101	11,043	2,144
1967	86,799	605	7	127,213	11,446	1,898
1968	88,767	786	9	131,462	13,346	2,673

Table 9.4
World Production of Steel with the Production and Percentage Produced by the United States, USSR Separate from Europe, Europe, Japan, and Other Nations, 1964–68 (U.S. Geological Survey and U.S. Bureau of Mines 1992)
(in million short tons)

Year	World	U.S.		USSR		Europe		Japan		Other
	Tons	Tons	%	Tons	%	Tons	%	Tons	%	%
1964	482.8	127.1	26	93.7	19	166.5	34	43.9	9	12
1965	506.2	131.5	26	100.3	20	173.4	34	45.4	9	11
1966	524.7	134.1	26	106.8	20	172.6	33	52.7	10	11
1967	544.1	127.2	23	112.7	21	180.9	33	68.5	13	10
1968	583.6	131.5	23	117.4	20	197.1	34	73.7	13	10

Table 9.5
The *Iron Age* Annual Average of Finished Steel Composite Prices, 1958–68
(in cents per pound)

1958	6.060	1961	6.196	1964	6.368	1967	6.464
1959	6.196	1962	6.196	1965	6.368	1968	6.600
1960	6.196	1963	6.273	1966	6.399		

9.33. Table 9.3 shows that the imports of steel that started in the 1959 strike, during the Eisenhower administration, and continued in the Kennedy administration also continued into the Johnson administration. Between 1964 and 1965 the imports increased 4 million long tons to 10.6 million, and by 1968 imports had reached 13 million long tons. The Johnson administration failed to recognize that starting in 1964 a substantial amount of this imported tonnage was dumping or unfairly subsidized steel. Such steel is always sold under the domestic price, and it forces domestic companies to cut prices to meet the competition to stop the import flow of steel selling at below cost. Selling below cost to restrict unfairly traded imports injures a domestic company seriously; it reduces the overall profit of the company to the extent that it leaves less funds for modernization and upgrading of technology. In the ferrous

146

metals division of the minerals industry, failure to keep modernizing the plant and keep abreast of technology is the "kiss of death"; it leads directly to bankruptcy. The Johnson administration failed to deal with the situation by passing trade laws to restrict unfairly traded steel imports, and subsequent administrations were also remiss. The failure of the U.S. government to deal with the situation adequately resulted in the development of a bleeding ulcer sapping the strength of the domestic steel industry by slow strangulation until, twenty-five years later, under the Reagan administration, the ulcer spewed a gangrenous mixture that forced restructuring of the domestic steel industry and a serious reduction in plant capacity.

9.34. Table 9.4 shows that by 1968 the U.S. share of world production of steel had dropped to 23 percent, the USSR share had increased from 19 to 20 percent, Europe's share stayed at about 34 percent, and Japan's share had increased 4 percentage points to 13 percent. A review of the production, imports, and exports of iron ore, pig iron, and steel from the second Eisenhower administration, starting in 1955, to the end of the Johnson administration in 1968 should be enough proof to even the most biased skeptic that the dominant industrial position of the United States was being taken over by the European continent, the Soviet Union, and Japan; the Soviet Union was utilizing their production to build a massive military striking force, and Europe and Japan were supplying the growing demand in their own nations and in Third World countries throughout the world. Excess production was being dumped into the United States. It was a fast-changing world during this thirteen-year period, and the United States was unable to make the necessary adjustments because of the actions by the three administrations that were in power at that time.

9.35. Table 9.5 shows in detail the failure of the Kennedy and Johnson administrations to recognize that the ferrous metals division of the minerals industry was in serious trouble. In 1958 the price of steel was at 6.06 cents per pound. During and after the steel strike, in 1959 and 1960, the price was 6.196 cents per pound. President Kennedy's action forced the price to remain at 6.196 cents per pound for two more years, 1961 and 1962. These four years were a critical time in the rebuilding of a restructured steel industry, and the industry was hand-cuffed by the inability to increase the price of steel to cover the cost of restructuring. The Johnson administration did not recognize or try to remedy the situation in any manner. In fact, they added to the problem.

After the disastrous years of the Kennedy administration, the ferrous metals division needed a large increase in the price of steel to get back on track and to correct the mistakes of the Kennedy administration. Instead of a large increase, the Johnson administration through their price guideline system held the industry to the same price in 1964 and 1965 and only minor increases up to 1968. In the ten-year period from 1959 to 1968 the price of steel was allowed to rise only 0.404 cents per pound. It was a miracle that the industry managed to retain 23 percent of its share of world production in 1968. That it was able to do so under the restrictions that were placed upon it during the Kennedy and Johnson administrations testifies to the absolutely dominant position it held in 1948, which gave it the strength to withstand ten years of erosion from 1959 to 1968.

9.36. It is obvious that the Johnson administration had little or no grasp of the problems facing the minerals industry. The Great Society program, which began after the overwhelming defeat of Mr. Goldwater, was noted primarily for the social legislation enacted; however, it also was the beginning of the environmental movement in the United States. Five environmental laws were passed in the years between 1964 and 1967 as follows: (1) the Wilderness Act of 1964, (2) the Water Quality Act of 1965, (3) the Clean Air Act of 1965, (4) the Clean Water Restoration Act of 1966, and (5) the Air Quality Act of 1967. The movement was slow in gathering a strong public following, but this was soon due to change, in 1969, because of a massive blunder by an oil company and their drilling crew in the Santa Barbara Channel offshore of the California coast.

9.37. Secretary of the Interior Udall, whose responsibility was to advise President Johnson on the minerals industry, appeared to be completely oblivious to the the necessity for restructuring in the ferrous metals division. In addition, Udall appeared to have no knowledge whatsoever of the developing problems of the liquid fuel division. One of the last actions by him seriously weakened the nation's ability to bargain effectively with the Middle East OPEC cartel in the early seventies. This was an Interior Department command barring all commercial activity on the federal domain in Alaska until the Alaskan native lands claims were resolved by Congress. The proclamation and the law that was eventually passed by Congress in 1971 delayed for five years the development of petroleum in Prudhoe Bay, Alaska, and placed the United States in a vulnerable position to the Middle East OPEC cartel.

148

Table 9.6
Annual Population Estimates in the United States, 1964–1968 (Bureau of the Census 1994)
(in thousands)

Year	Total Resident Population	Year	Total Resident Population	Year	Total Resident Population
1964	191,141	1966	195,576	1968	199,399
1965	193,526	1967	197,457		

This Department of Interior order and law passed by Congress was the biggest rip-off of the American public since Klaus Fuchs gave 2 billion dollars' worth of research on the atomic bomb to the Soviet Union. The independent enclaves created for the native Alaskans will require perpetual funding and be a festering problem that can never be solved as long as the enclaves exist.

9.38. At the end of the Johnson administration, if anyone were to ask what action could be taken to maintain what was then America's industrial position in the world, the only answer that could be given would be: "Let us pray." There were good reasons why this was the only answer. The population in the United States and the world had increased sharply during the years of the Johnson administration. However, it was not the domestic minerals industry that was supplying this increased population with steel produced from mineral commodities; it was Europe and Japan. The population growth in the United States is shown in table 9.6. The fact that the domestic steel industry was not supplying this increased population with steel was serious, but it was not as serious as the growth of the gross federal debt. The growth of this debt during the Johnson administration is shown in table 9.7.

9.39. Table 9.7 shows that the gross federal debt increased $52.6 billion from 1964 to 1968, which averages out to over $10 billion per year. This annual debt increase is, unfortunately, ample proof that President Johnson had made absolutely no provision whatsoever to pay for the social and environmental legislation that his administration enacted.

Table 9.7
Gross Federal Debt at the End of the Year, 1964–68 (Bureau of Public Debt 1992)
(in millions of dollars)

Year	Gross Federal Debt	Year	Gross Federal Debt	Year	Gross Federal Debt
1964	316,059	1966	328,498	1968	368,685
1965	322,318	1967	340,445		

As president he viewed the United States in the same manner as he had when he was a senator in the fifties: The United States was the dominant industrial nation in the world, and it would be the dominant nation forever; because it was the dominant industrial nation, it could carry any social and environmental programs that he decided to ask Congress to enact into law. There was apparently nobody in his cabinet who had the "guts" to advise him differently. President Johnson wanted his administration to be remembered. Certainly anybody who has any knowledge at all of the ferrous metals division of the minerals industry can never forget him, his cabinet, or his administration. The Kennedy and Johnson administrations had set the United States on a course of inflation and debt, which could harass the nation for the next fifty years. If a solution is not found by the end of that time, the nation may have to declare bankruptcy because of the failure to meet interest payments on the debt.

10

The Next Six Years (1968–74): Nixon

10.1. Richard Nixon was elected to the House of Representatives from the state of California in 1946. He was re-elected in 1948. He became nationally known in 1948 as the leader in an investigation of Alger Hiss, a State Department employee who was charged with passing sensitive State information to Soviet agents during the Roosevelt administration. The publicity Nixon received from the Hiss case helped get him elected to the Senate in 1950 and nominated to be Eisenhower's vice-presidential running mate in 1952. Nixon's adamant anticommunist stance had in six years gained him two terms (four years) in the House, two years in the Senate, and nomination to be vice president under Eisenhower. Nixon served as vice president under Eisenhower for both terms (1952–60).

10.2. In 1960 Mr. Nixon was the Republican candidate, but he was defeated by John Kennedy, the Democratic candidate, in a close race for the presidency. In 1968 Nixon was again the Republican candidate, with Spiro Agnew as a running mate. They defeated the Democratic candidate, Hubert Humphrey, and George Wallace. Nixon's primary promise during the race was that he would end "with honor" the Vietnam War started by Kennedy and expanded by Johnson. The defeat of Mr. Humphrey was assured when Mr. Nixon gained the financial backing of the liquid fuels division of the minerals industry (oil companies) by promising to support the oil depletion allowance law (see paragraph 4.16). Their support provided him with a well-heeled campaign chest, and it certainly was a factor in his election victory over Mr. Humphrey. This would again prove to be a poor choice by the electorate, and in the final analysis, it proved to be an absolute disaster for the liquid fuels division of the minerals industry.

10.3. President Nixon was intolerant of dissent, and he was distrustful to an extreme of everybody except a small group of individuals on the White House staff whom he considered his loyal followers. He had no confidence in the civil service employees who comprised the executive branch. Although he appointed the heads of the various departments and bureaus, he appeared to doubt that his political appointees had the ability to control the civil service bureaucracy.

10.4. President Nixon appointed cabinet members; however, it is difficult to determine whether he got his advice and recommendations on issues from cabinet officials or from his White House Staff. He appeared to turn to the staff that surrounded him in the White House for advice on most of his actions on major issues. His administration was an enigma. During the first term there were times when he handled serious and difficult problems with confidence and self-assurance equal to that of the great presidents in history. He succeeded in opening China to the West, and he also boldly assisted Israel during the Yom Kippur War. However, he imposed wage-price controls that doomed the nation's industrial world leadership. He also passed environmental legislation that developed into a litigious quagmire and at the same time placed the United States at the mercy of the Middle East petroleum producers. In the second term he refused to move to the forefront and supply the necessary foreign leadership to stop the oil embargo initiated by OPEC. To prove his innocence in the Watergate fiasco, he released the presidential transcripts that made him resemble the "godfather" giving orders to his "torpedos" to "rub out" his political enemies and detractors (Gold and Amster 1974, Staff of the *Washington Post* 1974).

10.5. The members of the staff who appeared to have constant access to Nixon in the Oval Office were the following: Dwight L. Chapin, presidential appointments secretary; Charles W. Colson, special counsel to the president; John W. Dean III, counsel to the president; John D. Ehrlichman, counsel to the president and later assistant to the president on domestic affairs; H. R. Haldeman, White House chief of staff; Henry Kissinger, assistant to the president for national security affairs; John N. Mitchell, attorney general; and Ronald L. Ziegler, White House press secretary.

10.6. The problems facing the Nixon administration were massive in character. It is doubtful if any other president in history had to face such an array of foreign and domestic political problems upon assuming the presidency. The problems associated with the Vietnam War were acute and tended to overshadow all others. President Nixon had to end in a manner that he termed "with honor" the Vietnam War, which had been in progress during two previous administrations. This entailed the withdrawal of over .5 million troops from South Vietnam while the war was still in progress. The arms race with the Soviet Union was continuing just as it had for the past twenty-five years, and the Soviets were actively supporting Cuba, North Korea, North Vietnam, Syria, and Egypt. In essence, Cuba was a colony of the Soviet Union. Gamal Abdel Nasser had succeeded in uniting the Middle East nations, and with Soviet military manpower and advisers serving in his armed forces he was threatening to go to war against Israel to win back the land Egypt and Syria had lost in 1967 during the Six-Day War.

10.7. The domestic problems confronting Mr. Nixon were as critical as the foreign problems but received less attention and, as a result, tended to worsen over time. The industrial world dominance that had been the position of the nation for so long was almost completely eroded by the Marshall Plan–funded and government-subsidized industries in Europe and government-subsidized industries in Japan because of the mistakes by the Kennedy and Johnson administrations. Inflation, a constant companion of the environmental and Great Society programs of the Johnson administration, was soaring and threatening to go completely out of control, and the imbalance in foreign trade because of increasing mineral commodity imports had become alarming. There was a growing opposition to the oil depletion allowance law (see paragraph 4.16), and a law repealing it was starting to move through Congress. Secretary of Interior Udall in a last-gasp action by the Johnson Administration had barred all commercial activity on the federal domain in Alaska until the Native Claims Act had been passed by Congress. In addition to the above problems, President Nixon was also faced with the "abundant life" program, which the public was pursuing with unabated enthusiasm. Both Presidents Kennedy and Johnson had refused to deal directly with this problem, apparently feeling that applying a brake to the program was politically unacceptable.

10.8. Although President Nixon appointed a secretary of state, he had no intention of making foreign policy through the State Department. Foreign policy was made and initiated through Henry Kissinger, assistant to the president for national security affairs (Kissinger 1982). H. R. Haldeman was President Nixon's chief of staff and had the power, and used it extensively, to screen access to the president. John Ehrlichman also held an extremely powerful position in the White House. He was first employed as counsel to the president and later as assistant to the president on domestic affairs. President Nixon appeared to trust him implicitly, and apparently a substantial amount of information and recommendations on domestic issues filtered through him before reaching the president. There is little doubt that in President Nixon's administration Messrs. Haldeman and Ehrlichman held an inordinate amount of power. This power could be and was exerted on Henry Kissinger as well as on cabinet secretaries (Kissinger 1982).

10.9. President Nixon and his White House aides barely had time to adjust their office chairs to the correct height before an oil well being drilled in the Santa Barbara Channel blew out in late January 1969. It proved to be an absolute disaster. The three major television networks covered it in detail. Human interest stories on the effect of the wildlife were nightly fare. Small children were shown sobbing as they looked at oil-covered birds, and dire predictions were made regarding the effect of the blowout on the California coast. Without doubt this single blowout gave the environmental movement the impetus it needed and later environmentalists were frank in stating, "We needed that." It became an even more serious situation when the administration withdrew the drilling permits on most of the leases in the channel. The withdrawals were destined to place a further reliance on Middle East petroleum in the early and middle seventies.

10.10. There was no procedure that could be set up for Mr. Nixon to act immediately on all the problems that were facing the nation, and certainly there were no historical guidelines available for withdrawing over .5 million troops from an ongoing war that a mostly young, highly vocal part of the American public had already labeled as lost and immoral. However, the administration failed to act immediately to end the Vietnam War. It did not require any political acumen to recognize that the nation was almost prostrate because of the war; it dominated all other political issues. President Nixon, his cabinet, and the White House staff failed to understand, or for that matter even recognize, that the nation needed to be reunited and the only way that this could be accomplished was by ending the Vietnam War forthwith. Whether it was, as he termed, "with honor" or without honor made absolutely no difference whatsoever to those voicing opposition to the war. They wanted just one action from Mr. Nixon, and that was to get the United States out of South Vietnam immediately!

10.11. President Nixon ignored those calling for immediate withdrawal and spaced out troop withdrawals over a period of four years. He wanted the South Vietnamese troops to replace the U.S. troops as they were withdrawn and continue the war against the North Vietnamese. The manner in which President Nixon was withdrawing the U.S. troops from Vietnam and replacing them with South Vietnamese troops had considerable support throughout the nation. However, whatever the breakdown of those for and against the war, the nation was divided, and it remained that way as long as there were troops in Vietnam and for a considerable length of time thereafter because of the spaced-time withdrawal method imposed by the administration.

10.12. President Nixon assigned the task of negotiating peace terms with the North Vietnamese to Henry Kissinger, assistant to the president for national security affairs. In addition, many other direct negotiations with foreign governments were handled by Mr. Kissinger. He overshadowed William Rogers, who was the secretary of state. There was confusion within the State Department in regard to the division of duties between Mr. Kissinger and the State Department. During President Nixon's second term, in August 1973, he cleared up this uncertainty by appointing Mr. Kissinger secretary of state.

10.13. President Nixon's concentration on the Vietnam War in 1969 left him no time for an in-depth analysis of the problems of the minerals industry. At the end of the Kennedy and Johnson administration (eight years), there was ample proof that America's industrial dominance was fading fast. Imports of mineral commodity products were beginning to flood into all ports in the United States, competing directly with the same products produced by domestic manufacturers. President Nixon's refusal to address the problem essentially killed off any revival of the industrial dominance. President Kennedy first put the throttling noose on the industrial superiority, President Johnson tightened the noose, and President Nixon sprang the trapdoor.

10.14. Although the first term of President Nixon's administration was dominated by the spaced-time withdrawal of troops from Vietnam, he still had time for those political issues that would win him votes. When he could set aside his intolerance of dissent, he was above all a wise and crafty politician, and he had an innate ability to spot an issue that would win him voter support. Although he was engrossed with the Vietnam War, he sensed the environmental awareness that was growing in the nation after the Santa Barbara Channel oil well blowout, and he apparently decided that he should join this movement prior to his run for a second term in 1972.

10.15. Almost a year after the blowout, on January 1, 1970, with considerable fanfare from his home in San Clemente, California, he signed into law the National Environmental Policy Act of 1969 (NEPA). This law contained a clause that required an "impact statement" be drawn up on all projects listing adverse effects. This single requirement in a policy act has now proven to have had the most profound and costly effect of any peacetime federal legislation enacted in the twentieth century.

10.16. The passage of NEPA in 1969 through Congress is cited in detail by Jack Anderson with James Boyd in their book, *Fiasco* (1983). According to them, the law moved to passage without any notice from the legislative and executive branches and, strangely enough, without arousing any lobbying activity. The only individual who recognized that the "impact statement" requirement could cause trouble with Interior Department solicitor Mitchell Melich; he advised Interior Secretary Hickel to recommend President Nixon veto the bill, but Mr. Hickel refused to intervene (Anderson and Boyd 1983). If this version is true, then Mr. Melich should have a bigger-than-life-size statue erected to him in the small park at the rear of the Interior building with the following inscription: ONE LAWYER AMONG THOUSANDS WHO KNEW HIS CRAFT.

10.17. The "impact statement" requirement in NEPA has been like a rabbit warren: each action breeds another action. It was a rallying point for environmentalists, and they banded together in a tight-knit group to form an environmental political bloc that has attained more power out-side of the two major political parties than any other political bloc in the history of the nation. It delayed the construction of the Alaskan pipeline to transport oil from Prudhoe Bay, Alaska. The original estimates for construction were $1 billion, but because of inflation the final cost five years later was over $5 billion, which was paid by the public in higher prices for gasoline and oil. In addition, NEPA triggered the passage of the following major environmental laws in 1970: (1) the Water Quality Improvement Act of 1970, (2) the National Air Quality Standards Act of 1970, and (3) the Resource Recovery Act of 1970. The water and air quality acts essentially represented a switch of power from the legislative to the executive branch. They were broad in context and empowered the executive branch with the authority to develop the rules and regula-tions under which the laws would be enforced.

10.18. To enforce the "impact statement" of NEPA and to develop and promulgate the needed rules and regulations for enforcement of the water and air quality acts, the Environmental Protection Agency (EPA) was formed. It rapidly became one of the major law enforcement agencies in the federal government. Regulations newly written or revised by the EPA became a standard part of the *Federal Register*. A close relationship developed immediately between the EPA and the environmental political bloc. A quick and easy way to receive a civil service appointment in EPA was to first become an activist in the environmental political bloc. As the bloc gained more strength and became more cohesive, many of the employees of EPA moved back into the bloc, sensing that here was where the big money was to be made, and certainly in this respect they were right.

10.19. NEPA and the first two acts cited above as they were enacted in sequence became the means whereby the environmental political bloc could challenge in court the operation of any industrial firm at any location in the United States and any project or program proposed or in progress by several of the agencies in the Department of the Interior, the Forest Service in the Department of Agriculture, and the AEC. No matter what the government project or program was, it could be delayed at least five to seven years and for all practical purposes nitpicked to death, and to cap it all off, under the Equal Access to Justice Act the environmental political bloc's legal fees and costs were paid with the public's tax dollars. It paid, and paid handsomely, for the environmental political bloc to go to court. The public appeared to look upon these lawsuits as "David fighting Goliath," and many individuals started to contribute funds to the various environmental organizations.

10.20. The suits brought by the bloc were a bonanza to the law profession. Law schools added branches teaching environmental law. Law firms added departments specializing in defending industrial firms against environmental suits, and the government had to add more lawyers to their staffs. For lawyers, it became the best of times. Seeking gold in "them thar hills" was a waste of time, because it was there for the taking on the courtroom floor by filing environmental lawsuits. Where did the money to pay for all this come from? It came from the public. In suits filed against the government, tax dollars paid the environmental lawyers, government lawyers, judges, and court expenses. In suits filed against industrial firms, the laws were such that the environmentalists won over 90 percent of the suits; thus the public's wallets were tapped by industrial firms, who increased the prices of their products to cover the court costs and lawyer fees.

10.21. President Nixon, his White House aides and cabinet secretaries, and Congress, throughout the development of this litigious quagmire and the syphoning of millions of dollars from the public to pay court costs and lawyer fees, remained calm and above the fray. They appeared to have the attitude that mistakes were not possible in their organization and there was no need to interfere in something that would eventually run its course. They made no move to correct the situation. The end result was the executive and legislative branches and the public becoming helpless against the eternal breeding NEPA "impact statement" requirement and other environmental laws it spawned. The judiciary branch became the primary governing body over the nation's public lands. The public and the executive and legislative branches became spectators, and federal judges seized the opportunity to usurp power from the executive and legislative branches.

10.22. It soon became apparent that the water and air quality acts were forcing utilities and many industrial firms that were using electricity to change from coal to oil to meet the rules and regulations being promulgated by the EPA. This meant more imports of petroleum and greater dependence on Middle East production. There were individuals in the Interior Department who were deeply concerned with the ever-increasing dependency on Middle East production. Hollis M. Dole, assistant Secretary for minerals, and others developed a Minerals and Metals Policy Act, which was passed through Congress and signed by the president in 1970. Under the law, the Bureau of Mines was required to publish an annual report on the state of the minerals industry. The first report was published in 1970. It received wide distribution to all states through the Bureau of Mines liaison officer program and the state geologists, but most of the governors and members of the state houses were not impressed. The Bureau of Mines has continued to publish the reports annually. They appear to have as little impact today as they did in 1970.

10.23. The 1970 *State of the Minerals Industry Report* pointed out that the United States was placing itself in an extremely vulnerable position. Although the report was ignored by the administration, Congress, and state governors, it was not ignored by the Middle East petroleum exporters. They began to realize that they held a bargaining position whereby if they united under OPEC, they could control the production and price of petroleum. In a series of clever maneuvers they began a campaign to exert leverage on certain vulnerable oil companies with considerable success (Bureau of the Census 1944-1994). They threatened to cut back allowable production unless their price raises per forty-two-gallon barrel of petroleum were accepted. The administration chose to ignore the situation, and the major oil companies without leadership from President Nixon did not appear to be able to band together to counteract the strategy of divide and conquer being employed by the Middle East oil-producing nations. The failure of President Nixon to take the lead and place the U.S. government into the forefront of the negotiations resulted in the price of petroleum, almost quadrupling in two months in late 1973.

10.24. In 1971 it became obvious to President Nixon that the United Nations was going to vote for the entry of China into that body in 1972. To avoid a political embarassment, he made a decision that surprised not only his adversaries but also his supporters. In a departure from the solid anticommunist stance that he had held publicly for a quarter of a century, he adopted a new policy toward China. He supported China's admission to the United Nations in October 1971, at the expense of Taiwan's membership. He then visited China in February 1972. It was a bold political venture, and because of detailed coverage by the print and electronic media it earned him a reputation as a wise and knowledgeable leader in foreign affairs. He emphasized several times in a statement to the media that he, a solid anticommunist, was the only one who could have taken this step to reestablish relations with China. This statement was certainly correct, because if anybody else had tried to reestablish relations with China, he, President Nixon, would have had him or her drawn and quartered for being soft on communism.

10.25. In 1971 President Nixon demonetized gold and allowed the value of the dollar to float on the world market. He made the same mistake as the Kennedy and Johnson administrations. He attempted to fight inflation from the top down. In 1971, he imposed wage-price controls, which in finality drove the nails in the coffin that buried America's world industrial leadership. It took three administrations just ten years to kill off completely an industrial superiority that had lasted for seventy years. President Nixon withdrew the controls in 1973, but it was too late. The damage had been done. The saddest commentary on the matter is that over the ten-year period none of the three presidents, their cabinet secretaries, White House aides, Congress, or a majority of the public had no idea whatsoever of what had been done.

10.26. President Nixon's White House aides were determined to retain the positions that they held. In the fall of 1971 the Committee to Re-elect the President (CREEP) was formed to campaign for the reelection of Richard Nixon. The campaign effort took an evil and illegal turn, and some employees were caught attempting to plant a listening device in Democratic Headquarters in the Watergate office complex in Washington, D.C.

10.27. President Nixon was well prepared for his campaign for a second term in 1972. The Republican Party renominated him on the first ballot, and the last ground combat troops were withdrawn from Vietnam in August 1972 (DeGregorio 1993). He had established himself as a environmentalist, and his success in China was still a topic of conversation in political circles. As it turned out, President Nixon's political preparations and the illegal activities of CREEP were unnecessary. The Democratic Party decided all by itself to self-destruct: it nominated George McGovern, a far left liberal senator from South Dakota, to run against President Nixon.

10.28. However, despite the fact that Senator McGovern had no chance at all to be elected, President Nixon, his White House aides, and CREEP did not view the political situation realistically. The vehement protests by those opposed to the Vietnam War and leaks of classified information concerned President Nixon and his aides far more than they would admit publicly. The protests were vehement, but those protesting did not by any measure have a large-enough number of votes to swing the election away from President Nixon, whose intolerance of dissent overrode his political know-how, and he placed himself in an impossible position by claiming that neither he nor his aides knew anything about the break-in at Watergate.

10.29. The attempted cover-up of the Watergate break-in by President Nixon and his White House aides placed the administration in the line of fire of a cannonade of charges that were continuous for almost two years and eventually led to the Watergate Hearings, starting on May 17, 1973 (Lubell, Sheridan, and Slosser, 1973). In an effort to clear himself of any involvement and to prove his innocence of participating in illegal activities, President Nixon released edited transcripts of conversations between himself and his advisers from September 15, 1972, to April 27, 1973, but they only exacerbated the situation (Staff of the *Washington Post* 1974, Gold 1974). A greater part of the public were shocked and dismayed at the subjects under discussion between President Nixon and his aides. The continuous broadside of charges being leveled against the administration forced Nixon to spend a considerable amount of time countering the attacks. Bowing to pressure, he asked for and accepted the resignations of Messrs. Haldeman and Ehrlichman on April 30, 1973. The edited transcripts did indicate that Henry Kissinger was never involved in the Watergate fiasco (Staff of the *Washington Post* 1974, Gold 1974). He denies knowing anything about Watergate until April 14, 1973 (Kissinger 1982).

10.30. Congress passed and President Nixon signed into law the 1973 Endangered Species Act. This law immediately gave the environmental political bloc the opportunity to control through the courts any tract of land within the borders of the United States. The 1973 Endangered Species Act exhibits craftsmanship far beyond the abilities of any elected senator or representative or their staffs. No matter whose names were on the act as sponsors, it was written by environmental activist trial lawyers for environmentalists with infinite care to assure that any lawsuit filed to protect what was termed an endangered species could be won by the environmental political bloc. Nothing was left to chance by the writers. This law was written in detail to protect both species and subspecies, no matter how many subspecies there might be. In addition, it protects the species and subspecies by specific area rather than nationwide. It is purely and simply a land control law disguised as a law to save endangered species.

10.31. On October 6, 1973, on Yom Kippur, Egypt, led by Anwar Sadat, and Syria, with strong support from the Soviet Union, attacked Israel in an effort to take back the land lost in the 1967 Six-Day War. Israel won the war, but it was a close call. War matériel support by the United States for Israel had to be by airplane to counter that being flown in by the Soviet Union. Prior to the start of the Yom Kippur War, OPEC had gained considerable strength, and the Middle East nations were allowing it to speak for them. Their intent was clear; they would use oil as a weapon to gain by oil embargo threats against the United States and Europe that which they could not win by force of arms against Israel. On October 16, 1973, OPEC raised the price of crude petroleum from $3.01 to $5.12 per forty-two-gallon barrel and announced that they would cut petroleum production each month until Israel withdrew from all occupied lands (Kissinger 1982, Bureau of the Census 1944-1994, Halberstan 1986). About two months later on December 23, they again raised the price per barrel, to $11.65 (Kissinger 1982, Bureau of the Census (1944-1994, Halberstan 1986).

10.32. It was obvious that at this time the United States was not operating from a position of strength, and the OPEC nations knew it. In charge was a president who had lost control, and a Congress and attentive public who were obsessed with the manner in which he had accomplished this loss of control. The statistics that showed the vulnerable position of the United States with respect to imported petroleum were available to all. From 1967 to 1974 imports of petroleum rose from 0.926 billion forty-two-gallon barrels to 2.222 billion barrels (see table 5 of appendix 8). The percentage of imports of U.S. production in this eight-year period doubled from 20 to 40 percent (see table 6 of appendix 8). This doubling meant that in 1974 the nation was dependent for two-fifths of the petroleum it consumed on the OPEC nations. The water and air quality acts were in a large part responsible for this huge increase (see paragraph 10.22).

10.33. To combat the oil embargo, the administration moved the Office of Oil and Gas out of the Department of the Interior and created the Federal Energy Administration (FEA). This agency prepared regulations to govern the use of oil during the embargo. It can be said without fear of contradiction that the regulations that were published were the most pitiful effort ever made by a federal agency to govern an industry about which they knew absolutely nothing. The regulations did not address the "abundant life" program and were an attempt to allow everybody to do what they had been doing but at a reduced rate. Fortunately, the embargo ended in March 1974, about five months after it started.

10.34. Henry Kissinger considered the petroleum price rise in December one of the pivotal events in the history of this century, primarily because of the huge amount of dollars that were siphoned out of the United States, Europe, Japan, and many developing countries (Kissinger 1982). He was correct in that it was a devastating blow to the economies of the world, but in regard to the United States, he was viewing the single effect of a more significant and subtle pivotal event that had occurred twenty years earlier, in 1953. That was the failure of the Eisenhower administration to follow through on the Truman administration's development of a materials policy with a strategic plan of action to guide the nation in development, mining, and importation of mineral commodities. The failures of Presidents Kennedy, Johnson, and Nixon to correct the omission resulted in the United States losing an industrial leadership that had lasted for seventy years, placing the nation in a vulnerable position, which could be exploited by OPEC, billions of dollars evaporating like steam vapor into the air by inflation, multimillions of dollars to meet the regulations of the clean air and water acts, millions of dollars burned up in lawsuits to meet the "impact statement" requirement of NEPA, and an annual increase in the national debt for twenty years. The petroleum price rise in December 1973 was nothing more than a continuation of losses of billions of dollars by the United States, which will continue indefinitely until some administration has enough sense to develop a materials policy with a strategic plan of action. An industry that is the very roots of our industrial civilization cannot be willfully ignored for twenty years without events such a those described above being a constant occurrence.

10.35. While President Nixon was engrossed in Watergate, Wall Street was caught in the coils of a bear market, which lasted almost two years, starting in January 1973 and ending in December 1974. The decline in the Dow Jones Averages was 45.1 percent, which was the greatest percentage drop since 1929. This bear market was caused by wage-price controls that Mr. Nixon imposed in 1971 and removed by the end of 1973.

10.36. The imposition of the wage-price controls definitely marked the end of the nation's world industrial dominance. Nixon supporters will argue that the dominance ended in the Kennedy or Johnson administration, but the available evidence will not support such an argument. The transition from Johnson to Nixon was marked by virtually no change in political policy, except that possibly Nixon was more pro-war than Johnson. Nixon continued the Vietnam War for four more years (40 percent of the total length of the war), and his preoccupation with the war and reestablishing relations with China during that period left little time for an in-depth analysis of domestic problems associated with the minerals industries. Even if there had been no war to stop, the fact that Mr. Nixon imposed wage-price controls is sufficient proof that he was not aware that a world industrial dominance was dying in the period between 1962 and 1972.

10.37. The death of the nation's industrial dominance completely changed the manner in which the United States would have to deal with other nations from 1972 on. Major nations in the world from 1962 to 1972 had industrialized in the ten-year period on a per capita basis fully equal to the industrialization of the United States. They were competing on a world basis and winning their share and more of the iron commodity and product export market. No longer would dominance in steel production be sufficient to control the U.S. export and domestic product market. From 1972 on, U.S. industry would be competing with that of other major nations of the world on a level playing field, with price, quantity, quality, and reliability being the dominant factors. Labor strikes could be costly and result in losing not only markets but also thousands of jobs forever. Environmental laws, excess taxes, or price controls could shut down an industrial company as quickly as the lack of energy. The death of the nations's industrial superiority forced a transition from reliance on dominance to reliance on leadership—leadership not only in the government but in industry and labor as well. The time had come for government, industry, and labor to unite in a common bond as a united front to win their share of the world export product market. Adversarial relationships, which were so common prior to 1972, would have to be scrapped and new relationships forged among government, labor, and industry, with each working toward the same goal.

10.38. There was sufficient evidence available on the nation's highways and byways to prove that the nation had lost its industrial dominance in steel production. Automobiles made in Europe were being imported, and by 1972 Japanese compacts and medium-size automobiles and other steel products were flooding into the West Coast ports. All of the imported automobiles were finding a ready market with the dissatisfied customers of General Motors, Ford, and Chrysler, and it was not long before Japanese automobiles dominated the small and medium car market. The era of "screw ya," which flourished during the Eisenhower, Kennedy, and Johnson administrations, was now proving to have been a massive customer relationship blunder by the automobile manufacturers and dealerships (see paragraph 7.39). It would prove to be a millstone around their necks for more than two decades. Even by 1992, the U.S. car manufacturers had not managed to convince at least 20 percent of the American public that "screw ya" was an era of the past, never to happen again; many, deeply scarred by the "screw ya" era, have shown little inclination to come back into the "buy American " fold.

10.39. The production, import, and export statistics for iron ore, pig iron, and steel during the Nixon administration are conclusive proof that America's dominance in iron commodities had been taken over by Europe, the Soviet Union, and Japan. Tables 10.1, 10.2, 10.3, and 10.4 also include the two years of the Ford administration, 1975 and 1976.

Table 10.1

Total Annual Production of Iron Ore in the United States, 1969–76, Compared to That
Produced by the Lake Superior District and the Mesabi Range (U.S. Geological Survey
and U.S. Bureau of Mines 1992)
(in thousand long tons)

Year	Total Tons	Lake Superior District Tons	Percentage of Total	Mesabi Iron Range Tons	Percentage of Total	Tons Accumulated
1969	88,328	68,730	78	55,275	63	2,723,741
1970	89,760	69,636	78	56,073	62	2,779,814
1971	80,762	64,034	79	51,283	63	2,831,097
1972	75,434	61,550	82	48,998	65	2,880,095
1973	87,669	72,414	83	60,021	68	2,940,116
1974	78,866	70,723	90	58,484	74	2,998,600
1975	78,866	66,735	85	51,177	65	3,047,777
1976	79,993	67,413	84	49,764	62	3,099,541

10.40. Table 10.1 shows the Mesabi Range reached an accumulated total production of 3 billion long tons of iron ore in 1975. The first billion was attained in forty-six years, the second in eighteen years, and the third in twenty years. The leveling off of production from the Mesabi Range, which was noticed first in the statistics during the Kennedy administration, had now become an established fact; production from 1969 to 1976 ranged from 50 to 60 million long tons, indicating that quite likely 60 million was close to the top annual production that could now be attained on the Mesabi Range. The total annual production ranged from 75 to 90 million long tons, indicating that close to 90 million was the top annual production of iron ore attainable in the United States; demand above 90 million would have to be attained through imports.

Table 10.2

Iron Ore Imported for Consumption into the United States by Continents, 1969–76
(U.S. Geological Survey and U.S. Bureau of Mines 1992)
(in thousand long tons)
(in thousand dollars)

Year	North America Long Tons	Value	South America Long Tons	Value	Europe And All Other Long Tons	Value
1969	18,978	219,347	13,936	147,154	7,818	35,677
1970	23,934	297,203	17,927	152,934	3,030	29,381
1971	20,342	267,424	16,616	150,318	3,166	32,902
1972	18,168	247,757	13,667	129,866	3,926	38,311
1973	21,628	311,893	18,037	185,681	3,631	35,914
1974	19,702	341,577	24,056	304,656	4,271	50,065
1975	19,111	420,116	23,145	371,050	4,487	69,330
1976	24,962	625,588	15,713	286,627	3,715	68,133

Table 10.3
Production, Imports, and Exports of Pig Iron and Steel in the United States, 1969–76
(U.S. Geological Survey and U.S. Bureau of Mines 1992)
(in thousand short tons)

Year	Pig Iron Production	Pig Iron Imports	Pig Iron Exports	Steel Production	Steel Imports	Steel Exports
1969	95,003	405	44	141,262	14,528	5,788
1970	92,213	249	310	131,514	13,861	7,657
1971	81,382	306	34	120,443	18,744	3,526
1972	88,876	637	15	133,241	18,158	3,546
1973	101,317	446	15	150,799	15,608	4,962
1974	95,477	342	101	145,720	16,746	6,992
1975	79,721	478	60	116,642	12,488	3,975
1976	86,848	415	58	128,000	15,038	3,671

Table 10.4
World Production of Steel with the Production and Percentage Produced by the United States, USSR Separate from Europe, Europe, Japan, and Other Nations, 1969–76 (U.S. Geological Survey and U.S. Bureau of Mines 1992)
(in million short tons)

Year	World Tons	U.S. Tons	U.S. %	USSR Tons	USSR %	Europe Tons	Europe %	Japan Tons	Japan %	Other %
1969	632.5	141.3	22	121.6	19	212.1	34	90.6	14	11
1970	655.2	131.5	20	127.7	19	221.2	34	102.9	16	11
1971	639.9	120.4	19	133.0	21	212.6	33	97.6	15	12
1972	692.7	133.2	19	138.4	20	230.8	33	106.8	15	13
1973	766.8	150.8	20	144.8	19	247.7	32	131.5	17	12
1974	780.4	145.7	19	150.1	19	257.7	33	129.1	17	12
1975	712.6	116.6	16	155.7	22	226.0	32	112.8	16	14
1976	742.1	128.0	17	159.6	22	237.6	32	118.4	16	13

10.41. Table 10.2 shows that the iron ore imports that started to increase in 1955, when the Mesabi Range direct shipping ore was depleted, continued during the Nixon administration. The total value of the iron ore imported into the United States to meet demand during the eight-year period was about $5 billion.

10.42. Table 10.3 shows that the steel imports into the United States that gained a foothold in 1959 during the steel strike were continuing to increase during the Nixon administration. They ranged from a low of 12 million in 1975 to a high of 19 million in 1971. Table 10.4 shows where these steel imports were coming from. Japan's share of world production in 1976 was 16 percent, just 1 percent below that of the United States. In twenty-eight years Japanese production of steel had increased from 1.9 million short tons to 118.4 million tons. With this increase in steel tonnage in less than three decades, it is easy to understand how Japanese imported automobiles became virtually a deluge in

Table 10.5

The *Iron Age* Annual Average of Finished Steel Composite Prices, 1969–76 (*Iron Age* 1974)

(in cents per pound)

Year	Cents Per Pound	Year	Cents Per Pound	Year	Cents Per Pound
1969	7.091	1972	8.999	1975	13.102
1970	7.650	1973	9.380	1976	14.213
1971	8.429	1974	11.141		

the early seventies on the West Coast. Table 10.4 also shows another startling statistic. In 1975 the Soviet Union passed the United States in production of steel; in percentage of world production, the United States was now ranked third, below Europe and the Soviet Union. It was obvious now why the Soviet Union was willing to start the Strategic Arms Limitation Talks (SALT) with the Nixon administration; they had as much as or more Yankee ingenuity and Yankee know-how than the United States. They were willing to reduce their nuclear arsenal because they had more strength in conventional weapons than the United States and, with steel production now greater than the United States, could replace the conventional weaponry at a faster pace. They would be sitting at the negotiation table in the dominant industrial position, which heretofore had been the position of the United States. They could negotiate from strength rather than from weakness, and the time that has been required on the SALT talks has reflected this dominant position of strength by the Soviet Union.

10.43. The *Iron Age* annual average of finished steel composite prices is shown in table 10.5. After President Nixon took office, the annual price of steel per pound started inching upward at a rate of about .5 cent a year until 1973. After 1973, when the wage-price controls were removed, prices exploded upward. Between 1973 and 1974 prices increased 1.761 cents per pound, between 1974 and 1975 they increased 1.961 cents per pound, and between 1975 and 1976 they increased 1.091 cents per pound. Although it was not realized at the time, these price increases had a far more devastating affect on the nation's economy than the petroleum price increases because of the oil embargo. They affected every mineral commodity and product produced in the nation.

10.44. President Nixon was unable to reduce the gross federal debt in any of the six years that he was president. The greatest annual increases in the debt occurred in 1975 and 1976, after Gerald Ford became president. Table 10.6 shows the gross federal debt in six years of the Nixon

Table 10.6
Gross Federal Debt at the End of Year, 1969–76 (Bureau of Public Debt 1974)
(in millions of dollars)

Year	Gross Federal Debt	Year	Gross Federal Debt	Year	Gross Federal Debt
1969	365,769	1972	435,936	1975	541,925
1970	380,921	1973	466,291	1976	628,970
1971	408,176	1974	483,893		

administration and the two years of the Ford administration. During the Nixon administration the gross national debt increased from $366 billion to $484 billion, a total of $118 billion in six years. During the Ford administration it increased from $484 billion to $629 billion, a total of $145 billion in two years. President Nixon's legacy of wage-price controls and the inflationary annual increases in the price of steel were the primary cause of the huge increase in the debt from 1974 to 1976. The increase was a carryover from the Nixon administration, and there was absolutely nothing that President Ford could have done about it.

10.45. The annual population estimates during the Nixon and Ford administrations are shown in table 10.7. The population grew on an average about 2.5 million annually.

10.46. However, by 1974 President Nixon was not interested in population estimates, the gross federal debt, steel prices, or any statistics on iron ore, pig iron, or steel. The Watergate fiasco was about to take its toll. Impeachment proceedings against him started in July 1974, and he resigned August 9, 1974. He was succeeded by Vice Pres. Gerald Ford, whom Nixon had appointed after Spiro Agnew was forced to resign. The downfall of Nixon's presidency was a tragic end for both him and the nation.

Table 10.7
Annual Population Estimates in the United States, 1969–76 (Bureau of the Census 1994)
(in thousands)

Year	Total Resident Population	Year	Total Resident Population	Year	Total Resident Population
1969	201,385	1972	209,284	1975	215,465
1970	203,810	1973	211,357	1976	217,563
1971	206,827	1974	213,342		

11

The Next Two Years (1974–76): Ford

11.1. Gerald R. Ford had been appointed vice president in October 1973, following the forced resignation of Spiro Agnew. After President Nixon resigned, Ford took the oath of office for the presidency on August 9, 1974 (DeGregorio 1993). He appointed Nelson A. Rockefeller vice president. Both Ford and Rockefeller were appointed under the provision of the Twenty-fifth Amendment. In September 1974 President Ford granted a "a full, free, and absolute pardon" to former president Nixon for all possible offenses against the United States (DeGregorio 1993). A large part of the public were still obsessed with Watergate. The televised Watergate hearings and in sequence the impeachment proceedings of President Nixon were highly rated television programs, and the pardon terminated the whole affair at the point of climax, leaving everybody to wonder what would have been the outcome if the impeachment process had been allowed to run its course. A barrage of criticism was hurled against President Ford, but he remained absolutely firm in his belief that he had done the right thing. There is little doubt but what the pardon of Nixon was one of the negative factors for President Ford in the 1976 election campaign.

11.2. President Ford's cabinet appointments were as follows: Secretary of State Henry Kissinger, Secretary of the Treasury William E. Simon, Secretary of Defense James R. Schlesinger, later replaced by Donald H. Rumsfeld, Attorney General William B. Saxbe, later replaced by Edward H. Levi, Secretary of the Interior Rogers C. B. Morton, later replaced by Stanley K. Hathaway, later replaced by Thomas S. Kleppe, Secretary of Agriculture Earl L. Butz, later replaced by John A. Knebel, Secretary of Commerce Frederick B. Dent, later replaced by Rogers C. B. Morton, later replaced by Elliot L. Richardson, Secretary of Labor Peter J. Brennan, later replaced by John T. Dunlop, later replaced by W. J. Usery Jr., Secretary of Health, Education, and Welfare Caspar W.

Weinberger, later replaced by F. David Matthews, Secretary of Housing and Urban Development James T. Lynn, later replaced by Carla A. Hills, and Secretary of Transportation Claude S. Brinegar, later replaced by William T. Coleman.

11.3. All of the inital appointees were holdovers from the Nixon administration; however, only two, Messrs. Kissinger and Simon, were still in the cabinet at the end of 1976. It soon became apparent to his cabinet officers and Congress that President Ford had definite and strong ideas on how the nation should be run. The cabinet officers who did not fit in were replaced, those in poor health resigned, and Congress discovered that passing a bill through Ford was not an easy task. He vetoed forty-eight bills during the two years of his term, saying most would be too costly (World Almanac 1993).

11.4. When Ford became president a large part of the public had shrugged off the oil embargo as an event that could not happen again, and they were again in hot pursuit of the "abundant life." They had good reason to view the oil embargo in this manner. On November 7, 1973, then-president Nixon, in response to the embargo, established Project Independence, with the goal of energy independence for the United States by 1980; this goal was to be reached through conservation and development of alternative energy sources (Halberstan 1986, Kissinger 1982). Although the proclamation lulled the Congress and public into thinking that by 1980 the United States could tell OPEC that they could "take their oil and shove it," that was certainly not the opinion of John Sawhill, administrator of the the FEA, which was formerly the Office of Oil and Gas under the secretary of the interior.

11.5. In November 1974, after Ford had been sworn in as president, Mr. Sawhill's agency published the *Project Independence Report* (Federal Energy Administration 1974). The report involved over five hundred professionals, public hearings in ten cities throughout the United States, and advisory committees of acknowledged experts in their energy specialties. According to the FEA, the report was the most comprehensive energy analysis ever undertaken, and that opinion would have to be shared by anyone who has read and studied the report. Although the report is titled *Project Independence Report*, it states frankly that the report is an evaluation of the nation's energy problem and does not recommend specific policy actions. In regard to President Nixon's promise of energy independence, the FEA wrote the following bureaucratic gibberish:

In response to the embargo and the realization of the potential costs of being increasingly dependent on foreign sources of energy, the President established the goal of energy independence for the United states by 1980. There was considerable divergence of opinion, however, regarding the meaning of energy independence, and there are likely to be even greater differences as to how the goal should be achieved once it is ultimately defined. To some, energy independence is a situation in which the United States receives no energy through imports, i.e., it produces all of its energy domestically. To others, independence is a situation in which the United States does import to meet some of its energy requirements, but only up to a point of "acceptable" political and economic vulnerability. The definition of independence and the criteria for evaluating it are central to the choice of a U.S. energy strategy. (Federal Energy Administration 1974)

11.6. For the FEA to assemble the professional talent that it did to prepare the *Project Independence Report* and then make a statement like the above was absurd. Since about 1948 the United States has had to depend on imports of petroleum to augment the domestic supply to maintain the "abundant life" program that the public had on full throttle forward for at least two decades. There is no way that any administration, including President Nixon's, could put the brake on this program without being driven out of office before the seats of their chairs were warm. Importation of petroleum to maintain the "abundant life" program was an absolute political necessity, and as time stretched into additional decades, the barrels of imported petroleum would have to increase.

11.7. One can only wonder why Mr. Sawhill did not ask President Nixon for his definition of "independence" before he had his agency prepare the report. The FEA offices were on Independence Avenue, and a ten-minute walk would have brought Mr. Sawhill to the White House. Certainly H. R. Haldeman would have been willing to allow Mr. Sawhill to see President Nixon on such a critical matter. If he did not want to walk or go through the onerous task of asking Mr. Haldeman for permission to enter the Oval Office, a telephone call could have been a simple alternative. There is absolutely no doubt that the answer he would have received would have been as follows: "Keep the 'abundant life' program on full throttle forward." That answer would have given him all the definition of "independence" that he needed. In regard to the recommendations of policy actions, Mr. Sawhill writes more nonsensical drivel in the preface as follows:

> This report does not recommend specific policy actions. FEA recognized that such an approach would not take account of the difficult tradeoffs the country faces in choosing an energy future. If we only proposed one course of action before allowing public debate on these choices, we would merely replay the endless debate without action which has characterized U.S. energy policy for the past several years. The problem in the past seems to have been that the public, the Congress, and the Executive Branch have focused arguments on particular measures, instead of a total energy policy. To correct this situation, we have prepared this report which we believe presents a comprehensive framework within which to evaluate individual issues.

11.8. It is obvious from the above quotes that Mr. Sawhill never had any intention of developing an energy policy when President Nixon assigned his agency the task of developing a program for attaining energy independence by 1980. Insofar as he was concerned, it was an impossible task, but he was not about to tell President Nixon that. Mr. Sawhill developed a remarkable strategy. He would bring in an overload of top advisers and other professionals, hold public hearings in some major cities, throw in a quantity of numbers, pad the report with a multitude of pages, and above all make certain that the FEA had protected themselves adequately by writing the type of bureaucratic gibberish and nonsensical drivel cited above. The amazing aspect of the whole affair is that the stratagem worked perfectly. The report was completed and insofar as can be determined accepted without objection by the Ford administration and Congress.

11.9. President Ford was well aware that Nixon had promised energy independence by 1980 and now had the FEA report on Project Independence, which by its own admission did not recommend specific policy actions but was "a comprehensive framework within which to evaluate individual issues." President Ford had less than two years before he had to make a run for election, and certainly it would be politically wise to make a move on energy that would grab public attention. Apparently he did not think that defining "energy independence" for the FEA would net him any political gain; therefore, it was now his turn to develop a strategy. The public and Congress needed to be lulled into thinking

172

that something was being done now about the nation's energy problems. It would be a safe move to reorganize the executive branch bureaus and agencies that were involved with atomic energy and petroleum.

11.10. Congress approved and he signed legislation that divided the AEC into two parts, regulatory and nonregulatory. The division with regulatory responsibilities was made an independent agency titled the Nuclear Regulatory Commission. The nonregulatory division of the AEC was combined with the FEA and hydrocarbon fuels and shale oil research functions of the Bureau of Mines; the combination was titled the Energy Research and Development Administration (ERDA). The reorganization received good publicity and served to convince Congress and the public that with the responsibility for energy under a single agency such an event as an oil embargo could not happen again. President Ford's stratagem, like that of Mr. Sawhill, worked perfectly. Insofar as can be determined, Project Independence was not given another thought by any of the four presidents who followed Ford in occupying the White House.

11.11. It was not difficult in 1974 to discover what petroleum was being used for. Published statistics by the Bureau of Mines showed that gasoline consumption far outranked use of every other petroleum product in the United States. Gasoline was nearly 40 percent of the product demand; distillate fuel oil consumption ranked second and accounted for about 20 percent of domestic demand for petroleum products (Staff of the Bureau of Mines 1975). Distillate fuel oil includes light home heating fuel oil and diesel fuel. To curb the high use of gasoline President Ford decided to increase the price of gasoline by placing a duty on petroleum imports. He proposed to raise the tariff on imported oils in one-dollar-per-barrel increments up to a total of three dollars per barrel. In April 13, 1975, the U.S. Court of Appeals ruled that he had exceeded his authority by imposing direct import control mechanisms (Staff of the Bureau of Mines 1975). Nevertheless, he did manage later to impose a duty on imported oil and signed into law a bill to gradually decontrol domestic oil prices. Decontrol of the domestic prices was expected to reduce the rate of domestic production decline.

11.12. The administration was still uncertain as to whether or not OPEC might attempt another oil embargo during the winter of 1975–76. The National Petroleum Council was requested to study the implementation of an emergency petroleum storage system. They recommended a 500-million-barrel petroleum storage system in Gulf Coast salt dome

Table 11.1

Prices of Bituminous Coal, Steel, and Petroleum, 1973–76 (U.S. Geological Survey and Bureau of Mines 1992, *Iron Age*)

Year	Bituminous Coal Average Value per Short Ton	Average of Finished Steel, Composite Price per Short Ton		Petroleum per 42-Gallon Barrel		
				Domestic	Imported	Composite
1973	$ 8.52	$187.60	May	$3.82	3.92	3.85
			Nov.	5.00	6.49	5.45
			Dec.	5.95	8.22	6.54
1974	15.75	222.82		7.18	12.52	9.07
1975	19.23	262.04		8.39	13.93	10.38
1976	19.43	284.26	Jan.	9.14	13.27	10.76
			Feb.	8.67	13.26	10.54
			Mar.	8.48	13.51	10.44
			Apr.	8.66	13.39	10.63
			May	8.56	13.20	10.53
			June	8.59	13.47	10.88

caverns to provide a three-to-six-month supply (Staff of the Bureau of Mines 1975).

11.13. The increase in the price of crude petroleum by OPEC in December 1973 was having a definite effect on all nations dependent upon Middle East imports. Airlines, maritime fleets, the armed forces, industry, and the populace in many nations throughout the world were engaged in conservation programs to reduce their consumption of petroleum. The price increases in petroleum were having a definite effect in the United States, but certainly the increases in the price of petroleum were not the only culprits in the inflationary upward spiral of prices. Table 11.1 shows the prices of three major mineral commodities during the period from 1973 to 1976.

11.14. *The tabulation under petroleum shows the refiner's acquisition cost per barrel for domestic, imported, and a composite of both as was maintained by the FEA.* In December 1973 the price of Middle East petroleum rose to $11.65 per forty-two-gallon barrel, but when the imported prices are averaged and combined with the domestic prices over a monthly period, the prices paid by the refiners per barrel of petroleum in the United States were considerably less than those paid by most other importers that had no domestic production. Prices for a barrel of imported petroleum in 1974 and 1975 rose steadily, but in 1976 they leveled off from a low of $13.20 to a high of $13.51. The price of the domestically produced petroleum moved upward in 1974 and 1975 by increments

174

granted by the Cost of Living Council (CLC) in an effort to stimulate additional production of domestic crude petroleum.

11.15. The rise in the price of petroleum is easily understood, because that was the price that OPEC was setting and the CLC was continuously granting increases to domestic producers. Not so easy to understand is the upward surge in prices in steel and coal. Bituminous coal almost doubled in price between 1973 and 1974, and steel prices increased $35.00 per short ton between 1973 and 1974, $39.00 between 1974 and 1975, and $22.00 between 1975 and 1976. Increases in the price of petroleum should not have had this much effect upon the prices of these two mineral commodities, especially coal; thus the three-year surge in prices must have been caused by the price controls that were imposed by the Nixon administration in 1971 and voided in 1973.

11.16. It is obvious from the data in table 11.1 that the inflation that was occurring in the United States during the Ford administration was not solely because of the increases in the price in petroleum. The increases in the prices of bituminous coal and steel were strong contributory causes, and, in fact, it is quite likely that the increases in the prices of these commodities had a greater inflationary effect than the increasing prices of petroleum. The data in table 11.1 present a strong argument for not focusing on the production and imports of a single mineral commodity. While attention is focused on one, situations may be developing in another that may cost the nation billions of dollars.

11.17. In August 1971 President Nixon had terminated the convertibility of U.S. dollars into gold in official transactions. President Ford, following through on the demonetization of gold, ended all regulations on private ownership of gold, which had been in force for forty years, on December 31, 1974. In the United States the price of gold had been held at $35.00 per troy ounce until 1967; this price when compared to constant 1973 dollars, as shown in table 11.2, presents an excellent time-price relationship to show the effect of inflation for the period from 1954 to 1974.

11.18. The Johnson, Nixon, and Ford administrations were somewhat similiar in that in each there was a domestic or foreign issue that plagued the president constantly. President Kennedy, because of his personal popularity, managed to escape much of the harsh criticism that the public leveled against the other three, yet in his short time as president he was the cause of much of the grief suffered by the following administrations: he was the first to force the steel industry to forgo price increases,

175

Table 11.2
Time-Price Relationship for Gold (West 1975)

	Average Annual Price, Dollars per Troy Ounce	
Year	Actual Prices	Constant 1973 Dollars
1954	35.00	60.24
1955	35.00	59.42
1956	35.00	57.47
1957	35.00	55.38
1958	35.00	54.01
1959	35.00	53.11
1960	35.00	52.32
1961	35.00	51.62
1962	35.00	51.02
1963	35.00	50.36
1964	35.00	49.65
1965	35.00	48.75
1966	35.00	47.43
1967	35.00	45.93
1968	39.26	49.51
1969	41.51	49.95
1970	36.41	41.56
1971	41.25	45.03
1972	58.60	61.88
1973	97.81	97.81
1974	159.74	144.82

which started the industrial dominance of the United States on a downhill course, which the following administrations were unable to check; he started the Vietnam War, which in the end defeated President Johnson and preoccupied President Nixon for a full term; and Kennedy's relationship with the Soviet Union brought us as close to nuclear war as possible without actually beginning such a war. President Johnson managed to pass social, educational, and environmental legislation, but the Vietnam War he inherited from President Kennedy destroyed him. President Nixon's preoccupation with the Vietnam War and, in the second term, the Watergate fiasco caused him to neglect pressing domestic issues, and he signed into law environmental legislation that resulted in a litigious quagmire and an increasing dependence on imported petroleum because of the replacement of coal with petroleum. President Ford inherited all of Nixon's unsolved domestic and foreign problems, plus an upward inflation surge that was threatening to go completely out of control. In addition, Nixon's Watergate fiasco instilled a public distrust of government that was like a millstone around President Ford's neck.

11.19. President Ford was well aware of the danger of inflation to the nation, and in 1974 he launched a campaign to "whip inflation now," but a recession forced him to abandon the program. He had too short a time in the White House to develop programs to solve the problems that he inherited from Nixon. Although the Watergate fiasco and Ford's pardon of Nixon were negative factors in his campaign for the presidency in 1976, it is possible that the import duty he imposed on foreign oil, which increased the price of gasoline, was an even more negative factor. The American public has for twenty years taken a dim view of any action that increases the cost of driving their automobiles: that is a serious impediment in their pursuit of the "abundant life." Driving an automobile is the only repetitive activity that does not give an American carpal tunnel syndrome, and he tends to become highly wrathful of a president who enacts any rule, regulation, or law that restricts or curtails use of his beloved automobile.

11.20. However, whatever the negative factors in President Ford's campaign, they must have been regarded as really serious by the public, because he lost to a Democratic Party dark horse candidate, Jimmy Carter. Mr. Carter was a candidate only a relatively small number of people in the United States knew anything about before he received the Democratic nomination.

Summary of the Era from 1946 to 1976

11.21. The period from 1946 to 1976 was the war years. Immediately after the end of World War II the Soviet Union became an enemy rather than an ally; it moved into a mode of continuous confrontation against the United States. Presidents Truman, Eisenhower, and Kennedy were constantly reacting to warlike actions by the Soviets. This constant confrontation led directly to the Korean War and the Vietnam War and close to nuclear war. Also, the United States entered into a "space race" with the Soviets, which culminated in moon landings under the Apollo Program at a tremendous cost in dollars. Social and environmental legislation was enacted in the sixties and early seventies without regard to cost or effect, steel was placed under various systems of price controls in the same period, and the nation blundered into a blackmail attempt by the Middle East petroleum-exporting nations in the seventies.

11.22. With the nation constantly in a defense posture and the public implementing on their own the quest for the "abundant life" as promised by Franklin Roosevelt, there was as great or even a greater demand for steel than during World War II. Figures 11.1 and 11.2 are

177

continuations of the graphs in chapters 3 and 5. Figure 11.1 shows the effect on iron ore production of the the steel strike in 1958 and the leveling-off in production after 1960, and figure 11.2 shows the gradually-increasing import tonnage of raw steel (series 2) starting in 1958. It is quite likely that one-half or more of this imported raw steel was dumped and sold under cost.

11.23. To cover the leveling-off of iron ore production, increasing tonnages of iron ore had to be imported. The total value of this imported iron ore from all sources is shown in figure 11.3. In 1976 the total annual value was $980.3 million. Comparing this value with the value of imported iron ore in 1950, it is easy to see the tremendous change that occurred in the production of steel from 1950 to 1976. The era of production of iron ore on demand that had been the characteristic of the Mesabi Range ended in 1958.

11.24. The most revealing graph in regard to America's industrial supremacy is figure 11.4, showing the annual percentage of steel produced in the world by country. Series 1 is the total produced by the United States, series 2 the USSR separate from Europe; series 3, Europe; series 4, Japan; and series 5, all other nations. After World War II, the United States was the greatest superpower the world had ever seen. In 1948 it was producing 52 percent of all the steel produced in the world. It could not, under any circumstances, hold this high percentage of world production as the Marshall Plan started rebuilding the war-ravaged countries of Europe. Rebuilding Europe's ferrous industries with Marshall Plan–funded dollars was a high priority, and added impetus was given to this restoration by the availability of cheap energy from the Middle East oil fields. However, the United States, with the strongest steel companies in the world, should have been able to maintain a 20 to 25 percent share of world production. But the price control programs, imported steel dumping, and inflation during the Kennedy, Johnson, and Nixon administrations so weakened the companies over a ten-year period that the world percentage share dropped below 20 percent. It required only ten years for the three above administrations to kill off an industrial supremacy that had lasted for seventy years.

11.25. As expected, Europe, separate from the USSR, surpassed the United States in tonnage production in 1957. The downward plunge of America's percentage share continued until 1961–62, when President Kennedy placed 18,000 combat personnel in the Vietnam war theater. The enormous demand for steel for the Vietnam War effort and the public's pursuit of the "abundant life" leveled off the decreasing percentage share until 1966, when again it resumed a downward plunge. The USSR surpassed the United States in annual production of steel in 1974 and it has retained this position of supremacy into the nineties. In 1975 Japan managed to equal the percentage produced by the United States, and a few years later Japan held the second highest single-nation percentage production in the world.

11.26. Figures 11.5 and 11.6 show the population and federal debt growth during the 1946–76 period. With the steady rise in resident population shown in figure 11.5 from below 150 million to over 200 million people, it is obvious from figure 11.4 that the domestic steel companies were not the companies that were filling the demand for steel to this increasing population. It was the European nations that had received the Marshall Plan–funded dollars and Japan.

11.27. Figure 11.6 shows that up to 1960 the federal debt was under reasonable control. It dropped between 1946 and 1952 and then increased on a gentle slope from 1953 to 1960. However, as soon as the Kennedy administration got the high-cost Apollo moon-landing program in full gear and the Johnson administration managed to get their social and environmental legislation through Congress without provisions to pay for it, the debt started rising at an increasing rate. The Nixon administration made no effort whatsoever to find means to pay for the Johnson administration social programs but continued to borrow funds to cover the costs. With the passage of more restrictive environmental legislation, the end result was the explosion upward of the debt between 1968 and 1976.

FIGURE 11.1--ANNUAL PRODUCTION OF IRON ORE 1946-1976 COMPARED TO THAT PRODUCED BY THE MESABI IRON RANGE

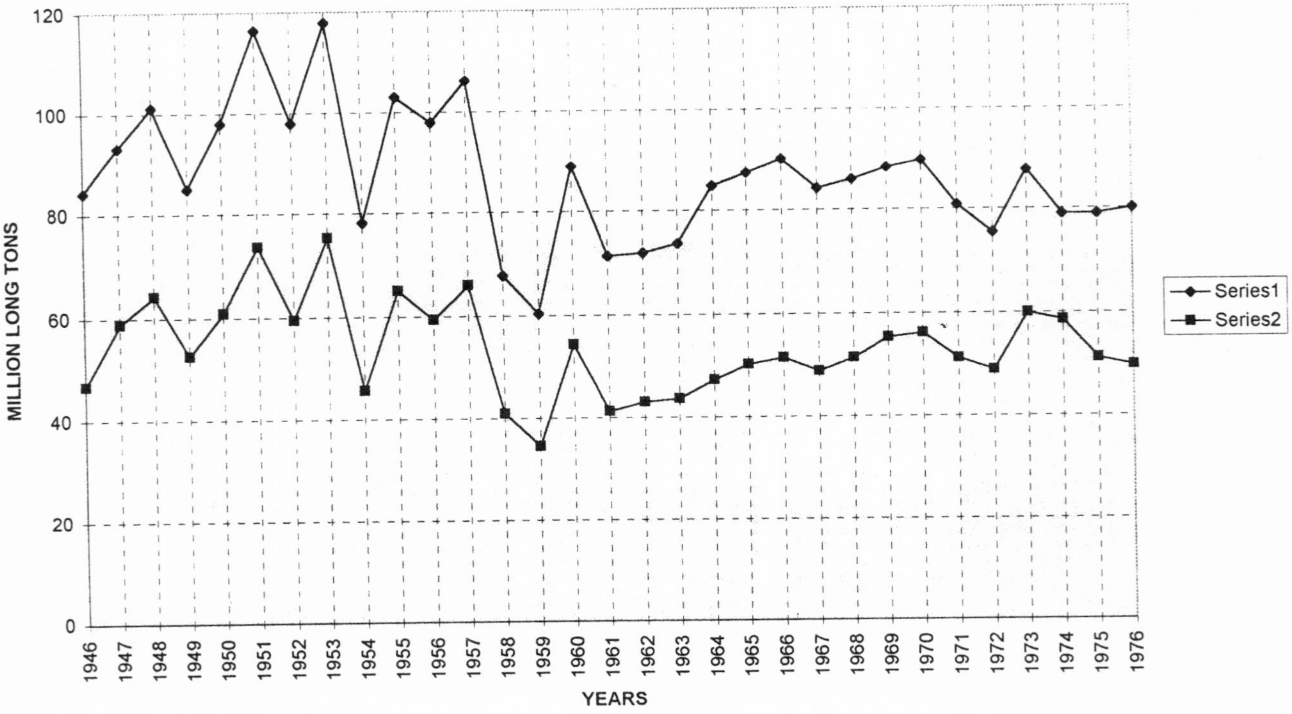

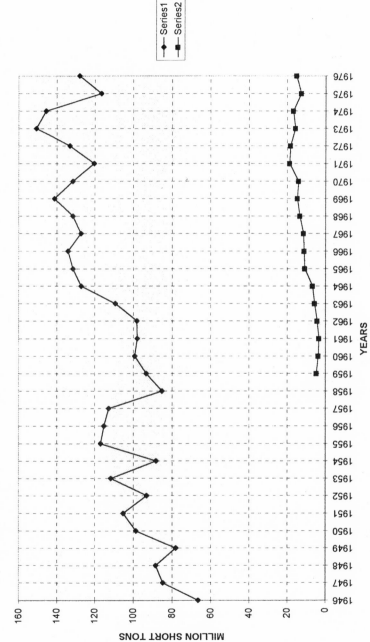

FIGURE 11.2--ANNUAL PRODUCTION OF STEEL 1946-1976 AND RAW STEEL IMPORTS 1958-1976

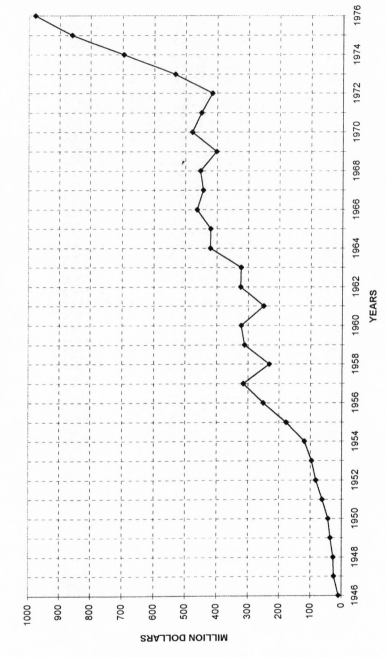

FIGURE 11.3--ANNUAL VALUE OF IRON ORE IMPORTED FOR CONSUMPTION INTO THE UNITED STATES 1946-1976

FIGURE 11.4--ANNUAL PERCENTAGE OF STEEL PRODUCED IN THE WORLD BY THE U.S., U.S.S.R. SEPARATE FROM EUROPE, EUROPE, JAPAN, AND OTHER 1948-1976

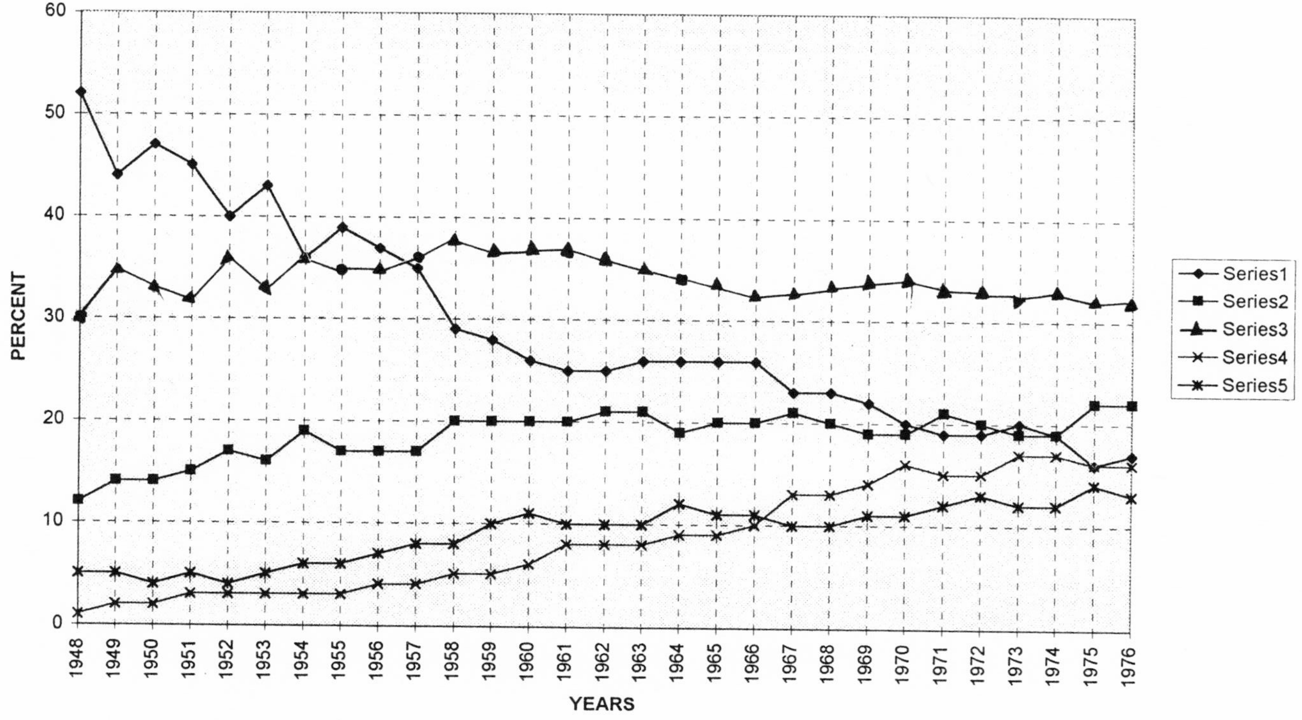

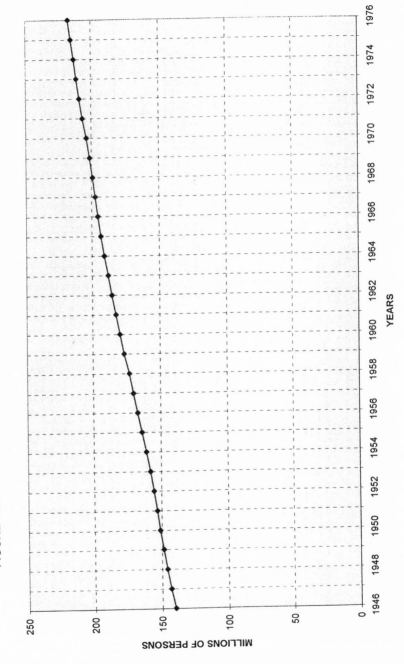

FIGURE 11.5--ANNUAL RESIDENT POPULATION ESTIMATES IN THE U.S. 1946-1976

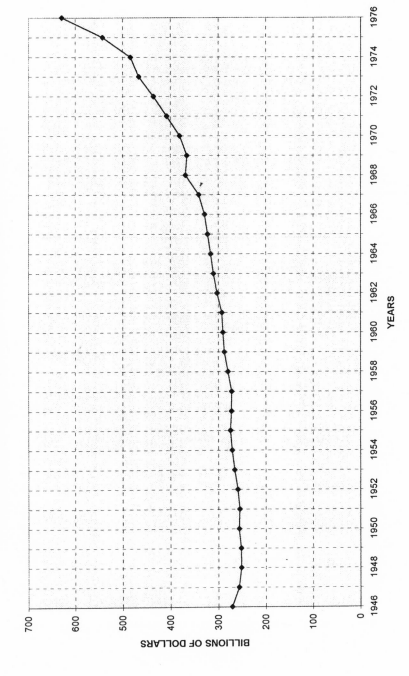

FIGURE 11.6--GROSS FEDERAL DEBT AT THE END OF YEAR 1946-1976

12

The Next Four Years (1976–80): Carter

12.1. Jimmy Carter graduated from the U.S. Naval Academy at Annapolis, Maryland, in 1946 and served in the navy from 1946 to 1953. He resigned from the navy to manage the farm and peanut brokerage business left by the death of his father and was highly successful in this business. Carter served in the Georgia State Senate for two terms, from 1963 to 1967, and he was elected governor of Georgia for one term (1971–75). In 1976 he demonstrated remarkable political ability in winning the Democratic Party nomination in several key states. He continued the political strategy he had used in the hustings into the Democratic convention and won his party's nomination for president on the first ballot. He chose Walter Mondale, a liberal senator from Minnesota, as his vice-presidential running mate. The ticket had excellent balance insofar as conservatism and liberalism were concerned. Hubert Humphrey had been the mentor of Senator Mondale, and the supporters of Hubert Humphrey in the Democratic Party would vote for Walter Mondale regardless of who was the nominee for president.

12.2. President Carter appointed the following cabinet members: Secretary of State Cyrus R. Vance, later replaced by Edmund S. Muskie, Secretary of the Treasury Michael Blumenthal, later replaced by G. William Miller, Secretary of Defense Harold Brown, Attorney General Griffin B. Bell, later replaced by Benjamin R. Civiletti, Secretary of the Interior Cecil D. Andrus, Secretary of Agriculture Robert S. Bergland, Secretary of Commerce Juanita M. Kreps, later replaced by Philip M. Klutznick, Secretary of Labor F. Ray Marshall, Secretary of Health and Human Services Joseph A. Califano Jr., later replaced by Patricia R. Harris, Secretary of Housing and Urban Development Patricia R. Harris, later replaced by Moon Landrieu, Secretary of Transportation Brock Adams, later replaced by Neil E. Goldschmidt, and Secretary of Education Shirley M. Hufstedler (DeGregorio 1993).

12.3. The public, in general, did not appear to ever grasp the idealistic approach that President Carter was attempting to bring to the presidency. However, the failure in understanding was primarily the fault of President Carter and his White House Staff. After Nixon's Watergate fiasco a reasonable amount of idealism was desirable in government, but in the real world of national and international politics idealism cannot be carried to an extreme, which, in effect, was what happened with the administration's foreign policy. The fundamental basis of Mr. Carter's foreign policy was human rights for all individuals throughout the world. This was certainly a desirable goal, but it was an impossibility. The Carter administration never did impose this policy evenly. Foreign aid to some nations was suspended, whereas others received only public denunciations in press releases or conferences. Denouncing a nation that has a history of violating human rights has about the same effect as lashing a tiger with a feather: they both continue doing what they were doing at an ever faster rate.

12.4. The public cannot be deceived by such maneuvers no matter how skillfully they are done, and, in fact, President Carter's administration was not at all skillful in attempting to impose this policy on sovereign nations. Actually, President Carter's human rights policy would have been much more successful when the United States was without doubt the dominant industrial nation in the world and immediately after the second atomic bomb had been delivered to Japan. For some reason, nations seem to heed the admonitions of a dominant industrial nation that has just made a solid demonstration that they mean business.

12.5. President Carter followed the lead of the Nixon and Ford administrations and concentrated his attention on energy, a product of the hydrocarbon fuels and uranium. The neglect of the problems of the ferrous metals division of the minerals industry by the Kennedy, Johnson, Nixon, and Ford administrations had resulted in deterioration to the point that the original status or ranking of the United States could never be reclaimed. The United States was no longer the dominant industrial nation in the world; Western Europe and the Soviet Union were leading in the annual production of steel, and Japan was threatening to surpass the United States in steel production before the end of President Carter's term. Inflation was shrinking the value of the dollar, the national debt was increasing, the balance of trade in dollars with Japan was increasing annually in Japan's favor, and a national energy policy had not been developed.

12.6. Despite these problems, President Carter's first act after becoming president was the pardon of 10,000 draft evaders of the Vietnam War era (DeGregorio 1993), which indicated that he was obsessed with the moral aspects of the Vietnam War. The pardon may have endeared him to the draft evaders and their families, but it certainly did not have the approval of a much larger number of war veterans. President Carter had strong guilt feelings about the Vietnam War, and he apparently thought that a majority of the public shared these same feelings. They did not, and although he did not realize it in 1977, this Vietnam War attitude and his pardon of the draft evaders would be negative factors in the 1980 election campaign, which at that time was four years away.

12.7. In 1977 President Carter signed legislation deregulating cargo airlines, and he also decided to do something about energy. A quick look into the actions of two previous administrations was all he needed for development of an energy policy. Mr. Nixon created the FEA by separating the Office of Oil and Gas from the Department of the Interior and then blandly ordered them to develop a program for energy independence by 1980. Mr. Sawhill, administrator of the FEA, had prepared a report on President Nixon's Project Independence but at the same time said he could not develop energy independence because he did not have a definition of independence. President Ford had reorganized the executive branch by melding the FEA, hydrocarbon fuels, and shale oil responsibilities of the Bureau of Mines and the AEC into a single agency, the ERDA. If the Congress and the public would accept this kind of posturing, then he, President Carter, would go the same route, but on a much larger scale.

12.8. In August 1977, he consolidated almost all of what he considered the major federal energy functions into one cabinet-level department. The consolidation included the ERDA, the Federal Power Commission (FPC), the Alaska, Bonneville, Southeastern, and Southwestern Power Administrations, the power-marketing functions of the Bureau of Reclamation, and certain functions of the Interstate Commerce Commission and the Departments of Commerce, Housing and Urban Development, Interior, and the Navy. The amalgam was labeled the Department of Energy. DOE was assigned the mission of providing the framework for a comprehensive and balanced national energy plan through the coordination and administration of the energy functions of the federal government. The department was responsible for the research, development, and demonstration of energy technology; the marketing of federal power; energy conservation, the nuclear weapons program; regulation of energy production and use; and a central energy data collection and analysis program (Office of the Federal Register 1981–82). James E. Schlesinger, President Carter's assistant for energy affairs, was appointed the first cabinet-level secretary, but he was later replaced by Charles W. Duncan Jr.

12.9. ERDA had the responsibility for the hydrocarbon fuels, shale oil, uranium, and nuclear energy. Melding this administration with other government bureaus, agencies, administrations, and commissions responsible for some type of federal energy function into a single department was an insanity. However, it did have the effect of ending posturing about doing something about energy by government reorganization, because there was little left to reorganize; therefore, the next move had to be development of an energy policy. The FEA, when functioning under Presidents Nixon and Ford, had already developed "a comprehensive framework within which to evaluate individual issues" in the *Project Independence Report* (Federal Energy Administration 1974). Thus all that was left for DOE to do was develop an energy plan for the nation utilizing the comprehensive framework previously provided by the FEA. It never happened, and President Carter's failure to solve the energy problem would plague him for the remaining three years of his term.

12.10. President Carter considered himself a very knowledgeable individual on energy. He had studied nuclear physics while in the navy, and this scientific background enabled him to readily understand briefings and written material on the subject. He had, without question, become knowledgeable on energy, but the difficulty was, it was knowledge of energy as a product. It was not the knowledge needed for development of an energy policy. It is unknown if President Carter decided alone to combine all federal energy functions and make energy a cabinet-level department or had advisers who convinced him this was the action to take. However, whichever it was, it has to rank as the most ill-advised government reorganization action ever taken by an administration and approved by Congress. The action of elevating this hodgepodge of energy functions to a cabinet department titled Energy can only be described as absurd.

12.11. The cabinet departments are primarily functional, such as State, Treasury, Defense, Justice, Agriculture, Commerce, Interior, Labor, Transportation, Health and Human Services, Education, and Housing and Urban Development. Energy is not a function—it is an abstract relationship, a connection between cause and effect. It has many meanings, such as the capacity of producing motion, heat, raising electricity, and an atomic explosion; it can also be an expression of the calorie content of food. To place it in the proper perspective, energy is a product. It is the product of the sun, wind, and oceans; it is one of the many products produced from the mineral commodities petroleum: natural gas, coal, peat, shale oil, and uranium. Energy is also one of the many products that can be produced from wood and other agricultural commodities. In fact, it is possible that ethanol, a product of corn, may become one of the prime products for producing motion in automobiles in densely populated areas. The regulations to govern the distribution of the products of petroleum during and after the "Arab oil embargo" were incredibly stupid, but making Energy a cabinet-level department topped them by 100 percent. Unbeknownst to President Carter and the Congress, they had compounded the problems with energy, and they had actually placed the nation in the position wherein development of an energy policy and a strategic plan of action on energy was an impossibility.

12.12. Congressional haste in approving the installation of Energy at cabinet-level status was an action in sheer panic. It was done at the time to placate the public, and it also was a belated effort to correct a situation that had existed since 1775. The minerals industry, a basic industry, had never had cabinet status. Congress, functioning in haste and focusing on one mineral commodity only, namely petroleum, attempted to correct the situation by making one of the products of petroleum a cabinet-level department. By this action the president and Congress fractionated the responsibility for the minerals industry in the federal government and created a condition that makes development of a rational government materials policy a difficult, if not impossible, task. A policy statement on any mineral commodity cannot start with the product it produces. It must start at the base point of the mineral commodity from which the product is produced. Development of a rational energy policy separately from all other mineral commodities is an impossible task. It cannot be done, and most certainly it cannot be done by starting with the product rather than with the mineral commodity from which it is produced.

12.13. In 1977 President Carter proposed to Congress an energy program calling for price increases and higher taxes on various energy products, mandatory efficiency standards on appliances, and outright power for the president to force on certain industries conversion from oil and gas to coal use (DeGregorio 1993). Congress did not act on this program until 1978, but when they did, President Carter did not receive the power to force conversion, and the higher taxes were rejected. In fact, in 1978 the nation was in the same consumption patterns of petroleum mineral commodities that it had been in during the Nixon and Ford administrations; nothing was changed except Energy was a cabinet department. However, President Carter was successful in 1978 in obtaining deregulation of commercial airlines and natural gas prices.

12.14. In March 1979 the cooling system of the Pennsylvania Three Mile Island nuclear power plant failed to function. The breakdown was an environmental disaster comparable to the Santa Barbara oil well blowout. The effect was predictable. Nuclear plant construction was suspended until a better design and stricter safety standards were developed. This action again added to the nation's energy woes, because it removed from the energy equation an energy source that had been projected as one of the major systems for producing energy in the future.

12.15. The Democratic-controlled Congress had given President Carter very little of what he had asked for in energy legislation, except approval of Energy as a cabinet department. In 1979 his top advisers apparently convinced him that he had to take some kind of direct action on energy. Posturing, such as more government reorganization, was not going to placate the public. In July of 1979 he settled in at Camp David and started interviewing a steady stream of prominent and influential citizens, including members of Congress, governors, and representatives of special interests, over a period of about ten days (Hamilton 1982). Whatever Carter learned from this ten-day seminar is unknown, but if it was what he said in a nationally televised speech from the White House on July 15, 1979, it was a waste of time.

12.16. There is nothing wrong with obtaining input from U.S. citizens on their opinions of government, but what Mr. Carter needed in this case was basic information on the mineral industries. Since the Mesabi Iron Range came on line in 1890, the public's awareness of the value of mineral commodities in our industrial society had dwindled annually. By 1979 a huge percentage of the populace, including members of Congress and the executive and judicial branches of government, had little or no knowledge of the mineral industries; they were unaware that mineral commodities were the roots of our modern industrial civilization and the basic key to our standard of living. The awareness and knowledge of the populace and Congress on the mineral industries has been discussed in almost all of the preceding chapters of this book.

12.17. In the televised speech President Carter claimed that America was suffering from a malaise, a crisis of confidence in government. The people were losing faith in the government and also their ability to be shapers and rulers of democracy; therefore, a large percentage were not voting. The causes of this lack of confidence were events that had occurred in the past twenty years, including the Vietnam War, the assassinations of John and Robert Kennedy and Martin Luther King Jr., Nixon's Watergate fiasco, inflation, growing dependence on imported petroleum, and the current situation on energy. Carter cited what he termed six basic policy decisions, designated as Points 1–6, to solve the energy problem (Hamilton 1982). Most of the program died in Congress.

12.18. President Carter's guilt feelings on everything bad that had happened in the United States in the past twenty years apparently led him to assume that the major percentage of the public shared this guilt with him. This assumption led him to the conclusion that the populace was suffering from a malaise, a crisis of confidence, and they were losing faith in the government. Rediculous! The people were not losing faith in the government. They were losing faith in the two-party system and specifically in the system of choosing the party nominees. They were losing faith in the small number of people heading the parties, who in the end made the decision as to who was to be the party nominee. To state it more bluntly, they were losing faith in the system that had placed him, his White House staff, and his cabinet in the White House. At the time that President Carter gave his speech most of the American public had shrugged off the evil events of the past twenty years, just like they had the barbarous horrors of World War II and the Korean War. The vast majority of Americans, unlike Mr. Carter, did not carry guilt over events or occurrences that they considered beyond their control.

12.19. The malaise that President Carter was viewing in the American public was not a crisis of confidence; it was disgust. The people were disgusted with government. During the "oil embargo" at least 90 percent of the public had come to the conclusion that the oil companies were the sole and direct cause of the gasoline shortage. The shortage of gasoline during the Carter administration served to convince them that they were wrong in their original placement of blame. They were now discovering that it was not the oil companies that were to blame for the shortage; it was the U.S. government. They were disgusted that the federal government was doing nothing, they were totally fed up with six years of promises that were never delivered, and they wanted the government to get out of the way and let the oil companies deliver gasoline to the service stations just as they had been doing before the "oil embargo." It was as simple as that.

12.20. The gasoline shortage interfered with the average individuals' pursuit of the "abundant life," and they had come to the point where posturing by the government was no longer acceptable. They wanted gasoline in their automobile tank so that they could come and go as they pleased. Above all, they did not want higher prices and more taxes tacked onto each gallon of gasoline. They wanted to go back to the good old days, when they drove into a service station and said, "Fill 'er up," and without undue delay a gurgling sound could be heard above the traffic noise on the adjoining thoroughfare. Once that was achieved they would forgive and forget for the time being and no longer be disgusted with the government. However, for about 20 percent of the populace, getting gasoline without a hassle was not about to cure their loss of faith in the two-party system of selecting candidates.

12.21. Instead of asking for amendments or repeal of the environmental laws that were causing the industrial conversion from coal to oil, President Carter wanted presidential authority to reverse the trend. That such a reversal would in all probability place undue hardships upon an industrial company to meet the requirements of the clean air and clean water acts did not appear to concern him, but it did concern certain industrial firms targeted for the reversal, and without doubt they voiced their concerns to Congress in a heavy-handed manner. However, President Carter did succeed in forcing some industries and utilities back to using coal as an energy source. This is discussed further in appendix 8.

12.22. President Carter did not appear to understand that the causes of the difficulties he was experiencing could be traced back to 1952, with each administration from that time on contributing to the difficulty. President Carter was not alone in his failure to understand the difficulties he was experiencing; about 90 percent of the members of Congress had no idea at all of what was the matter.

12.23. A nation, no matter how rich, cannot ignore a basic industry for twenty-five years when almost every year of the twenty-five the statistics were virtually shouting that something was going wrong. The statistics on the production, imports, and exports of iron ore, pig iron, and steel

Table 12.1
Total Annual Production of Iron Ore in the United States, 1977–80, Compared to That Produced by the Lake Superior District and the Mesabi Range (U.S. Geological Survey and U.S. Bureau of Mines 1992)
(in thousand long tons)

Year	Total Tons	Lake Superior District		Mesabi Iron Range		
		Tons	Percentage of Total	Tons	Percentage of Total	Tons Accumulated
1977	55,750	43,952	79	30,943	56	3,130,484
1978	81,583	72,727	89	55,316	68	3,185,800
1979	85,716	77,151	90	59,320	69	3,245,120
1980	69,613	62,282	89	45,162	65	3,290,282

Table 12.2
Iron Ore Imported for Consumption into the United States by Continents, 1977–80
(U.S. Geological Survey and U.S. Bureau of Mines 1992)
(in thousand long tons)
(in thousand dollars)

	North America		South America		Europe and Remainder	
Year	Long Tons	Value $	Long Tons	Value $	Long Tons	Value $
1977	25,283	693,384	10,008	216,242	2,614	46,958
1978	19,236	555,657	11,270	230,622	3,110	58,760
1979	22,602	683,286	8,359	181,643	2,815	52,497
1980	17,311	581,759	6,112	160,841	1,635	30,244

during the four-year term of the Carter administration were no different from those of the past five. They shouted for attention and received none. The statistics follow in tables 12.1, 12.2, 12,3, and 12.4.

12.24. During the Carter administration a very significant development in domestic iron ore production was taking place. Table 12.1 shows that the Lake Superior District was becoming the primary domestic source of iron ore. Production from the district had increased from 79 percent of the total ore produced in 1977 to 89 percent in 1980. The

Table 12.3
Production, Imports, and Exports of Pig Iron and Steel in the United States, 1977–80
(U.S. Geological Survey and U.S. Bureau of Mines 1992)
(in thousand short tons)

	Pig Iron			Steel		
Year	Production	Imports	Exports	Production	Imports	Exports
1977	81,494	373	51	125,333	19,930	3,098
1978	87,690	655	51	137,031	22,027	3,271
1979	86,975	476	105	136,341	18,428	3,400
1980	68,699	400	73	111,835	16,355	4,729

Table 12.4

World Production of Steel with the Production and Percentage Produced by the United States, the USSR Separate from Europe, Europe, Japan, and Other Nations, 1977–80 (U.S. Geological Survey and U.S. Bureau of Mines 1992) (in million short tons)

Year	World	U.S.		USSR		Europe		Japan		Other
	Tons	Tons	%	Tons	%	Tons	%	Tons	%	%
1977	741.6	125.3	17	161.7	22	232.4	31	112.9	15	15
1978	787.2	137.0	17	166.9	21	243.7	31	112.6	15	17
1979	821.2	136.3	17	164.4	20	255.6	31	123.2	15	17
1980	789.5	111.8	14	163.0	21	247.0	31	122.8	16	18

trend had been noticed during the Nixon and Ford administrations, and now it was obvious. Iron ore deposits in districts other than Lake Superior were either reaching exhaustion or were unable to compete against the cheaper imported iron ore, and there were no new discoveries coming on line. Almost all of the iron ore coming from the Lake Superior District was coming from the huge taconite plants. The maximum capacity of these plants to produce iron ore pellets was set. Any demand for iron ore above the maximum had to be met by imports. Now was the time for the assistant secretary of energy and minerals at the Department of the Interior to be studying the situation and deciding how firm the maximum iron ore production was in the district. A host of questions would have to be answered by the study, some of which would be as follows: Were the companies in good shape financially? Were they going to be able to continue to compete in the domestic market against foreign imports? If one or more of the plants were to close down, would the government want to offer a subsidy to keep them running or provide funds for mothballing to maintain them in a state of readiness? There is no record that Interior made any such kind of study.

12.25. Table 12.2 shows that in the four years of the Carter administration a total of 130 million tons of iron ore valued at 3.5 billion was imported. The largest supplier was Canada, which would have been pertinent information to the answer of whether a subsidy should or should not be given to keep a domestic plant in operation. Table 12.3 shows that an average of about 19 million tons of steel per year was being imported into the United States during the Carter administration. A large percentage of the imports came from Japan. In addition to being a major supplier to the United States, Japan was the sole supplier to its own domestic market, and it had captured a large part of the Asian and South American steel market. The U.S. domestic steel industry exported an

Table 12.5
The *Iron Age* Annual Average of Finished Steel Composite Prices, 1977–80

Year	Cents per Pound	Year	Cents per Pound
1977	15.577	1979	20.006
1978	17.957	1980	21.655

average of 3.8 million tons annually, which was somewhat less than exports during the Nixon administration but roughly the same exports as during the Ford administration. The domestic steel industry in competition with Europe and Japan had been unable to capture much of the steel export market since the end of World War II and was having difficulty in holding its own in the domestic market.

12.26. The reason the United States could not capture much of the steel export market is well illustrated in table 12.4. In 1980 Europe produced 247 million short tons of steel, the Soviet Union 163 million tons. The percentage share of each of world production was Europe, 31 percent; the Soviet Union, 21 percent; Japan, 16 percent; other nations of the world, 18 percent; and the United States, 14 percent. Viewing Europe as a European Common Market, the United States in 1980 was ranked fourth in steel production. In 1948 it had been ranked number one and was producing 52 percent of total world production. In thirty-two years it dropped 38 percentage points, an average of almost 1.2 percentage points per year. The United States dropped these percentage points year by year through seven administrations, and it is doubtful if any president, White House aide, cabinet member, or more than a dozen members of Congress after the Truman administration knew it was happening.

12.27. It is a certainty that the Carter administration did not know that it was happening. The increasing trend of steel prices, which was beginning to develop in the Ford administration, was now in full bloom during the Carter administration. Table 12.5 shows that during the Carter administration the price for finished steel increased an average of 1.5 cents per pound per year. This was a tremendous increase amounting to $120 per short ton over a four-year period, and it was raising the price of every product produced in the United States. Although President Carter, his White House staff, his cabinet, and Congress did not realize it, an annually increasing price of steel of this magnitude was far more critical than the energy problem that was occupying most of their attention and sent Mr. Carter to the "mountaintop" at Camp David to obtain

Table 12.6
Time Price Relationship for Steel, 1963–79 (U.S. Bureau of Mines 1980)
(in cents per pound)

Year	Actual Price	1978 Constant Cents	Year	Actual Price	1978 Constant Cents
1963	6.273	13.324	1972	8.999	13.683
1964	6.386	13.317	1973	9.380	13.481
1965	8.368	13.028	1974	11.141	14.601
1966	6.399	12.676	1975	13.102	15.669
1967	6.464	12.438	1976	14.213	16.162
1968	6.601	12.156	1977	15.577	16.716
1969	7.091	12.434	1978	17.957	17.957
1970	7.650	12.731	1979	20.006	18.363
1971	8.429	13.347	1980	21.655	

information for a televised speech. The devastating effect of the rising price of steel is shown in table 12.6. In addition to the annually increasing prices of steel, the gross federal debt was also increasing at a fast rate. From 1977 to 1980 the debt increased $202 billion, as shown in table 12.7.

12.28. Early in November 1979, an Iranian political group took the U.S. embassy staff in Teheran hostage. The reaction of the administration and Congress and the continuous television coverage of the affair convinced the Iranian government, which was undergoing a religious revolution at the time, that they should milk this situation for all it was worth. The "tail of the Great Satan" would be twisted mercilessly for over a year, and every minute detail of the twisting was covered on television. The whole affair outraged President Carter to the extent that he went completely out of character and ordered a military action to rescue the hostages. It was bungled. During the entire 1980 election campaign, the hostage situation was nightly fare on television. There is no doubt that it did great harm to Carter's Presidency.

12.29. In his State of the Union Address before Congress in January 1980, President Carter warned that the United States was prepared to use military force, if necessary, to repel any attempt by an outside nation

Table 12.7
Gross Federal Debt at the End of the Year, 1977–80 (Bureau of Public Debt)
(in millions of dollars)

Year	Gross Federal Debt	Year	Gross Federal Debt
1977	706,398	1979	828,923
1978	776,502	1980	908,503

to gain control of the Persian Gulf region (DeGregorio 1993). This statement was made while the political group still held the embassy hostages and the nation was being taunted malevolently on nightly television. There was something ludicrous about the president of a nation sounding off about going to war and at the same time totally impotent with a nation like Iran. The warning must have given Leonid I. Brezhnev and the Central Committee of the Soviet Union a "belly laugh" that could be heard on the eastern border of Siberia.

12.30. President Carter signed into law the Alaska Land Act of 1980, withdrawing 104 million acres for wilderness and other single uses (DeGregorio 1993). This action was taken without a materials policy program and strategic plan of action on the mineral industries. It was also taken while the merchandise trade with Japan adjusted to balance of payments basis was increasing from a minus $8.6 billion in 1979 to a minus $10.5 billion in 1980 (U.S. Department of Commerce, Economics, and Statistics Administration 1993). This was an increase in the imbalance of trade with Japan of almost $2 billion in one year. Apparently, President Carter was unaware of the situation and nobody in his cabinet or on the White House staff or Council of Economic Advisers bothered to inform him of the imbalance. To ignore such a trend is to invite an increasing imbalance in succeeding years, and that is exactly what happened. In the nineties it would reach such a figure that rectifying the imbalance would force Japan to stall and delay in attempts to remedy the situation, because for them that was virtually a political impossibility.

12.31. In view of this increasing imbalance of trade with Japan and the difficulties that President Carter had experienced with energy in the first three years of his administration, one would have thought that he would never withdraw any land from a multiple-use classification. In his "malaise" speech in July 1979, he stated in Point 1 of his six basic policy decisions the following: "Beginning this moment, this nation will never use more foreign oil than we did in 1977." Where did he expect the petroleum was going to come from to fill the demand while research was perfecting some of the idealistic alternative sources he cited in his speech? The full term of his administration had been plagued by a petroleum shortage, and he had calmly taken an action that would make the nation more dependent on petroleum imports in the future.

12.32. It is also a certainty that the withdrawal will force the United States in the future to import more ferrous and nonferrous mineral commodities By signing the act into law, Mr. Carter removed from multiple-use classification 162,500 square miles of land, which is 4,267 square miles larger in area than the state of California. There is little doubt that in this huge area there are deposits of ferrous and nonferrous mineral commodities. These deposits are now locked up, and they cannot contribute to lowering the national debt by creating wealth. The gross national debt increased $202 billion during the Carter administration, and by withdrawing the Alaskan land from multiple use Carter had ensured that the debt would continue to increase in the succeeding administration, whether he was re-elected or not.

12.33. President Carter's withdrawal of the Alaskan public lands from a multiple-use classification was a continuation of the environmental actions that began after Johnson signed the Wilderness Act and Nixon signed the NEPA of 1969 into law, on January 1, 1970. The passage of NEPA was instrumental in forming the environmental political bloc; in just eleven years this bloc managed to make the most profound changes in the United States ever made by a political group operating outside the two major political parties. Within three years they had pushed through a willing Congress the clean air and water acts, which forced many industries to change from coal to petroleum to meet the terms of the acts. The huge increase in imports of petroleum placed the nation in a position wherein OPEC used exports of petroleum as a lever on the United States and the rest of the world in an attempt to force Israel to return lands won in the Six-Day War of 1967.

12.34. In the fourth year the environmental bloc managed to push through Congress the Endangered Species Act, which allows the bloc to control every acre of land in the United States through the judicial branch, no matter what classification the land may have. In the tenth year the Three Mile Island nuclear power plant accident gave the bloc an excuse for demanding that additional nuclear plant construction be placed on hold until stricter safety standards were adopted. In the eleventh year the bloc managed to "hit the jackpot" in land withdrawal. They convinced Congress and the president to withdraw 162,500 square miles of land from exploitation, the land to be preserved for single use. In an election year both President Carter and Congress yielded to the demands of the powerful environmental political bloc. If the withdrawn

Table 12.8
Annual Population Estimates in the United States, 1977–80 (Bureau of the Census 1994)
(in thousands)

Year	Total Resident Population	Year	Total Resident Population
1977	219,760	1979	224,567
1978	222,095	1980	226,546

land area was given official status as the fifty-first state, it would rank third in size after Alaska and Texas, relegating California to fourth.

12.35. Although the acreage of the land withdrawal is delinated by border lines on a map, the actual size of the withdrawn area is far greater than is stated in the act that legalizes the withdrawal. The environmental political bloc will immediately start court action on any mining company that starts operation within a two-to-three-mile buffer zone around the withdrawn acreage claiming violation of the Clean Air Act, Clean Water Act, or Endangered Species Act. Federal land managers, fearing the court actions of the bloc, have made the buffer zones as sacrosanct as the withdrawn lands; thus, for all practical purposes, the withdrawn area is considerably larger than that stated in the act. This situation has been tolerated by all administrations and congresses since passage of the Wilderness Act during the Johnson administration.

12.36. The population growth during the Carter administration averaged about 1.7 million per year. The annual population estimates are shown in table 12.8.

12.37. In the November 4, 1980, election President Carter was defeated by Ronald Reagan, the Republican candidate for president, in an electoral vote landslide. Reagan received 51 percent of the popular vote, Carter 41 percent, and John Anderson, an independent, 7 percent (DeGregorio 1993). Carter's percentage of the popular vote indicated that he had not received any independent votes, and he had lost about 2 to 3 percent of the solid Democratic voters in the election. The loss of Democratic voters in a presidential election is an unusual occurrence in the Democratic party. Normally the Democratic "regulars" will stay with the ticket to the bitter end, no matter what the record of the Democratic candidate.

13

The Next Eight Years (1980–88): Reagan

13.1. President Carter started the 1980 campaign for re-election with three strikes against him; for all practical purposes he was beaten before he started. Inflation was in double digits, gasoline was in short supply, and Iran still held the embassy staff hostage. It is doubtful if a reincarnation of Franklin Delano Roosevelt, the most successful Democrat of them all, could have won the election carrying this kind of political baggage. However, President Carter appeared to feel that if he held the solid Democratic vote and picked up enough anticonservative votes he could defeat Mr. Reagan, Carter did not receive the solid Democratic Party backing that he anticipated, and he did not pick up any anticonservative votes.

13.2. President Carter also seriously misjudged the public's feelings in regard to the Vietnam War. In a debate with Mr. Reagan, Carter stated that the Vietnam War was immoral; Mr. Reagan countered with the statement that it was a noble effort by America. The vast majority of the people were more inclined to agree with Mr. Reagan's assessment of the tragic affair rather than President Carter's. Carter's strategy in bringing the matter up in the first place had to be questioned. President Kennedy, a revered Democrat, had placed the first combat troops in Vietnam and President Johnson, also a Democrat, had expanded the troop commitment, but it was President Nixon, a Republican, who withdrew the combat troops out of Vietnam. It took him a long time to do it, but nevertheless he was the one who did it. The individuals who were against the Vietnam War made a lot of noise and created considerable disturbance throughout the United States, but their numbers in no way compared to the noise and disruption they caused. In brief, their noise and disruptive behavior could not be translated into votes.

13.3. Ronald Reagan had had a successful career in radio, television, and film acting. During most of his working career he was interested

201

in politics, and in 1964 he was the cochairman of California Republicans for Barry Goldwater (DeGregorio 1993). Reagan was elected governor of California for two terms, 1967–75. In 1976 he attempted to obtain the Republican presidential nomination, but he lost to Gerald Ford, who had become president when Nixon resigned. Reagan won the 1980 Republican nomination and defeated Carter by an electoral landslide. Reagan was sixty-nine years old when he became President. A book by Larry Speakes on the Reagan presidency presents an excellent insight into the relationships of the White House staff and cabinet and infighting among the staff and cabinet members to hold onto their prerogatives against those who were always seeking mor power (Speakes 1988).

13.4. President Reagan appointed the following cabinet members: Secretary of State Alexander M. Haig Jr., later replaced by George P. Shultz, Secretary of the Treasury Donald T. Regan, who later became chief of staff by trading positions with James Baker, Secretary of Defense Caspar W. Weinberger, later replaced by Frank C. Carlucci, Attorney General William French Smith, later replaced by Edwin Meese, later replaced by Richard Thornburgh, Secretary of Energy James B. Edwards, later replaced by Donald P. Hodel, who later became secretary of the interior and was replaced by John S. Herrington, Secretary of Agriculture John R. Block, later replaced by Richard E. Lyng, Secretary of Commerce Malcolm Baldridge, killed in an accident and replaced by C. William Verity Jr., Secretary of Labor Raymond J. Donovan, later replaced by William E. Brock, later replaced by Ann Dore McLaughlin, Secretary of Health and Human Services Richard S. Schweiker, later replaced by Margaret M. Heckler, later replaced by Otis R. Bowen, Secretary of Transportation Andrew Lewis, later replaced by Elizabeth H. Dole, later replaced by James H. Burnley, Secretary of Education Terrel H. Bell, later replaced by William J. Bennett, later replaced by Lauro F. Cavazos, Secretary of the Interior James G. Watt, later replaced by William P. Clark, later replaced by Donald P. Hodel, who had been secretary of energy, and Secretary of Housing and Urban Development Samuel R. Pierce Jr.

13.5. President Reagan's White House and cabinet appointments were baffling. During the campaign for the presidency he claimed to be a conservative, cleaving closely to the political philosophy of Barry Goldwater, but the only true conservative appointment that Reagan made was James Watt as secretary of the interior. If Reagan had applied the Barry Goldwater conservative litmus test to all the others, he would have discovered that they were moderate Republicans more aligned with the political philosophy being expressed by George Bush than Reagan's own political philosophy. After Mr. Reagan's preelection conservative campaign rhetoric, the appointments just did not make sense.

13.6. President Reagan's cabinet was not what could be called an ideal example of a stable entity during his two terms in office. Samuel Pierce was the only secretary to serve the full eight years. In all probability Malcolm Baldridge, an original appointee as secretary of commerce, would have also served the full eight years if he had not been killed in an unfortunate accident. After the original appointments there was one change of secretaries each in the Departments of State and Defense and two changes each in the Departments of Transportation, Energy, Education, Health and Human Services, Labor, and Interior, attorney generalship, and Treasury.

13.7. President Reagan also had difficulty with his political appointees in other than cabinet positions, which points directly to poor staff work in checking out the history and political philosophy of the prospective appointees. Knowledge in the duties of the position is not the only prerequisite needed for political appointees. They have to know that tact and patience in dealing with members of Congress are absolute necessities. In addition, they must be aware that the U.S. political system has constraints that they must operate under for the full period of their appointed term.

13.8. During the campaign Mr. Reagan had promised to abolish both the Departments of Energy and Education. He did not keep his promise. At the end of his two terms both departments were flourishing as they had under the Carter administration. Reagan was of the opinion that the regulations that the Department of Energy was imposing on the petroleum companies and the nation were unnecessary and the business of distributing the products of petroleum should be left to the companies as it was before the "oil embargo." This certainly was an excellent idea, but he failed to follow through on the idea and abolish the regulations. After all his campaign rhetoric about keeping the government out of business, he muffed the chance to get rid of the most incredibly stupid regulations ever imposed upon a business in the United States.

13.9. James Edwards, President Reagan's original appointee as secretary of the Department of Energy, had no experience that would enable him to manage the department capably. Edwards attempted to promote nuclear energy, but he had no influence whatsoever in the administration, and his promotion attempts were ignored. He was replaced by Donald Hodel, a highly capable administrator who, under Mr. Nixon, had been the administrator of the Bonneville Power Administration in Oregon. There is little doubt but what Mr. Hodel would have followed through on President Reagan's promise to abolish the petroleum regulations if the president had given the word to do so. Mr. Hodel was later reassigned in the cabinet to secretary of the interior.

13.10. James Watt, original appointee to the Department of the Interior, was more in tune with President Reagan than any other cabinet member. Watt was a political conservative in the Goldwater tradition. He wanted restrictions on the continuing growth of government, opposed the withdrawal of public lands for single use, and wanted to open these lands to private development. However, Mr. Watt apparently did not understand the constraints of the political system under which he had to work. He either underestimated the power of the environmental political bloc or thought that he could counter their political actions by presenting to Congress and the public a farsighted program that they would accept on the basis of its advantages to the nation. He went into direct confrontation with the bloc and also with some strong environmental bloc supporters in Congress. When he decided to go this route some of his more politically savvy friends in Interior should have told him that it would be prudent for him to also send a letter of resignation to President Reagan. There were no sitting members of Congress at that time who were going to admit that they were wrong in voting for withdrawal of any public lands. Under the Carter administration, in 1980, they had voted to withdraw a land area larger than the state of California, and certainly they were not going to admit that the withdrawal had been a mistake. Mr. Watt could present to them all the solid arguments in the world for multiple-use classification of public lands, but they would not be heeded.

13.11. Mr. Watt did not appear to understand that a majority of Congress had been voting for withdrawal of public lands for single use since the passage of the Wilderness Act in 1964, during the Johnson administration. Each time that the congressional hearings on the different withdrawals were held, there were mineral industry lobbying groups voicing concern that the constant withdrawals were shrinking the nation's domestic resource base of mineral commodities, but this was of little concern to many members of Congress. Regularly they had been going back home and telling their constituents that they had voted to preserve public lands for their children and grandchildren. Such information always received an enthusiastic reception from those who were against any commercial use of the public lands. In addition, the vote to withdraw got high marks from the environmental political bloc, which were always positives to have on the record at re-election time. The majority of Congress wanted to continue the withdrawals, and no matter who was president at the time, he was going to receive from Congress laws to sign that withdrew public lands for single-use purposes.

13.12. Even with the environmental political bloc and congressional sniping at Mr. Watt, President Reagan stood by him until Mr. Watt made a remark about the political correctness of the appointed members of a Department of Interior advisory panel on the use of public lands. The manner in which he made the statement angered Congress, and President Reagan had to replace him to keep peace within his own party. The fact that Mr. Watt was not removed because of his proposed programs on public lands outraged the environmental political bloc. They would have preferred to have him discredited for his beliefs rather than for an ill-advised statement; however, they were willing to accept his departure under any terms so as to remove a thorn in their side. His successor, William Clark, managed to strike a middle course, and the direct confrontations with Congress ceased. Donald Hodel succeeded Mr. Clark as secretary and served from 1985 to the end of Mr. Reagan's second term. The environmental political bloc was not at all pleased by the appointment of Mr. Hodel. They continued to monitor closely Mr. Hodel's efforts to expand the nation's domestic resource base in petroleum by permitting petroleum producers to explore for oil on public lands.

13.13. President Reagan was apparently convinced to adopt the theory of supply-side economics by Sen. Jack Kemp of New York (Stockman 1986). According to David Stockman, director of the Office of Management and Budget (OMB), when the theory was placed into practice, hard money policies would pull down the high rate of inflation inherited from the Carter administration; a tax cut and other policies would push up the rate of output and corresponding employment expansion (Stockman 1986).

13.14. Very few, if any, supply-side economists agree in total with each other on the details of the theory of supply-side economics, and this certainly was the case as it was expounded by Mr. Stockman; he had his own interpretation of the theory. Probably the best way to broadly define the basic theory of supply-side economics is by saying that it focuses on production as a means of revitalizing the economy. Production is increased by tax cuts to increase personal savings and investment, which is supposed to supply funds for modernizing industrial plants and equipment, thus increasing productivity. The improved productivity coupled with drastic reductions in government spending is supposed to bring down the inflation rate and enable the administration to balance the budget.

13.15. Inasmuch as Mr. Reagan was a new recruit into the supply-side camp, he had to be taught the "buzz" words and phrases that supply-siders use. During the campaign against Carter for the presidency he managed to express enough of the necessary words and phrases to make him sound like an authentic supply-sider. The press promptly labeled the theory "Reaganomics," and George Bush, when he was campaigning for the Republican nomination against Mr. Reagan, labeled it "voodoo economics." Mr. Reagan apparently forgave Mr. Bush for trashing his economic theory, because he chose him to become his running mate on the ticket.

13.16. The fact the Mr. Reagan could talk like a supply-side economist certainly did not mean that he fully understood what he was saying. To make the supply-side theory work, drastic reductions had to be made in government spending. This meant deep cuts in all government entitlements and the social programs that had been enacted under the Johnson administration and additional social programs added to the original legislation over a period of twenty years. In addition, all cabinet departments and independent agencies, such as NASA, the EPA, and the Veterans Administration, were going to have to take their share of monetary reductions.

13.17. All members of Congress, whether Democrat or Republican, have to play to many constituencies, and there were powerful constituencies on the home front who were guarding defense industries, military installations, government entitlements, and social programs like a tiger guarding the carcass of newly slain deer. Each constituency had added to the initial ten the eleventh commandment, which stated as follows: "Thou shalt not cut the appropriations to our program." There was little doubt but what President Reagan was going to encounter strong resistance to his supply-side program in Congress from members of both parties; however, there is considerable doubt that either he or Mr. Stockman realized the total amount of congressional resistance that they would encounter. This failure is difficult to understand, because anybody who had been governor of California for two four-year terms must have encountered the same situation every year that the budget was prepared.

13.18. However, there is ample proof that both President Reagan and Mr. Stockman were about as naive as they could possibly be about the reception of their supply-side economic program. To make the program work, President Reagan needed the wholehearted cooperation of his cabinet, White House aides, and other agency political appointees, but of all of those appointed he did not appoint one who believed in the supply-side theory. In fact, he received as much (or more) resistance to his program from his own cabinet members, White House aides, and other political appointees as he did from Congress. All of the first cabinet appointments refused to cooperate except by token reductions in their appropriations. The White House aides divorced themselves from the budget reduction process and thus by inaction left the OMB director to make the fight for budget reductions alone. This adamant stance by most of the cabinet members forced President Reagan to make the decision on the reductions, and he ended up trying to placate both Mr. Stockman, OMB director, and cabinet secretaries rather than making the necessary hard choices (Stockman 1986). Reagan's supply-side program died in the Oval Office as he waffled on the government spending reductions that had to be made. He discovered early in his first term that parroting the "buzz" words and phrases of supply-side economics was a lot easier than putting the program into action.

13.19. However, the most amazing aspect of President Reagan's supply-side program was not his waffling on the necessary monetary reductions, the intransigeance of the cabinet members, White House aides, and other political appointees, or the opposition in Congress; it was the absolute fact that for supply-side economics to work, domestic mining, the most basic part of the mineral industries, has to be healthy or the necessary increases in production can never be achieved. Apparently there was nobody in President Reagan's political entourage who knew this. A book, *The Triumph of Politics: How the Reagan Revolution Failed,* written by former OMB director David Stockman in 422 pages never stated that he or the gurus of supply-side economics Sen. Jack Kemp and Arthur Laffer knew that domestic mining had to be healthy for the agenda to work; in fact, the book never did cite any needed prerequisites for the supply-side theory to be successful (Stockman 1986).

13.20. Both the ferrous and nonferrous divisions of the minerals industry had been whipsawed by the six previous administrations until they were but a mere shadow of what they had been under the Truman administration. In 1981, 21 million short tons of raw steel and 28 million long tons of iron ore were being imported. Since the Kennedy administration the ferrous division of the minerals industry had been suffering from lack of capital for adequate maintenance, building of new plants, and upgrading the technology of old plants. The nonferrous division was in an even worse predicament. Production and processing of many of the base metals was shifting to the Third World countries, which had huge ore reserves of copper, lead, and zinc. Coupled with this sad state of affairs in the minerals industry was a negative balance of trade with Japan in 1981 in the amount of $17 billion and an inflation rate of 13 percent. It is impossible for the supply-side agenda to work under such a load of negatives. There are those who argue that these negatives should not be harmful to the economy of the United States. It is pointed out that Japan is a superstate with virtually no mineral self-sufficiency; this is true, but Japan has become a superstate only by the largesse of the United States and some European nations, who allow Japan to have a positive balance of trade of billions of dollars. Force Japan to even the trade balance with other nations and the superstate status will disappear like a feather in a hurricane.

13.21. President Reagan did manage to bring down the inflation rate with the help of a drop in oil prices and by action of the Federal Reserve raising interest rates. However, the economy was so weak that the high interest rates caused a severe recession, which did not reach bottom until the end of 1982. The administration did reduce taxes and also cut government spending by reducing the federal funds allotted to states. However, to cover this loss of revenue, the states promptly raised state taxes, which effectively canceled out the reduction in federal taxes. The end result with all of the negatives cited above was a lack of funds for modernizing plants and equipment, and thus the very heart of supply-side economics, increased productivity, could not be achieved. The failure to increase productivity made it impossible for Reagan to balance the budget, which he pledged to do during his campaign for the presidency. Also, the supply-side agenda was of no help to the ferrous metals division of the minerals industry. The division had to undergo a complete

Table 13.1
Total Annual Production of Iron Ore in the United States, 1981–88, Compared to That Produced by the Lake Superior District and the Mesabi Range (U.S. Geological Survey and U.S. Bureau of Mines 1992)
(in thousand long tons)

| Year | Total Tons | Lake Superior District | | Mesabi Iron Range | | Tons Accumulated |
		Tons	Percentage of Total	Tons	Percentage of Total	
1981	73,174	67,462	92	51,025	70	3,341,457
1982	35,433	31,013	88	23,898	68	3,365,205
1983	37,562	35,594	95	26,255	70	3,391,460
1984	51,269	49,679	97	36,697	72	3,428,157
1985	48,751	47,388	97	34,910	72	3,463,067
1986	38,862	37,600	97	27,042	70	3,490,109
1987	46,895	46,017	98	33,724	72	3,523,833
1988	56,606	55,853	98	40,794	72	3,564,627

restructuring to stay alive, and in the period from 1982 to 1986 they lost $12 billion. Tables 13.1, 13.2, 13.3, and 13.4 on the production, imports, and exports of iron ore, pig iron, and steel, show the sharp decline in steel production.

13.22. During the Carter administration, in 1978–80, there was an oversupply of steel in the world. Several nations in the European Community (EC) were forced into restructuring their steel industries with government aid. In contrast, the United States produced 137 million short tons in 1978 and close to the same tonnage in 1979. Production dropped 25 million short tons to 112 million in 1980. Table 13.3 shows that in 1981, the first year of the Reagan administration, steel production increased to 121 million and imports rose almost 5 million to 21 million

Table 13.2
Iron Ore Imported for Consumption into the United States by Continents, 1981–88
(U.S. Geological Survey and U.S. Bureau of Mines 1992)
(in thousand long tons)
(in thousand dollars)

| Year | North America | | South America | | Europe and Remainder | |
	Long Tons	Value	Long Tons	Value	Long Tons	Value
1981	18,845	707,974	7,228	201,929	2,255	38,074
1982	9,281	359,728	2,697	64,837	2,523	46,302
1983	8,832	339,472	2,609	73,131	1,805	33,128
1984	11,190	423,473	4,064	86,585	1,933	29,007
1985	8,557	325,248	4,893	93,703	2,321	33,286
1986	8,696	311,757	6,186	117,726	1,861	31,160
1987	8,108	246,181	7,153	132,001	1,858	30,601
1988	9,303	285,961	8,964	159,246	2,239	39,336

Table 13.3
Production, Imports, and Exports of Pig Iron and Steel in the United States, 1981–88
(U.S. Geological Survey and U.S. Bureau of Mines 1992)
(in thousand short tons)

Year	Pig Iron			Steel		
	Production	Imports	Exports	Production	Imports	Exports
1981	73,755	468	16	120,828	20,818	3,557
1982	43,432	322	54	74,577	17,385	2,367
1983	48,770	242	6	84,615	17,964	1,589
1984	51,961	702	57	92,528	27,488	1,413
1985	49,963	338	32	88,259	25,707	1,266
1986	44,287	295	41	81,606	22,145	1,201
1987	48,308	355	50	89,151	21,534	1,419
1988	55,745	700	72	99,924	22,310	2,576

Table 13.4
World Production of Steel with the Production and Percentage Produced by the United States, the USSR Separate from Europe, Europe, Japan, and Other Nations, 1981–88
(U.S. Geological Survey and U.S. Bureau of Mines 1992)
(in million short tons)

Year	World	U.S.		USSR		Europe		Japan		Other
		Tons	%	Tons	%	Tons	%	Tons	%	%
1981	779.6	120.8	15	163.6	21	239.4	31	112.1	14	19
1982	709.9	74.6	11	162.2	23	217.5	31	109.7	15	20
1983	730.6	84.6	12	168.1	23	217.3	30	107.1	15	20
1984	784.0	92.5	12	170.2	22	234.5	30	116.4	15	21
1985	791.4	88.3	11	170.5	22	235.2	30	116.0	15	22
1986	785.6	81.6	10	177.0	23	225.9	29	108.3	14	24
1987	809.4	89.2	11	178.5	22	226.5	28	108.6	13	26
1988	860.0	99.9	12	179.7	21	239.6	28	116.5	14	25

tons. The sharp increase in the imports of steel started investigations to determine if the imported steel was being dumped or unfairly subsidized. There is no doubt whatsoever that it was, but the cumbersome bureaucratic system for detecting the dumping and unfair subsidization was not functioning properly. The government agencies charged with the responsibility to stop such practices were always dealing with the situation after the dumping occurred rather than developing a system to stop it before it occurred.

13.23. It was not until 1982 that the recession that started after Reagan took office affected the steel industry. When it did hit, it hit hard. Table 13.4 shows that steel production decreased 46 million short tons, from 121 million tons in 1981 to 75 million tons in 1982. Europe also cut back production a total of 22 million tons, but neither the Soviet Union nor Japan reduced production in amounts comparable to the reduction in the United States and Europe. Third World nations increased production in this period by constructing direct-reduction plants (see appendix 4). Tables 13.1, 13.2, and 13.3 reflect the same huge decrease in domestic production and imports of iron ore and production of pig iron. The end result was that America's share of the world's steel production dropped from 15 percent in 1981 to 11 percent in 1982. The Soviet Union's share rose to 23 percent, Japan's to 15 percent, and other nations' to 20 percent. Europe's share of world production remained the same at 31 percent.

13.24. Table 13.4 shows that in 1983 and 1984 steel production began to recover from the low level in 1982, but the increase did not result in profit for the steel companies. Imports of steel in 1984 rose to over 27 million tons, the highest level of imports ever experienced in the United States. This import figure amounted to almost one-quarter of total steel consumed domestically. The huge increase in imports forced the domestic steel companies to seek protection through trade laws, and the Reagan administration began a program to control injury to the domestic industry and to restrict dumping and unfairly traded imports (U.S. Geological Survey and U.S. Bureau of Mines 1992). This program was, in reality, about twenty years too late, when steel imports increased almost 4 million short tons from 6.6 million in 1964 to 10.6 million in 1965 (see paragraph 9.33).

13.25. There is no doubt that the high level of imports in 1984 caused injury to the domestic steel industry. Prices were constrained at import subsidized steel level, and many companies were losing money. To survive under the conditions that were existing, the Republic and Jones & Laughlin steel companies merged and older plants were closed. The closing of these older plants reduced domestic capacity, and this reduction is shown in the production figures for 1985–86 in table 13.3.

13.26. Under the restructuring program started in 1984, the domestic steel industry managed to show a profit of about $1 billion in 1987 and about $2 billion in 1988; however, this total of $3 billion in profits in 1987–88 in no way made up for the $12 billion in losses suffered in the period from 1982 to 1986 (U.S. Geological Survey and U.S. Bureau of Mines 1992). Also in the two-year period 1987–88, the industry managed to increase steel capacity by upgrading existing facilities and starting up new minimills, but the domestic capacity did not even approach the capacity that was available in the late seventies. More than twenty years of unrestrained imports of subsidized steel flowing into the United States

Table 13.5
The _Iron Age_ Annual Average of Finished Steel Composite Prices, 1981–95 (_Iron Age_ 1974)

Year	Cents per Pound	Year	Cents per Pound
1981	24.224	1985	27.582
1982	25.271	1986	24.792
1983	26.190	1987	25.236[a]
1984	27.313	1988	24.594[b]
		1993	25.156[c]
		1994	26.108[d]
		1995	27.305[e]

a. Price on January 4, 1987. b.Price on August 1, 1988. c. Price on April 4, 1994. d. Price on April 4, 1994. e. Price on November 6, 1995.

had taken their toll on the domestic steel industry. Presidents Kennedy, Johnson, Nixon, Ford, and Carter had ignored the situation throughout their administrations. The end result was the oozing ulcer gushing blood in a torrent in 1984, when over 27 million tons of subsidized steel were dumped into the United States. No matter how solid the domestic ferrous metals division companies were, they could not remain stable forever in a market where they were competing against the continuous erosive action of imported, below cost, subsidized steel.

13.27. Table 13.5 shows that during the Reagan administration steel prices continued to rise for the period from 1981 to 1985, but at a lesser rate than during the Carter administration. In 1986 the price dropped sharply, 2.78 cents per short ton. This indicates that President Reagan did have some success in bringing the high inflation rates that had prevailed during the Carter administration under control. After 1988 prices started to increase, reaching 27.305 cents per pound near the end of 1995. The devastating effects of inflation are shown in table 13.6, wherein the time price relationship for steel is shown based on constant 1983 dollars.

13.28. After the restructuring of the ferrous metals division of the minerals industry, the domestic steel capacity had shrunk 48 million short tons from the high of 160 million tons in 1977 to 112 million in 1987–88 (U.S. Geological Survey and U.S. Bureau of Mines 1992). Land withdrawals, stringent environmental laws, and indifference to the plight of the ferrous metals divisions by the seven administrations following Mr. Truman had forced the larger of the iron mining companies to be active in searching for iron ore deposits outside the United States. The largest of the steel companies, U.S. Steel, was the most successful of all. Their exploration subsidiary in 1967 discovered an iron ore deposit at

Table 13.6
Time Price Relationship for Steel, 1963–83 (Staff of the Bureau of Mines 1985)
(in cents per pound)

Year	Actual Prices	Based on Constant 1983 Dollars	Year	Actual Prices	Based on Constant 1983 Dollars
1963	6.273	18.878	1973	9,380	19.131
1964	6.368	13.317	1974	11.141	20.878
1965	8.368	18.468	1975	13.102	22.461
1966	6.399	17.979	1976	14.213	23.163
1967	6.464	17.632	1977	15.577	23.986
1968	6.601	17.248	1978	17.957	25.744
1969	7.091	17.621	1979	20.006	26.403
1970	7.650	18.042	1980	21.655	26.175
1971	8.429	18.933	1981	24.224	26.772
1972	8.989	19.406	1982	25.271	26.345
			1983	26.190	26.190

Carajas, Brazil, in the middle of a virgin tropical forest 890 kilometers southwest of the Ponta da Madeira marine terminal near Sao Luis on the Atlantic Ocean (*Business Week* 1984, Paley 1952, Suttill 1995). The development and operation of the orebody is a 50.9 percent: 49.1 percent joint venture between Brazil and U.S. Steel (Suttill 1995). It is now the world's largest known source of high-grade iron ore (Suttill 1995). Estimates of the ore reserves are that it will exceed by almost six times the tonnage of merchantable ore that was found on the Mesabi Iron Range. The World Bank underwrote a $500 million loan to the Brazilian state-owned mining company in 1982 to start development of the project (*Business Week* 1984). Over half of the capital cost of the project was for a 890-kilometer railroad from the mine site to the marine terminal (Suttill 1995). The immediate effect that the project will have on the world steel market is difficult to judge, but it is highly likely that foreign steelmakers importing the Carajas Project iron ore will be able to under-sell some of America's domestic producers on the world market.

13.29. With the huge loss in steel capacity, imports of large tonnages of subsidized steel, and the eventual threat that cheaper imported steel might soon be available there was absolutely no chance that supply-side economics could work. The necessary gain in production to make the economic agenda work simply could not be achieved. Even if the other requirements of the agenda, tax reduction and reduction in government spending, had been successful, the loss in steel production was too great to overcome, and this is certainly reflected in the increase in the national debt that occurred during the the eight years of the Reagan

Table 13.7
Gross Federal Debt at the End of the Year, 1981–88 (Bureau of Public Debt 1940-1992) (in millions of dollars)

Year	Gross Federal Debt	Year	Gross Federal Debt
1981	994,298	1985	1,816,974
1982	1,136,798	1986	2,120,082
1983	1,371,164	1987	2,345,578
1984	1,564,110	1988	2,600,760

administration. Table 13.7 shows the annual increases in the gross federal debt from 1981 to 1988.

13.30. The federal debt increased from $994.3 billion in 1981 to $2.6 trillion in 1988—an increase of $1.6 trillion during President Reagan's two terms. The average annual increase amounted to $200.8 billion; it was the largest annual average increase in the history of the nation. In addition to this huge increase in the gross federal debt, President Reagan's administration was plagued by a yearly increase in the imbalance of trade with Japan. About 60 percent of the imbalance was attributable to automobiles. Table 13.8 shows the yearly negative imbalance of merchandise trade, adjusted to balance of payments basis. Two years of the Carter Administration, 1979–80, are included in the table to show that the problem did not surface only under the Reagan Administration; however, it did increase sharply under the Reagan Administration.

13.31. The imbalance of trade with Japan received little or no attention during the Carter administration, but it did receive considerable attention during the Reagan administration. Japanese automobile exports were clobbering the U.S. automobile industry and, in the process, destroying the little that was left of the administration's supply-side agenda, that is, if there was anything left to destroy. Supply-siders are free-traders to the nth degree, but the administration recognized that the domestic automobile industry was unable to compete in a free market with Japan

Table 13.8
Merchandise Trade with Japan Adjusted to Balance of Payments Basis, 1979–88 (U.S. Department of Commerce, Economics, and Statistics Administration 1993) (in millions of dollars)

Year	Imbalance	Year	Imbalance	Year	Imbalance
1979	− 8,629	1982	−16,989	1985	−43,505
1980	−10,465	1983	−21,556	1986	−54,401
1981	−15,802	1984	−36,980	1987	−56,948
				1988	−52,615

and, therefore, the government would have to come to its rescue. To avoid being labeled as against free trade, the administration adopted the plan of coercing Japan into volunteering to limit their automobile exports into the United States (Stockman 1986).

13.32. One would not have to wonder why the administration was forced to drop all pretense of being a free-trader and press Japan to accept a quota on exports of automobiles. In 1986–88 the imbalance rose to over $50 billion. An imbalance in trade of this magnitude with one nation and fully 60 percent of it being a finished product, coupled with the loss of 48 billion short tons of steel capacity, would sink out of sight not only a supply-side economic agenda but any kind of economic theory. However, Reagan was in the same position as Hoover in 1928. Reagan was the sitting president when the ulcer gushed blood because of thirty-five years of neglect of the Ferrous Metals Division of the Minerals Industry by seven previous administrations. He was the sitting president when those who were ripped off during the era of "screw ya" retaliated with a vengeance against the domestic automobile industry. It would have made no difference what kind of economic theory Reagan had on the agenda; it could not have stopped the Japanese assault on the automobile industry, the percentage decrease in steel produced as compared with the rest of the world, or the loss of steel capacity. To some extent if he had not reduced federal taxes, he could have controlled the increase in the national debt, but the debt was bound to move higher when the nation lost 48 million tons of steel capacity and the imbalance in trade with Japan rose to the $50 billion figure.

13.33. As the restructuring of the steel industry was being completed during the last years of the Reagan administration, unemployment had dropped significantly to 5.3 percent, and it is estimated that a record 20 million new jobs had been created (DeGregorio 1993). This is a tremendous number of new jobs; however, numbers of workers employed is not the only criterion by which employment should be judged. More important criteria are the type of job and the earnings received. A most disturbing trend in workers' jobs started in 1979 and continued through the eighties to 1990. The Economics and Statistics Administration, Bureau of Census, reports the following: "There was a sharp rise between 1979 and 1990 in the proportion of year-round, full-time workers with low annual earnings. The rate rose from 12.1 ($\pm$ 0.3) percent in 1979 to 14.6 ($\pm$ 0.3) percent in 1984, to 16.3 ($\pm$ 0.3) percent in 1989, and 18.0 ($\pm$ 0.3) percent in 1990" (1992).

215

Table 13.9
Annual Population Estimates in the United States, 1981–88
(in thousands)

Year	Total Resident Population	Year	Total Resident Population	Year	Total Resident Population
1981	229,637	1984	236,477	1987	243,427
1982	231,996	1985	238,736	1988	245,785
1983	234,284	1986	241,107		

13.34. These statistics show that beginning in 1979 an extremely serious situation was developing as the nation was annually losing its industrial superiority more and more. Jobs with low annual earnings were replacing the lost industrial jobs with high annual earnings. It can be assumed that a large percentage of the low-annual-earnings jobs were in the service sector of the economy, a trend that was likely to continue into the future until some administration woke up and realized that as the minerals industry goes, so goes the nation and a terrible price is extracted the longer the minerals industry is ignored.

13.35. In any event, the low unemployment rate and the increase in any kind of jobs in the U.S. economy were welcome, and Table 13.9: "Annual Population Estimates in the United States, 1981–88," shows why.

13.36. During the eight years that President Reagan was in office, the population increased an average of 2 million per year, reaching a total of 245.8 million people in 1988. High employment was necessary to supply this amount of people with food, shelter, and clothing and also to provide almost all people above age fifteen with an automobile. Fully 75 percent of the people would be paying for the automobile in annual payments of anywhere from eighteen to thirty-six months' duration. It could be of foreign or domestic make, a new one, a slightly used one, a well-used one, or a "beater," but whichever it was, it had to be one that would get a person to and from work each weekday and from here to there and there to here over the weekend.

13.37. Unbeknownst to the administration and Congress, a highly significant change was occurring in the daily lives of a large segment of the American people during the Carter and Reagan administrations. The pursuit of the "abundant life" by many families required that there had to be two persons in the family bringing home a paycheck to maintain the standard of living to which they had become accustomed. Those who held high-paying industrial jobs discovered that when they were the victims of lay-offs the only jobs that were available paid considerably less, with little or no medical coverage. It required two working in the family to provide the funds that were originally available under the higher-paying industrial job. If the mother in the family was tied down at home with small children, then to meet payments on the home and automobile the father often had to hold down two service jobs. It was a dramatic change in lifestyle for many that appeared to go unnoticed by both the Carter and Reagan administrations and the senators and representatives who served during the terms of both presidents. In Congress it was deadlock as usual on trivial matters that had nothing whatsoever to do with how a person could maintain the standard of living to which he had become accustomed.

13.38. At the end of the Reagan administration the pursuit of the "abundant life" for many was becoming a nightmare of lost homes, repossessed automobiles, and interest payments on charge cards that had them in almost total despair. To them the "abundant life" had become an elusive will-o'-the-wisp. The only way that they could go back to the good old days was by hitting it big in the state-run lotteries that were becoming highly popular throughout the nation. To a large extent the ones who were playing the lottery heavily were the ones who could least afford it, but it was understandable why they were making the gamble. Living the "abundant life" was a whole lot more fun than living the way they were now.

14

The Next Four Years (1988–92): Bush

14.1. George Bush was nominated on the first ballot by the Republican Party. He surprised leaders of both parties by selecting Sen. Dan Quayle from Indiana to be his running mate. Mr. Bush had wide experience in government, having served in the House and as ambassador to the United Nations, chairman of the Republican Party, chief U.S. liaison in China, director of the Central Intelligence Agency, and vice president during the Reagan administration. Bush's performance in all these posts was successful, and there was very little that could be criticized. At times Mr. Bush appeared to have difficulty in reaching a definite decision on certain matters, but this apparent indecisiveness did not surface in the 1988 campaign. He defeated Michael Dukakis in the November 8, 1988, election.

14.2. Bush's selection of Senator Quayle as his vice president proved to be an unfortunate choice. Quayle became the focal point for criticism of the Bush-Quayle ticket during the campaign. The venomous treatment of Quayle in both the electronic and print media reached such a crescendo prior to the election that it continued off and on for the full four-year term. He was constantly the butt of jokes by electronic media comics and print media cartoonists and columnists. In effect, he became a millstone around the administration's neck.

14.3. The venomous media campaign against Quayle did have an odd twist. His political enemies and the media painted him as a mediocre politician and lackadaisical bungler. However, if one took time to look at his political record, his achievements did not square with these general characterizations. In 1988 he won the nomination for vice president over several prominent Republicans. He defeated a two-term Democratic representative, J. Edward Roush, for the House seat of Indiana's Fourth Congressional District in 1976 and was reelected in 1978. In 1980 Quayle did the unthinkable and unacceptable to the Democratic Party faithful: he defeated Birch Bayh, a revered three-term Democratic senator from Indiana. At the time, Bayh was a powerful man in the Senate and a Senate sage and pundit who often appeared on television dispensing his wit to all who would listen. Some political analysts attributed this victory over Bayh to the popularity of Ronald Reagan, but in reality Quayle soundly defeated Bayh on his own. In 1986 the Democratic Party was further chagrined when Quayle defeated another Democrat, Jill Long, by the largest majority of any elected senator in Indiana history (DeGregorio 1993). If Quayle was as bad as he was being painted, Roush, Bayh, and Long must have seemed bungling politicians beyond any description to the Indiana electorate.

14.4. President Bush appointed the following cabinet members: Secretary of Defense Richard Cheney, Attorney General Richard Thornburgh, later replaced by William Barr, Secretary of the Interior Manuel Lujan, Secretary of Agriculture Clayton Yeutter, later replaced by Edward Madigan, Secretary of Commerce Robert Mosbacher, later replaced by Barbara Franklin, Secretary of Labor Elizabeth Dole, later replaced by Lynn Martin, Secretary of Health and Human Services Louis Sullivan, Secretary of Housing and Urban Development Jack Kemp, Secretary of Transportation Samuel Skinner, later replaced by Andrew Card, Secretary of Energy James Watkins, Secretary of Education Lauro Cavazos, later replaced by Lamar Alexander, and Secretary of Veterans' Affairs Edward Derwinski.

14.5. Several of the original appointments, with the exception of Mr. Cavazos, changed to other positions in the administration or ran for elected office. Mr. Cavazos resigned apparently because President Bush was dissatisfied with his leadership in the department (DeGregorio 1935). In general, President Bush made political appointments to government positions that were more in tune with his political philosophy than did President Reagan. Bush's first choice for secretary of defense was former senator John Tower of Texas. The appointment was political; it was a payoff for support from the right wing of the Republican Party. Tower's conduct, style of operation, and right wing stance while he was in the Senate had netted him many enemies but very few friends. The Senate Democrats seized the opportunity to exact revenge on Mr. Tower: they rejected the appointment. President Bush appeared unperturbed about the rejection. He calmly appointed Mr. Cheney, who would have been his first choice if he had not had to make the political payoff. More than likely President Bush regarded the rejection with relief. The Senate had done something he could not do: they removed Mr. Tower from any consideration as a cabinet officer. President Bush had made his political payoff, but he did not have to live with it for four years.

14.6. President Bush took office at a critical time in the history of the minerals industry. The mistakes of seven administrations had come to a head during the Reagan administration. A total of 48 million short tons of steel capacity had been lost; subsidized steel imports were increasing; the U.S. share of world steel production had dropped to 11 percent; foreign iron ore imports were threatening the investments made in taconite plants of some iron ore producing companies in the Lake Superior District; the steel export market was decreasing as Third World nations continued to increase their domestic capacity; and domestic mines producing nonferrous ores were closing as nonferrous metal imports increased. The loss of these vital basic industries had resulted in a large segment of the populace suffering a drop in their standard of living. What had once been the pursuit of the "abundant life" was now turning into the pursuit for a job, just any kind of job.

14.7. There were no quick solutions to any of the problems that had developed over the past thirty-five years in the mineral industries. In view of the indifference of the Bush administration to the problems of the minerals industry, the most that could be hoped for was that America's diminishing share of world production of steel had reached bottom. It was an absolute impossibility for the United States to regain its industrial superiority in steel production. Western Europe, Japan, and Third World nations had discovered that Yankee ingenuity and Yankee know-how paid paid handsome dividends. The more steel they produced, the higher their standard of living. If they produced more than they could use in their own country, all they had to do was dump it at reduced prices into the United States. In addition, the products they produced from steel or with products and machines made of steel had a ready market in the United States, which was the focal point for almost one-third of the world's imports and was the most buoyant import market in the world.

14.8. To some extent the president's indifference to the problems of the minerals industry was understandable. He had a Congress that was controlled by the Democratic Party, and it was hopelessly deadlocked on such programs as taxes, capital gains, welfare, Social Security, Medicare, abortion, gun control, school prayer, term limits, and universal health care. If he could get anything done during his administration, it would have to be regarded as an accomplishment.

14.9. Almost before President Bush had an opportunity to lay out the broad outlines of his policies to his cabinet he was confronted with an environmental disaster, a financial debacle, and disintegration of the USSR. Dealing effectively with these three *d* events in sequence would test the skill of any president. In March 1989 the supertanker *Exxon Valdez*, after running aground in Prince William Sound, Alaska, spilled millions of gallons of crude oil. It was a far greater disaster than the Santa Barbara Channel well blow-out, which had occurred under the Nixon administration. The aftermath of the disaster was predictable. It increased the strength of the environmental political bloc, there was a report by a commission calling for more government regulation of the petroleum tanker industry, and the courts managed to clear everybody without funds of responsibility for the accident. Exxon, the owner of the supertanker and the only participant in the case that had folding money, was found to be solely liable for the accident. The manner in which the learned judges of America's justice system reach decisions on liability cases is simple: they fasten liability only on those that have deep pockets. It is somewhat difficult to understand why a judge needs a law degree to reach these kinds of decisions in liability cases. It is merely a matter of adding up the green, and the one with the most green is guilty. A high school graduate could do just as well.

14.10. As the cleanup and court cases proceeded on the *Exxon Valdez* disaster, a financial debacle occurred. President Bush had to sign into law and create a new office under Treasury to bail out many savings and loan institutions throughout the United States that failed to survive after banking deregulation laws were passed several years earlier. The ultimate cost of the bail-out was estimated to be $500 billion (DeGregorio 1993). Whatever the cost, the nation had to foot the bill, and a considerable amount of the payments would have to be made to institutions in the state of Texas. Texas had more bungling inept managers of savings and loan institutions than any other state in the union.

14.11. And while President Bush was still dealing with the environmental disaster and financial debacle, the USSR suddenly started to disintegrate. It caught every nation in the world by surprise except China. Chinese government leaders had been predicting for several years that unless the Soviet Union changed its form of government, it would cease to be a major power. These predictions were regarded

221

in world diplomatic circles as nothing more than rhetorical utterances because the Soviet Union did not follow as strict a party line as China. Probably the most surprised government official in the world was Fidel Castro of Cuba, although his surprise might well have been matched by every person in the United States, including the president and his aides, personnel in the State Department and the CIA, all of Congress, print and electronic media editors, commentators, and correspondents, and everybody in think tanks and universities from the janitor on up or the president on down. Normally such lapses in knowledge are grist for the mill by the opposition party, but there was no finger pointing on the failure of the Bush administration to have prior knowledge of the disintegration. The reason was simple. Nobody had the "guts" to start railing at the stupidity of the administration, because that would end up exposing their own ignorance; they would never be able to say, "We told you so," or, "Our party has been expecting this to happen for years." Better just to keep one's silence and join the millions who were hiding their ignorance in the same way.

14.12. There were good reasons for the world to be unaware of what was happening in the Soviet Union. Travel within the borders of the nation was restricted to designated areas, and their leaders at times appeared to go out of sanity balance. *Lunacy* is probably the best word to describe their actions beginning in 1946, immediately after the end of World War II. They started a buildup of their armed forces, atomic warhead rocketry, and outer space exploration that would surpass the United States in all respects. At the time they started this buildup they were producing about 20 million short tons of steel annually; the United States was producing over four times this amount. It was a superhuman effort for twelve years, requiring 75 percent or more of their mineral industry production be diverted from civilian use to the effort. Raising the standard of living of the populace went on hold, and the final result was that the Soviets ended up with a huge industrial complex suited primarily for war and outer space exploration but of little use for anything else.

14.13. From 1946 to 1962 their constant menacing actions forced Presidents Truman, Eisenhower, and Kennedy, especially Eisenhower and Kennedy, to be constantly acting or reacting to some threat. After attaining what they thought was equal or near-equality with the United States in armed forces and atomic warhead rocketry, the Soviets became bolder and during the Kennedy administration nearly plunged the world into atomic warfare. They supported North Vietnam during the Kennedy, Johnson, and Nixon administrations, and although they signed arms limitation agreements, there was never any guarantee that they were obeying the terms of the agreements.

14.14. Their constant menacing actions toward the rest of the world forced them to be continuously improving the technology of their atomic warhead rocketry and increasing their naval forces. Also, the need to impose their political philosophy by force on neighboring nations forced them to continue to build and maintain huge air and land forces utilizing conventional arms and ground troop deployments such as those employed in World War II.

14.15. During the Reagan administration, the Soviet Union began experiencing serious economic problems. These problems were flowing over into the European border countries surrounding the Soviet Union, upon which the Soviets had imposed their form of government by military force. In Poland the economic condition of the nation had become intolerable, and they started to set up their own type of government to cope with the situation. Economic deterioration in the Soviet Union had progressed to the point wherein the Soviets were unable to stop Poland's movement to free itself from Soviet domination. The other border countries in Europe, including Czechoslovakia, Hungary, Yugoslavia, Romania, Bulgaria, and later East Germany and Albania, followed the example set by Poland and abolished the government imposed upon them by force of arms.

14.16. The inability of the Soviet Union to stop the border nations from breaking away gave impetus to the disintegration within the USSR. A total of fifteen republics comprised the union prior to the disintegration. They were as follows: The Russian Soviet Federated Socialist Republic, the Ukraine, Kazakhstan, Bylorussia, Uzbekistan, Georgia, Azerbaijan, Lithuania, Moldavia, Latvia, Kirghizia, Tadzhikistn, Armenia, Turkmenistan, and Estonia. The Baltic Republics, Lithuania, Latvia, and Estonia were the next after Poland to break off, and they were followed by the Russian SFSR, the Ukraine, and Byelorussia withdrawing from the union and forming a Commonwealth of Independent States (DeGregorio 1993).

14.17. The Soviet Union's spending half a century preparing for war completely destroyed their economy, but exactly what the final result of the disintegration will be is difficult to determine. However, it is possible to misjudge completely the effect that the disintegration will have upon the new Commonwealth of Independent States. Before disintegration, the Soviet Union with its fifteen constituent republics was 8.6 million square miles in area; this compares with the U.S. area of 3.6 million square miles. The Russian SFSR constituted 76.7 percent of the area and over 60 percent of the population of the former union. It is a huge landmass 6.6 million square miles in area extending from the Baltic Sea in Europe to the Pacific Ocean in Asia. It has now joined with the Ukraine and Bylorussia Republics in a Commonwealth of Independent States, and these three combined are 6.9 million square miles in area, or 80 percent of the former union.

14.18. Although the Asian Republics have seceded from the union, their secession will have little or no effect upon the Commonwealth of Independent States that has developed from the original union. The Soviet Union, prior to disintegration, paid little or no attention to the Far Eastern Asian Republics. No attempt was made to develop their resources and improve the standard of living of the inhabitants. The Central Committee that governed the nation was just too busy preparing for war against Western Europe and the United States for fifty years to give any thought to improving the standard of living of the people of the Asian Republics. It was the most insane fifty-year program of any nation in the history of the world. Some of the former Asian Republics, especially Kazakhstan, are rich in mineral resources, and if they open their borders to investment and development, they will experience real changes from their secession from the union.

14.19. Disintegration of the Soviet Union forced them to stop their menacing actions toward Western Europe and the United States. The North Atlantic Treaty Organization (NATO) and the Soviet Union and its former satellite nations signed a mutual nonaggression pledge and an arms control treaty. These agreements signaled the end of what the media had called for fifty years the "cold war" but which, in actuality, was never "cold" and never should have had that designation. If the former Soviet Union's actions during the Korean and Vietnam Wars and attempt during the Kennedy administration to place nuclear missiles within sixty miles of the borders of the United States were cold war actions, then *cold* needs to be redefined.

14.20. The disintegration of the Soviet Union has raised many problems that concern all nations of the world. They have plutonium-producing plants and huge arsenals of nuclear warhead missiles, which must be deactivated and all products stored in a securely guarded area. Also, many of their nuclear power plants are now operating beyond their life expectancy and with outmoded technology. Ironically, the production of the nuclear warhead missiles by the Soviet Union forced the United States to spend billions of dollars yearly to counter the threat, and now they are pledging billions of dollars for deactivation of the threat. Unless some kind of different approach is taken, it appears that the seceding republics of the former Soviet Union will be on the backs of the American people well into the next century. There is something wrong with this scenario, and either the legislative or the executive branch of government should stop bickering about abortion, term limits, gun control, and school prayer long enough to give the matter some thought. Provide the necessary technology to deactivate the atomic warhead missiles, improve the technology or dismantle the nuclear power plants, and furnish a safe secure storage area for the plutonium and deactivated warheads, but let the independent republics and Commonwealth of Independent States support themselves. They maneuvered themselves into the mess, and now we should let them maneuver themselves out of it. The Commonwealth of Independent States is still a giant of a country with vast mineral resources and air and land forces still capable of overrunning Western Europe. The world must remain wary until the final effects of the disintegration shake out.

14.21. In August 1990 President Bush was faced with another major crisis when Iraq invaded and overran Kuwait. Saddam Hussein, the Iraqi president, had built the largest armed force in the Middle East, and he needed the petroleum fields of Kuwait to support it. After the invasion, diplomats of many nations throughout the world attempted to persuade Saddam to retreat back to the original border, but the entreaties were to no avail. In January 1991 the allied army started an air bombardment, which lasted close to a month. The subsequent ground invasion lasted only 100 hours before President Bush called for a cease-fire.

14.22. For some reason President Bush made no effort to remove Saddam Hussein from his leadership position in Iraq but left it up to the Iraqi people to force his resignation. Saddam's loyal army troops were never on the front line. They had apparently suffered no casualties from the month-long bombardment, and the end result was, war or no war, Saddam remained just as powerful as he ever had been in Iraq. To show the allied armies that he was still in control and that he held them in contempt, he ordered his retreating army to set fire to the oil wells in

Table 14.1

Total Annual Production of Iron Ore in the United States, 1989–92, Compared to That
Produced by the Lake Superior District and the Mesabi Range (U.S. Geological Survey
and U.S. Bureau of Mines 1992)
(in thousand long tons)

| Year | Total Tons | Lake Superior District | | Mesabi Iron Range | | |
		Tons	Percentage of Total	Tons	Percentage of Total	Tons Accumulated
1989	58,099	56,081	96	40,716	70	3,605,343
1990	55,517	53,765	97	44,446	80	3,649,789
1991	55,867	54,760	98	42,314	76	3,692,103
1992	54,717	54,151	99	40,424	74	3,732,527

Kuwait. By that time President Bush had called for a cease-fire and informed Congress that the war was over; thus all he could do was whine from the Oval Office that Saddam should be tried for environmental terrorism. That statement certainly must have given Saddam and his generals a moment of triumph in their humiliating defeat.

14.23. The administration and Congress revised the Clean Air Act in 1990. The original Clean Air Act was passed during the Johnson administration. The antipollution standards were intensified in the revision passed during the Nixon administration and further enhanced in a revision passed in 1977 during the Carter administration. The standards were markedly increased in measure by the revision in 1990. The compliance standards were to be phased in over a period of ten years starting on January 1, 1995. As the standards increase in measure, the cost to the American people will also be measured in billions of dollars.

14.24. There was no improvement in the status of the minerals industry under the Bush administration. The same sequence of tables on the steel industry that has been presented in previous chapters is presented in this chapter.

14.25. Table 14.1 shows that in 1992 a total of 99 percent of the iron ore produced in the United States was being produced in the Lake Superior District and 74 percent of this production was from the Mesabi Range. Table 14.2 shows that by 1992 imports of iron ore from Europe were 343 thousand long tons. Most of the imports were coming from Canada and South America. Table 14.3 shows that the trade protection laws enacted during the Reagan administration to stop the imports of subsidized steel were having some effect. In 1984–86 the percentage of steel produced domestically and imported was as follows: 1984 and 1985: domestic 77 percent, imported 23 percent; and 1986: domestic 79 percent, imported 21 percent. In 1990 and 1991 the percentage of steel

Table 14.2
Iron Ore Imported for Consumption into the United States by Continents, 1989–92
(U.S. Geological Survey and U.S. Bureau of Mines 1992)
(in thousand long tons)
(in thousand dollars)

Year	North America		South America		Europe and Remainder	
Year	Long Tons	Value	Long Tons	Value	Long Tons	Value
1989	8,675	292,866	9,802	206,732	1,432	22,664
1990	9,493	339,622	8,104	202,819	746	17,084
1991	7,416	266,496	5,592	155,798	539	14,484
1992	6,726	242,877	5,078	140,290	343	9,171

Table 14.3
Production, Imports, and Exports of Pig Iron and Steel in the United States, 1989–92
(U.S. Geological Survey and U.S. Bureau of Mines 1992)
(in thousand short tons)

Year	Pig Iron			Steel		
Year	Production	Imports	Exports	Production	Imports	Exports
1989	55,873	488	12	97,943	17,333	4,578
1990	54,750	382	15	98,906	17,162	4,303
1991	48,637	478	17	81,895	15,741	6,346
1992	52,224	548	36	92,948	17,075	4,288

Table 14.4
World Production of Steel with the Production and Percentage Produced by the United States, USSR Separate from Europe, Europe, Japan, and Other Nations, 1989–92 (U.S. Geological Survey and U.S. Bureau of Mines 1992)
(in million short tons)

Year	World Tons	U.S. Tons	%	USSR Tons	%	Europe Tons	%	Japan Tons	%	Other %
1989	866.6	97.9	11	176.4	20	239.9	28	118.9	14	27
1990	849.5	98.9	12	170.2	20	222.9	26	121.6	14	28
1991	811.8	87.9	11	146.2	18	197.7	24	120.9	15	32
1992	796.3	92.9	12	118.9	15	188.0	24	108.2	14	36

Table 14.5
Gross Federal Debt at the End of the Year, 1989–92 (Bureau of Public Debt)
(in millions of dollars)

Year	Gross Federal Debt	Year	Gross Federal Debt
1989	2,867,493	1991	3,598,303
1990	3,206,207	1992	4,001,941

Table 14.6
Merchandise Trade with Japan Adjusted to Balance of Payments Basis, 1989–92
(Bureau of Public Debt)
(in millions of dollars)

Year	Imports	Year	Imports
1989	−49,666	1991	−45,040
1990	−42,564	1992	−50,513

Table 14.7
Annual Population Estimates in the United States, 1989–91 (Economics and Statistics Administration 1992)
(in thousands)

Year	Total Resident Population	Year	Total Resident Population
1989	248,239	1991	252,177
1990	248,710		

imports had dropped to 15 and 16 percent, respectively, although in 1992 the percentage of imports had increased to 18 percent.

14.26. Table 14.4 shows that the United States in 1989, 1990, 1991, and 1992 was able to hold its share of world steel production at 11 and 12 percent. The former USSR, which is now the Commonwealth of Independent States, would be expected to lose steel production because of the secession of the Baltic and Asian Republics from the union; however, the commonwealth is still the largest single-nation steel producer in the world by a wide margin. The "Other" production, which includes China and the Third World nations; increased to 36 percent in 1992, and this increase is indicative that China and the Third World nations have every intention of continuing to produce more Yankee ingenuity and Yankee know-how.

14.27. Table 14.5 shows that the average annual increase in the national debt during the Bush administration was $283.8 billion. The national debt totaled over $4 trillion in 1992. This is a mammoth figure totally beyond the comprehension of fully 99 percent of the electorate. Congress appears to regard the debt as less important than school prayer, abortion, gun control, term limits, and getting elected to office.

14.28. The gargantuan size of the national debt becomes even more critical when it is realized that the ability of the United States to repay the debt is constantly being eroded by the failure to maintain the domestic minerals industry in a prosperous and viable state. The ferrous metals division of the minerals industry is fighting to maintain its share of world production, but it is beset on all sides by forces that tend to undermine its ability to function. Domestic iron ore production is being threatened by cheaper imported iron ore; subsidized steel is constantly being imported; there is little possibility to increase steel exports because Third World nations are increasing domestic steel capacity to meet their requirements; and as the standards of the revised Clean Air Act increase in measure starting on January 1, 1995, the ability to compete in the domestic market will become even more difficult. The nonferrous division is continuing to lose the domestic mining industry, and to add insult to injury, the negative balance of trade with Japan reached −$50.5 billion in 1992, as shown in table 14.6. With the domestic minerals industry in the state that it is and the balance of trade with Japan negative in the amount of a −$50.5 billion, there is absolutely no chance that payments of any sizable amount can be made on the national debt.

14.29. The conservative wing of the Republican Party and most of the independent voters had become totally disenchanted with President Bush's administration. The Republican Party platform could be everything that they desired, but they had no intention of voting for him, even if it meant electing a Democrat. Bush's failure to remove Saddam Hussein from the leadership of Iraq could have been a negative, but little about the failure was mentioned during the campaign. The venomous media treatment of Dan Quayle, which never ceased during the four-year term, reached the same crescendo that marked the ending of the initial campaign in 1988.

14.30. Quayle refused to give Bush an out by withdrawing from the vice presidency but clung like a burr to the president's back. Bush denies that he ever considered dumping Quayle from the ticket; however, a former Bush campaign adviser claims that they tried to get Quayle to resign voluntarily from the ticket, but he refused to do so (*Business Week* 1994). If he was removed from the ticket, Bush was going to have to be the one to do it (*Business Week* 1994). For some reason or other, President Bush lapsed into what could be termed an indecisive languid campaign, somewhat reminiscent of the type of campaign waged by his Democrat opponent, Michael Dukakis, in 1988. However, keeping Quayle on the ticket and the type of campaign that Bush ran had nothing to do with the eventual outcome; his defeat was caused by the entry of Ross Perot into the race as a third-party candidate under the banner of United We Stand America. He lost the election to Bill Clinton.

Summary of the Era from 1976 to 1992

14.31. The era from 1976 to 1992 was an epoch of enormous growth of the national debt and minus trade balance with Japan. It was the period when the debt, energy, and inflation problems generated by the Kennedy, Johnson, and Nixon administrations were passed on to four administrations. All four appeared to recognize that the debt and minus trade balance were growing, but the recognition involved no direct action to correct the situation. The era of rising debt has not ended, and it is now doubtful if it will end by year 2000. The national debt has reached such magnitude that it is beyond the understanding of a large part of the American public.

14.32. Figures 14.1 and 14.2 are continuations of figures 11.1 and 11.2. Figure 14.1 shows that by 1977 the primary domestic producer was the Mesabi Iron Range. The sharp downturn in production in 1982 reflects the recession that occurred after President Reagan took office. Figure 14.2 shows that raw steel imports in 1984 amounted to almost 30 million short tons, and it was necessary for the domestic industry to seek protective laws to stop dumping and selling raw steel under cost.

14.33. Figure 14.3: "The Annual Value of Iron Ore Imported for Consumption" shows that the need for imported iron ore dropped sharply after the loss of a large amount of steel capacity under the Reagan administration. North America (Canada) and South America had become the primary suppliers. Europe and other nations were importing only a small tonnage.

14.34. Figure 14.4 is a continuation of figure 11.4. Series 1 is the percentage production of the United States, Series 2 that of the USSR, separate from Europe, series 3 that of Europe, series 4, that of Japan, and series 5, that of all other nations. Figure 14.4 shows that the annual percentage of steel produced in the United States as compared to the rest of the world continued to drop. Other nations started a strong move upward in the midseventies by producing steel by direct reduction methods. This group includes China, who by this time was indicating that it was going to join in the race in the production of Yankee ingenuity and Yankee know-how. Japan passed the United States in percentage of steel produced in 1981, and by 1982 the United States was fifth in percentage produced behind Europe, the USSR, Japan, and other nations.

14.35. Figure 14.5 shows that the annual resident population increased from 220 million in 1977 to over 250 million in 1991. The increases in percentages of world steel production by Europe and Japan indicate that most of the steel required by the increase in resident population was being supplied by these nations.

14.36. Figure 14.6 shows that the gross federal debt at the end of the year had reached a trillion dollars by 1981, and in eight years of the Reagan administration it had exploded past $2.5 trillion. It kept going up at the same rate during the Bush administration, reaching $4 trillion in 1992.

14.37. The merchandise trade with Japan adjusted to balance of payments basis is shown in figure 14.7 for years 1979 to 1992. In 1992, at the end of the Bush administration, the minus trade balance totaled $50 billion. The upward trend of the period between 1990 and 1992 in figure 14.7 is not expected to continue its current course under the Clinton administration.

FIGURE 14.1--ANNUAL PRODUCTION OF IRON ORE 1976-1992 COMPARED TO THAT
PRODUCED BY THE MESABI RANGE

FIGURE 14.2--ANNUAL PRODUCTION OF STEEL AND RAW STEEL IMPORTS 1976-1992

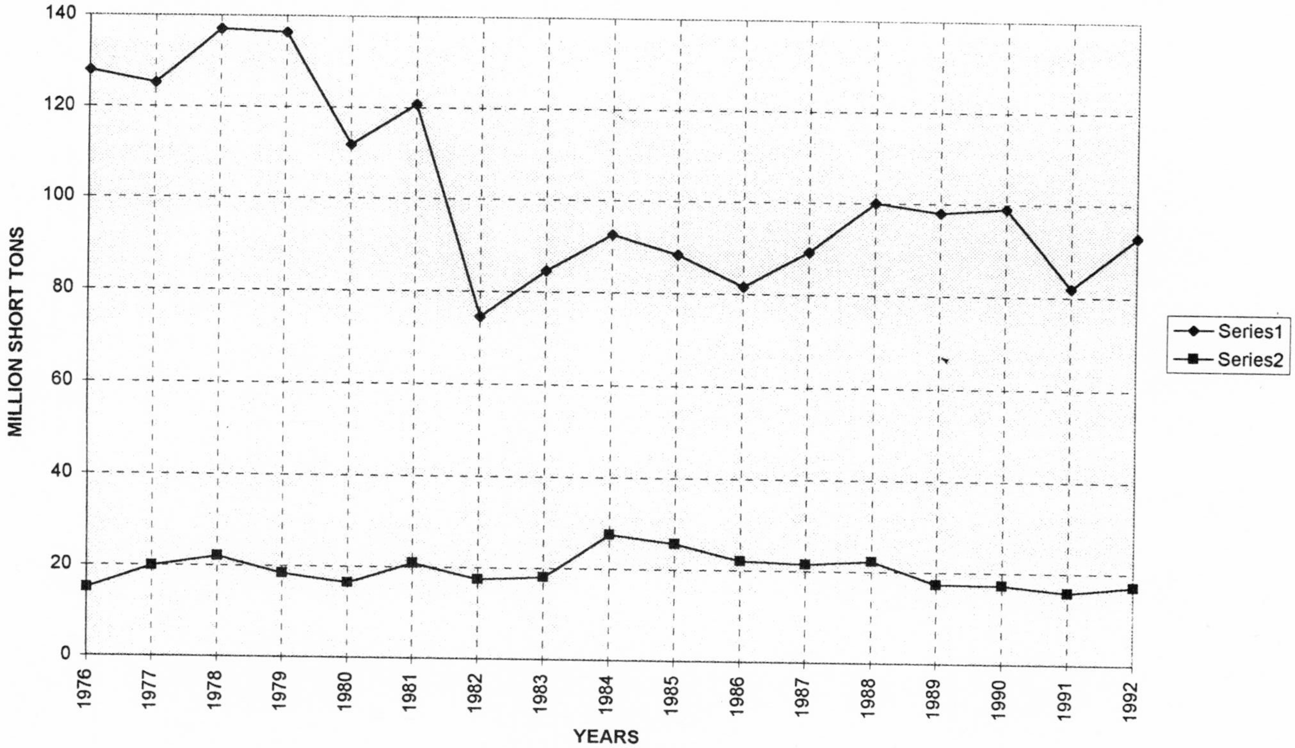

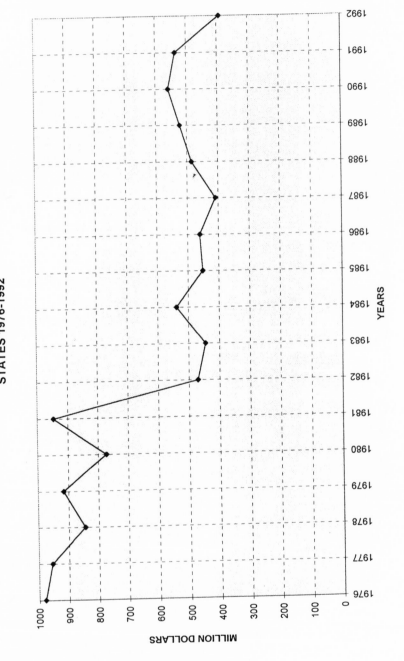

14.3--ANNUAL VALUE OF IRON ORE IMPORTED FOR CONSUMPTION INTO THE UNITED STATES 1976-1992

FIGURE 14.4--ANNUAL PERCENTAGE OF STEEL PRODUCED IN THE WORLD BY THE U.S., U.S.S.R. SEPARATE FROM EUROPE, EUROPE, JAPAN, AND OTHER, 1976-1992

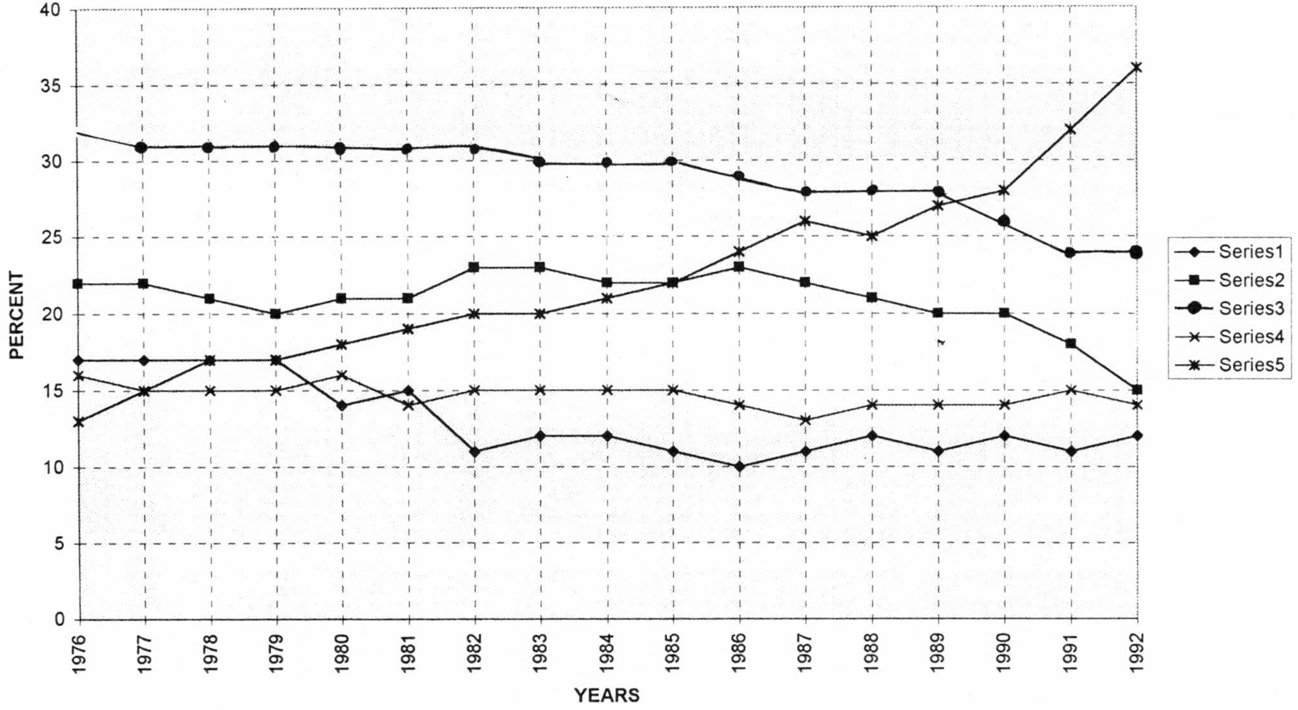

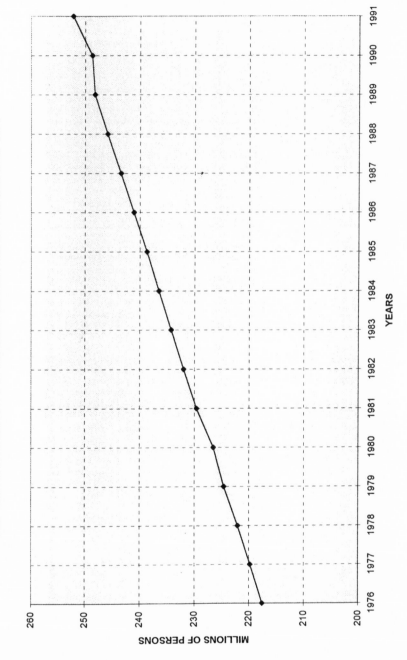

14.5--ANNUAL RESIDENT POPULATION ESTIMATES IN THE U.S. 1976-1991

MILLIONS OF PERSONS

YEARS

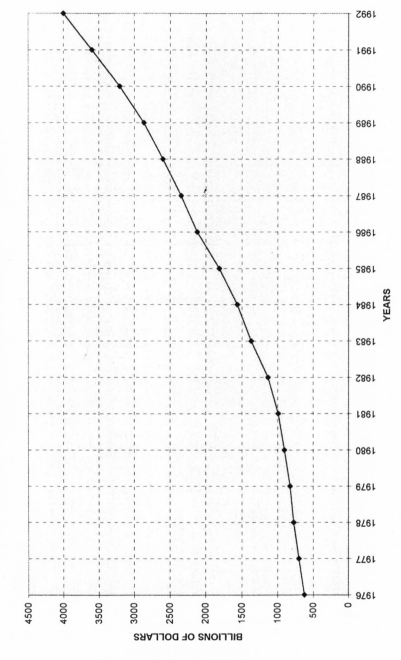

FIGURE 14.6--GROSS FEDERAL DEBT AT THE END OF YEAR 1976-1992

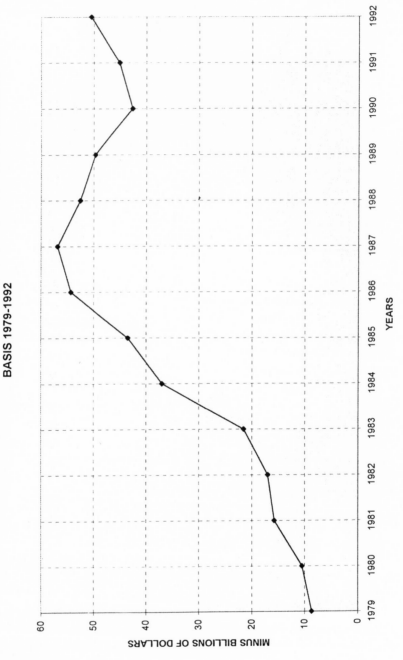

FIGURE 14.7--MERCHANDISE TRADE WITH JAPAN ADJUSTED TO BALANCE OF PAYMENTS
BASIS 1979-1992

MINUS BILLIONS OF DOLLARS

YEARS

15

The Next Four Years (1992–96): Clinton

15.1. In the 1992 campaign for the presidency a third-party ticket headed by Ross Perot surfaced to run against the Democratic candidate, Bill Clinton, and the Republican incumbent, George Bush. The electoral vote was: Clinton, 370; Bush, 168; Perot, 0. The popular vote was split Clinton 43.2 percent, Bush 37.8 percent, and Perot 19.0 percent. The 19 percent obtained by Mr. Perot was in a large part a combined independent and anti-Bush vote. The Democrats had been waiting for this moment for twelve years. Mr. Clinton called the victory a "clarion call" for change, and the party workers were jubilant even though 56.8 percent of the voters marked their ballots for opposing candidates.

15.2. Mr. Clinton had campaigned in Texas for George McGovern, the Democratic nominee for president in 1972 (DeGregorio 1993). Clinton's support of Senator McGovern indicates that he was far to the left in political philosophy in his late twenties. He was a law professor at the University of Arkansas from 1973 to 1976, attorney general of Arkansas from 1977 to 1979, and governor of Arkansas from 1979 to 1981 (DeGregorio 1993). He was forty-six years old when he was elected president. He appointed a group of young White House aides who displayed considerable amount of "gung ho" and exuberance but very little in the way of political "smarts" or knowledge at the federal level. Although a Rhodes scholar, President Clinton at the start of his administration had considerable trouble with numbers representing percentages of a whole. It would require two years and the elections in 1994 to convince him that only a little more than 43 percent of the people were responsive to his programs and this percentage simply did not represent enough voters to win an election if it was only a two-party contest.

15.3. During the campaign Mr. Clinton sang the same song as all the others that preceded him. He called for change. He would solve the social and economic problems facing the nation, and in the course of the campaign he managed to promise everything to everybody. As soon as he took office, it became obvious how he was going to do it. He would levy taxes, reduce government costs, and redistribute this wealth through health care reform and other social programs. Payments on the national debt would be made by utilizing the savings obtained from reducing government costs and by increasing economic growth. How he intended to increase economic growth and at the same time raise taxes on those he was depending upon to increase the growth was never explained. His program was nothing more than a rerun of the Kennedy and Johnson administrations: levy taxes, develop and enact into law new social, including health, programs, but at the same time make no effort whatsoever to create more wealth.

15.4. President Clinton appointed the following cabinet members: Secretary of State Warren Christopher, Secretary of the Treasury Lloyd Bentsen, Secretary of Defense Les Aspin, Attorney General Janet Reno, Secretary of the Interior Bruce Babbitt, Secretary of Agriculture Mike Espy, Secretary of Commerce Ronald H. Brown, Secretary of Labor Robert B. Reich, Secretary of Health and Human Services Donna Shalala, Secretary of Housing and Urban Development Henry G. Cisneros, Secretary of Transportation Federico Pena, Secretary of Energy Hazel R. O'Leary, Secretary of Education Richard W. Riley, and Secretary of Veterans' Affairs Jesse Brown.

15.5. With the exception of Treasury Secretary Lloyd Bentsen, the cabinet appointees were in general in tune with President Clinton's political philosophy. Mr. Bentsen was from the conservative wing of the Democratic Party and further to the right than George Bush; in political philosophy Clinton and Bentsen were polar opposites.

15.6. Mr. Clinton had chosen Al Gore to be his running mate. Senator Gore was a strong environmentalist, and he had a considerable amount of influence in the administration in regard to environmental policies and the appointment of individuals in environmentally sensitive departments. Gore had expressed his views on environmental issues in a book. The selection of Gore and the influence that he had in the administration on environmental policies indicates that President Clinton may be a strong environmentalist himself.

15.7. Clinton's presidency got off to a rough start. His inexperienced, weak, and sloppy White House staff failed to properly screen his first two female appointees for attorney general. Both withdrew their nominations because of similiar violations of what could be called the "nanny law" (DeGregorio 1993). The botched affair was somewhat amazing. The first nominee had a salary well into six figures with a private company, the second was a judge, and both had working husbands with comparable incomes. Neither the first nor second nominee would have had any hardship whatsoever in hiring a citizen, paying reasonable wages, and making the necessary Social Security payments as required by law.

15.8. Clinton was determined to be the first president to appoint a female attorney general, and come hell or high water he was going to keep choosing women lawyers with the proper political credentials until he found one who had a clean record. He finally settled on Janet Reno, who was the state attorney for Dade County, Florida. That she was the third choice for the cabinet post did not appear to bother Miss Reno.

15.9. President Clinton appointed his wife, Hillary, as head of the Task Force on National Health Reform. The task force was charged with the responsibility of developing a national health care system. For some reason or other, the task force started out as if there were no other health care programs in existence anywhere. By their actions it appeared as if they were going to reinvent the stethoscope, and the final program that resulted from the evolution indicated that they had made an effort to do so. The final program completed by the task force in late 1994 was described in a thick document containing more than one hundred pages, which few people attempted to plow through. Without reading the document, the Democrats universally proclaimed it the answer to all national health care problems. Without reading the document, the Republicans universally proclaimed it to be an abomination.

15.10. For forty years the U.S. government has had a remarkably successful health care program for all of its employees and retirees. Over the forty-year period this program has been amended and improved to fit various conditions. Now it is a well-organized and smooth-running health care plan. One would have thought that this program would have been a model for the task force, but it was ignored completely. This successful program would have to be altered completely to fit into the program devised by the task force. The task force certainly must have had enough political sense to realize beforehand that any program dealing with national health care would receive a barrage of criticism from many different constituencies, and that they would take off into "never never land" is not understandable. If they had adopted what was already a successful working health care program, they would have had a solid base upon which to build an expanded health care plan for the nation. The program developed by the task force was declared dead on arrival at the end of 1994. Whether it will be resurrected in 1995 or 1996 remains to be seen, but it appears that it will have little chance of even being considered by the new Congress. There is only a single word needed to describe the whole sad affair: *botchery.*

15.11. To some extent that single word is also relevant to Clinton's first year as president. After one year it was obvious that the confidence he exuded and the excitement he tended to generate among his fellow Democrats was nothing more than a thin shell, a patina, that covered up ignorance of government at the federal level. The programs he campaigned on were merely figments that were sketched out roughly and hastily for presentation in a speech while campaigning for the presidency. It was his method of promising everything to everybody on the spur of the moment. He was well to the left of center in political ideology, but actually he occupied no identifiable political groove. He zigged and zagged, but he was always zigging when he should have zagged and zagging when he should have zigged. In regard to the minerals industry, he was traveling down the exact same path taken by the eight administrations that had preceded him, and three years into his term, no cabinet member had surfaced to advise him differently.

15.12. Certainly Sen. Dale Bumpers from President Clinton's home state of Arkansas was not competent to advise him on any aspect of the minerals industry. Senator Bumpers had his own ax to grind. He was more concerned with mining law revision than delving into the massive problems facing the minerals industry. Judging from the original Senate Bill for Mining Law Revision, his intent was to change drastically the current mining law and impose a royalty fee on all mineral commodities mined on the public domain.

15.13. There is nothing wrong with revising what has been an eminently successful law to bring it up-to-date to fit current conditions as long as those who are making the revisions know what they are doing. A mistake in the revision can create irreparable damage to America's most basic industry. Senator Bumpers's bill for revision as it was submitted to Congress was certainly solid proof that he had no knowledge whatsoever of the minerals Industry. Today the prices for many metallic and nonmetallic mineral commodities are set on an international basis (see paragraph 1.3), and now with NAFTA and GATT in force, international pricing of all mineral commodities is a real probability. A domestic mining company either meets these prices or shuts down; it has no other option, unless the mining company or government for some reason wants to subsidize the operation to keep it producing. Thus if the articles of the proposed new mining law are too harsh and the royalty payments are set too high, domestic production of mineral commodities on public lands will stop, and the exploration and development of domestic mineral deposits on public lands will also cease.

15.14. Those concerned with revising the mining law must be highly aware that a mistake in revising the provisions of the law and setting the amount of the royalty payments can result in absolute devastation of America's most basic industry. They must also assess carefully what the intent is in applying the royalty payment system in the first place. If the purpose is to obtain funds for government operation, reducing the debt, and providing funds for entitlement programs, then it would be prudent for Congress and the administration to make another detailed study of the situation.

15.15. At the present time and under the best of circumstances a royalty fee system is not going to be a "horn of plenty." Currently the international competition that is now in the marketplace for the sale of mineral commodities is intense, and most commodities are selling on the international market at a reasonable price. Thus the royalty charges are going to have to be modest in order to maintain a viable domestic mining industry on the public lands. In actuality, at this period in time, wherein we casually talk about billions, the total dollar amount obtained from moderate royalty charges will be little more than a pittance and will have little effect on the balance sheet of the nation. Certainly the consequences that excess royalty charges might have at this time would not be worth the risk of destroying a law that is still effective for one that could result in a partial or full cessation of mining operations on public lands. There is also another aspect in regard to revising the mining law that Congress should examine closely, and that is the withdrawal of public lands to prevent exploration, development, and mining. Withdrawal of all public lands to bar mining is the goal of the environmental political bloc. However, if much more land is withdrawn for single-purpose use, there will be no reason to revise the mining law. The prime land for exploration that may contain minerals will be under one of the withdrawal categories, and there will be no available land upon which to file a viable claim. If such occurs, the long-term trend for the United

States is, like Japan, the expending of wealth to import the greater part of their needed mineral commodities.

15.16. The problems of the minerals industry that started with the Kennedy administration and burst into a bleeding ulcer during the Reagan administration were passed on through the Bush administration into the Clinton administration. In addition, the sharp rise in the proportion of year-round full-time workers with low annual earnings that occurred during the Carter, Reagan, and Bush administrations appeared to be continuing on the same upward trend. Despite the improving economy, many feel that they are strapped for money, and an ominous trend in American life is developing wherein highly qualified middle-aged individuals find themselves downsized into lower-paying jobs (Lewis 1994). Job downsizing has a most devastating effect on an individual and tends to leave him or her discouraged and bewildered as to what to do next.

15.17. Under the Clinton administration there has been little, if any, improvement in the problems of the U.S. automobile industry with respect to Japanese imports. The era of "screw ya" gave the Japanese and European automobile manufacturers a huge opening into the U.S. market, which to this date they have not relinquished and which, in fact, they have continued to expand upon. The U.S. car manufacturers have discovered that merely correcting the problems that spawned the era of "screw ya" is not all that has to be done to bring the American public back into the "buy American" fold. They must prove beyond all question that the automobile they are producing is a better automobile than that being produced by the Japanese and European industries. This is an extremely difficult task, and without doubt the American automobile industry is headed for a knockdown, drag-out fight that may well define the structure of the industry in the future.

15.18. In 1981 the supply-side economists of the Reagan administration, to avoid being labeled as anti–free trade, managed to obtain from the Japanese a voluntary restriction on the number of automobile exports to the U.S. market. The Japanese immediately started to maneuver around this restriction by constructing assembly plants in the United States. The major components of the automobiles come from Japan, and in 1992 20 percent of the automobiles produced in the United States were from these Japanese assembly plants (Sullivan 1992). The American automobile industry is in a competitive market battle not only with Japan but also with Europe, which may well determine the structure of the industry for a long period of time in the future. The "screw ya" era is proving to be the greatest blunder in customer relations made by an industry since the Mesabi Iron Range went on line in 1892. It appears that the shoddy automobile product experiences are being handed down from parents to offspring by memorabilia. If this proves to be the case, the effects of the "screw ya" era could continue for generations.

15.19. The elections in 1994 had a profound effect upon President Clinton, and in some respects he appears to have settled into a political groove that he did not occupy before. The Republicans gained control of the Senate and House of Representatives. For the first time during his presidency Clinton appeared to realize that if it was only a two-party contest, receiving 43 percent of the popular vote in a three-party election was not a "clarion call" for change in government policy, as he had been interpreting it; rather, it was a "clarion call" to change one's political philosophy and change it fast in case the 1996 election became a two-party contest for the presidency.

15.20. President Clinton wasted no time but after the 1994 elections moved from the left to the absolute center of political ideology. This is an exceptionally long jump for a McGovern Democrat, and it indicates that whatever political ideology it is, from alpha to omega, Clinton can swallow it. He made the transformation so fast that he left the left-of-center group in the Democratic Party gasping for breath in the vacuum he created. In addition, for the time being, he appeared to have placed on hold the more controversial domestic programs that he campaigned for in 1992. He apparently felt that if he stayed in the political center, he would force the far right members of the Republican Party to field a third-party candidate again in 1996. His strategy was certainly sound. Whether Clinton's programs succeeded or failed would have no bearing on the outcome of the election. The final result would be determined by whether or not there was a third-party candidate. Apparently he decided that he was able to jump from the left to the center in 1995 without difficulty; therefore after the election he should be able to jump back.

15.21. To reinforce his claim on the ideological political center, President Clinton consistently reiterated in press conferences and interviews that the nation should not go back to the "trickle down economics" of the Reagan administration. Up to that point in time Clinton had failed to realize that as long as he continues to ignore the minerals industry he will be continuing along the same general political path that has characterized the past eight administrations. If he insists on a label to distinguish his administration from that of Reagan, his could be labeled as "dribble down economics," because there is little variance between the two. President Clinton, like the previous eight presidents, failed to understand that the only way in which massive change can occur in the United States is by reversing the current downward trend of the U.S. minerals industry.

15.22. However, the fact that President Clinton was ignoring the problems of the minerals industry does not mean that the problems would be addressed in the 1996 election for the presidency. Those who were maneuvering to become the Republican Party nominee appeared to have no greater grasp of the major problems facing the nation than Clinton. The Republican Party was as divided as ever on abortion, school prayer, welfare, gun control, and other minor matters. If the party had managed to avoid the formation of a third party and win the election, its label might well have been "ooze down economics"; otherwise, the "dribble down economics" of the Clinton administration would continue. Whichever it was, "dribble down" or "ooze down," there would be no more difference than between twenty and a score.

15.23. The crop of Republicans attempting to position themselves in January 1995 to be the party's nominee for president in 1996 contained a real surprise. Dan Quayle, vice president under Bush, started to survey the field to assess his chances of becoming the Republican nominee. However, by February 9, 1995, reality set in and he withdrew when he discovered that there were no backers with deep pockets to finance his run for the nomination. If optimism was a virtue, Mr. Quayle would certainly be a candidate for the most virtuous individual in the history of the nation. If he thought for one moment that the media was going to admit that they were wrong in savaging him when he was vice president, he was living in a dream world of his own making. If he had entered the race to be the Republican nominee, the media would have started on him right where they left off in 1992, and the barrage would have been just as venomous as ever. With the media blasting away as they did in 1992, Mr. Quayle would have a better chance of being elected pope by the College of Cardinals than being chosen as the nominee of the Republican Party or, for that matter, elected president by the electorate of the United States. In any event, the efforts by the various Republicans went for naught. Perot entered the race, and President Clinton won easily.

15.24. On January 1, 1995, the increased measures of the Clean Air Act passed during the Bush administration were supposed to kick in, but there was a resistance building up across the nation against the action (Regan and Woodruff 1994–95). Whether or not this show of opposition will gel into an all-out effort to quash the more stringent measures of the act remains to be determined. The environmental political bloc has a body of favorable judicial decisions dating back twenty-five years, and it is not likely that they will stand idly by and let the EPA water down the measures or allow Congress to start tinkering with changes. After all, they wrote the act and if there is to be any tinkering, the measures will be intensified, not diminished. The bloc's motto is "we will see you in court if you disagree with us," and it is almost a certainty that watering down the measures will spur the bloc to live up to its motto.

15.25. The Clean Air Act also mandates on January 1, 1995, the use of reformulated gasoline (RFG). Step one of the act requires the addition of ethanol to gasoline to lower the emission of carbon monoxide in high-density-traffic areas. (The use of ethanol in gasoline is discussed in appendix 9.)

15.26. It has been forty-three years since Harry S Truman decided not to run for another term. When President Truman retired, awareness in the public and government of the minerals industry as the roots of our industrialization and standard of living died. He was president when the domestic minerals industry was at the very height of its productive capacity, yet he started a program to develop a strategic plan of action to ensure that there would always be available a plentiful supply of mineral commodities to maintain the industrial base and a high standard of living for the populace (see paragraph 6.28). In addition, he started the DMA and DMEA programs to develop increased domestic production of certain mineral commodities on public and private lands (see paragraph 6.19).

15.27. Contrast President Truman's program for the minerals industry with those of his nine successors. None of them paid any attention to the minerals industry except when petroleum was in short supply, they withdrew millions of acres of public land for single-use categories barring mining, and they passed environmental laws that have resulted in quagmire of lawsuits. The programs promulgated and recommended by President Truman are polar opposites in philosophy to those executed by his nine successors. Very little common sense is needed to decide who was right and who was wrong. The actions of President Truman's nine successors have placed Uncle Sam in hock up to his eyebrows, caused a sharp rise in percentage of workers with low annual earnings, forced a large segment of middle-aged workers into downsized jobs, placed the nation constantly in fear of runaway inflation, set the nation up so that it is continuously in a vulnerable position in regard to petroleum supply, generated a negative balance of trade with Japan in amounts running over $50 billion per year, and demoted the nation from a dominant industrialized position in the world to a point where it is questionable if it can maintain its current status at number four. As a statesman and president Truman stands so far above his nine successors that they are not even in the picture. By the complete record of his presidency during war and peace he proved that he can take his place in line with the greatest presidents in U.S. history.

15.28. Pundits rationalize the drop in the nation's industrial position in the world with "buzz" words such as "we are leaders in the information highway" and "our economy is changing from a resource-based to an information service economy." It is incomprehensible that anyone would utter or, for that matter, believe such hogwash. As long as the United States is an industrial nation, its economy will be resource-based and tied directly to the use of mineral commodities. Information service economies, or any other industrialized economy, cannot exist without mineral commodities, and as such the commodities are the base or roots of the economy. As the nation moves on toward a higher and higher industrialized technology, mineral commodities become more and more important, and as the population increases, the need for mineral commodities is certain to increase. As long as we remain an industrialized nation with a high standard of living, the minerals industry will be the basic foundation of the economy. If mineral commodities are not mined domestically, wealth will have to be expended to import them.

16

Probability for Change

16.1. From 1952 to 1994, four Democrats and five Republicans have held the presidency since Harry S Truman decided not to run for a second term. In the forty-two-year span not one of the nine presidents, Democrat or Republican, has attempted to correct the slow but continuous annual deterioration of the minerals industry. None have recognized the minerals industry as the roots of our standard of living. None have recognized that a plentiful supply of mineral commodities has made possible the "American dream" and living the "abundant life," which was promised by Franklin Roosevelt sixty years ago. However, slowly but inexorably the "American dream" is dying for many. The death hits home when individuals suddenly find themselves jobless in their calling with no prospects of changing the situation, downsized into lesser-paying jobs, and when they become painfully aware that their offspring have great difficulty in finding work in their fields of study after graduation from high school or college.

16.2. Today maintaining the armed forces, outer space program, atomic energy program, entitlement, social, and educational programs and the standard of living attained through the "abundant life" program requires imports of mineral commodities and products costing billions of dollars. Prior to the Truman administration the nation did not need to expend billions for the mineral commodities, as they were mined domestically, creating the maximum amount of wealth from each commodity produced. The massive wealth producers of the past are no longer active or are now producing mineral commodities at a much lower rate. The end result is that wealth has to be expended to import mineral commodities that were huge wealth producers in the past.

16.3. There is nothing wrong with importing mineral commodities as long as it is recognized by the president, Congress, and the public that wealth has to be expended to obtain them and the wealth they produce when made into a product is far less than it would be if they were mined within the nation's borders. Manufactured products produced from an imported mineral commodity are no different from those produced from the same commodity mined domestically. Gasoline produced from Middle East petroleum is the same as that produced from West Texas. The primary difference is the amount of wealth each provides to the nation.

16.4. It is certain that the Kennedy and Johnson administrations did not recognize that less wealth was being produced by an imported mineral commodity than by a commodity mined domestically. Presidents Johnson and Kennedy proposed and the Congress enacted social, educational, and entitlement programs just as if they had the same wealth that was being created during the Truman and Eisenhower administrations. That the wealth was not there to fund the programs did not appear to concern them at all, and they made no effort to determine what was causing the shortfall. The procedure that they set up to cover the shortfall was to annually borrow the necessary funds and attempt to redistribute available wealth by levying more and higher taxes. At no time was either the Kennedy or Johnson administration able to balance the budget during their terms.

16.5. In subsequent administrations the final course set by President Johnson was continued. An increasing trade deficit with Japan, inflation, and high interest rates on the borrowed funds added to the problem. The national debt continued to rise as each year passed and as each new administration took office. At no time did any of the administrations adjust their annual budgets to cover the increasing shortfall of funds caused by increasing importation of mineral commodities. The end result has been a continuously increasing annual shortfall of available funds for the social, educational, and entitlement programs that were passed by the Johnson administration and the same type of programs enacted by later administrations. To provide money for the shortfall the only source of funds was through borrowing and redistribution of wealth by additional taxes.

16.6. At the present time the nation has a huge trade deficit with Japan, is mired in massive debt, and has an annually increasing shortfall of funds for ongoing social, educational, and entitlement programs. There is little opportunity for the minerals industry to produce more wealth because of the huge withdrawal of lands under various classifications for single use and the strangling effect of environmental laws, such as the Environmental Policy Act of 1969, the Clean Air Act of 1990, and the Endangered Species Act.

16.7. It is difficult to understand why the administrations since the Eisenhower administration took the actions that they did in regard to land use. Always before them there had been the land use programs of Western Europe. These nations withdraw only small tracts of land within city or town boundaries for single designated use, such as parks, playgrounds, and tree-lined lanes. Almost all other lands are multiple-use. A prime example is their mountainous areas. These lands are used for every conceivable purpose, including restaurants, recreation, mining, agriculture, hunting, fishing, villages, scenic trails, roads, and railways. It is not unusual to find restaurants on mountain crests accessible by mountain railways or by trail and cable cars. The Western European countries have had no difficulty whatsoever in combining scenery viewing with economic use. They view mining not as a land-raping, polluting nuisance but as a wealth producer for the maintenance of their standard of living. Often to avoid importing a mineral commodity a mining project is subsidized by the government to create wealth domestically and to avoid the cost of importation.

16.8. If the land withdrawal program of the United States is difficult to understand, the massive foreign trade deficit with Japan is even more difficult to fathom. For many years the United States and Europe have been the prime supporters of the high standard of living attained by the Japanese. The efforts to date to change the situation by any administration have been feeble and border on the ridiculous. The elected and appointed officials of the U.S. government have moved so far away from recognition of what nourishes and maintains America's standard of living that they are unable to understand Japan's attitude toward foreign trade. Japan's need to import huge quantities of mineral commodities to maintain their industries and standard of living is the key to their intrasigeance in regard to the removal of restrictions on imports of products from other countries.

16.9. Third World countries from which Japan imports a substantial amount of mineral commodities can accept only a limited amount of Japanese manufactured products; thus their prime trading partners for these products must be their own population and the populations of the United States and Europe. Because of the huge cost outlay to obtain imported mineral commodities, they want no competition for the sale of products at home, and they must maintain a trade surplus with their

251

primary trading partners. If they cannot maintain a trade surplus with these nations, especially the United States, then they will be unable to retain their high standard of living. The United States and Europe, in effect, have been the major factors in the development and continued support of the Japanese high standard of living over the past forty years.

16.10. Japanese producers, like U.S. industries, view unsold inventory of manufactured products as costly; thus they will use their major trading partners to dump products at below manufacturing cost to avoid inventory buildup and accompanying interest costs. No matter what kind of trade treaty Japan signs with other countries, it will be one that they interpret as giving them the opportunity to maintain a trade surplus, and regardless of the terms of the treaty, dumping of excess inventory products will continue unabated. Lowering the standard of living of the people is as politically impossible in Japan as it is in the United States.

16.11. The nine administrations following Truman have continued on the same course as set by the Eisenhower administration and continued and enlarged upon by the Kennedy and Johnson administrations. Regardless of political affiliation, none have deviated from this course, and they have piled mistake upon mistake as each succeeding administration moved further and further away from recognition of the mineral industries as the roots that nourish the standard of living of the American people. The political parties are supposed to be different; thus there is no rational explanation of why both would move in the same direction. The composition of the president's cabinet made little or no difference; the course set in regard to the minerals industry remained the same. The never-ending withdrawal of lands from mining and the continuous enactment of restrictive environmental laws indicate that each succeeding political party, except for a few minor variations, was a clone of the other.

16.12. Even the most casual observers of city, county, state,and federal governments have to know that something has gone wrong with the present political system in the United States. Politicians will spend at least 70 percent of their speech time during an election campaign or in a television interview blaming the other political party for everything from depletion of the ozone layer to the national debt; in fact, on television their eyes will shine with delight and their faces become radiant with pleasure as they denigrate the opposing party. Politicians campaigning for office promise to make real economic and social changes that will solve the problems at that particular level. When they campaign for re-election they plead for more time because, in reality, they have accomplished nothing in the way of changes and rarely, if ever, solved anything of consequence.

16.13. At the national level they may have voted to enact laws that were supposed to cure the social ills of the nation, but in the final analysis, all the laws did was raise the national debt and throw more funds into a mess that became a bigger mess because there was more money to mess with. Congress is deadlocked on such issues as health care reform, women's rights, gay rights, abortion, school prayer, gun control, capital gain taxes, crime, racial problems, annual budgets, national debt, foreign policy, and entitlements of all kinds. There are now a growing number of skeptics in the United States who sense that elected office holders are unable to cope with the growing economic and social problems that are facing the nation today. These skeptics are uncertain of the course of action to take, but as a last resort they appear to be joining independents and moving in the direction of a third political party.

16.14. The Constitution of the United States contains nothing about political parties. The party system developed naturally as a system to nominate and subsequently elect individuals of a certain age and citizenship to serve a specified term in office. However, over a period of time the current two-party system as it has evolved has developed political alignments that are difficult to understand. In the Democratic Party, conservative southern factions in Congress coexist with northern liberals. Also, in the Republican Party ultraconservatives coexist with a larger but less conservative faction. The ultraconservative faction will bolt the party and refuse to vote if they consider the Republican ticket too liberal.

16.15. The strategy now in both parties is to nominate a president whose political ideology is midway between the extremes of the party and then choose an individual who has conservative approval for a vice-presidential running mate. When the parties deviate from this strategy they suffer humiliating defeats, such as the Republicans with Goldwater in 1966 and the Democrats with McGovern in 1972. Senator McGovern was an ultraliberal in the Democratic Party; even Hubert Humphrey, the staunchest of staunch Democrats, said publicly that some of McGovern's ideas where "screwy." The defeat of McGovern in 1972 started a chain of events that even in American politics has to be considered strange. Four years later the Democratic Party nominated Jimmy Carter,

a conservative southerner, who apparently drew votes from the ultraconservative faction that had supported Wallace in the 1968 election and
Nixon in the 1968 and 1972 elections. Carter was also strongly supported
by the two major black organizations, the NAACP and the Urban
League, and prominent blacks throughout the nation. Carter defeated
Ford, a conservative Republican with close ties to the ultraconservative
right wing faction of the Republican Party. Ford was a member of the
House of Representatives for many years, with a good voting record on
civil rights. There is no rational political explanation of such a sequence
of events.

16.16. An individual who created one of the strangest twists in
American political history was Earl Warren. Mr. Warren was a Republican governor of California and he was also Thomas E. Dewey's vice
presidential running mate on the Republican ticket in 1948. After Warren was appointed to the Supreme Court and no longer had to have the
approval of voters to hold office, he became an instant liberal in political
ideology. Mr. Warren was a political compromiser, not a judge, and he
should have never been appointed to the Supreme Court; some of the
decisions on which he held strong views that were handed down by
the Supreme Court during his tenure as Chief Justice reflected this
characteristic. The meanings were obscure and often raised more questions than they solved. Mr. Warren's tendency to compromise on virtually
anything that he was asked to obtain a consensus on is well illustrated
by his report to the nation on John F. Kennedy's assassination. The report
resolved nothing except to confirm that President Kennedy was killed
by gunfire.

16.17 The strange alignments in both parties are not confined
solely to the candidates running for or elected to office. Each party must
have a large cadre of voluntary workers at the grassroots level for making
direct contact to the voter. These volunteers have different objectives in
working for the various candidates. Some are angling for political jobs,
others enjoy politics and the prestige, and many are "winner worshipers"
who want to get involved in the political system and especially want to
be on the winning side.

16.18. When primary campaigning begins, the volunteers will select candidates at all levels of government and start working for them at
grassroots level, hoping that their candidates can win the party's nomination for office. During the primary campaign, volunteers will denigrate
rival candidates of the same party who are running for the same office.

At the end of the primaries, if their candidates lose, volunteers will on the following day start gushing superlatives about the winners, despite the fact that twenty-four hours earlier they were calling them dunces. This is what is called "presenting a united front to the opposing party."

16.19. The manner in which Sen. Gary Hart was forced out of the Democratic primaries in 1988 is probably the best example of the adaptibility of the volunteer party worker to change fealty to another candidate on a moment's notice. Senator Hart made a run for the Democratic presidential nomination in 1984, which was won by Walter Mondale. In the following four years Senator Hart kept himself well in the spotlight with the intent of making a strong run for the nomination in 1988, and during the time that campaigning in the primaries began it looked like he had an excellent chance to win. He had a strong organization and many loyal and eager workers at the grassroots level. They were praising his virtues and babbling that he was a sure winner because he was talking about the "issues."

16.20. However, everything turned upside down for the senator. The *Miami Herald* printed a story that a young lady had come to visit him while his wife was away. The affair received wide publicity, and although Senator Hart admitted she did visit him, he claimed nothing happened. In the end, it forced him out of the race. His volunteer workers went to work for other candidates. Later Senator Hart reentered the race, but it proved to be futile. His workers would not return, and in addition, they claimed that instead of talking about the "issues" he was being "devisive." Senator Hart's lady visitor must have been a remarkable person, because just by a casual visit she changed him in the eyes of his loyal and trusty followers from a man who discussed "issues" to a man who was "dividing the Democratic Party." This is without doubt feminine power with a capital F.

16.21. One can only wonder why Senator Hart did not seek the advice of fellow Democratic senator Ted Kennedy, who has weathered several affairs much more serious than Hart's. Kennedy could have told him to get a prestigous university to provide a forum and an audience and then indulge in a little self-flagellation—however, not too much, just enough to display some contrition. If the self-flagellation gambit fails, then deny everything, even if there is a book by a longtime coworker detailing a ten-year period of transgressions (Burke 1992). Piously state that the author was a disgruntled staff member; claim that you do not smoke, drink, sniff, or chew or go with the girls who do. This proved to be a highly successful line of action for Kennedy in his campaign to retain his Senate seat in the 1994 Massachusetts election. Kennedy's case was also helped by his getting married a few months before the election. It showed the gullible electorate that playing the field was now over; he had now found himself a safe little nook.

16.22. The vagaries of the politicians, the coexistence of various factions in both parties, and the chameleon loyalties of the grassroots workers are well known and seemingly tolerated without complaint by a large majority of the voting public. The conservative factions have forced both parties to be constantly in a fluid state of compromise. The framers of party platforms must always be ready to delete or insert statements that are objected to or favored by the factions. The party platforms have become nothing more than bombastic phrases that mean little insofar as action on issues facing the nation is concerned. However, somehow or other, for a long period of time a large percentage of the population have managed to find something in the platform of one of the parties that they are willing to support by casting their vote for the nominee of that party. The situation as it exists today has gone on so long that the parties, in the eyes of some members, have become permanent institutions and are revered in the same manner as the Constitution of the United States.

16.23. The members who revere and adore the parties are "regulars." No matter what the situation is in the nation, the "regulars" will vote the ticket "straight," that is, for all nominees of their party at all levels of government; without doubt, such voters are the backbone of the party. Each party is highly aware of the percentage of voters that they can depend on to back them without fail in a national election. In the 1992 election with Mr. Perot a third-party candidate, the vote was split roughly 43 percent for Clinton, 38 percent for Bush, and 19 percent for Perot. For all practical purposes these percentages represent the "regulars" in each party and roughly the independents and growing number of skeptics who are becoming dissatisfied with either the Democratic or Republican Party.

16.24. The result of the growing discontent with both parties was that in 1992 the "regulars" in the Democratic Party voted the Clinton-Gore ticket into office with only 43 percent of the national vote. If the third-party movement continues, the political party that manages to hold the greatest number of "regulars" is quite likely to consistently win the national election. For a third party to be successful, it must wean from both parties at least 40 percent of their "regulars." Desertion of the "regulars" from either party on such a scale appears at this time to be an impossibility.

16.25. For some time it has been obvious that instead of voting for the candidate, the majority of voters are voting for the system of nominating and electing a candidate—that is, they are voting for the party, not the candidate who is running for election. Graft and corruption within the system are widespread. Apparently unbeknownst to or unrecognized by the party voter, the party system has become a sieve for the entry of manipulators and money into the process, and these have become the controlling factors in determining who is nominated and who wins the election. The candidates need only the party's blessing and sufficient campaign funds for television and radio advertising, and they are certain to receive the votes of at least the party "regulars."

16.26. The high cost of campaigning makes the candidates beholden to those that supply the funds. Recognizing the opportunity, special interest groups have become active in both parties through what are called Political Action Committees (PACs) and have achieved a considerable amount of power within the parties by backing their selected candidates with funds through the election process. The most powerful and well-funded PACs often succeed in getting their candidates on the ticket and elected. An excellent example of a winning candidate backed by a powerful, well-funded PAC was Richard Nixon running against Hubert Humphrey in 1968 (see paragraph 10.2). It is also an excellent example of how the backing turned sour. Most of the PACs have a narrow self-interest, and many are formed solely to advance or impede certain social programs and continuance or elimination of entitlements.

16.27. The narrow self-interest of the PACs in the social and entitlement programs has infected them with tunnel vision, because they do not appear to require anything from the candidates other than that they support the views on the issues for which the PACs are lobbying. Such a system of selecting candidates for government office is proving to be devastating to the nation. Far too often the one- or two-issue candidates are being swept into office with PAC backing. They may have other interests, but the issues that got them elected occupy the greater part of their time. The minerals industry is discussed by most members of Congress only when they vote to withdraw lands from mining to create wilderness areas or to change the Mining Act of 1872, when petroleum starts

257

to be in short supply, when a mine, gravel pit, or oil well is likely to be situated in a location that is objectionable to their constituents, or when in a speech or interview on television they label mining a terrible polluting, foul-smelling, and land-raping industry.

16.28. The social and entitlement programs backed by many of the PACs do not produce wealth; they are consumers of wealth. This is also true of many of the programs backed by professional associations, such as the National Education Association (NEA), American Bar Association (ABA), American Medical Association (AMA), National Association for the Advancement of Colored People (NAACP), and Urban League. Year after year wealth has been expended on many of the programs backed by the PACs with no provision whatsoever to create wealth to cover their cost. To fund them, money has been borrowed or raised by raising or levying new taxes, and now the nation finds itself deep in debt, with interest costs increasing annually. Regardless of the national debt and its future consequences, the PACs continue their one-issue lobbying seemingly oblivious to the fact that borrowing funds for their programs cannot go on forever.

16.29. The Republican and Democratic Parties as they are now constituted are not going to be able to reverse the process. Almost all of the currently elected members of Congress and state governors are committed to the party system as it has evolved. They have voted for the environmental laws that have been passed and beholden to one or more PACs for the campaign funds that placed them in office. In most elections, nominees for president are drawn from either the state governors or from Congress; thus there is little hope that another administration is going to be any different from the last nine. The political parties change little over time. If one of them has been out of power for a considerable length of time, it makes no difference whatsoever, because when they again regain power, the same individuals who previously held key positions in the executive branch resurface and move back into the same positions. These individuals have not changed at all. They continue to make the same mistakes and pursue the same objectives as when they were previously in power. The beloved political party system as it has evolved over the past century has meandered into a political quagmire from which it is experiencing difficulty in extracting itself. The Democratic and Republican Parties are today's dinosaurs blundering into a tar pit, and they are in grave danger of becoming fossils, dead, but still the primary systems for selecting candidates for office.

16.30. The current political party system is also bolstered strongly by the electronic and print media. All will claim that they are neutral insofar as political affiliation is concerned, and to prove it the print media will carry both conservative and liberal columns on their editorial pages. However, even for the most disinterested of observers, after purusing the printed pages for a couple of weeks it is not difficult to discern the media's political preferences. During campaigns the editorial endorsements of candidates by the printed media have a familiar ring. The candidates always inherit their honorable intentions, social awareness, and integrity from their mother. They are patriotic beyond all questions. If their birthplace was a small town, they developed their values (whatever they are) growing up in this environment. If their birthplace was the Midwest, they developed their values in the heartland of America. In describing the candidates, to avoid saying that they are simple, they state that they are complex and drop it at that point.

16.31. The changing demographics of the western states erase any possibility that a political bloc can be formed in the West with enough clout to accomplish a change in the way the minerals industry is regarded in Congress. Many of the western states have had large concentrated population increases, which, if they do not now, will dominate the states politically in the near future. With this new electorate, a candidate campaigning for more wilderness areas will get elected over the one who campaigns for multiple use of the lands that constitute the federal domain.

16.32. Excellent examples of concentrated population increases that dominate the states politically are Washington and Oregon. In Washington the increase has centered primarily on the west side in the I-5 corridor running the full width of the state from the Canadian border, through Seattle, to Vancouver, on the Columbia River. These new state citizens will not support basic industries. Insofar as commercial fisheries and logging are concerned, both can be shut down; *mining* is not even in their vocabulary.

16.33. In Oregon the growth has also centered on the west side in the I-5 corridor from Portland, through Salem, to Eugene and at some future date may extend to the southern border. For over twenty-five years Oregon has been a state with high environmental awareness, and the new citizens are moving here primarily for what they call the quality of life that Oregon offers. Gov. Tom McCall is credited with starting the environmental movement in 1970, and today his full-size (six-foot-five) portrait in the Capitol Building in Salem depicts him walking on water. Stock raising on public lands has already come under fire, and mining, as always, will encounter strong citizen resistance. More areas are certain to be set aside for wilderness.

16.34. The results of a recent (1995) special election in Oregon to fill the vacancy left when Sen. Bob Packwood was ousted from the Senate for amorous advances toward women is an excellent example of how a highly populated area can rule a state politically. Ron Wyden, running solely on protecting the environment, Medicare, and Medicaid, won the election over Gordon Smith, a conservative businessman from eastern Oregon. Wyden carried the major populated counties surrounding the city of Portland and in the northwest corner of the state and some of the coastal counties. All other counties were carried by Smith. Wyden won despite the fact that on television in a debate he was unable to describe where Bosnia was located. The faithful who voted for him did not expect him to know that. All he had to do was protect the environment, Medicare, and Medicaid; let some other senator from another state be tuned into what was going on in Bosnia.

16.35. Almost all the western states have also had concentrations of population similiar to those of Washington and Oregon that have changed the voting patterns. In a direct contest between support of the mineral industries and environmental issues, the dominant electorate in these states, like those in Washington and Oregon, will tend to support land withdrawals and other environmental issues. They tend to view mining as a land-raping and air-and water-polluting industry, which admittedly is necessary, but it is better that it be outside of the borders of the state in which they reside. This public attitude tends to place in the Senate and House individuals who hinder development of a western-state political bloc favorable to the minerals industry that can make a significant change in how Congress regards the minerals industry.

16.36. The outlook is grim. The environmental political bloc has attained massive power within the system. Their very existence is dependent upon retaining the present system by any means available to them. They have entry into the development of environmental laws and land withdrawals far beyond those of any other political bloc, and they have succeeded in locking the minerals industry into a regulatory quagmire of laws and regulations. They have available a constant stream of monetary contributions from the public, environmental equipment makers, and law firms and large grants from endowed institutions. The environmental organizations provide little information on how these funds are being spent. The environmental laws enacted and the lawsuits they bring to force action on these laws are their life blood. The more lawsuits they file against the government, the more payments the government makes to them under the Equal Access to Justice Act. They have little accountability for their actions or how they spend funds. They can bring suit, and it is unknown by the presiding judge who has contributed funds to start the legal action. Just the statement that they are an environmental organization appears to be satisfactory information for the court. The executive, legislative, and judicial branches of government have tolerated this situation for twenty-five years, and it now appears that it will continue indefinitely at a more accelerated pace than heretofore.

16.37. The environmental political bloc has no difficulty whatsoever in obtaining support from the public for their programs. Claims that any changes in the clean water and air acts will result in contaminated drinking water and impure air win them widespread political support, which, in turn, translates into strong support in all three branches of government. Currently the environmental political bloc's most successful "bugbears" are global warning and ozone depletion. With these the bloc can predict scourges that will result in skin cancer afflictions and floods that will devastate the world. Just the thought that these events could take place raises the consciousness of the public to the point that their emotional reaction is: "Why take a chance? Let's make the environment safe enough so that what they are predicting won't occur." This portends that congressional decisions made on these "bugbears" will be based solely on emotion and not on scientific data.

16.38. The environmental political bloc has also been remarkably successful in the courtroom. On June 29, 1995, the U.S. Supreme Court ruled that the government has the right to stop private property owners from destroying endangered species habitat. This decision was an important victory for the bloc. It established at the highest court level the validity of the Endangered Species Act and gave the government control over private land, which may contain endangered species. Once a plot of land is declared to contain an endangered species, the owner of the land suddenly discovers that he has lost control of the land and it is now in the hands of the government. With this land control established in the Endangered Species Act, it is not going to be easy to amend the act to remove the provisions that provide for the "taking of private property."

Many congressional members have been seeking this kind of power for years, and now that they have it, they intend to keep it.

16.39. Public land withdrawals up to August 1994 were made under forty-three classifications, which bar mining on more than 218 million acres; the total acreage withdrawn comprises 62 percent of the public lands (Lee 1994). It is doubtful if more than 10 percent of the members of Congress are aware of all the classifications or even aware of the total acreage that has been withdrawn. Under one or more of the classifications in concert with the Endangered Species Act and other environmental law, the land agencies of the federal government can to continue to make additional withdrawals without congressional approval. There is no end to this practice in sight. In October 1996 President Clinton withdrew 1.7 million acres of land in southern Utah under a ninety-year old law designating the area as a National Land Monument. The area is known to contain large reserves of coal. This was purely and simply a political action prior to the election, and in all probability Vice President Gore urged the president to do so.

16.40. Change can occur only if enough people are affected by the current system to change their views on the environmental movement and political party affiliation. It will require a gut-wrenching decision by the party "regulars," but if they want to stop the decline in their standard of living and comparable decline in their standard of living of their children, the decision to change is going to have to be made and made now. Individuals who have on their agenda creating wealth, eliminating the PACs, and curtailing the power of the environmental political bloc must be elected at federal and state levels. Sweeping changes must be made in the executive, legislative, and judicial branches. The laws enacted to create wilderness areas in the Federal Domain must be repealed and the land returned to multiple-use status, the strangling environmental laws must be repealed or amended, and legislators who have voted for these laws must be removed from office. Their ignorance has mired the nation in debt and placed it in jeopardy.

16.41. The probability of any of these changes occurring up to the year 2000 is remote. However, as more and more people suffer a declining standard of living and downsizing in their jobs, I hope party loyalties will decline at the same rate. If this occurs, then there is a possibility that this will impact the political parties sufficiently to force substantial changes in the political system at some time in the future. One can only hope that the changes will occur before the national debt reaches a total that is beyond the ability to repay.

16.42. As of August 1995, a total of six Democrats and one Republican were scheduled to retire from the Senate in 1996. Both political parties would attempt to fill these upcoming vacancies with individuals who had been loyal to the party. Dissidents would not be tolerated, and they would have no chance whatsoever of becoming the party nominee. One of the retirees, Bill Bradley, announced he was disgusted with the politics of both political parties and might consider a run for president in 1996 as an independent. He was in the Senate for three terms and voted for every environmental and land withdrawal law passed by Congress at that time. He or anybody else who has been in the House or Senate and may make any effort to run for the presidency has no more idea of what has gone wrong with the nation than the nine men who succeeded to the presidency since Harry S Truman retired.

Appendixes

Appendix I
Metallic, Nonmetallic, and Industrial Mineral Commodities

The commodities of the minerals industry are most commonly classified as metallic and nonmetallic mineral commodities. The metallic commodities are further classified as ferrous and nonferrous and the nonmetallic mineral commodities as other than fuels and hydrocarbons. The metals listed under the ferrous mineral commodities in table 1 are those whose primary use is alloying with iron and steel. There are many other metals that are alloyed with iron and steel, but alloying is not their primary use. Such metals include aluminum, copper, lead, and rare earths. Aluminum is an additive for deoxidation and grain-size control. Copper, lead, and rare earths are used to obtain various properties, such as hardness, machinability, and resistance to corrosion.

Steel is an alloy of iron. It is listed with iron because it is the primary alloy of iron; also, all other ferrous metals and some nonferrous metals are alloyed with it, and it has the greatest use of any other metal or alloy. Iron ore is also listed with iron because it constitutes one of the major bulk commodities transported in the United States; this is also the reason that cement and lime are included with calcium, phosphate rock is included with phosphorous, potash is included with potassium, cinder is included with pumice, salt is included with sodium, and sand and gravel are listed together. These combination listings are all underlined in table 1.

The rare-earth metals are listed under "Nonferrous Mineral Commodities," although they are extensively used in steel production. The ion-exchange process must be used to separate them from one another; thus they are often used in steel production as a metal mixture in what is termed *misch metal*. There are fifteen of them, as follows: lanthanum, cerium, praseodymium, neodymium, promethium, samarium, europium, gadolinium, terbium, dysprosium, holmium, erbium, thulium, ytterbium, and lutetium.

Table 1
Mineral Commodities Used in the United States (Staff of the Bureau of Mines 1985)

METALLIC MINERAL COMMODITIES

Ferrous Mineral Commodities:

Chromium	Cobalt	Columbium	Iron, steel, iron ore
Manganese	Molybdenum	Nickel	Rhenium
Silicon	Tantalum	Tungsten	Vanadium

Nonferrous Mineral Commodities:

Aluminum	Antimony	Arsenic	Beryllium
Bismuth	Cadmium	Cesium	Copper
Gallium	Germanium	Gold	Hafnium
Indium	Lead	Magnesium	Mercury
Platinum	Palladium	Rhodium	Ruthenium
Osmium	Radium	Rubidium	Rare-earth metals
Scandium	Selenium	Silver	Tellurium
Thallium	Thorium	Tin	Titanium
Uranium	Zinc	Zirconium	

NONMETALLIC MINERAL COMMODITIES

Nonmetallic Mineral Commodities (other than fuels):

Argon	Asbestos	Barium	Boron
Bromine	Chlorine	Clays	Calcium, cement, lime
Corundum	Emery	Diatomite	Diamond-industrial
Feldspar	Flourine	Garnet	Gemstones
Graphite	Gypsum	Helium	Hydrogen
Iodine	Kyanite	Lithium	Mica
Nitrogen	Oxygen	Perlite	Phosphorus, phosphate rock
Potassium,	Pumice,	Quartz	Sand and gravel
potash	cinder	crystal	
Sodium, salt	Stone	Strontium	Sulfur
Talc	Soapstone	Pyrophillite	Vermiculite

Nonmetallic Mineral Commodities (hydrocarbons):

Anthracite	Bituminous coal	Carbon	Coke
Lignite	Natural gas	Peat	Petroleum
Shale oil			

Certain mineral commodities are often termed *industrial minerals*; they are those used in their mineral form. The nomenclature of the industrial minerals is confusing. Some will be listed under an all-inclusive term, like abrasives, special sands, sillimanite group, or insulators, others as minerals, and some under their metallic and nonmetallic term, such as chromite, titanium, and sulphur. Technically, cement, limestone, phosphate rock, nitrogen compounds, rare earths, and potash, which have been listed in table 1, are also industrial minerals. However, how industrial minerals are classified is not all that important, because they, like the metallics and nonmetallics, occur in the Earth's crust as minerals containing two or more elements.

Industrial minerals can be best understood by seeing them listed as a group followed by a short explanation of their use. The purpose of table 2 is solely informational. A selected group of industrial minerals is listed under the names that are commonly used by industry. Their primary uses are recorded under the same number as listed.

Table 2
Industrial Minerals and Rocks Used in the United States (Dolbear and Bowles 1949)

1. Abrasives	2. Asbestos	3. Barium minerals	4. Bauxite
5. Bentonite	6. Bleaching clay	7. Borax and borates	8. Cement materials
9. Chalk and whiting	10. Chromite	11. Clays	12. Crushed stone
13. Diatomite	14. Dimension stone	15. Feldspar	16. Secondary fertilizer materials
17. Fluorspar and cryolite	18. Granules	19. Graphite	20. Gypsum
21. Heat and sound insulators	22. Lime	23. Lithium minerals	24. Magnesite and related minerals
25. Manganese ore	26. Mica	27. Mineral fillers	28. Mineral pigments
29. Minor industrial minerals	30. Monazite	31. Native bitumens	32. Nitrates and nitrogenous compounds
33. Phosphate rock	34. Potash	35. Precious stones	36. Pumice and pumicite
37. Pyrophyllite	38. Quartz crystal	39. Refractories	40. Salt
41. Sand and gravel, crushed stone	42. Sillimanite group	43. Slate	44. Natural sodium carbonate and sodium sulphate
45. Special sands	46. Strontium minerals	47. Sulphur and pyrites	48. Talc and ground soapstone
49. Titanium	50. Tripoli	51. Zeolites	52. Zircon
53. Vermiculite	54. Rare earths		

1. Abrasives—the mineral commodities that are used to abrade, as follows: diamond, corundum, emery, garnet, flint, sandstone, silica sand, granite, basalt, feldspar, siliceous shale, and manufactured abrasives such as boron carbide, tungsten carbide, steel wool, and brass wool.

2. Asbestos—uses declining because of health danger from asbestos fibers.

3. Barium minerals—used in oil well drilling muds, production of glass, as a pigment in paints and inks, and as a filler in paints.

4. Bauxite—primary ore for metallic aluminum but also used as aluminous chemicals, aluminous abrasives, and aluminous refractories.

5. Bentonite—used in oil well drilling and in foundries as a bond and conditioner for molding sand.

6. Bleaching clay—used in the oil industry for adsorbing coloring matter from oil. There are three common types as follows: Fuller's earth, activated clay, and activated bauxite.

7. Borax and borates—Used as a cleansing agent, medicine, pharmacy, mouthwashes, tooth powders, cosmetics, lotions, ointments, deodorants, and medicated lint and gauze.

8. Cement materials—the minerals from which concrete is made, such as volcanic ash, limestone, shale, marl, blast-furnace slag, and gypsum.

9. Chalk and whiting—used as a fillers or extenders in paints, rubber, putty, paper, linoleum, oil cloth, window shades, white shoe dressing, dolls, dyes, crayons, and leather gods.

10. Chromite—used primarily for the production of stainless steel but in mineral form used extensively in the chemical industry and in refractries.

11. Clays—used in manufacture of stoneware, earthenware, porcelains, fillers for paper and rubber, fireclays, facing brick, tile.

12. Crushed stone—aggregate in highway construction, concrete, railroad ballast, and riprap.

13. Diatomite—filtration, insulation, fillers, and admixtures.

14. Dimension stone—used as blocks and slabs, including cut stone, building stone, paving, curbing, flagging.

15. Feldspar—basic raw material for the manufacture of burned clay products.

16. Secondary fertilizer materials—limestone, gypsum, sulphur, borax, copper sulphate, magnesium sulphate, manganese sulphate, and zinc sulphate.

17. Fluorspar and cryolite—fluorspar is primarily used as a flux in the steel industry; cryolite is used in the enamel and glass industry.

18. Granules—protective and decorative coating on composition roofing.

19. Graphite—graphite crucibles, lubricants, paints, lead pencils, crayons, electrodes, and dry batteries.

20. Gypsum—building material and agriculture.

21. Heat and sound insulators—vermiculite, perlite, cellular glass, mineral wool, glass wool, rock wool, and slag wool.

22. Lime—building construction, industrial, and agriculture.

23. Lithium minerals—pharmaceutical, chemical industries, glass making, and ceramics.

24. Magnesite and related minerals—magnesium compounds in fertilizers, chemical industry, and refractories.

25. Manganese ore—steel industry, dry batteries, fertilizers, glass making, chemical industry, pottery, and tile.

26. Mica—electrical industry, insulation.

27. Mineral fillers—used in composition floorings, fertilizers, plastics, and textiles.

270

28. Mineral pigments—paints, stains, roofing granules, linoleum, plastics, and floor tile.

29. Minor industrial minerals—alum minerals, bromine, calcium chloride, epsonite, iodine, meerschaum, quartz, Iceland spar, tourmaline, fluorite, selenite, mica, air, helium, and carbon dioxide.

30. Monazite—source of the rare-earth elements and thorium.

31. Native bitumens—native asphalts, gilsonite, mineral waxes, native asphalts containing mineral matter, bituminous residues obtained from the distillation of petroleum.

32. Nitrates and nitrogenous compounds—fertilizers.

33. Phosphate rock—agriculture.

34. Potash—agriculture and industrial uses.

35. Precious stones—decorative purposes, mainly in jewelry.

36. Pumice and pumicite—concrete aggregate, decorative, and abrasives.

37. Pyrophillite—ceramics and refractories.

38. Quartz crystal—semiprecious gemstones, industrial uses.

39. Refractories—furnace linings.

40. Salt—a basic product needed for humans and animals.

41. Sand and gravel, crushed stone—the most common of all construction materials.

42. Sillimanite group—andalusite, kyanite, sillimanite, dumortierite, and topaz used in refreactories and chemicals.

43. Slate—roofing and decoration.

44. Natural sodium carbonate and sodium sulphate—source of soda, chemical industry, paper industry.

45. Special sands—molding sands in foundries, glass sand, filter sand, abrasive sand, sand for sheet asphalt, sand to stop drive wheels from slipping on rail, and furnace sand.

46. Strontium minerals—drilling mud weighting agent.

47. Sulphur and pyrites—widespread industrial use.

48. Talc and ground soapstone—roofing, ceramics, paper, rubber, cosmetics, textiles, and insecticides.

49. Titanium—titanium metal, white pigment.

50. Tripoli—abrasives, inert filler.

51. Zeolites—lightweight building and decorative stone.

52. Zircon—pigment, chemical, ceramic.
53. Vermiculite—insulation, cement, and plaster aggregate.
54. Rare earths, including lanthanides, yttrium, and scandium—batteries, magnets, oxide fuel cells.

Appendix II

Process Systems and Subsystems for Obtaining the Marketable Commodities of the Minerals Industries

The subsystems listed under the secondary systems in table 1 are many of the known processes that are now in use to recover mineral commodities. Certain subsystems are suitable only for recovery of certain mineral commodities. For instance in the search processes under "Prospecting: Search and Discovery," it may be necessary to use only the land geophysical and geological surveys to select the most promising mineral deposite sites. Under "Refining: Extraction and Purification and Material Development," commodities are listed under the subsystems that are now being used for their recovery.

Table 1
Primary, Secondary, and Tertiary Process Systems to Obtain Mineral Commodities

1. PROSPECTING: SEARCH AND DISCOVERY

    1.1. Search processes: Searching for rocks and minerals having industrial value and/or rocks bearing valuable minerals.

        1.11. Exploration: A sequence of search processes designed to locate a valuable mineral deposit contained in a small subsurface area within a large land mass.

            1.111. Selection of target area: may be one-quarter to hundreds of square miles in area.

            1.112. Literature search for available reports and maps by government agencies.

            1.113. Determination of applicable land exclusion, land withdrawal, land use, labor, environmental, and industry operation laws in force by all branches of the government.

            1.1131. At this point certain laws may eliminate any further consideration of the target area or specific land withdrawal or exclusion areas within the target area.

            1.1132. If there are land withdrawals or exclusions within the target area, omit the search processes in these areas.

            1.114. Geologic remote sensing: to determine if there is probable mineralization or a favorable stratigraphic structure over an immense area of land.

            1.1141. Satellite photography (Rowan 1975).

            1.1142. Electromagnetic radiation (Taranik and Trautwein 1976).

            1.115. Aerial geophysical surveys: To define the limits of the probable mineralized areas discovered by remote sensing.

            1.1151. Aerial photography

            1.1152. Magnetic, radioactive, and infrared surveys.

            1.1153. Side-looking radar and others.

            1.116. Determine public acceptance of a mining operation on the probable areas containing valuable mineral deposits.

            1.117. Land geophysical surveys of the probable mineral deposit areas to select the most promising mineral deposit sites.

                1.1171. Gravitational, magnetic, seismic, electrical, radioactivity, and others.

                    1.11711. Determination of rock structure and detection of mineral occurrences.

            1.118. Geological, geochemical, and biogeochemical surveys of the most promising mineral deposit sites to select the site for the discovery processes.

1.2. Discovery processes: the finding of a valuable mineral in place.

    1.21. Finding: sequence of discovery processes designed to determine the occurrence and specific location of a valuable mineral deposit below the surface of the Earth.

        1.211. Surface trenching, borehole drilling (rotary, churn, diamond), and continuous sampling.

        1.212. Electric, magnetic, temperature, radioactivity, and acoustic waveform borehole logging.

        1.213. Obtaining of core or cuttings for metallurgical testing and petrographic studies, including age determination and fossil identification.

        1.214. Determination of physical and mechanical properties of the mineral-bearing rock and the rock surrounding the mineral deposit.

2. PLANNING: MINE PLANT DESIGN

    2.1. Plant design processes.

        2.11. From the PROSPECTING SYSTEM data determine the size, shape, depth, continuity, volume, and average grade of the mineral deposit. Determine the MINING SUBSYSTEM best suited for extraction of the material from the Earth, and on the basis of the available data on the mineral deposit and the selected MINING SUBSYSTEM determine the daily, monthly, and annual production and the expected life of the mine.

        2.12. On the sampled material obtained in the PROSPECTING SYSTEM run laboratory tests to determine the amenability of the material to REFINING SUBSYSTEMS. Determine the REFINING SUBSYSTEM best suited for enhancing the value of the rock or mineral and/or extraction and recovery of the valuable mineral from the rock. Determine the REFINING SUBSYSTEM capacity on the basis of the production from the mine.

        2.13. Determine the volume of solid waste expected from all sources and provide safe areas for its storage and disposal.

        2.14. Determine the drainage area required for all water discharge, temporary storage, and disposal.

            2.141. Determine the treatment, if any, needed for the water discharge.

        2.15. Determine the maximum area required for the mine plant.

        2.16. Determine the transportation system that will best serve the plant (surface and subsurface) and the required roadway network on the surface that will cause the least erosion.

        2.17. Prior to construction and operation of the mine plant conduct environmental studies in and around the projected mine plant area establishing the environmental base of the following: (1) plant and animal life; (2) subsurface and surface water quality; and (3) eroded soil areas and soil analyses.

            2.171. File this baseline environmental data with all units of government responsible for enforcing environmental laws.

        2.18. Determine the size and capacity of the power plant, if one is needed. Select the equipment needed for the DEVELOPMENT, MINING, AND REFINING SYSTEMS and

275

surface plant, and determine the type and design of buildings needed to house the mine plant.

2.19. Develop a mined land reclamation plan.

3. VALUATION: ENVIRONMENTAL AND ECONOMIC ANALYSES

3.1. Environmental analyses processes.

3.11. From the baseline environmental data obtained under the DESIGN SYSTEM evaluate insofar as possible the impact on the environment that the mine plant will have on the surrounding area under full operation.

3.12. Determine if the mine plant under full operation can meet all environmental laws.

3.121. If it cannot, determine the changes in design that are needed.

3.2. Economic analyses processes.

3.21. Determination of commercial value of the mineral deposit.

3.211. Determination of present, annual, and future worth of the mineral deposit.

3.212. To be commercial the deposit must yield a commodity that will recover capital outlay at a fair rate of compound interest, pay all operating costs and taxes, and yield a reasonable profit.

3.22. Decision to abandon, hold, or continue on the basis of total costs and net profit after taxes.

3.23. If decision is to continue, start the federal and state permitting procedures.

3.231. Time required for these procedures varies from one to four years.

4. DEVELOPMENT: PREPARATION FOR MINING

4.1. Preparation for mining processes.

4.11. Drilling platform construction for continental shelf drilling.

4.111. Offshore installation.

4.12. Borehole drilling (rotary, churn, and diamond)

4.13. Driving into the rock with shafts, tunnels, drifts, crosscuts, and adits of sufficient size to be transportation ways for removing the rock bearing the valuable minerals from the Earth.

4.14. Overburden stripping.

4.15. Continuous sampling.

4.16. Continuous checking and rechecking the data obtained in the PROSPECTING SYS-TEM to substantiate the MINING AND REFINING SUBSYSTEMS selected under the DESIGN SYSTEM.

4.17. Purchase of equipment and mine plant construction.

276

5. MINING: EXTRACTION OF ROCK AND MINERAL FROM THE EARTH'S CRUST

    5.1. Extraction processes.

        5.11. Rotary drilling.

            5.111. Water flooding, horizontal drilling, and pumping.

                5.1111. Liquid and gaseous hydrocarbons.

            5.112. Superheating with water and pumping.

                5.1121. Sulphur.

        5.12. Underground mining: The method selected is dependent upon the physical characteristics of the ore deposit, the rock enclosing the deposit, and the depth of the deposit below the surface of the Earth.

            5.121. Open, timbered, filled, and shrinkage stopes.

                5.1211. Metallics, nonmetallics, and coal.

            5.122. Caving methods.

                5.1221. Top slicing (mostly nonferrous metallic deposits).

                5.1222. Sublevel (ferrous, and nonferrous metallic deposits). Sublevel caving, where applicable, will yield high extraction and an ore product with minimum contamination, and with the exception of block caving it is the cheapest of underground mining methods.

                5.1223. Block caving (mostly nonferrous metallic deposits). Block caving, where applicable, is the cheapest of all underground methods of mining.

                5.1224. Longwall (coal).

        5.13. Combined methods.

            5.131. Metallics, nonmetallics, and coal.

        5.14. Surface mining.

            5.141. Quarry.

                5.1411. Rocks and nonmetallics.

            5.142. Open pit and open cast.

                5.1421. Metallics, nonmetallics, and coal.

            5.143. Dredging (placer).

                5.1431. Gold and platinum metals.

                5.1432. Monazite, rutile, cassiterite, ilmenite, rutile, garnet, and zircon minerals.

5.15. Chemical

    5.151. Metallics and nonmetallics.

6. REFINING: EXTRACTION AND PURIFICATION AND MATERIAL DEVELOPMENT

6.1. Extraction and purification processes of petroleum, natural gas, and natural gas liquids (Staff of the Bureau of Mines 1985).

    6.11. MINERAL PRODUCT development by distillation, thermal cracking, catalytic cracking, alkylation, catalytic reforming, solvent refining, and chemical treatment.

        6.111. Mineral products: Gasoline, kerosene, jet fuel, distillate fuel oil, lubricants, wax, residual fuel oil, coke, asphalt, road oil, aliphatics, petrochemicals, aromatics, and inorganics, including ammonia, carbon black, and sulfur.

6.2. Extraction and purification processess for solid fuels, nonmetals, and metals (Staff of the Bureau of Mines 1985).

    6.21. Hydrometallurgy: beneficiation of rocks and minerals to enhance their marketable qualities and extraction and recovery of minerals from rock containing valuable minerals by wet and chemical processes to separate the minerals from the rock.

        6.211. Crushing, grinding, comminution, classifying, washing, screening, sizing, sorting, trimming, grading, drying, blending, cleaning, gravity, laundering, heavy media, and tabling.

            6.2111. Coal, rocks, nonmetallics, and metallics.

        6.212. Flotation.

            6.2121. The method most in use for selective recovery and concentration of metallic minerals.

        6.213. Magnetic.

            6.2131. Primarily separation of iron minerals from rock.

        6.214. Cyanidation and precipitation.

            6.2141. Leaching gold from rocks.

        6.215. Electrolysis.

            6.2151. Aluminum and other metallics.

        6.216. Other: solvent extraction, ion exchange, liquefaction, precipitation, filtration, amalgamation, electrostatic, catalytic, crystallization, condensing, dissolution, evaporation, leaching.

            6.2161. Metallics and nonmetallics.

    6.22. Pyrometallurgy: thermal treatment of concentrated and separated mineral.

        6.221. The primary point for return of metallic scrap.

6.222. Smelting, distilling, furnace (blast, basic oxygen, open hearth, electric, rotary, other), direct reduction, agglomeration, heating, roasting, calcining, leaching, sintering, drying, gaseous diffusion.

       6.2221.   Metallics and nonmetallics.

6.3. Material development processes.

  6.31. Physical Metallurgy: physical and mechanical properties of metals as affected by temperature, composition, and mechanical working.

    6.311. Ingots, alloying.

      6.3111. METAL PRODUCT development by casting, rolling, forging, shaping, forming, extrusion, plating, and coating.

        6.31111. Shapes, forms, bars, beams, angles, rods, pipes, wire, cable, sheets, plates, and rails.

Table 2
Management of a Mineral Commodity–Producing Plant (Planning, Organizing, and Directing Human Effort and Machines to Obtain Optimal Health, Safety, Environmental, and Production Efficiency)

1. Planning processes: mine plan design.

    1.1.   Basing the MANAGEMENT SYSTEM on the life and size of the mine plant as established under the PLANNING SYSTEM.

    1.2.   Outline the various possible separate management functions and the responsibility of each separated function, and outline an expression of managerial policy of what is expected of the supervisor of each segmented function.

    1.3.   Outline an in-house research and development discovery program within the mine to ensure that all valuable mineral at the site has been found; outline an in-house refining research and development program to maximize the percentage recovery of valuable mineral from the rock; outline a prospecting program in the immediate vicinity of the mineral deposit site.

    1.4.   Develop health and safety guidelines to conform with the federal Office of Health and Safety (OSHA) and state mine safety laws; outline the solid waste management requirements necessary to conform to all regulatory and environmental laws.

    1.5.   Outline the water waste management requirements necessary to conform to all regulatory and environmental laws; outline methods of ground and surface water monitoring.

    1.6.   Final development of the mined land reclamation plan to conform to all regulatory and environmental laws.

2. Organizing processes: differentiation and segmentation of the management functions that will be the most efficient and will achieve the best interaction among all components of the system.

    2.1.   Administrative.

        2.11.   Taxes (outside advisory).

        2.12.   Legal (outside advisory).

        2.13.   Accounting and treasury.

        2.14.   Personnel.

    2.2.   Engineering and geological.

        2.2.1.   Surveying and geological mapping.

        2.22.   Sampling.

        2.23.   Grade of ore control.

        2.24.   Environmental—regulation and control.

        2.25.   Health and safety—administration, regulations, and enforcement.

        2.26.   Industrial engineering—time studies, design of process systems for maximum efficiency, redesign of all systems as needed, continous education of relationship of operator to machine, and development of computer software to model all primary and secondary process systems to improve their operating efficiency.

    2.27.   Mine ventilation—design and control.

    2.28.   Research and development.

  2.6.   Mining operation.

  2.7.   Refining operation.

  2.8.   Maintenance.

  2.9.   Purchasing and supplies.

3.   Directing processes.

  3.1.   Assignment of necessary human effort and machinery to the segmented functions.

  3.2.   Establishment of lines of communication between all segmented functions of the system.

  3.3.   Budget allocation for all segmented functions.

  3.4.   Finalizing and adoption of the planned expression of managerial policy for all supervisors of the segmented functions of the total system; keeping all lines of communication open between the segmented functions of the system and immediate notification of any changes in the managerial policy.

  3.5.   Finalizing and adoption of the health, safety, and environmental guidelines for use by all personnel.

  3.6.   Finalizing and adoption of mine water and solid waste regulations that will meet the requirements of all regulatory laws.

  3.7.   Adoption of ground and surface water monitoring systems.

  3.8.   Start the in-house research and development programs and the immediate vicinity prospecting program.

  3.8.   Continuous operations research projects through computer modeling to develop better systems and subsystems in mining, refining, management, health and safety, and environmental control to obtain optimal operating efficiency.

  3.9.   Selection of a time point in the depletion of the mineral deposit for planning and instituting outside prospecting for additional mineral deposits to keep the organization intact.

  3.10. Selection of personnel for continuous education in the latest technology in mining engineering, mining geology, mine health and safety, environmental, mined land reclamation, and computer software and regulatory and environmental laws; maintain a reference library of selected books, journals, and business and news publications.

Appendix III
Radiation-Electromagnetic Waves (Glasstone 1950)

By 1925 research in Europe on the quantum theory of radiation had become well advanced and had developed into quantum mechanics. This was just twenty years after the decade that marked the beginning of modern physics (see paragraph 3.29). An excellent description of the existing technology on electromagnetic waves during that period is contained in the *Sourcebook on Atomic Energy,* by Samuel Glasstone, who was commissioned to prepare the book by the AEC (1950). The source for the discussion below is Dr. Glasstone's publication.

Radiation (radiant energy) is a form of energy that is transferred through space from a sending to a receiving point. The most familiar forms of radiation are light and radio waves. The theory of light is that it travels through space by wave motion at about 186,000 miles per second. The wave motion has a series of crests and troughs; however, the wave does not move the medium it travels through. The distance between the crests or troughs is the wave length. The number of waves passing a point in one second is the frequency. Visible light has a range of wave lengths and frequencies, but all traveling at the same speed. Invisible radiations having longer wave lengths than visible light are infrared and short-wave and long-wave radio. Invisible radiations having shorter wave lengths than visible light are ultraviolet, X-ray, and gamma rays. All of the radiations, including visible light, are termed *electromagnetic radiations*.

A fundamental relationship exists among invisible radio waves, visible light rays, the invisible infrared and ultraviolet light, and X-ray and gamma-ray radiation. They all travel at the same speed, and there is no sharp division or line of demarcation between each radiation; there is only a gradual transition from one to the other. This relationship between the radiations had been established prior to 1930 in Germany, which was the only nation in the world at that time that had university professors qualified to teach quantum mechanics.

Appendix IV

Iron and Steel–Making Processes (Staff of the Bureau of Mines 1985, Liddell and Doan 1933, Morse 1956)

Iron ore is rock containing one or more of the oxide and carbonate minerals of iron, such as hematite, magnetite, siderite, and limonite. Iron is obtained from the iron ore by smelting in a blast furnace. Smelting is a process involving melting and, through the melting process, producing a chemical change. The process may be carried out in either an oxidizing atmosphere or a reducing atmosphere. Because the iron minerals are oxides, they must be smelted in a reducing atmosphere in the blast furnace to separate the pig iron (matte) from the slag (gangue) containing the oxides.

A blast furnace resembles a large-diameter cylindrical pipe standing upright about one-hundred feet high lined with firebrick. Air is forced into the pipe through openings near the bottom. Molten iron is drawn out through openings near the bottom from a hole. Slag is drained from the pipe from another hole higher up the pipe. Vents at the top of the pipe allow gases to escape. The basic charge introduced at the top of the blast furnace is iron ore, containing one or more of the iron oxide minerals, coke, and limestone. Impurities in the charge are oxides of phosphorus, manganese, sulphur, aluminum, and silica. The coke is burned, giving off carbon monoxide, which combines with the oxides, reducing the iron ore to molten metallic iron. The molten iron (pig iron) produced by the blast furnace assays as follows: about 92 percent iron; 3 to 4 percent carbon; 0.5 to 3 percent silicon; 0.25 to 2.5 percent manganese; 0.25 to 2.0 percent phosphorus; and possibly some sulfur. The molten pig iron is either poured into molds or directly charged to steel furnaces in the molten state.

Table 1
Types of Steel and End Uses (Thrush 1968)

LOW CARBON STEEL	USE
.04 to .12 percent carbon	drawing, stamping, nails, rivets
.08 to .25 percent carbon	structural

HIGH CARBON STEEL OR CARBON STEEL	USE
0.25 to 0.50 percent carbon	steel castings, machine parts
0.50 to 0.75 percent carbon	railway, spring wire
0.75 to 1.25 percent carbon	drills, cutting tools, ball bearing
1.25 to 2.25 percent carbon	files, drawing dies, tools

Steel is an iron-base alloy containing manganese, usually carbon, and often other alloying elements. There are thousands of different qualities and types of steel. It is extremely difficult for the layman to understand the various classifications used by the ferrous metallurgist to define steel. For general purposes, steel can be classed by its carbon content. The carbon content controls the ductility and the hardness of the steel and thus also controls the type of product that can be produced from the steel. Table 1 illustrates, in general, the different types of steel and the products made from those specific types.

When steel is alloyed with other ferrous metals (see the list of ferrous metals in appendix 1), it is normally classed on the basis of the percentage of carbon and alloying metals in the steel. Table 2 illustrates the difference between low-alloy and high-alloy steel.

In some steels containing less than 0.04 percent carbon the manganese content is the principal differentiating factor rather than the carbon content. Steel should not be confused with the cast irons, containing above .25 percent carbon, or the pure irons, containing less than .25 percent carbon. The production of steel from pig iron by any of the steel-making processes is essentially a control of the carbon percentage in the molten metal. The various processes that are in use and have been used for producing steel are discussed below.

Table 2
Types of Ferrous Alloy Steels (Thrush 1968)

LOW-ALLOY STEEL	HIGH-ALLOY STEEL
2.0 percent CARBON	2.5 percent CARBON
Less than 5 percent alloying ferrous metals	More than 5 percent alloying ferrous metals

Bessemer Process

In 1860 Henry Bessemer invented the Bessemer steel-making process in England. It was the first practical process for making steel in large quantities. About twenty-five tons of molten pig iron is poured into a twenty-foot-high pear-shaped lined furnace. The process refines pig iron by oxidation. Air is blown upward through the charge of molten pig iron. The time for oxidation of a twenty-five-ton charge is about ten minutes. Silicon is removed in the first stage and manganese, which removes the oxygen from the molten metal, in the second. The quality of Bessemer steel is inferior to that of steel produced by the open hearth method.

Open Hearth Process

Much better control of the molten pig iron is obtained in the open hearth process, and a better quality of steel can be obtained. The open hearth furnace is, for example, an elevated, covered, rectangular brick hearth about eight feet high twenty feet wide, and thirty-five feet long. Such a furnace would have a capacity of about two-hundred tons of steel per twenty-four hours. The furnace is charged with molten pig iron, scrap steel, limestone, and fluorspar. The metal is kept molten by oxidizing flames. Additional oxygen is supplied by charging iron ore into the molten mass. Chemically the action consists of lowering the carbon content of the charge by oxidation and removing silica, phosphorus, manganese, and sulfur, which combine with the limestone to form a slag. Tests can be made of the molten metal at various stages in the process. When the proper degree of purification has been reached, the molten metal can be drawn off separately into a ladle and thence into ingot molds.

During the time period that the molten steel is in the ladle and prior to pouring into the ingot molds, certain ferrous metals can be added to the molten mass to produce a special type of ferrous alloy steel.

Electric Furnace Process

The composition of ferrous alloy steels for specialized purposes must be precisely controlled. The electric furnace is best for this process. In an electric furnace the electric charge has no other function than the production of heat. Combustion gases are absent, and the steel refined in the electric furnace is governed by the materials used. The electric furnace is operated in a reducing atmosphere, which holds the steel at high molten temperatures as the oxides and slag materials float out.

Basic Oxygen Process

The basic oxygen furnace (BOF) is used to produce steel in the basic oxygen process (BOP). This process is now the dominant steel-making process in the United States. Pure oxygen is blown into a refractory lined furnace through the bath of molten iron, oxidizing the impurities and maintaining the temperature through the heat produced in the oxidation process. Fluxes are added to form a slag. A total of 300 tons of steel can be produced in an hour.

Direct-Reduction Processes

There are a dozen or more types of direct-reduction processes. Direct-reduction processes reduce iron oxides to metal using gaseous or solid reductants at temperatures below the melting point of iron. As the name direct reduction implies, the need for a blast furnace in the steel-making system is eliminated. Third World nations often prefer this process because they can produce iron in quantities as small as 20,000 metric tons per year; however, most of the plants in operation in 1990 have capacities of 350,000 to 850,000 metric tons per year (U.S. Geological Survey and U.S. Bureau of Mines 1992). World production of direct-reduction processes more than doubled in the decade from 1980 to 1990 to about 18 million metric tons (U.S. Geological Survey and U.S. Bureau of Mines 1992).

Appendix V

Rolled Steel Shapes Available from One Company in the United States in 1929

A steel company producing various sizes of rolled products, such as plates, bars, tees, zees, angles, I-beams, U-channels, wheels, and other special shapes and forms has the ability to produce products for almost any industry, including agriculture, construction, power generation, appliance manufacturing, shipbuilding, automobile, motor truck, motor bus, and railroad. The same shapes and forms are used in all industries but in various sizes. Thus a nation that has a strong shipbuilding industry would have no difficulty at all in developing shapes and forms to manufacture automobiles and appliances, machinery for agriculture, and railroad engines and rails. It would only be a matter of "downsizing" the various shapes and forms in thickness, length, and width to fit the purpose for which they would be used. The rolled products of shapes, plates, bars, and rails available in 1929 by one company in the United States are shown in table 1.

Table 1
Carnegie Shape Book Listing Rolled Products of Shapes, Plates, Bars, and Rails (Carnegie Steel Company 1929)

Number of Different Sizes Available	Shapes and Uses
75	I-beams (building and ship construction)
100	U-channels (ships, cars, and car wheels)
27	Equal angles (Structural)
71	Unequal angles (Structural)
88	Tees—structural
22	Zees—structural
60	Bars of all shapes
217	Various automobile parts
140	Sash and casements for windows
56	Flat rolled carbon steel rectangular plates from one-quarter-inch to twenty-four inches thick
35	Flat rolled nickel steel rectangular plates one-quarter-inch to two inches thick
121	Automobile rim sizes
96	Miscellaneous automobile parts, magnets, door latches, hinges, brake shoes, and clamps
40	Rails
53	Railroad accessories, bars, frogs, and clips
48	Miscellaneous parts for cars, draw bars, floor parts, and various steel thickness of steel sheet
	Many miscellaneous other steel shapes, such as beveled, half-circle, oval, half-oval, bars

Appendix VI
Aluminum

Aluminum is a light metal. It ranks first in tonnage among the primary nonferrous metals produced in the United States. It is commonly referred to as belonging to the light metals division of the minerals industry. Other metals in this division are magnesium and titanium. Primary aluminum production increased almost continuously up to about 1971, but since that time it has varied between 3.9 and 5.1 million short tons. It was one of the strategic commodities used to meet Pres. Franklin Roosevelt's goal of 55,000 airplanes per year. The production of aluminum from 1883 to 1990 is shown in table 1. In table 1, the net imports are the imports minus the exports. In most of the years from 1949 to 1990 more metal was imported than exported.

All of the bauxite used for producing aluminum must be imported; thus the wealth created by producing aluminum metal is in the refining and management systems less the cost of the bauxite (see paragraph 1.13, table 1). Production of aluminum metal is by an electrolytic process that reduces aluminum oxide (alumina) to metal. During the Roosevelt administration aluminum plants were constructed near the TVA, Grand Coulee, and BPA projects to utilize the cheap electricity produced by these projects. After World War II, Canada and the Soviet Union through their vast resources for developing water power also became substantial producers of aluminum.

Table 1
U.S. Production of Aluminum from 1883 to 1948 and As Compared to Rest of the World Production from 1949 to 1990 (U.S. Geological Survey and U.S. Bureau of Mines 1992)
(in pounds 1883–1909) (in thousands of short tons 1910–90)

Year	World Production	U.S. Production	U.S. Percentage of World Production	Net Imports
		pounds		
1883		83		
1884		150		
1885		283		
1886		3,000		
1887		18,000		
1888		19,000		
1889		47,468		
1890		61,281		
1891		150,000		
1892		259,885		
1893		333,629		
1894		550,000		
1895		920,000		
1896		1,300,000		
1897		4,000,000		
1898		5,200,000		
1899		6,500,000		
1900		7,150,000		
1901		7,150,000		
1902		7,300,000		
1903		7,500,000		
1904		8,600,000		
1905		11,347,000		
1906		14,910,000		
1907		17,211,000		
1908		11,152,000		
1909		34,210,000		
		thousands of short tons		
1910		24		
1911		24		
1912		33		
1913		36		
1914		40		
1915		50		
1916		not available		
1917		not available		
1918		not available		
1919		not available		
1920		69		
1921		28		
1922		37		
1923		65		
1924		75		

291

Table 1 (continued)

Year	World Production	U.S. Production	U.S. Percentage of World Production	Net Imports
1925		70		
1926		73		
1927		80		
1928		105		
1929		114		
1930		115		
1931		89		
1932		52		
1933		43		
1934		37		
1935		60		
1936		112		
1937		146		
1938		143		
1939		164		
1940		206		
1941		309		
1942		521		
1943		920		
1944		776		
1945		495		
1946		410		
1947		572		
1948		623		
1949	1,442	603	42	88
1950	1,651	719	44	
1951	1,975	837	42	
1952	2,259	937	41	141
1953	2,725	1,252	46	346
1954	3,090	1,461	47	194
1955	3,460	1,566	45	206
1956	3,720	1,679	45	197
1957	3,710	1,648	44	197
1958	3,865	1,566	41	211
1959	4,480	1,954	44	138
1960	4,985	2,014	40	−188
1961	5,185	1,904	37	17
1962	5,580	2,118	38	118
1963	6,075	2,313	38	174
1964	6,720	2,911	38	104
1965	6,951	2,754	40	305
1966	7,583	2,968	39	349
1967	8,343	3,269	39	173
1968	8,875	3,255	38	442
1969	9,885	3,793	38	−17

292

Table 1 (continued)

Year	World Production	U.S. Production	U.S. Percentage of World Production	Net Imports
1970	10,641	3,976	37	−144
1971	11,373	3,925	35	397
1972	12,115	4,122	34	465
1973	13,364	4,525	34	53
1974	14,516	4,903	34	105
1975	13,387	3,879	29	110
1976	13,913	4,251	31	265
1977	15,189	4,539	30	425
1978	15,577	4,804	31	520
1979	16,044	5,023	31	67
1980	16,944	5,130	30	−770
1981	16,596	4,948	30	68
1982	14,807	3,609	24	144
1983	15,331	3,696	24	348
1984	17,314	4,518	26	886
1985	16,973	3,858	23	1,398
1986	16,990	3,348	20	2,639
1987	18,099	3,685	20	1,028
1988	19,290	4,347	23	411
1989	19,863	4,442	22	−160
1990	19,630	4,462	23	−159

293

Appendix VII
Bituminous Coal and Lignite

Bituminous coal and lignite are nonmetallic mineral commodities (hydrocarbons). For classification purposes they are termed as belonging to the solid fuels division of the mineral industries. Other mineral commodities in this division are anthracite, carbon, coke, peat, and shale oil.

Similiarly to the production of iron ore, iron, and steel, the true start of America's industrialization can be traced in the production of bituminous coal and anthracite. From 1870 through 1890, production increased from 17 million to 111 million short tons, an increase of 94 million tons in a twenty-one-year period. However, after the Mesabi Iron Range came on-line in 1892, from 1890 through 1910 production per year increased from 111 million to 417 million, an increase of 306 million short tons in a twenty-one-year period. With such statistics can there be any doubt as to the massive change that the Mesabi Iron Range wrought in the United States?

Production from 1910 to 1965, a period of fifty-five years, varied from a low of 310 million short tons in 1932, the third year of the Great Depression, to a high of 630 million tons in 1947. After 1965 yearly production stayed above 500 million tons per year and continued to gradually increase, reaching a total of over 1 billion tons in 1990. During the period from 1910 to 1965 coal was being replaced as an energy source in residential, commercial, industrial, and utility uses. The clean air and clean water acts tended to retard coal production growth between 1965 and 1975, but after the OPEC oil embargo and the realization that the Mideast was an uncertain energy source, the conversion from coal to petroleum lessened, and new utility and industrial plants tended to turn to the more secure energy source: domestically mined coal.

The percentage of underground mechanically loaded coal, shown in column 4 of table 1, is also an excellent indicator of why Appalachia was hit so hard during the Great Depression. In 1928 the percentage of underground mechanically loaded coal was 4.5 percent. During the depression years the percentage continued to increase, reaching 31 percent by 1939. Thus in place of rehiring underground miners as the depression abated, the underground mining companies were laying off laborers. By 1976 the percentage of underground mechanically loaded coal had reach 99.9 percent, and for practical purposes it can now be assumed that 100 percent is mechanically loaded.

The percentage of coal surface mined increased from 0.6 percent in 1915 to 24.8 percent in 1955, a period of forty years. The massive physical metallurgy research programs of the fifties and early sixties resulted in improved metals for both underground and surface mining equipment, and the percentage surface mined increased to 50 percent in 1971.

Table 1
U.S. Production of Bituminous Coal and Lignite Each Five Years from 1870 to 1910 and Annually from 1910 to 1993 (Staff of the Bureau of Mines 1985, Energy Information Administration 1984, 1993)

Date	Millions of Net Tons	Average Value/Ton (Dollars) (FOB Mines)	Percentage Underground Mechanically Loaded	Percentage Surface Mined
1870	17.4	2.34		
1875	29.9	1.84		
1880	42.8	1.36		
1885	72.8	1.13		
1890	111.3	0.92		
1895	135.1	0.86		
1900	212.3	1.04		
1905	315.1	1.06		
1910	417.1	1.13		
1911	405.9	1.11		
1912	450.1	1.15		
1913	478.5	1.18		
1914	422.7	1.17		
1915	442.6	1.13		0.5
1916	502.5	1.32		0.8
1917	551.8	2.26		1.0
1918	578.4	2.58		1.4
1919	465.9	2.49		1.2
1920	568.7	3.75		1.5
1921	415.9	2.80		1.2
1922	422.3	3.02		2.4
1923	564.6	2.68	0.3	2.1
1924	483.7	2.20	0.7	2.8
1925	520.0	2.04	1.2	3.2
1926	573.4	2.06	1.9	3.0
1927	517.8	1.99	3.3	3.6
1928	500.7	1.86	4.5	4.0
1929	535.0	1.78	7.5	3.8
1930	467.5	1.70	10.5	4.3
1931	382.1	1.54	13.1	5.0
1932	309.8	1.31	12.3	6.3
1933	333.6	1.34	12.0	5.5
1934	559.4	1.75	12.2	5.8
1935	372.4	1.77	13.5	6.4
1936	439.1	1.76	16.3	6.4
1937	445.5	1.94	20.2	7.1
1938	348.5	1.95	26.7	8.7
1939	394.9	1.84	31.0	9.6
1940	460.8	2.19	35.4	9.2
1941	514.1	2.19	40.7	10.7
1942	572.7	2.36	45.2	11.5
1943	590.2	2.69	48.9	13.5
1944	619.6	2.92	52.0	16.3

Table 1 (continued)

Date	Millions of Net Tons	Average Value/Ton (Dollars) (FOB Mines)	Percentage Underground Mechanically Loaded	Percentage Surface Mined
1945	577.6	3.06	56.1	19.0
1946	533.9	3.44	58.4	21.1
1947	630.6	4.16	60.7	22.1
1948	599.5	4.99	64.3	23.3
1949	437.9	4.88	67.0	24.2
1950	516.3	4.84	69.4	23.9
1951	533.7	4.92	73.1	22.0
1952	466.8	4.90	75.6	23.3
1953	459.3	4.92	79.6	23.1
1954	391.7	4.52	84.0	25.1
1955	464.6	4.50	84.6	24.8
1956	500.9	4.82	84.0	25.4
1957	492.7	5.08	84.8	25.2
1958	410.4	4.86	84.9	28.3
1959	412.0	4.77	86.0	29.4
1960	415.5	4.69	86.3	31.4
1961	403.0	4.58	86.3	32.3
1962	422.1	4.48	85.7	33.4
1963	458.9	4.39	85.8	34.1
1964	487.0	4.45	87.4	33.9
1965	512.1	4.44	89.2	35.0
1966	533.9	4.54	91.7	36.6
1967	552.9	4.62	94.5	36.8
1968	545.2	4.87	95.7	36.9
1969	560.5	4.99	96.6	38.0
1970	602.9	6.26	97.2	43.8
1971	552.2	7.07	98.2	50.0
1972	595.4	7.66	99.0	48.9
1973	591.7	8.53	99.3	49.4
1974	603.4	15.75	99.7	54.0
1975	648.4	19.23	99.8	54.8
1976	678.7	19.43	99.9	56.5
1977	691.3	19.82	99.9	61.5
1978	665.1	21.78	99.9	63.6
1979	776.3	23.65	99.9	58.7
1980	823.6	24.52		59.1
1981	818.4	26.29		61.4
1982	833.5	27.14		59.4
1983	778.0	25.85		61.5
1984	891.8	25.51		60.6
1985	879.0	25.10		60.3
1986	886.1	23.70		59.5
1987	915.2	23.00		59.4
1988	946.7	22.00		59.8
1989	977.4	21.76		59.8

Table 1 (continued)

Date	Millions of Net Tons	Average Value/Ton (Dollars) (FOB Mines)	Percentage Underground Mechanically Loaded	Percentage Surface Mined
1990	1,025.6	21.71		58.7
1991	992.5	21.45		59.1
1992	994.1	20.98		59.2
1993	943.0	20.56		59.0

Appendix VIII
Petroleum and Natural Gas

Petroleum and natural gas are closely linked because they are often produced from the same well; there are, however, some wells that produce only natural gas. As a combination they are often classified as belonging to the liquid fuels division of the minerals industry.

Table 1 shows the percentage of total energy used in the United States derived from various energy sources from 1900 to 1954. The growth of petroleum and natural gas relative to bituminous and anthracite coal and water power is clearly shown in table 1. In 1930 crude petroleum and natural gas provided 34.1 percent and bituminous and anthracite 62.5 percent of the total. By 1952 the figures were almost exactly reversed, with petroleum and natural gas providing 61.7 percent and bituminous and anthracite 34.2 percent. The table also illustrates the growth in the use of natural gas as an energy source from 1950 to 1954.

Table 1
Percentage of Total Energy Used in the United States Derived from Various Energy Sources (Staff of the U.S. Bureau of Mines 1985)

Date	Percentage Crude Petroleum Produced and Imported	Percentage Natural Gas	Total Percentage Petroleum and Natural Gas	Percentage Coal, Bituminous and Anthracite	Percentage Water Power
1900	4.7	3.2	7.9	88.9	3.2
1910	7.9	3.6	11.5	89.0	3.5
1920	14.5	3.0	18.4	78.2	3.4
1930	24.8	9.3	34.1	62.5	3.4
1940	32.1	11.3	43.4	53.1	3.5
1950	36.6	18.6	55.2	40.5	4.3
1951	37.6	20.3	57.9	38.2	3.9
1952	39.6	22.2	61.7	34.2	4.1
1953	40.5	23.0	63.5	32.6	3.9
1954	54.8	25.0	66.8	19.3	3.9

Table 2
Natural Gas Consumption in the United States in Five-Year Increments, 1930–93
(Energy Information Administration 1993)
(in million cubic feet)

Year	Residential	Commercial	Industrial	Utilities	Total
1930	295,700	80,707	721,782	120,290	1,866,504
1935	313,496	100,187	790,563	125,239	1,854,413
1940	443,646	134,644	1,181,352	183,156	2,575,133
1945	607,400	230,099	1,819,838	326,190	3,740,543
1950	1,198,369	387,838	2,498,259	628,919	5,766,542
1955	2,123,952	629,219	3,410,975	1,153,280	8,693,657
1960	3,103,167	1,020,222	4,534,530	1,724,762	11,966,537
1965	3,902,802	1,443,648	5,955,417	2,321,101	15,279,716
1970	4,837,432	2,398,510	7,850,660	3,931,860	21,139,386
1975	4,924,124	2,508,293	6,968,267	3,157,669	19,537,593
1980	4,752,082	2,610,895	7,171,661	3,681,595	19,877,293
1985	4,433,377	2,432,382	5,901,288	3,044,083	17,280,943
1990	4,391,324	2,622,721	7,018,414	2,786,153	18,715,090
1991	4,555,659	2,728,581	7,230,962	2,789,014	19,035,156
1992	4,690,065	2,802,751	7,526,898	2,765,608	19,544,364
1993	4,957,208	2,911,321	7,941,916	2,682,440	20,298,119

Table 2 depicts natural gas consumption in the United States from 1930 to 1993 in five-year intervals (Energy Information Administration 1993). The last column in table 2 is the total consumption for all uses, including lease and plant fuel, pipeline fuel, and vehicle fuel. Tables and graphs on natural gas production and consumption are difficult to interpret because of the extremely high numbers that have to be expressed in cubic feet for annual production or consumption. For example, from 1930 to 1935 the growth in consumption in electric utilities was close to 5 billion cubic feet, whereas from 1965 to 1970 the growth in consumption was over 1.6 trillion cubic feet.

However, the data in table 2 from 1965 to 1993 tell an interesting story. In general, residential use stablilized between 4 and 5 trillion cubic feet, commercial use between 2 and 3 trillion cubic feet, industrial use between 6 and 8 trillion cubic feet, and electric utilities between 2 and 4 trillion cubic feet. There was only a 1 trillion cubic foot variance in residential and commercial consumption during the period, but there was a 2 trillion cubic foot variance in industrial and electric utility use. Most of the higher variance in the latter two occurred between 1970 and 1974, the OPEC oil embargo years. Industrial use decreased for the next five years to 1980 and then started in an upward trend to 1993. In contrast, electric utility use after 1974 went into a slow but somewhat steady decline in use over the nineteen-year period. The consumption use patterns of the commercial users and electric utilities are attributable primarily to the passage of the clean air and clean water acts during the Johnson administration and their revision under the Nixon administration. These patterns were caused by commercial and utilities users seeking a cleaner-burning fuel to meet the terms of the clean air and clean water acts. Federal environmental laws have had and continue to have a strong effect upon the minerals industries.

Table 3 depicts the domestic production of crude petroleum from 1859 to 1993. The production figures in the first column do not include natural gas plant liquids; thus the production figures will not match the production figures in table 4, which do include natural gas plant liquids. The growth in production for all practical purposes can be considered almost continuous until production reached 3.517 billion barrels in 1970. Production from 1970 to 1988 varied in the 3 billion barrel range but dropping gradually, until in 1988 it was 2.971 billion barrels. By 1993 domestic production had dropped to 2.496 billion barrels. The reason for this decreasing production is covered in the discussion of table 4.

During the Great Depression years of 1929–40 the price of petroleum at the well varied from a high of $1.27 to a low of $0.65. The figures indicate that most certainly the cost of energy should not have been a factor in causing the Great Depression.

The third column of table 3 is the total value per year at the well of all crude petroleum domestically produced. Examination of the figures in this column in combination with the percentage figures shown in table 4 gives a rough indication of the cost to the nation of imported petroleum. For example, in table 4 in 1993, 50 percent of our petroleum was imported. Table 3 shows that in 1993 the petroleum domestically produced was valued at $35.5 billion. This was wealth produced within the nation. To obtain the other 50 percent, the United States had to expend another $35.5 billion or more (depending on the OPEC cartel price) to foreign nations to keep our industries in operation and our automobiles moving. This was wealth leaving the nation.

The columns, on domestic petroleum production, imports, and exports in table 4 were taken directly from the 1993 *Annual Energy Review* published by the Energy Information Administration. The figures are in million forty-two-gallon barrels per day. The production figures in the second column include natural gas plant liquids, and the import figures

Table 3
Petroleum Produced in the United States, 1859–1993 (Staff of the Bureau of Mines 1985, Sletto 1995)
(thousand of forty-two-gallon barrels)

Year	Quantity Crude Petroleum	Value at Well	
		Total Value per Year (thousand dollars)	**Average Value per Barrel (Dollars)**
1859–75	74,072	215,781	2.91
1876	9,133	22,963	2.52
1877	13,350	31,789	2.38
1878	15,397	18,045	1.17
1879	19,914	17,211	.86
1880	26,286	24,601	.94
1881	27,671	25,448	.92
1882	30,350	23,631	.78
1883	23,450	25,790	1.10
1884	24,218	20,596	.85
1885	21,859	19,198	.88
1886	28,065	19,996	.71
1887	28,283	18,877	.67
1888	27,612	17,948	.65
1889	35,164	26,963	.77
1890	45,824	35,365	.77
1891	54,293	30,527	.56
1892	50,515	25,907	.51
1893	48,431	28,950	.60
1894	49,344	35,522	.72
1895	52,892	57,632	1.09
1896	60,960	58,519	.96
1897	60,476	40,874	.68
1898	55,364	44,193	.80
1899	57,071	64,604	1.13
1900	63,621	75,989	1.19
1901	69,389	66,417	.93
1902	88,767	71,179	.80
1903	100,461	94,694	.94
1904	117,081	101,175	.86
1905	134,717	84,157	.62
1906	126,494	92,445	.73
1907	166,095	120,107	.72
1908	178,527	129,079	.72
1909	183,171	128,329	.70
1910	209,557	127,900	.61
1911	220,449	134,045	.61
1912	222,935	164,213	.74
1913	248,446	237,121	.95
1914	265,763	214,125	.81
1915	281,104	179,463	.64

Table 3 (continued)

Year	Quantity Crude Petroleum	Value at Well	
		Total Value per Year (thousand dollars)	Average Value per Barrel (Dollars)
1916	300,767	330,900	1.10
1917	335,316	522,635	1.56
1918	355,928	703,944	1.98
1919	378,367	760,266	2.01
1920	442,929	1,360,745	3.07
1921	472,183	814,745	1.73
1922	557,531	895,111	1.61
1923	732,407	978,430	1.34
1924	713,940	1,022,683	1.43
1925	763,743	1,284,960	1.68
1926	770,784	1,447,760	1.88
1927	904,129	1,172,830	1.30
1928	901,474	1,054,880	1.17
1929	1,007,323	1,280,417	1.27
1930	891,011	1,070,200	1.19
1931	851,081	550,630	0.65
1932	785,159	680,460	0.87
1933	905,656	608,000	0.67
1934	908,065	904,826	1.00
1935	996,596	951,440	0.96
1936	1,009,686	1,199,820	1.09
1937	1,279,160	1,513,340	1.18
1938	1,214,355	1,373,060	1.13
1939	1,264,962	1,294,470	1.02
1940	1,353,214	1,385,440	1.02
1941	1,402,228	1,602,000	1.14
1942	1,386,645	1,643,420	1.19
1943	1,505,613	1,809,020	1.20
1944	1,677,904	2,032,960	1.21
1945	1,713,655	2,094,250	1.22
1946	1,733,939	2,443,550	1.41
1947	1,856,987	3,557,890	1.93
1948	2,020,185	6,245,080	2.60
1949	1,841,940	4,674,770	2.54
1950	1,973,574	4,963,380	2.51
1951	2,247,711	5,690,410	2.53
1952	2,289,836	5,785,230	2.53
1953	2,357,082	6,327,100	2.68
1954	2,314,988	6,424,930	2.78
1955	2,484,428	6,870,380	2.77
1956	2,617,283	7,296,760	2.79
1957	2,616,901	8,070,259	3.09
1958	2,448,837	7,410,422	3.03
1959	2,574,500	7,473,336	2.90
1960	2,574,938	7,420,181	2.88

303

Table 3 (continued)

Year	Quantity Crude Petroleum	Value at Well	
		Total Value per Year (thousand dollars)	Average Value per Barrel (Dollars)
1961	2,621,758	7,565,582	2.89
1962	2,676,189	7,774,051	2.90
1963	2,752,723	7,965,743	2.89
1964	2,786,800	8,030,000	2.88
1965	2,848,500	8,150,000	2.86
1966	3,027,800	8,720,000	2.88
1967	3,215,700	9,390,000	2.92
1968	3,329,000	9,790,000	2.94
1969	3,371,800	10,420,000	3.09
1970	3,517,500	11,190,000	3.18
1971	3,453,800	11,710,000	3.39
1972	3,455,400	11,710,000	3.39
1973	3,360,900	13,070,000	3.89
1974	3,202,600	22,000,000	6.85
1975	3,056,900	23,450,000	7.67
1976	2,968,200	24,370,000	8.19
1977	3,009,425	25,790,000	8.57
1978	3,178,055	28,600,000	9.00
1979	3,121,500	39,450,000	12.64
1980	3,137,900	67,930,000	21.59
1981	3,128,800	99,400,000	31.77
1982	3,156,800	90,030,000	28.52
1983	3,171,100	83,050,000	26.19
1984	3,240,800	84,100,000	25.88
1985	3,274,400	78,880,000	24.09
1986	3,168,200	39,630,000	12.51
1987	3,047,400	46,930,000	15.40
1988	2,971,100	37,480,000	12.58
1989	2,778,700	44,070,000	15.86
1990	2,648,000	53,770,000	20.03
1991	2,707,000	44,700,000	16.54
1992	2,617,400	41,970,000	15.99
1993	2,495,500	35,540,000	14.25

in the third column include petroleum product imports. The fifth column is the percentage of imports of the total produced and imported. It is the amount of the total that must be imported to meet the daily or yearly petroleum demand. The sixth column is the amount of the total produced and imported that is exported. The year 1948 was the first in which petroleum imports exceeded exports; from that year on, imports always exceeded exports.

Table 4 shows that from 1949 through 1968, a period of twenty

304

Table 4

U.S. Petroleum Production, Imports, and Exports, 1949–93 (Energy Information Administration 1993)
(in million barrels per day)

Year	Production	Imports	Total	Exports	Percentage Imports to Total	Percentage Exports to Total
1949	5.48	0.65	6.13	0.33	11	5
1950	5.91	0.85	6.76	0.30	13	4
1951	6.72	0.84	7.56	0.42	11	6
1952	6.87	0.95	7.82	0.43	12	5
1953	7.11	1.03	8.14	0.40	13	5
1954	7.03	1.05	8.08	0.36	13	4
1955	7.08	1.25	8.83	0.32	14	4
1956	7.95	1.44	9.39	0.43	15	5
1957	7.98	1.57	9.55	0.57	16	6
1958	7.52	1.70	9.22	0.28	18	3
1959	7.93	1.78	9.71	0.21	18	2
1960	7.96	1.81	9.77	0.20	19	2
1961	8.17	1.92	10.09	0.17	19	2
1962	8.35	2.08	10.43	0.17	20	2
1963	8.64	2.12	10.76	0.21	20	2
1964	8.77	2.26	11.03	0.20	20	2
1965	9.01	2.47	11.48	0.19	21	2
1966	9.58	2.57	12.15	0.20	21	2
1967	10.22	2.54	12.76	0.31	20	2
1968	1060	2.84	13.44	0.23	21	2
1969	10.83	3.17	14.00	0.23	23	2
1970	11.30	3.42	14.72	0.26	23	2
1971	11.16	3.93	15.09	0.22	26	1
1972	11.18	4.74	15.92	0.22	30	1
1973	10.95	6.26	17.21	0.23	36	1
1974	10.46	6.11	16.57	0.22	37	1
1975	10.01	6.06	16.07	0.21	38	1
1976	9.74	7.31	17.05	0.22	43	1
1977	9.86	8.81	18.67	0.24	47	1
1978	10.27	8.36	18.63	0.36	45	2
1979	10.14	8.46	18.60	0.47	45	2
1980	10.17	6.91	17.08	0.54	41	3
1981	10.18	6.00	16.18	0.59	37	4
1982	10.20	5.11	15.31	0.82	33	5
1983	10.25	5.05	15.30	0.74	33	5
1984	10.51	5.44	15.95	0.72	34	5
1985	10.58	5.07	15.65	0.78	32	5
1986	10.23	6.22	16.45	0.78	38	5
1987	9.94	6.68	16.62	0.76	40	5
1988	9.76	7.40	17.16	0.82	43	5
1989	9.16	8.06	17.22	0.86	47	5
1990	8.91	8.02	16.93	0.86	47	5
1991	9.08	7.63	16.71	1.00	46	6
1992	8.87	7.89	16.76	0.95	47	6
1993	8.57	8.53	17.10	1.00	50	6

years, the percentage of imports of the total domestically produced and imported petroleum increased from 10 to 21 percent, which is an average increase of a little over .5 percent per year. From 1968 through 1977, a period of ten years, the percentage of imports increased from 21 to 47 percent, which is an average increase of slightly more than 2.5 percent per year. In the ten-year period from 1968 through 1977 the percentage of imports was more than double the imports of the previous twenty-year period. The reason for the increase was the clean air and clean water laws passed during the Johnson administration and revised during the Nixon administration. These laws forced industrial companies and utilities using coal to seek a cleaner-burning fuel in order to meet the terms of the laws. They found the cleaner energy source in petroleum imported from the Middle East.

President Johnson paid no attention whatsoever to the two-percentage-point rise in imported petroleum in the last year of his administration. He compounded the problem by allowing Secretary of the Interior Udall's withdrawal of 384,500 acres of national parkland (DeGregorio 1993) and a ban on all transactions in Alaska until the Native Alaskan Claims Act was considered and passed by Congress. He had effectively stopped the building of the petroleum pipeline from Valdez, Alaska, to the North Slope.

President Nixon and his staff completely ignored the rising percentages of imported petroleum during his first term, passed the NEPA, and revised the clean air and clean water acts. In passing these laws they set the United States up like a clay pigeon for a blackmail attempt by the OPEC nations. With the Watergate scandal plaguing him in his second term, he and his staff ignored the six-percentage-point rise in imports in 1973. The end result was Presidents Johnson and Nixon passed on to Presidents Ford and Carter the difficult task of correcting the massive mistakes made in handling the problems of the liquid fuels division of the minerals industry. The federal government was wholly to blame in every respect for the OPEC oil embargo. The OPEC nations merely attempted to take advantage of a convenient situation handed to them on a king-size platter by the U.S. government. Undoubtedly OPEC'S thinking was: *If the government of the United States is that stupid, let's line our pockets with their green until they wise up.*

After 1977 the percentage of imports dropped to 45 percent in 1978 and 1979. In 1979 President Carter, in his July 15 "malaise" speech to the nation, in point 1 of his six basic policy decisions said that this nation would never use more foreign oil than we did in 1977 (Hamilton 1982). The reason, of course, that Mr. Carter selected the 1977 figure was because it was the highest import amount in the history of the nation up to 1979.

By choosing the 1977 import figure President Carter, whether he realized it or not, had defined independence for the Department of Energy. He had stated explicitly that the maximum amount of foreign oil imported in any year after 1979 would be 3,215,650,000 barrels (8.81 million per day). With this explicit import figure the Department of Energy should have been able to finish the *Project Independence Report* that was started by the FEA, although there is no record that they ever did so.

It is too bad that Mr. Sawhill, administrator of the FEA in 1974, did not use President Carter's method of defining independence, that is, just selecting a high import number. The report could have been completed in 1975, and the nation would have had nothing to fear from OPEC because the *Project Independence Report* would have assured the public that the nation was independent as long as the amount imported did not exceed the selected figure. Ah yes, indeed, the nation would have been safe and sound because the *Project Independence Report* said the nation was independent. President Carter would never have had the energy problems that he had during his administration because Project Independence said the nation was independent, and the nation would have been spared from listening to his "malaise" speech on July 15, 1979. That most certainly would have been a real bonus.

The handling of the problems of the liquid fuels division of the minerals industry by the Johnson, Nixon, Ford, and Carter administrations has to rank as one of the most pitiful efforts to govern in the history of the United States. The whole botched affair by the governing bodies reached a low point when President Carter delivered his "malaise speech," trying to clear his skirts and blame the American public for the botchery.

To President Carter's credit, his selection of a high import figure and his energy programs of conservation and getting the nation's utility and industrial companies to switch to other fuels (primarily coal) were successful in holding the amount of imported petroleum below the maximum amount that he set. In 1993, thirteen years after he left the presidency, the percentage of petroleum imports to the total produced and imported was 50 percent, yet it was still 102,200,000 barrels per year (280,000 barrels per day) below the maximum figure. Without doubt President Carter was most wise to have selected the highest amount of petroleum ever imported as his definition for independence. However, imports are now edging close to Carter's maximum amount that he set in 1979; thus, either President Clinton or his successor must be prepared to redefine independence by setting a higher import number. If the 1977 figure for petroleum imports is exceeded and a new higher import number is not selected, either President Clinton or former president Carter will have to give another "malaise speech" on television so that the public will know that they are the ones that have botched the handling of the petroleum problem again.

Appendix IX

Analysis of Alternative Sources of Energy and Environmental Trade-offs

Alternative Sources of Energy

In the United States the public in general is highly aware of the value and use of the mineral commodities gold, silver, platinum, and gemstones. They have a name familiarity with products used in their homes that are produced from the mineral commodities copper, steel, iron, aluminum, cement, and stainless steel and also those that produce heat for their home or energy to power their automobile, such as oil, gasoline, natural gas, and coal. However, it is doubtful if more than a small percentage of the public recognize these materials as mineral commodities or products of mineral commodities. The Arab oil embargo served to heighten the public awareness of the need for petroleum, but the awareness dropped exponentially as the gallons of gasoline increased in the automobile gas tank.

All nations in the world are dependent to some extent upon an agricultural or mineral commodity from which energy is produced. At the present time the mineral commodities are the hydrocarbon and nuclear fuels. In many nations water power supplements the energy obtained from these commodities. The higher the industrialization and correlative standard of living of the nation, the greater the energy use. Geothermal energy is being produced in nations that contain areas where geologically recent volcanic activity is evident, but in the larger nations it is a minor percentage of the total energy consumed.

In the United States environmental laws, such as the air quality and water quality acts, have induced many manufacturing plants and electrical power-producing utilities to change to fuels that burn cleaner, have less emission of particulates, and leave no radioactive residue. Most often the change has been from coal or nuclear fuels to petroleum or natural gas. At this time there are no utilities or industries in the United States changing to plants or building new plants fueled by nuclear energy. In addition, the construction of dams on rivers and streams to produce electrical power has almost ceased in the United States because of opposition by the environmental political bloc.

There are alternative sources of energy that can be developed. The most obvious are wind, solar, shale oil, and ocean tides. Energy produced from the wind and sun has received considerable publicity in the past several years, and there are research projects in progress on these sources. It is quite possible that in the future solar energy may be one of the primary systems for heating homes and/or heating water. But although the wind and the sun are limitless sources for producing energy, they are certainly no panacea to the energy problem.

Wind power can be classified as another form of solar power, since winds are generated by solar heating (U.S. Geological Survey and U.S. Bureau of Mines 1992). To harness the wind, sites with constant strong winds are necessary to drive the turbines that in turn power the generators that produce electricity. Constructing giant turbines at these sites meets strong objections from the environmental political bloc and often, in the western part of the United States, from Native Americans. In addition, the requirements for metallic mineral commodities to construct the turbine structures, generators, and distribution lines will be substantial, and the maintenance costs will be constant over the life of the turbines and generators. Denmark, which has almost constant wind in some areas, has managed to produce about 3 percent of the nation's total energy requirement with wind-driven turbines (Sletto 1995). The United States will be indeed fortunate if just 1 percent of its total energy requirements can be obtained from wind-driven turbines.

Developing energy from the sun has been actively researched for several years, and there are systems on the market for heating homes and water. The available systems for heating homes and water capture the electromagnetic radiation from the sun and convert it into electricity, which is then used as a heat source. The primary difficulty with such a method is the energy unit loss from the point of capture of the sun's radiation to the point where the energy unit is utilized. The reason for the energy loss is the purity of the metals used to transfer the electricity to the point of use. Ultra high-purity metals can be and are produced, but their cost is far in excess of that of the metals used in normal trade. It is quite possible that in the future the energy-loss problem can be

310

solved and solar-produced energy may become one of the primary methods for home heating in warmer parts of the nation.

Solar One, a plant in the Mohave Desert funded by the Department of Energy, concentrates sunlight by mirrors on a boiler to produce superheated steam; however, the cost of production is far above the cost of conventional sources. This type of solar furnace technology has been actively researched by the French National Center for Scientific Research. Their installation in the Pyrenees Mountains of France was the first of the type, constructed in early 1970 (Black 1995).

Solar systems like the systems to harness the wind will require substantial amounts of other mineral commodities. The installation at a single home will require a moderate amount of construction materials, but to blanket the nation with these systems the amount of material required for a single home must be multiplied by millions. Also, for every solar energy system installed it is quite likely that a backup system utilizing electricity, natural gas, oil, or coal will have to be installed or retained to cover needs during protracted cold and low-sun-radiation periods. Nationwide energy savings attained from solar energy will be moderate at best and will not even be close to that which is being predicted by many of the enthusiasts of harnessing the sun's eletromagnetic rays.

Oil shales of the Green River Formation occurring in Colorado, Utah, and Wyoming are the world's largest known hydrocarbon deposit. Estimates of the amount of oil in the formation range beyond 2,000 billion barrels (Staff of the Bureau of Mines 1985). However, there are serious problems that have to be solved before active mining can begin. Water demand in an area of water scarcity will be high, and wastes from mining will constitute almost 100 percent of the original material mined and will probably be over one and one-third times the volume of the material in place.

Such an operation will have strong opposition from the environmental political bloc and also the governors and a large percentage of the citizens in the three states. Nevertheless, shale oil constitutes a tremendous energy resource that is far more viable than wind, solar, or any other alternative energy source, and the federal government and states involved should have final plans developed for mining and processing the shale oil and replacing the wastes. The time will come when the resource has to be utilized. Unless there are radical changes in the current environmental laws, intent to mine should start twenty years prior

311

to the date of actual rock breaking to clear away the litigation that will be instigated by the environmental political bloc. For a nation that has allowed the environmental political bloc to nitpick the nuclear industry almost into extinction with the "impact statement" clause in the National Environmental Policy Act, even a twenty-year lead time may not be sufficient.

Ocean tides generate a tremendous amount of renewable energy. Where exceptionally high tides are normal occurrences harnessing the generated energy is a possibility; however, an equal return on energy units expended to construct and maintain the facility to energy units generated may be difficult to obtain. One system of harnessing the wave power that may have promise has been developed by Ocean Power Technologies of Princeton, New Jersey (*Popular Science* 1995). The system uses piezolectric material, which generates electricity when pressure is applied. The rise and fall of the ocean waves generate the pressure. The system is in the early stages of development.

Environmental Trade-offs

Electric-Powered Vehicle

There are now research projects in progress to develop an electric-powered vehicle to take the place of the gasoline-powered automobile in densely populated areas. Such a vehicle will not have the type of emissions that are characteristic of the gasoline-powered automobile; however, it will not save energy. In fact, actual unit of energy consumption per mile traveled by the electric-powered vehicle will be greater than that consumed by the gasoline-powered automobile.

An electric-powered vehicle has to have a constant source of electricity to stay in motion. Under current technology this source can be obtained in different ways; however, at this time, batteries for furnishing the electric power appear to be the most viable. Battery-powered vehicles operating on narrow-gauge railroad track for pulling ore cars have been standard technology in underground mines for over sixty-five years. However, the design of the vehicle is considerably different from what the design of a pleasure vehicle would be. The battery pack almost constitutes the total vehicle, with the operator occupying a small attached

uncovered seat in the front or rear. This technology can be easily transferred, but for the usual comforts of a pleasure vehicle a much smaller
battery pack will be necessary. The battery-powered vehicle must come
from the factory with power-source batteries installed, and they constitute
a deadweight that has to be freighted constantly while the vehicle is in
motion. The units of energy consumed to produce the vehicle with
batteries, freighting the batteries for the life of the vehicle, and recharging
the batteries will consume more units of energy than that consumed by
the gasoline-powered automobile. It will have no emissions, but there
will be more emissions at the utility plant from which the electricity for
recharging is obtained.

When all factors are considered, the only advantage that will be
gained with a battery-powered vehicle is the trade-off of transferring emissions from a high-density to a low-density populated area, and no matter
what the supporters claim, it will not save energy. It will consume more
energy. In addition, at every collision or wreck point there exists the
possibility of a hazardous material cleanup because of leakage from
the batteries.

Ethanol

Ethanol, an energy product distilled from corn, has been used as
an additive in gasoline to decrease undesirable emissions from automobiles in densely populated areas. However, utilizing ethanol as an additive in gasoline will not save energy. Like the battery-driven automobile,
the use of ethanol will increase the use of the mineral commodities that
now produce energy. The hydrocarbon fuels will be needed for land
preparation, fertilizing, seeding, growing, harvesting, and distillation of
the corn. The production of ethanol will never achieve a positive energy
balance—that is, more units of energy will be consumed to produce the
ethanol than will be available in the finished product. However, it will
lower undesirable emissions in densely populated areas when used as an
additive in gasoline.

General Discussion

It is not uncommon in times of shortage of petroleum for the environmental political bloc to blame industry for not developing alternative

energy sources. It is easy to say that the sun, wind, and ocean are there, so all we have to do is find a way to harness all the energy going to waste, but developing the system that will use the source and at the same time save in energy is a totally different matter. All alternative energy systems will require huge amounts of mineral commodities, including the hydrocarbon fuels. Easy solutions to the current energy problem are just not available at this time, and solutions are not likely to get any easier in the future. *In any way that the alternative energy sources are analyzed, shale oil is the most viable alternative source.*

To analyze properly the various alternative energy–producing systems the nation is in dire need of a materials policy and strategic plan of action on the minerals industry. Adoption of an alternative energy system that will use more units of energy than it will ever produce or produce only a small amount of units of energy on the positive side makes no sense at all. In addition, because of the critical situation in regard to energy it makes no sense at all to omit nuclear power from the energy equation. The federal government should encourage utilities to make nuclear plants at least 25 percent of their energy-producing capacity and at the same time repeal laws that are utilized by the environmental political bloc to keep the utilities constantly in court or before the state utility commissioners. Harassing actions by the bloc must become a direct concern of the federal government and laws, rules, and procedures that allow such actions have to be changed. Also, the government should have in progress and pursue vigorously a well-funded research and development program on advanced nuclear energy systems.

The lack of nuclear-produced energy and the clean air and water quality acts in the United States have served to place a tremendous demand on petroleum. The result has been increased vulnerability to Middle East production and petroleum producers scrambling to find deposits that are not subject to the ever-changing political winds of the Middle East. As they are unable to discover new deposits in the contiguous landmass of forty-eight states, their prospecting changed to the outer continental shelf and North Pole area, which has met consistent opposition by the states and the environmental political bloc.

Scientists claim that the polar area is becoming polluted by contaminants emitted into the air by industries located in all nations of the world and prospecting, development, and additional production of minerals in the region will make the situation worse. On the basis of preliminary sampling the concern appears to be valid. Thus what has occurred is the environmental political bloc by its constant and never-ending opposition to every prospecting site selected in the lower forty-eight has actually forced the mineral producers into the North Pole area. The problem is that the same emotional moaning, groaning, and whining is heard at every prospecting site selected, and whether the opposition is valid or not is lost in the moans, groans, whines, and dire predictions that have been heard over and over again. In brief, the environmental political bloc shouts "wolf" at all sites with the same dire predictions of what will happen if mineral prospecting and development are allowed to proceed. The bloc must come to the realization that it must make environmental trade-offs. The question is how to decide where and when to make the trade-off. The decision must be answered before the fact, not after the fact.

The only way that the decision can be answered before the fact is by having a viable minerals industry materials policy and strategic plan of action, and it should be apparent that to develop such a plan the minerals industry must be viewed as a total system. A policy developed on a single mineral commodity or on the general term energy has little value except as a presentation on statistics of production and consumption.

Appendix X

Common Stock Prices by Year of Major Steel Companies after Price Rise Denial in 1962

President Kennedy's demand in 1962 that the steel companies rescind their proposed price increase on steel had a devastating affect on many of the steel companies that comprised the ferrous metals division of the minerals industry. To demonstrate what occurred after the steel companies were forced to buckle under and rescind the price increase, the annual common stock price ranges for six companies were plotted over various yearly periods. Stock splits and mergers with other companies were the controlling factors of the yearly period of the graph. The six companies were as follows: U.S. Steel, Bethlehem Steel, Inland Steel, Jones & Laughlin Industries, Republic Steel, and National Steel. These companies were selected to obtain a cross-section of companies that were dependent on domestic deposits, a combination of domestic and foreign deposits, and primarily foreign deposits.

U.S. Steel held an exceptionally strong position in the Lake Superior District and in foreign investments. In contrast, Bethlehem Steel had no domestic deposits in the Lake Superior District, but they did have underground deposits in Pennsylvania. However, they held a strong position in foreign deposits, and the greater part of their iron ore was imported. Republic had a mix of both domestic and foreign deposits. Inland, Jones & Laughlin, and National obtained their ores primarily from domestic deposits and Canada. At the time, U.S. Steel was by a wide margin the dominant steel producer of the group. Table 1 shows U.S. Steel's annual production and the percentage of their production to the total produced in the United States.

The graphs of all companies show a sharp drop in common stock value after the price rise denial by President Kennedy in 1962. However, after 1962 the graphs are distinctive, depending upon the many factors that exercise control over the company. The trendlines in the graphs are

Table 1
U.S. Steel Production and Percentage of Production to the Total in the United States, 1957–69*

Year	U.S. Steel Production Per Year (net tons in millions)	Percentage of U.S. Steel's Production of Total Produced in the United States
1957	32.7	29.9
1958	23.8	27.9
1959	24.4	26.2
1960	27.3	27.5
1961	25.2	25.7
1962	25.4	25.8
1963	27.6	25.3
1964	32.4	25.6
1965	32.6	24.8
1966	32.8	24.4
1967	30.9	24.3
1968	32.4	24.7
1969	34.7	24.6

*Moody's Industrial Manual, 1969.

of the linear regression type in order to show the average trends of the value of the stock over the time span of the graph. The trendlines show how the company fared under the price control practices and the importation of below-cost steel products during the Kennedy, Johnson, and Nixon administrations. The slopes of the trendlines are the determinant of whether or not the company was able to overcome the effects of price controls and below-cost imports. If the slope is above the horizontal, the company had managed to overcome the price controls to a certain extent and increase the value of its stock; horizontal, the company had managed to some extent to counteract the price control practices but was unable to increase its stock value; and below the horizontal, the price control and imports of below-cost steel programs of the administrations were forcing the value of the company's common stock consistently to lower dollar amounts. The amount of decrease in common stock value was dependent on the degree of the slope of the trendline below the horizontal.

U.S. Steel stock in 1949 had split, and from that date on it was steadily increasing in price, reaching a high of $108 7/8 in 1959. During the three years of the Kennedy administration the yearly high value of the stock dropped steadily to a high of $57 1/2 in 1963, and then it continued on a downward trend to $34 3/4 in 1972. After 1973 the annual stock price moved sharply upward when U.S. Steel's exploration subsidiary discovered what was expected to be the largest and highest-grade iron ore deposit ever found in the world at Carajas, Brazil. (This

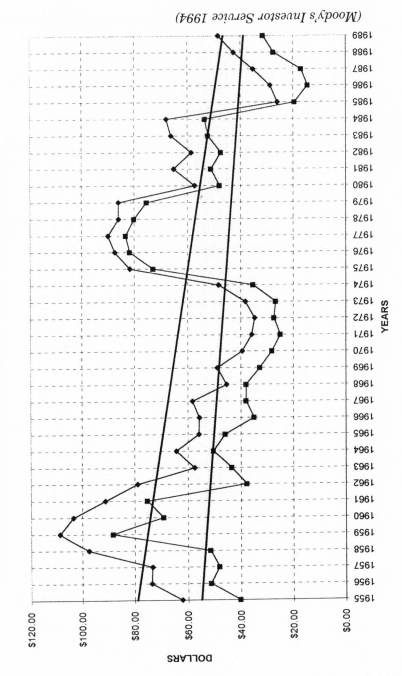

FIGURE 1--U.S. STEEL CORP. COMMON STOCK PRICE RANGE BY YEAR

(Moody's Investor Service 1994)

FIGURE 2--BETHLEHEM STEEL CORP. COMMON STOCK PRICE RANGE BY YEAR (74)

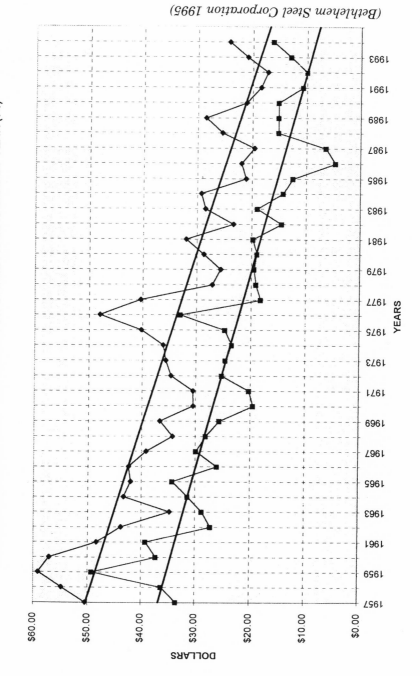

(*Bethlehem Steel Corporation 1995*)

FIGURE 3--INLAND STEEL INDS. COMMON STOCK PRICE RANGE BY YEAR

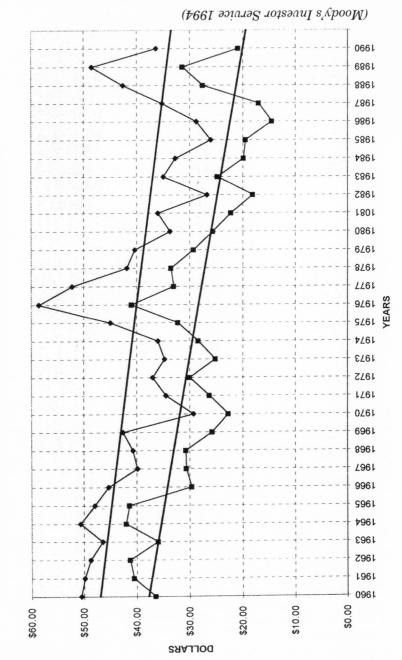

(*Moody's Investor Service 1994*)

FIGURE 4--J & L INDUSTRIES INC. COMMON STOCK PRICE RANGE BY YEAR

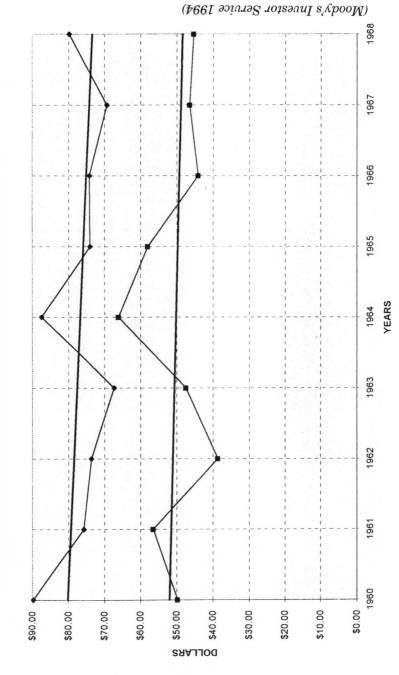

(*Moody's Investor Service* 1994)

FIGURE 5--REPUBLIC STEEL CORP. COMMON STOCK PRICE RANGE BY YEAR

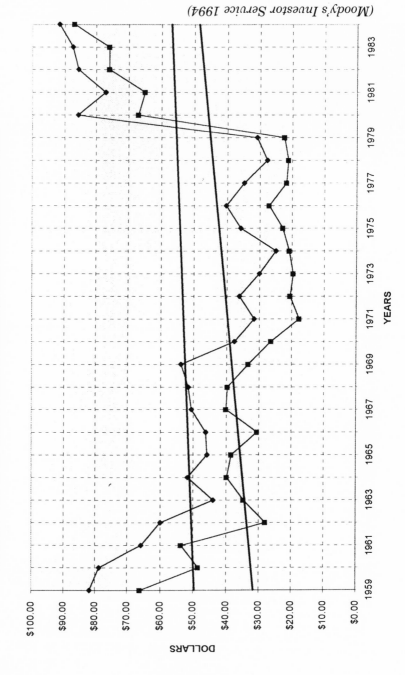

(Moody's Investor Service 1994)

FIGURE 6--NATIONAL STEEL CORP. COMMON STOCK PRICE RANGE BY YEAR

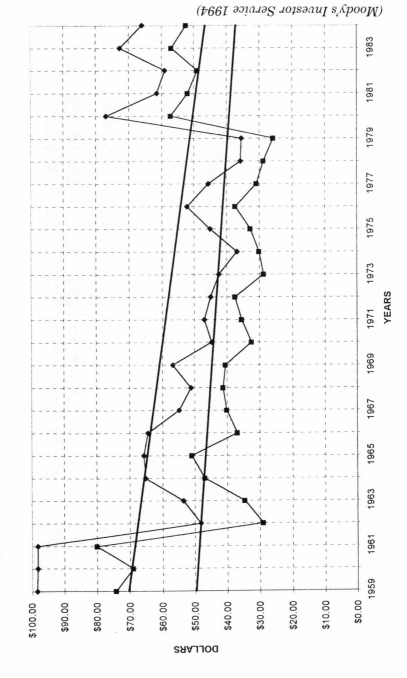

deposit was discussed in more detail in chapter 13). However, the report of a discovery of an iron ore deposit that was claimed to be six times larger than the Mesabi Iron Range was not enough to fend off the effect of the price control and import programs that were part and parcel of the Kennedy, Johnson, and Nixon administrations. By 1985 the stock had dropped to an annual high of $26. After 1986 the value of the stock was steadily moving upward. The trendline shows that the value of the stock could not recover from the price control and import programs of three administrations in twenty-nine years.

In view of the developments in petroleum during the Nixon administration, U.S. Steel purchased the Marathon Oil Company in 1982, thus widening its base in the minerals industry at a vital time in U.S. history. But even this purchase did not stop the stock from dropping to the low point in 1986. However, the purchase of Marathon Oil did apparently help the stock surge upward in price after the low point in 1986.

The graph of Bethlehem Steel, the second-largest steel company at that time, is shown in figure 2. Bethlehem's stock split three for one in 1947 and four for one in 1957. Its stock dropped sharply in the three years of the Kennedy administration and then continued on a downward trend to 1992. The downward slope of the trendlines is steeper than that of U.S. Steel. In thirty-three years the stock steadily lost value, and it was unable to overcome the price control and import programs of the Kennedy, Johnson, and Nixon administrations.

The graph of Inland Steel is shown in figure 3. Inland Steel stock split in 1946, and it split three for one in 1959. The trendlines of the stock values resemble those of Bethlehem Steel but at a less steep slope. However, Inland, like Bethlehem, was unable to overcome the price control and import policies of three administrations.

Jones & Laughlin (figure 4) was purchased by LTV Corporation in 1972, and Republic Steel (figure 5) was purchased by the same corporation in 1984. Thus their graphs tend to be skewed because of the takeover activity. In 1969, prior to their takeover in 1972, Jones and Laughlin paid a 100 percent stock dividend; thus the time span of the graph has been limited to eight years, from 1960 to 1968. Prior to merging with LTV, Jones & Laughlin was managing to almost hold its own against the price control and steel importation policies of the Kennedy and Johnson administrations. The average trendline of the yearly highs is just slightly below the horizontal. However, in the eight-year span there was no increase in value of the common stock.

Republic Steel is the only one of the six companies to show a gain in common stock value. However, for nineteen years, 1960–79, the common stock value decreased. When takeover talks started in 1979, the stock value jumped from an annual high in 1979 of $31.00 to $85 3/4 in 1980. By 1984 the stock value annual high had reached $91 5/8. This four-year period of high stock value (even higher than it was in 1959) was enough to place the average trendline for the twenty-five-year period on a gentle slope above the horizontal.

The graph of National Steel in figure 6 shows that the company was hit hard in 1962 by President Kennedy's demand that they rescind the price raise. In 1961 their stock price range was $80.00 and $98 1/8 per share. In 1962, after National was forced to rescind the price raise, the stock price range dropped to $29.00 and $48 1/8 per share. The low of $29.00 per share was so low that it only broke below that point once in seventeen years, to $25 3/4 per share, in 1979. Even with a sharp recovery in the value of the stock in 1980, the average trendlines were still below the horizontal. In 1984, National sold the assets of its Weirton Steel Division to Weirton Steel Corporation, a newly formed corporation owned by former employees.

The graphs of the stock price ranges in figures 1–6 of the six steel companies depict with startling clarity what interference in the market-place can do. In 1960 the companies were in a position whereby decisions on investing in new plants, remodeling of old plants, and investing in reliable sources of iron ore could be done with the expectation that the sale of their stock would net them sufficient capital to carry through on the planned programs. By 1962 their stock had devalued to the point that all programs had to be put on hold. The price control and steel import programs of the Kennedy, Johnson, and Nixon administrations kept them in this mode for over two decades. The refusal of the Ford and Carter administrations to rectify the situation resulted in a serious loss of steel capacity and heavy monetary losses during the Reagan administration.

References

Several of the references cited below list the total number of pages contained in the volume. Such listings indicate that the reference was used primarily to determine the state of technology of the minerals industry at a specific time period and the correct titles of individuals that have been cited in the book.

American Legion, The. 1992. The Bataan "Death March." *American Legion Magazine* 132, no. 4 (April): 19–21, 52.

Amster, Linda. 1974. *Chronology of Watergate-Related Events.* New York: Viking, pp. 813–77.

Anderson, Jack, and James Boyd. 1983. *Fiasco.* New York: Times Books.

Berman, Edgar, M.D. 1979. *Hubert: The Triumph and Tragedy of the Humphrey I Knew.* New York: G.P. Putnam's Sons, pp. 102–6.

Bethlehem Steel Corporation. 1995. *Common Stock Prices by Year, 1905–1995.* Bethlehem, PA: Bethlehem Steel Corporation.

Black, Wendi E. 1995. "Looking Back, 25 Years Ago, World's Largest Furnace." *Popular Science* 246, no. 2 (February 1995): 100.

Bunch, Bryan, ed. 1986. *The Science Almanac.* Garden City, NY: Anchor Books, Anchor Press/Doubleday, pp. 299–300.

Bureau of Public Debt. The *Historical Tables.* Washington, DC: U.S. Government Printing Office, table 7.1: "Federal Debt at the End of Year, 1940–1999." p. 89.

Bureau of the Census. 1994. *Updated National State Population Estimates.* Washington, DC: Economics and Statistics Administration, United States Department of Commerce, Public Information Office, News Release CB 94–43, March 15.

Burke, Richard E., with William and Marilyn Hoffer. 1992. *The Senator: My Ten Years with Ted Kennedy.* New York: St. Martin's Press.

Business Week. 1959. "A Long, Bitter Steel Strike." *Business Week,* July 18, pp. 23–25.

Business Week. 1960. "Steel Now—Bill Still to Come," January 9, pp. 27–28.

Business Week. 1984. "The Death of Mining: America Is Losing One of Its Most Basic Industries," "Merger of Republic and Jones & Laughlin

Steel," "The Big Chill in Washington: The Question Is: Will the Budget of the Budget Process End Up Frozen?," "Don't Ignore the Supply Side's Other Side." *Business Week*, December 17, pp. 64–70, 42, 28–29, 14.

Business Week. 1994. "Politics as Usual: Dump Quayle? Never Crossed His Mind," November 7, p. 4.

Carnegie Steel Company. 1929. *Carnegie Shape Book: Profiles, Tables, Data for Rolled Products, Shapes, Bars, and Rods*, 10th ed. Pittsburgh, PA: Carnegie Steel Company, 271 pp.

Cummins, A. B., and I. A. Givens. 1973. *SME Mining Engineering Handbook*, 2 vols. New York: Society of Mining Engineers of the AIME.

Davis, Nuel Pharr. 1968. *Lawrence and Openheimer*. New York: Simon and Schuster, pp. 26–27, 96–97.

DeGregorio, William A. 1993. *The Complete Book of U.S. Presidents*, 4th ed. New York: Wings Books.

Dolbear, S. H., and Oliver Bowles. 1949. *Industrial Minerals and Rocks*. New York: AIME, 1156 pp.

Economics and Statistics Administration, Bureau of Census. 1992. *Current Population Reports, Consumer Income Series*, P-60, no. 178, March. Washington, DC: U.S. Department of Commerce.

Energy Information Administration. 1984. *Coal Production*. Washington, DC: U.S. Government Printing Office, Table B2: "Coal Production Trends," p. 104, table B1: "Coal Mining Trends," p. 103.

Energy Information Administration. 1993. *Annual Energy Review*. Washington, DC: U.S. Department of Energy, pp. 141, 146, 147, 213–225.

Energy Information Administration. 1993. *Natural Gas Annual*. Washington, DC: Office of Oil and Gas, U.S. Department of Energy, p. 213.

Federal Energy Administration. 1974. *Project Independence Report*. Washington, DC: U.S. Government Printing Office, pp. ii, 18.

Finch, J. W. 1933. *Ore Deposits of the Western States*, 1st ed. New York: AIME, 797 pp.

Fuerstenau, D. W. 1962. *Froth Flotation, 50th Anniversary Volume*. New York: AIME, chapter 3, p. 39.

Glasstone, Samuel. 1950. *Sourcebook on Atomic Energy*. Princeton, NJ: D. Van Nostrand, pp. 344–45.

Gold, Gerald. 1974. *The White House Transcripts*. New York: Viking, 1974.

Gorrie, Jack. 1952. *The Objectives of United States Material Resources Policy and Suggested Initial Steps Taken in Their Accomplishment: A Report by the Chairman of the National Security Resources Board Based on the Report of the President's Materials Policy Commission and Federal Agency Comments Thereon*. Washington, DC: U.S. Government Printing Office, December 10.

Halberstan, David. 1986. *The Reckoning.* New York: William Morrow, pp. 451–59.

Hamilton, Charles V. 1982. *American Government.* London: Scott Foresman, pp. 12–29.

Iron Age. 1974. 119th annual issue, Iron Age. 1951. *The Iron Age Metal Industry Facts.* January. "Metal Facts section," p. 292.

Iron Age. 1955. Annual review and forecast issue, January 6, p. 2.

Jespersen, James, and Jane Fitz-Randolph. 1981. *Mercury's Web.* New York: Antheneum, pp. 40–49, 71–75.

John A. Roebling Son's Company. 1930. *Roebling Catalog: Roebling Wire Rope and Wire.* Trendton, NJ: John A. Roebling Son's Company, January 1, 279 pp.

Kissinger, Henry, 1987. *Years of Upheaval:* Boston: Little Brown, pp. 73, 414, 415, 872, 874, 895.

Lee, Courtland L. 1994. "Lack of Access Makes Mining Law Reform Irrelevant." *AMC Journal* 80 (November 8, August): 12–16.

Lewis, Robert. 1994. "Harsh Fate Awaits Many; Caught up in Downsizing." *AARP Bulletin* 35, no. 11 (December): 1.

Liddell, D. M., and G. E. Doan. 1933, *The Principles of Metallurgy.* New York: McGraw-Hill, 625 pp.

Lubell, John, Robert Sheridan, and Robert Slosser, eds. 1973. *The Watergate Hearings, Break-in and Cover-up: Proceedings of the Senate Select Committee on Presidential Campaign Activities.* New York: Bantam, October.

McCarthy, Eugene J. 1969. *The Year of the People.* Garden City, NY: Doubleday, pp. 16, 99–100, 294–95.

McKay, Douglas, John Foster Dulles, Sinclair Weeks, and Arthur O. Fleming. 1954. *Report of the Cabinet Committee on Minerals Policy.* Washington, DC: United States Department of the Interior, Office of the Secretary, November 30.

Meyer, Jane, and Doyle McManus. 1988. *Landslide: The Unmaking of the President, 1984–1988.* Boston: Houghton Mifflin.

Miller, William "Fishbait," as told to Frances Spatz Leighton. 1977. *Fishbait: The Memories of the Congressional Doorkeeper.* Englewood Cliffs, NJ: Prentice-Hall, pp. 26, 105–6, 245–46, 298, 301.

Moody's Investor Service. 1994. *Moody's Industrial Manual 1948–1994.* New York: Moody's Investor Service.

Morse, J. L. 1956. *An Abridgement of the New Funk & Wagnalls Encyclopedia, the Universal Standard Encyclopedia.* New York: Standard Reference Works.

Office of the Federal Register, National Archives and Records Service, General Services Administration, Department of Energy 1981/82. *The United States Government Manual.* Washington, DC: U.S. Government Printing Office, p. 249.

Paley, William S., Chairman. 1952. *Resources for Freedom:* vol. 1, *Foundations For Growth and Security;* vol. 2, *The Outlook for Key Commodities;* vol. 3, *The Outlook For Energy Sources;* vol. 4, *The Promise of Technology;* vol. 5, *Selected Reports to the Commission.* Washington, DC: U.S. Government Printing Office, June.

Peele, Robert. 1941. *Mining Engineers' Handbook,* 3d ed., vols. 1 and 2. New York: John Wiley.

Perkes, Dan, and Laurence Urdang. 1974. *The Official Associated Press Almanac.* Maplewood, NJ: Hammond Almanac, pp. 51–161.

Pfleider, E. P. 1968. *Surface Mining,* 1st ed. New York: AIME, 1061 pp.

Pogue, Forrest C. 1987. *George C. Marshall, Statesman 1945–1959.* New York: pp. 14, 18–25.

Popular Science. 1995. "Science and Technology, Energy, Wave Power." *Popular Science,* September, pp. 2, 24.

Regan, Mary Beth, and David Woodruff. 1994–95. "May Old Clean-Air Laws Be Forgot: The New Year's Deadline Sparks a Revolt across the U.S.A." *Business Week,* December 6, 1994/January 2, 1995.

Ridge, J. D. 1968. *Ore Deposits of the United States, 1933–1967,* 1st ed., 2 vols. New York: AIME, vol. 1, 991 pp., vol. 2, 1,880 pp.

Rowan, Lawrence C. 1975. "Application of Satellites to Geologic Exploration." *American Scientist.* 63, no. 4 (August): 393–403.

Sattill, Keith R., international ed. 1995. "Iron in the Selva, World's Largest Iron-Ore Project at Carajos." *Engineering and Mining Journal* 196, no. 11 (November): 32–35.

Semat, Henry. 1958. *Introduction to Atomic and Nuclear Physics,* 3d ed. New York: Rinehart, p. 3.

Sheppard, Carol R. 1993. "Hall of Fame Inductees Include AMC Leader Clyde Weed." *AMC Journal* 78, no. 10, p. 22.

Simons, Theodore. 1924. *Ore Dressing Principles and Practice,* 1st ed. New York: McGraw-Hill, 292 pp.

Sletto, Jacqueline Wiora. 1995. "Denmark." *Rotarian* 167, no. 1 (July) : 18–23.

Smith, Page. 1984. *The Rise of Industrial America: A People's History of the Post-Reconstruction Era,* vol. 6. Saint Louis: McGraw-Hill.

Speakes, Larry, with Robert Pack. 1988. *Speaking Out: The Reagan Presidency from inside the White House.* New York: Charles Scribner, Macmillan.

Spitzer, Dana L. 1996. "Lead: We All Need It." *Mining Voice* 2, no. 1 (January/February).

Staff of the Bureau of Mines. 1985. *Mineral Facts and Problems,* bulletin 556. Washington, DC: U.S. Department of the Interior, Bureau of Mines.

Staff of the *Washington Post,* The. 1974. *The Presidential Transcripts: The Complete Transcripts of the Nixon Tapes, Sept. 15, 1972–April 30, 1973.* New York: Dell.

Standard and Poor's Corporation. 1980. *Stock Guide.* New York: Standard and Poor's.

Stockman, David A. 1986. *The Triumph of Politics: How the Reagan Revolution Failed.* New York: Harper and Row, pp. 49, 72, 154–58.

Sullivan, Edward J. "Car Wars: Can American Auto Industry Be Saved?" *American Legion,* October 1992, p. 25.

Taranik, James V., U.S. Geological Survey, and Charles M. Trautwein, Technicolor Graphics, Inc. 1976. *Integration of Geological Remote-Sensing Techniques in Subsurface Analysis.* United States Department of Interior, Geological Survey, Open-File Report 76–402, Sioux Falls, South Dakota, May, p. 3.

Thrush, P. J. 1968. *A Dictionary of Mining, Mineral, and Related Terms.* Washington, DC: U.S. Department of the Interior, Bureau of Mines.

U.S. Bureau of Mines. 1993. *Commodity Data Summaries.* Washington, DC: U.S. Government Printing Office.

U.S. Department of Commerce. Economics and Statistics Administration. 1993. *Survey of Current Business,* June, Table 2: "U.S. Merchandise Trade." Washington, DC: Bureau of Economic Analysis.

U.S. Geological Survey and U.S. Bureau of Mines. 1992. *Mineral Resources of the United States and Minerals Yearbook: Mineral Resources 1882–1925, Minerals Yearbook 1925–1992.* Washington, DC: U.S. Government Printing Office.

West, J. M. 1975. *Mineral Facts and Problems.* Bulletin 667. Washington, DC: U.S. Bureau of Mines, table 6.

Williams, Robert Chadwell. 1987. *Klaus Fuchs, Atom Spy.* Cambridge, MA: Harvard University Press, 267 pp.

World Almanac. 1993. *The World Almanac and Book of Facts.* New York: World Almanac.

Index

335

341

Subsystems of: 275
Venezuela Ore Shipments: 6.312
Vermilion Iron Range: 3.9
Vietnam War:
   Acute Problems: 10.6
   End with Honor: 10.6
   Escalation of: 9.17–9.22
   Expansion of Troops: 8.12
   Ideology: 8.13
   Noble Effort: 13.2
   Peace Negotiations: 9.29
   Support of War: 8.14
   Withdrawal from: 10.10–10.12
Volcanic: 1.2
Volstead Act: 4.21, 4.9, 5.2
Volunteer Workers: 16. 17, 16.18
V1 and V2, German Rockets: 7.30

W

Wage and Price Controls: 10.25, 10.36
Walt, James, Secretary of the Interior:
     13.5, 13.10–13.12
War:
1812:2.7
   Six-day: 10.31
   Spanish American: 3.24
Warren, Earl: 16.16
Washington, George: 2.4
Water, Clean Water Restoration: 9.11
Water and Air Quality Acts, Effects of:
   10.22

Water Quality Act of 1965: 9.11
Watergate: 10.35, 10.46
   Cover-up: 10.29
Whitney, Eli: 2.13
Wilderness Act: 9.16
Wilderness Withdrawal: 16.32
Wilson, Charles E., Secretary of Defense:
   7.5
Wind Power: 309
Work Project Administration: 5.3
World Bank, Loan for Brazilian Iron Ore
   Deposit: 13.28
World War I: 3.38
World War II:
   Beginning: 5.14
   End: 6.3, 6.6
   Invasion of Norway: 5.14
   Invasion of the Netherlands, Belgium &
     France: 5.14
Wright, Wilbur & Orville: 3.34

Y

Yankee Ingenuity, Yankee Know-how: 3.39,
     4.12, 4.13, 6.6, 6.31, 6.41, 7.12,
     8.22, 10.42, 14.7, 14.26
Yom Kipper War: 10.31
Yttrium: 2.19

Z

Zinc: 2.20, 2.23
Zirconium: 2.19